MARKS OF AN ABSOLUTE WITCH

To my parents, with love

Marks of an Absolute Witch
Evidentiary Dilemmas in Early Modern England

ORNA ALYAGON DARR
Carmel Academic Center, Israel

ASHGATE

Published by
Ashgate Publishing Limited
Wey Court East
Union Road
Farnham
Surrey, GU9 7PT
England

Ashgate Publishing Company
Suite 420
101 Cherry Street
Burlington
VT 05401-4405
USA

www.ashgate.com

British Library Cataloguing in Publication Data
Darr, Orna Alyagon.
 Marks of an absolute witch : evidentiary dilemmas in early
 modern England.
 1. Trials (Witchcraft)–England–History–16th century.
 2. Trials (Witchcraft)–England–History–17th century.
 3. Evidence (Law)–England–History–16th century.
 4. Evidence (Law)–England–History–17th century.
 5. Witch hunting–England–History–16th century.
 6. Witch hunting–England–History–17th century.
 7. Trials (Witchcraft)–England–Case studies. 8. Witch hunting–England–Case studies.
 I. Title
 345.4'20288-dc22

Library of Congress Cataloging-in-Publication Data
Darr, Orna Alyagon.
 Marks of an absolute witch : evidentiary dilemmas in early modern England / Orna Alyagon Darr.
  p. cm.
 Includes bibliographical references and index.
 ISBN 978-0-7546-6987-6 (hardcover) – ISBN 978-1-4094-3024-7 (ebook)
 1. Trials (Witchcraft)–England. 2. Witchcraft–England–History.
 3. Witch hunting–England–History. I. Title.
 KD371.W56D37 2011
  345.42'0288–dc22

2011015949

ISBN 9780754669876 (hbk)
ISBN 9780754630247 (ebk)

Printed and bound in Great Britain by the
MPG Books Group, UK

Contents

List of Figures

Introduction

The terms 'witch trial' and 'witch hunt' long ago acquired a meaning broader than that of a specific historical occurrence. They have become a powerful metaphor denoting diverse instances of unfair and unjust treatment, including scapegoating, labelling, discrimination and persecution, either by the authorities or by private people. The witch symbolizes a victim who is not only innocent, but also helpless, singled out for physical or symbolic extermination by powerful forces. The actual historical trials are commonly perceived as the epitome of injustice and disregard for the truth. A widespread yet inaccurate belief is that in the Middle Ages an accusation of witchcraft automatically led to burning at the stake. This myth is imprecise on several levels. In England, as in Continental Europe, the prosecution of witches transpired in the early modern era, not in the Middle Ages. In many cases formal legal proceedings were delayed or withheld. By the time they were brought to trial, many of the accused had a long-standing reputation for being witches, which implies that fellow villagers endured their suspicious neighbours for many years before they eventually took any formal action.

In England, the location of this research, the conviction and execution rates were relatively low.[1] English witches who were sentenced to death were hanged

---

[1]   On the Home Circuit, only 22 per cent of the accused were executed. Macfarlane established that between 1560 and 1680, of the 291 people tried for witchcraft at the Essex Assizes, 151 were either acquitted or the bill of presentment against them was dismissed. Of the remaining 140, 129 were convicted, of whom 74 were executed and 55 imprisoned. After 1620 the percentage of acquittals rose enormously. Malcolm Gaskill, 'Witchcraft and Evidence in Early Modern England', *Past and Present*, no. 198 (2008): p. 40; Christina Larner, *Witchcraft and Religion: The Politics of Popular Belief* (New York, NY: Blackwell, 1984), p. 72; Brian P. Levack, *The Witch-Hunt in Early Modern Europe*, 2nd edn (New York: Longman, 1995), p. 23; Alan Macfarlane, *Witchcraft in Tudor and Stuart England: A Regional and Comparative Study* (New York: Harper & Row, 1970), pp. 57, 62; James A. Sharpe, *Instruments of Darkness: Witchcraft in England 1550–1750* (London: Hamish Hamilton, 1996), pp. 112, 233. It should be noted that the low English conviction and execution rates may be applicable to other felonies too. Generally, in Elizabethan England only 25 per cent of those who were tried for felony were executed. During the first half of the eighteenth century this rate dropped even further, to about 10 per cent. J.S. Cockburn, 'Introduction', in J.S. Cockburn (ed.), *Calendar of Assize Records*, 11 vols (London: Her Majesty's Stationery Office, 1985), p. 113; Cynthia B. Herrup, *The Common Peace: Participation and the Criminal*

rather than burned at the stake. In addition, the English law against witchcraft had two degrees of criminality. Only illegal acts of a more serious degree were capital, whereas others were punishable by a year's imprisonment and four pillory sessions. Prosecution of witches was conducted by central judges, a method that effectively supervised and restrained local pressures. There were Continental parallels to restriction of witchcraft prosecution by higher instances that imposed higher standards of justice and due process on the lower provincial magistracy, a notable example being the appeals taken to the Parlement of Paris in witchcraft cases.[2] In early modern England defendants were not yet granted a statutory right to appeal. There, however, witch trials were initially held before the assize judges, mostly fully trained, experienced and senior legal practitioners, who, as itinerant judges, were less prone to community pressures than the local magistrates.

Two key characteristics of the English witch trials distinguish them from the popular stereotype of accusations necessarily leading to convictions. The first is procedural, the barring of torture in criminal witchcraft cases. The second is the onset of a social debate that surrounded the trials. The question of what the best evidence was to prove the crime, and what the standard of proof should be, was seriously debated. The determination of guilt was not automatic, and proof of witchcraft was not a matter to be taken lightly. Even the most adamant believers in the reality of witchcraft expressed concern regarding false conviction and discussed the best way to tell real witches from those falsely accused. It was not a mere legal quandary, but a much wider social dilemma discussed by many.[3]

Law in Seventeenth-Century England, Cambridge Studies in Early Modern British History (Cambridge, UK: Cambridge University Press, 1987), ch. 6; J.A. Sharpe, *Crime in Early Modern England*, in J. Stevenson (ed.), *Themes in British Social History* series (London: Longman, 1984), p. 65. In Continental Europe the execution rates in witchcraft trials, which varied across regions, were typically higher than in England. Robin Briggs, *The Witches of Lorraine* (Oxford: Oxford University Press, 2007), p. 52; Levack, *The Witch-Hunt in Early Modern Europe*, pp. 23–4. Cf. Wolfgang Behringer, *Witches and Witch-Hunts* (Cambridge: Polity Press, 2004), p. 150.

[2]   Brian P. Levack, 'Crime and the Law', in Jonathan Barry and Owen Davies (eds), *Witchcraft Historiography*, Palgrave Advances (Houndmills, UK: Palgrave Macmillan, 2007); Brian P. Levack, 'The Decline and End of Witchcraft Prosecutions', in Bengt Ankarloo and Stuart Clark (eds), *Witchcraft and Magic in Europe: The Eighteenth and Nineteenth Centuries* (Philadelphia: University of Pennsylvania Press, 1999).

[3]   For an overview of the witchcraft debate in the European context, see Peter Maxwell-Stuart, 'The Contemporary Historical Debate, 1400–1750', in Jonathan Barry and Owen Davies (eds), *Witchcraft Historiography*, Palgrave Advances (Houndmills, UK: Palgrave Macmillan, 2007).

The prevailing legal theory regards the rules of evidence as a rational and objective truth-finding tool.[4] Typically, the social context of evidence law is neglected and referred to mainly for the limited purpose of grounding the rationale of some of the evidential rules in social policy. Yet, even studies that explore social policy and moral considerations in evidence law, as well as interdisciplinary studies of fact-findings, still tend to regard truth-seeking as an overriding consideration and assume the conscious and deliberate design of evidence law to be in the best interest of society.[5] A bolder argument was explicitly articulated in the recent work of Alex Stein, who analysed the law of evidence as a tool for apportioning the risk of fact-finding errors between the parties. Stein dared to doubt the basic axiom of the truth-finding rationale by pointing to sharing risk and reducing cost as major considerations. Yet, Stein's model presupposes a society whose members share the same vision of the general social well-being, where expressions such as 'utility', 'fairness' or 'morality' have the same meaning to different social actors. Stein also assumed the existence of an instrumental relationship between evidence and fact-finding.[6]

Starting from classical treatises on evidence, such as Wigmore's, to the recent writings of Stein, these works are a-historical and detached from changes in the social and cultural context in which evidence law developed. Furthermore, they presuppose an image of a homogeneous society that tailors the rules of evidence in an intentional and deliberate manner, best serving a general common good. The existence of diverse interests in a society and the struggle between social groups to achieve distinct goals are missing from these studies of evidence law.

This book, in contrast, is grounded in a specific historical social and cultural context – the debate concerning the proof of the crime of witchcraft in early modern England. The analysis examines the social embeddedness of evidentiary techniques and uncovers a divided society, where various social groups have diverse goals and interests. My findings indicate that evidentiary methods are shaped in the course of a symbolic struggle between the various social players and that evidentiary techniques are not necessarily the fruits of an intentional or consistent design. They are rather an amalgam of interrelating concepts and the outcome of sometimes competing and sometimes complementary

[4] As expressed in the classic treatise by John Henry Wigmore, *Evidence in Trials at Common Law*, 4th edn, 10 vols, vol. 1, *Wigmore on Evidence* (Boston: Little, Brown and Company, 1983), pp. xx, 8; see also p. 9, fn. 5.

[5] William Twining and Alex Stein (eds), *Evidence and Proof*, The International Library of Essays in Law and Legal Theory, edited by Tom D. Campbell (New York: New York University Press, 1992), pp. xxi–xxv.

[6] Alex Stein, *The Foundations of Evidence Law* (Oxford: Oxford University Press, 2005), esp. pp. x–xi.

interests. The period under study was a formative age for evidentiary law, and the witchcraft debate explicitly presented the basic assumptions of the different participants regarding the dilemma of this serious but hard-to-prove crime. However, it is important to bear in mind that this research is not limited to the narrow perspective of the evidentiary techniques that were actually used in court, but endeavours to expose the broader perspective of contemporary thought regarding the methods of proving witchcraft within the framework of the dilemma posed by such problematic crimes.[7]

A fruitful way of demonstrating the social embeddedness of evidentiary methods is to examine an open and public debate about ways of proof. When the methods of proof become the subject of social controversy, they are no longer taken for granted, and their underlying rationales and implications rise to the surface, making it easier to examine possible connections between the speakers, their socio-cultural attributes and their evidentiary dispositions. The category of cases that I have termed 'serious but hard-to-prove crimes' typically triggers fierce public debates that reflect a great degree of social tension, diverse opinions and manifold interests. Thus, those debates provide an excellent research setting.

Some crimes are widely acknowledged as especially serious, and scarcity of evidence in such cases generates a pressing conflict. Using the standard evidentiary methods may jeopardize any chance of prosecuting and convicting extremely dangerous criminals. On the other hand, loosening the evidentiary standards may warrant convictions but may also lead to the absurdity of demanding less-convincing proof for the conviction of the more serious crimes. A standard of too-meagre proof in order to convict may result in the conviction and punishment of innocent people. A false accusation may be sufficient to make anybody the next convict. Social cohesiveness and trust cannot be maintained when each person is permanently vulnerable and susceptible to false accusations made by hostile opponents.

Mistrust in the legal system is socially and politically undesirable. Lower evidentiary standards may subsequently give rise to resentment and rage against a regime that seems arbitrary and unjust. Higher evidentiary standards may impede effective law enforcement, and people may seek private justice outside the legal system. Any imbalance undermines the legitimacy of the regime. Thus,

---

[7]   Throughout this work, the terms 'proof techniques' or 'evidentiary methods' are used rather than the terms 'evidence law' or 'rules of evidence'. The former terms are broader and include informal and popular proof practices. In addition, the field of evidence law was non-existent in the middle of the sixteenth century. By the eighteenth century this legal branch had already emerged, including basic principles that still apply today, such as the hearsay rule or the confession rule.

we see that serious but hard-to-prove crimes pose a special challenge not only to the legal system, but also to society at large.

The dilemma of such crime is not specific to the early modern era. Societies today are no less tormented by incarnations of the dilemma in dealing with crimes such as terrorism or sex offences where physical evidence is lacking. The prospect of paedophiles and terrorists walking about freely terrifies many. Yet, sometimes mere suspicions, albeit troubling ones, are all there is. Such cases stir fierce arguments about the need to tilt the scales between freeing society of dangerous criminals and establishing guilt only by legitimate and prudent means. Here, too, the public debate exposes a variety of social interests mobilizing various lines of reasoning on the ways of proof that fit such cases.

The early modern English and their Continental counterparts were very explicit in describing the dilemma and its evidentiary implications, namely, the modification of the regular ways of proof in cases of crimes such as witchcraft, rape and poisoning.[8] The renowned judge Sir Matthew Hale referred to both rape and witchcraft as the 'crimes that give the greatest difficulty ... wherein many times persons are really guilty, yet such an evidence, as is satisfactory to prove it, can hardly be found; and on the other side persons really innocent may be entangled under such presumptions, that carry great probabilities of guilt'.[9]

The fear of convicting the innocent was not specific to witchcraft. Langbein regarded this concern as the background of the procedural reforms of the 1690s and 1730s, which ameliorated the defendant's status.[10] Nevertheless, because the dilemma was especially severe in witchcraft cases, witchcraft was a significant element in the context surrounding the nascent evidence law. To paraphrase Christina Larner's words concerning gender and witchcraft, the dilemma was 'witchcraft related' though not 'witchcraft specific'.[11] Perhaps this fact explains why the debate about proving witchcraft continued into the eighteenth century, although prosecution had already diminished.

---

[8]   Katharine Eisaman Maus, 'Proof and Consequences: Inwardness and Its Exposure in the English Renaissance', *Representations*, no. 34 (1991): p. 34.

[9]   Hale also maintained that rape 'is an accusation easily to be made and hard to be proved, and harder to be defended by the party accused, tho never so innocent' (cited by Gilbert Geis and Ivan Bunn, *A Trial of Witches: A Seventeenth-Century Witchcraft Prosecution* (London: Routledge, 1997), p. 121). The total of rape cases amounted to 1 per cent of indicted felonies and had an exceedingly low conviction rate. Garthine Walker, *Crime, Gender and Social Order in Early Modern England* (Cambridge: Cambridge University Press, 2003), p. 55.

[10]   John H. Langbein, *The Origins of Adversary Criminal Trial*, Oxford Studies in Modern Legal History (Oxford: Oxford University Press, 2003), p. 172.

[11]   Christina Larner, *Enemies of God: The Witch-Hunt in Scotland* (Baltimore, MD: Johns Hopkins University Press, 1981), pp. 3, 92.

This book introduces a triple-layered argument regarding the social and cultural context of evidentiary methods. First, it suggests that the dilemma of the crime of witchcraft was a viable tension in early modern English society. This tension was clearly expressed in a heated debate regarding the appropriate ways of proof. The second layer of the analysis places the dilemma within a wider social context. The claim is that the social and cultural position of the participants in the debate influenced their evidentiary dispositions. I discuss in particular the significance of social class, central versus peripheral locale and professional affiliation. Third, as a general conclusion from the particular instances of social and cultural influences on evidentiary techniques, I argue that the common-law rules of evidence do not necessarily possess real objective value and do not develop exclusively by virtue of their inner judicial logic. Instead, I argue that evidentiary techniques are socially constructed through a symbolic struggle between various social and cultural groups.

Why Witchcraft

I chose the crime of witchcraft in England from the mid-sixteenth to the mid-eighteenth century as the focus of this book, and as a key example of a serious but hard-to-prove crime, for several reasons. The crime was both exceptionally serious and extremely hard to prove. In early modern Europe it was considered one of the most serious crimes, highly dangerous in several respects. First, it was a spiritual and religious crime. The alliance with the devil was heresy, a rejection of the Christian faith. Second, it was a common belief that witches had the power and motivation to inflict death, illness and damage to cattle, crops and property. Third, the use of magic or prophecies was sometimes deemed a potential risk to the reign of the monarch.[12]

In early modern England the term witchcraft had conveyed various meanings and concepts. It was a secular crime, a religious sin, a variety of popular beliefs and a subject of learned treatises. Even within the same discipline, demonology, for example, different writers had different foci. Although a pact with the devil was a cornerstone of all demonological treatises, some writers stressed the heretical nature of witchcraft, some emphasized the organization of the witches, some called attention to the sexual relationship with demons, and still others

---

[12]   Cecil L'Estrange Ewen, *Witch Hunting and Witch Trials: The Indictments for Witchcraft from the Records of 1373 Assizes Held for the Home Circuit A.D. 1559–1736* (New York: Lincoln Mac Veagh: The Dial Press, 1929), pp. 19, 21, 39; Macfarlane, *Witchcraft in Tudor and Stuart England*, p. 16; Barbara Rosen (ed.), *Witchcraft, Stratford-Upon-Avon Library* (New York: Taplinger, 1972), p. 57.

viewed the sabbath as an essential element. However, for the purposes of this book, which concentrates on the debate about methods of proving the crime, a witch is simply someone who was accused or prosecuted as one.

Yet, to better understand the matter of proof, it is essential to clarify the meaning of two key elements of the concept of witchcraft:

- *maleficium* – causing harm to others, bewitching neighbours, inflicting illnesses and death on them, injuring cattle and crops, and so on. The notion of *maleficium* was prominent in popular beliefs. It was also present in learned demonological treatises, albeit as an element secondary to the pact with the devil.
- pact with the devil – in demonological theory, the forming of a contractual-like relationship with the devil was the initial and constitutive step in becoming a witch. The alliance empowered the witches with supernatural abilities to cause harm. The worship of the devil followed the compact. English demonologists were relatively moderate in their descriptions of the acts of worship: 'These writers did not involve themselves in those more extreme fantasies which mark the pages of so many Continental tracts: the orgiastic sabbath, infanticidal midwives, unbridled copulation between witches and demons and so on.'[13]

Despite a widespread agreement as to its seriousness, proving a clandestine and often witnessless crime was extremely thorny. The wording of the secular anti-witchcraft laws was not particularly helpful. The Henrician 1542, the Elizabethan 1563 and the Jacobean 1604 acts listed outlawed behaviours (focusing on malefic elements) but did not specify how to prove them.[14] Without a confession, both elements, *maleficium* and the pact, were difficult if not impossible to prove. In fact, there was a controversy among demonologists as to whether the appointment with the devil was a physical reality or a spiritual experience that was impossible to witness.[15] Contemporaries also feared that the devil might attempt to shed innocent blood and implicate jurors in murder and perjury by causing them to convict innocent defendants. In sum, it was extremely hard, to use a contemporary term, to 'discover' witches.

The problem of proof became the subject of a heated public debate. Lawyers, judges, clerics, doctors, gentlemen, villagers, suspects and even royals participated in this debate, expressing different attitudes and ideas regarding witchcraft and

---

[13] Sharpe, *Instruments of Darkness*, pp. 87–8.

[14] 33 Hen. VIII, c. 8, 1542 (repealed five years later by the 1 Edw. VI. c. 12, 1547, s. 3); 5 Eliz., c. 16, 1563; 1 Jac. I, c. 12., 1604.

[15] Levack, *The Witch-Hunt in Early Modern Europe*, pp. 46–7.

the right ways to prove it. The public debate that unfolded in the England of 1542 to 1736 regarding the appropriate ways of proof presents us with a rare opportunity to uncover the basic assumptions and systems of meaning regarding such controversial crimes.

The prism of witchcraft offers an additional advantage in studying the ways of proof of similarly difficult crimes in general. The belief in the reality of witches and demons, so widespread in the early modern period, is no longer shared by most members of society. On the contrary, today's hegemonic perspective adheres to the views of scholars from the era of the Enlightenment, who considered the witch trials to be legal murders committed out of barbarity and ignorance. Hundreds of years have passed since the time of witch trials, and we are now able to examine the bare mechanisms of proof without attributing to the judicial practices or their underlying ideology any inherent truth value or sense of necessity. Such a sense of detachment would be much harder to acquire if, for example, the focus were on current sex crimes against children.

At this point I would like to make an important distinction. Although not sharing the early modern belief in witchcraft, and reserving the right to view the witch trials as miscarriages of justice leading to the loss of innocent lives, I did not write this book from the perspective of the Enlightenment. An irrational phenomenon, said Ginzburg, 'could be studied in a rational, but not rationalistic key'.[16] It is erroneous to view the witchcraft beliefs and the witch trials as mere expressions of ignorance. The witch hunters – the ideologists, prosecutors and judges of the witch trials – were the intellectual elite of the period, educated men of reason. The prosecution was an organized judicial effort that operated according to standard procedures and many times with a desire to find the truth. The debate and perceptions of the contemporaries cannot be understood unless they are analysed in the terms and social context of the era in which they were constructed and enacted. As Macfarlane stated, 'To understand all is not *necessarily* to forgive all'.[17]

Why England of circa 1550–1750

The witch trials varied in form and in consequence from country to country and even from one region to another. Recent scholars have expressed reservations as to the traditional distinction between English and Continental witchcraft, which portrayed the former as malefic and the prosecution of the latter as a monolithic

---

[16]   Carlo Ginzburg, *Clues, Myths, and the Historical Method* (Baltimore, MD: Johns Hopkins University Press, 1989), p. viii.

[17]   Macfarlane, *Witchcraft in Tudor and Stuart England*, p. 241.

effort against the heretical pact. This was one of Sharpe's main conclusions in his survey on English witchcraft. He demonstrated similarities between English and Continental beliefs and the extent of Continental influence on English prosecution.[18]

However, one significant procedural attribute makes England much more interesting than the Continent for studying the societal debate. Although the suspect's confession provided one of the easiest solutions to the dilemma of proof, English law resisted the temptation to extort witchcraft confessions by force. In fact, despite the tendency of English writers to portray their law as torture-free, torture was infrequently practised legally. Torture warrants could be issued by the monarch or the Privy Council, and they were used mostly in crimes against the state (such as treason), and in some serious criminal cases as well.[19] However, there is no evidence that torture was used in run-of-the-mill witchcraft cases. Private torture by accusers or fellow villagers was considered categorically illegal. Yet, we know of many cases in which suspects were subjected to private ordeal-type tests such as swimming or scratching during the pre-trial stage. This book, therefore, considers torture to be a legally unacceptable option, as indeed it was in criminal witchcraft cases, but exceptions existed and should be remembered. Unlike their Continental counterparts, the English could not use the strappado, the rack or the thumbscrews to obtain confessions and thus were forced to confront the full extent of the problem of proving guilt.

In England, the early modern period was characterized by a paradigmatic change in the legal system and society at large. After the ordeal was abolished in 1215, adjudication was transferred from the hands of God to fallible humans. The guilt of the defendant in the criminal trial could no longer be declared by the hand of God, but needed to be proved. Fact-finding was done by lay jurors, and a substitute system of evidentiary techniques and standards of proof began

---

[18]   Sharpe, *Instruments of Darkness*, p. 32. See also Jonathan Barry, 'Introduction', in Jonathan Barry, Marianne Hester and Gareth Roberts (eds), *Witchcraft in Early Modern Europe: Studies in Culture and Belief* (Cambridge, UK: Cambridge University Press, 1996), p. 24; Robin Briggs, 'Many Reasons Why: Witchcraft and the Problem of Multiple Explanation', in Jonathan Barry, Marianne Hester and Gareth Roberts (eds), *Witchcraft in Early Modern Europe* (Cambridge, UK: Cambridge University Press, 1996), pp. 60, 63; Malcolm Gaskill, 'Early Modern Kent', in Jonathan Barry, Marianne Hester and Gareth Roberts (eds), *Witchcraft in Early Modern Europe* (Cambridge, UK: Cambridge University Press, 1996), p. 285; James A. Sharpe, 'Introduction: The Lancashire Witches in Historical Context', in Robert Poole (ed.), *The Lancashire Witches: Histories and Stories* (Manchester: Manchester University Press, 2002), p. 10.

[19]   John H. Langbein, *Torture and the Law of Proof: Europe and England in the Ancien Regime* (Chicago: University of Chicago Press, 1977), pp. 73–139. See also Elizabeth Hanson, 'Torture and Truth in Renaissance England', *Representations*, no. 34 (1991).

to be formulated. The structure of the legal system was also in flux. Criminal and civil procedures began to diverge; most criminal cases were actions of the crown against the defendants and not suits between private individuals. The state began to construct an apparatus of investigation and prosecution. A system of judges arriving at the periphery from the centre to spread royal justice increased the standardization of procedures and evidentiary methods. The doctrine of evidence law, non-existent before the mid-sixteenth century, was evolving during this period. By the mid-eighteenth century a set of evidence rules had already been established. During this era of transformation the evidentiary methods were not obvious, natural or taken for granted, but rather a subject of heated debate. This era of transformation overlapped the life span of the anti-witchcraft legislation, and much of the debate focused around this crime.[20] The gravity and the probative difficulty associated with the crime of witchcraft stimulated many to express their opinions. Therefore, much of the debate about evidentiary methods was in the context of witchcraft.

The prosecution of witches was debatable to begin with, and controversies surrounded the crime from the start. England lagged behind the Continent in the formation of both elaborate demonological theory and organized judicial witch prosecution. Therefore, the English arena was characterized by multiple and frequently conflicting attitudes. Both the judicial and the religious establishments were divided on the question.[21]

Corpus and Method

The foundation of this book is a body of 157 pamphlets, tracts and legal manuals written and published from 1561 to 1756. The publication of pamphlets during those two centuries was not systematic or even. Between the years 1627 and 1642 no known pamphlets or other witchcraft literature were published.[22] About half the texts depict specific cases of either witchcraft or possession.

---

[20]   It has been suggested that the factor that most shaped the history of the witchcraft crime was its evidentiary status. Gaskill, 'Witchcraft and Evidence in Early Modern England'.

[21]   Barry, 'Introduction', p. 23.

[22]   Two translations published in London during that time were *A Certaine Relation of the Hog-Faced Gentlewoman ...* (London: J.O., 1640) and *A Relation of the Deuill Balams ...* (London: R. Badger, 1636). Sharpe explained that in the 1620s and 1630s witchcraft was a dying subject that was revived by the conditions left by the Civil War. Sharpe, *Instruments of Darkness*, p. 146. Interestingly, despite the decline in prosecution since the 1660s, the writings about witchcraft, including theological and philosophical treatises, continued until the beginning of the eighteenth century.

More than 50 publications are learned treatises (legal, medical, theological and philosophical tracts). This category includes both the demonologist and the sceptic literature. Texts that address no evidentiary issues (for example, those that discuss the question of good versus evil in the world) are excluded from the corpus. Where the discussion of evidentiary issues is limited (for example, in James I's *Daemonologie*), I focus on the relevant portions of the text. The remainder of the texts include legal manuals that do not treat witchcraft, but are very useful in portraying the early modern criminal procedure and evidence, and translated pamphlets from the Continent and materials from New England that were published in England during the relevant period. The latter are included for the limited purpose of demonstrating potential influence on the English debate, but the ways of proof they discuss are clearly beyond the scope of this book. The categories of pamphlets, tracts and legal manuals are not necessarily mutually exclusive, and it is not always easy to fit the text into one category. For example, a pamphlet related to a specific witch trial may be soaked in demonological rhetoric, or a demonological tract may contain practical instructions to jurors and examples of particular cases.

Any analysis should take into account the nature of the pamphlets as an historical source and the benefits and shortcomings of such a diverse body of texts. The textual accounts of specific cases vary in length (from a single page to hundreds of pages) and in literary genre. There is a broad distinction between early pamphlets, which aimed to provide an accurate picture of the proceedings and the protocol, and the pamphlets from the 1590s onward, which were narratives in the third person and not legal in style.[23] Whereas the early pamphlets focus on the trial and the witch, the later ones revolve around the victim's suffering.[24] Some pamphlets linger over the background of the indictment (the facts constituting the offence, the suspect's history and reputation, the relationship between the neighbours) and then briefly treat the legal proceedings. Sometimes the detailed introduction is followed by a mere statement that the witch was tried and notes the result of the trial. Some pamphlets do not even describe the sentence; others describe the proceedings in detail. Only a few provide a detailed factual description of the trial procedure. However, other pamphlets describe fragments of the trials and pre-trial procedures.

Some texts strive to be morally meaningful; others are sensational descriptions, a sort of early modern tabloids. Some openly advocate a legal or

---

[23]   Stuart Clark, 'Introduction', in Stuart Clark (ed.), *Languages of Witchcraft: Narrative, Ideology, and Meaning in Early Modern Culture* (New York: St. Martin's Press, 2001), p. 11; Marion Gibson, *Reading Witchcraft: Stories of Early English Witches* (London: Routledge, 1999), p. 114; Rosen (ed.), *Witchcraft*, p. 213.

[24]   Gibson, *Reading Witchcraft*, p. 187.

moral stand, whereas others try to seem neutral. Some relate to one case, some to a few cases. Some cases are discussed in a few pamphlets, others in none. Unlike indictments or court records, the pamphlets have no standardized form or style. Their reliability depends on the author's legal knowledge and the level of accuracy and detail. Some pamphlets were written by authors familiar with the legal process and some by ignorant writers who did not know the difference between a grand and a petty jury. Their accuracy is dependent on the author's understanding, sources, presence in court (first- or second-hand information), bias, level of selectivity in providing the information, and so on.

Although the pamphlets and tracts cannot provide a full and systematic picture of the prosecution, these literary texts are probably the richest existing documentation of conflicting attitudes toward the proof of witchcraft in English society.[25] The tracts and pamphlets reflect a lively socio-legal debate, and the pamphlet literature provides us with reports written by many participants: judges, lawyers, divines, laymen and other members of the public.[26] This spectrum is important when we examine issues of proof, not only from the narrow legalistic discourse within the boundaries of the legal profession, but from a wider social perspective. The social and intellectual currents that are reflected in the pamphlets possibly influenced the judges' and juries' decisions and sometimes clashed with them. The fact that those participants wrote from their own subjective perspectives is no impediment to this research, but rather an advantage.

One of the main advantages of the pamphlets is that they provide a much broader social context to the witch trials than court records.[27] The court cases are just the tip of the iceberg of the witchcraft phenomenon. Many of the beliefs, suspicions and concerns never made it to court. Among the many reasons for unwillingness to prosecute a suspected witch were fear, lack of evidence, the cost and trouble for the complainants, intimidation on behalf of the suspect, the severity of the capital punishment, informal out-of-court arbitration and informal sanctions.[28] When a case did reach court, the charges of the indictment

---

[25]   Sharpe, *Instruments of Darkness*, p. 105. Recent research is innovative in its use of legal records (statutes, indictments, examinations, orders, and so on) for historical purposes and also in its study of law through the help of non-legal sources such as broadsides, pamphlets, ballads, plays, personal letters and diaries, and so on.

[26]   Gibson regarded controversy as the most important aspect of the Jacobean pamphlets. Gibson, *Reading Witchcraft*, p. 181.

[27]   J.S. Cockburn, 'The Nature and Incidence of Crime in England 1559–1625: A Preliminary Survey', in J.S. Cockburn (ed.), *Crime in England, 1550–1800* (London: Methuen & Co. Ltd, 1977), p. 56.

[28]   Langbein, *Origins*, p. 151.

were often just a small selection of the suspicions, but the information in the pamphlets went beyond the scope of the indictment.

Pamphlets are an excellent source for the purposes of this research, as they contain many references to evidentiary techniques, including informal or illegal methods, with frequent comments about their probativeness or propriety. Theoretically, court records could have been an important source of information about evidentiary practices because they are a systematic body of standardized texts. Unfortunately, the contemporary court records, of which many are missing or damaged, are an insufficient source of knowledge about evidentiary methods.[29] The records contain no verbatim transcripts, descriptions of the proof offered or the testimonies. Not all official records were preserved. Only 'true bills', those that became indictments, were kept. The 'ignoramus bills', which could teach us about legal insufficiency, were not preserved,[30] but rather 'rent into peeces immediately'.[31] The depositions of examinations did not survive either.[32] The records do not state the plea, but it could be reconstructed from the standard codes of the clerks.[33] Using court records 'is vital when building up serial statistical evidence about crime and punishment, but it is less useful in providing qualitative insights'.[34] Thus, the court records are insufficient as a source of information regarding proof techniques, and the dearth of information presented in the indictments and records renders impossible the reconstruction of the evidence submitted.

Comparison of data contained in the pamphlets and court records reveals that the pamphlets' information 'of such facts as names, familial relationships, status, charges, pleas, verdicts and sentences usually tally with legal records with

---

[29]   With the exception of a few celebrated treason trials. Ibid., pp. 14–15.

[30]   John Hamilton Baker, 'Criminal Courts and Procedure at Common Law 1550–1800', in J.S. Cockburn (ed.), *Crime in England, 1550–1800* (Princeton, NJ: Princeton University Press, 1977), p.19.

[31]   Sir Thomas Smith, *De Republica Anglorum* (London: Printed by Henrie Midleton for Gregorie Seton, 1583), p. 68.

[32]   Cockburn, 'Introduction', p. 11; Herrup, *The Common Peace*, p. 67, fn. 1; John H. Langbein, *Prosecuting Crime in the Renaissance: England, Germany, France*, Studies in Legal History (Cambridge, MA: Harvard University Press, 1974), p. 31.

[33]   If an accused pleaded guilty, then a jury trial was obviated and there would be no list of jurors for that case. In addition, the clerks marked the indictment with standard abbreviations, including the following: *cogn[ovit]* for a guilty plea, *po[nit] se [super patriam]* for a not guilty plea and request for jury trial, *cul[pabilis]* for a guilty verdict and *sus[pendatur]* for to be hanged. Cockburn, 'Introduction', pp. 195, 116, 124. An acquittal (*quietus*) was not marked on the indictment.

[34]   J.A. Sharpe, 'Witchcraft and Women in Seventeenth-Century England: Some Northern Evidence', *Continuity and Change* 6, no. 2 (1991): p. 184.

some glaring exceptions'.[35] Macfarlane, who compared the pamphlets to the Essex court records, also concluded that those two sources support each other. The pamphlets usually contain more details, but in some cases the indictments contain information that was omitted from the pamphlets. Contradictions among the sources exist but are few in number.[36] On the basis of that comparison Macfarlane concluded that '[p]amphlets, therefore, are a vital and reliable source, providing otherwise inaccessible material and correcting the somewhat narrow impression of witchcraft prosecutions given by the indictments'.[37] Unfortunately, this unequivocal inference must be regarded with some reservation.

Pamphlets should be read with caution. They contain broad information that is not necessarily available in other sources. The boundary between documentation and fiction may not always be apparent, and it is often impossible to know whether certain details were invented. However, a comparison to other sources tends to verify many factual details. So, despite the difficulties, the pamphlets enjoy what Notestein dubbed 'trustworthiness' or, in Cockburn's more critical terms, 'heavily qualified' reliability.[38]

Nevertheless, for the purposes of this research, qualified reliability is no obstacle. Although we cannot be sure that certain asserted facts are true, we may confidently construct the general intellectual and social paradigms behind the pamphlet. For example, we may not be sure that the accused cursed the victim before he got sick. But we can conclude that some of the contemporaries believed in the reality of bewitchment and that witchcraft can cause illness. We may not be certain whether a specific suspect was thrown into the pond and whether she floated or sank (this fact could also be a matter of the viewers' interpretation). However, we can conclude that at least some of the people of early modern England regarded the swimming test as probative. We may doubt that the pamphlet is accurate in stating that the alleged witch confessed freely and voluntarily. Yet, we can learn that some contemporaries regarded such confessions as a satisfactory basis for conviction. The social landscape is not necessarily painted by accurate representations of reality but can be reconstructed from the stereotypes presented in the pamphlets. Factually misleading and highly fictional accounts also reflect ideas and interests and are well suited to the goal of this research.

---

[35] Gibson, *Reading Witchcraft*, p. 9. See also Langbein, *Prosecuting Crime in the Renaissance*, p. 47.

[36] Macfarlane, *Witchcraft in Tudor and Stuart England*, pp. 85, 92, fn. 19.

[37] Ibid., p. 86.

[38] Cockburn, 'Introduction', p. 98; Wallace Notestein, *A History of Witchcraft in England from 1558 to 1718*, 1911, 2nd edn (New York: T.Y. Crowell Co., 1968), p. 37, fn. 6.

In addition, the analysis of the pamphlet and tract literature also helps to identify paradigmatic gaps between the legal system and social and intellectual currents. For example, the anti-witchcraft statutes of 1542 and 1563 were based on malefic notions. The demonic pact with the devil became a statutory element only by the Jacobean law of 1604. Yet, an analysis of early pamphlets reveals that the demonic theme of the pact with the devil had already appeared in the 1560s. The phenomenon of witchcraft was not limited to the statutory definition, but belonged to a wider intellectual and theological discourse.

The pamphlets provide a much wider picture of the cultural and social context of the witch trials than that provided by court records. The pamphlets and tracts not only describe the different evidentiary practices, but also offer a broad perspective of the intellectual, theological and social paradigms behind them. Holmes maintained that a sensitive reading of this literature can detect to what degree popular culture was moulded by elite concerns.[39] In Sharpe's words, the pamphlets locate the witch beliefs and witch trials in a 'moral framework'.[40]

Exploring the different views and controversy around witchcraft is essential for a good historical study that is not written solely from the perspective of the prevailing concepts or figures, but rather uncovers those voices that were silenced. My interpretation of the texts considers the value that the different speakers attributed to the various evidentiary methods and how natural or taken for granted they perceived them to be. In addition, my analysis takes into account the social identity of the participants in the debate about how to prove witchcraft (in particular, their professional affiliation, social class and position along the centre/periphery axis). Identification of voice and authorship must also take into account the possibility of multiple voices in the texts, implicit messages and biases of the authors.[41] The analysis of evidentiary methods in a mixture of diverse perceptions helps to expose the logic and rationale behind them. Such a comprehensive view helps to unravel general patterns and modes of thought about proving the crime of witchcraft. Such analysis enables us to examine how the wider social and cultural power grid interacted with the intellectual currents and echoed in the social and legal views expressed by the pamphleteers

---

[39]   Clive Holmes, 'Popular Culture? Witches, Magistrates and Divines in Early Modern England', in S.L. Kaplan (ed.), *Understanding Popular Culture: Europe from the Middle Ages to the Nineteenth Century* (Berlin: Walter de Gruyter & Co., 1984), p. 94.

[40]   Sharpe, *Instruments of Darkness*, p. 100.

[41]   Gibson, *Reading Witchcraft*, various locations, esp. pp. 37–49. Identifying voice and authorship may help to approach what Briggs called 'the most difficult problem of all ... of detecting behind-the-scenes manipulation by persons who may never appear at all, or attacks on substitutes for the real targets'; Briggs, 'Many Reasons Why: Witchcraft and the Problem of Multiple Explanation', p. 57.

and the authors of tracts. Tracing compatibility between social groups and their evidentiary preferences and dispositions helps to uncover hidden interests and rationales at the basis of established ways of proof. Treating the stories in the pamphlets as cultural narratives helps to go beyond an accumulation of judicial documentation and moves toward an understanding of the contemporaries' concepts and beliefs. My analysis endeavours to extract from these texts how the diverse social approaches to the issue of proof offered answers to the need for securing convictions on the one hand and for maintaining a claim to a just legal system, a rational procedure and a moral society on the other.

Intellectual and Disciplinary Framework

The period in which witchcraft was a crime coincided with major developments in legal procedure, criminal evidence and the structure of the English legal system. The legal literature routinely presumes the rules of evidence to be general and unaffected by the severity of the crime or by probative difficulties. Broad studies of English legal history discuss witchcraft only to a limited extent and from the perspective of the Enlightenment, viewing the early modern witchcraft beliefs as part of a superstitious and cruel past.[42] A long tradition of scholarly works written from an internal legal perspective examines the internal processes in the English legal system. The theoretical concept of the serious but hard-to-prove crime allows an examination of the proof question not through a narrow legalistic prism, but as a wider societal dilemma, exploring the interrelations between different cultural, ideological and intellectual currents, including law and various social players. Witchcraft is an outstanding example of such a problematic crime, and it therefore provides an excellent case study for the social embeddedness of ways of proof.

Recent studies have examined legal history in either a social or intellectual context. Some have examined law in a specific social and political context and focused on the practices and social affiliations of different players in the justice system – lawyers, grand jurors, trial jurors, magistrates and judges. Jurors were at the focus of much research; but many other actors in the legal arena were

---

[42]   Sir William Searle Holdsworth, *A History of English Law*, 17 vols (London: Methuen & Co., 1924), vol. IV, pp. 507–11; Sir Frederick Pollock and William Maitland, *The History of English Law Before the Time of Edward I*, 2 vols (Cambridge, UK: The University Press, 1895); Sir James Fitzjames Stephen, *A History of the Criminal Law of England* (London: Macmillan, 1883), pp. 410, 436–7. Baker's more recent comprehensive study, also written from an internal legal perspective, does not include witchcraft; John Hamilton Baker, *An Introduction to English Legal History*, 3rd edn (London: Butterworths, 1990), p. 6, fn. 7.

also studied.[43] Lawyers were studied by Langbein, who portrayed a shift from lawyer-free to lawyer-dominated criminal proceedings.[44] The transformation was not the result of a change in worldview, but rather of a series of coincidental judicial decisions in response to various procedural difficulties (such as pre-trial investigation or the procedural inferiority of the defendant). Langbein showed how this 'lawyerization' resulted in what we now know as the law of criminal evidence. Langbein related evidential developments to social players, yet he remained within the bounds of the legal profession, referring to lawyers but not to other professions or social categories. Although Langbein did not refer to witchcraft, his book was of immense importance to this work, as he traced the creation of four basic rules of criminal evidence: the character rule, the corroboration rule, the confession rule and the hearsay rule. Langbein uncovered the basic presumptions and weaknesses of the adversary system and the links between the substance of the adversary trial and the structure of the legal system.[45] A related branch of socio-legal history studies the history of crime in general, aiming to uncover its social meanings, or mentalities.[46]

Scholars who study legal history often demonstrate the gap between formal and informal law, between law in books and law in action.[47] Jury nullification,

---

[43]   Cockburn, 'Introduction', in J.S. Cockburn and Thomas Andrew Green (eds), *Twelve Good Men and True: The Criminal Trial Jury in England, 1200–1800* (Princeton, NJ: Princeton University Press, 1988), esp. pp. 130–34; George Fisher, 'The Jury's Rise as Lie Detector', *The Yale Law Journal*, no. 107 (1997): pp. 575–713; Thomas Andrew Green, *Verdict According to Conscience: Perspectives on the English Criminal Trial Jury, 1200–1800* (Chicago: University of Chicago Press, 1985).

[44]   Langbein, *Origins*.

[45]   Other works are Norma Landau's research on the role of the justices of the peace in a social and political framework, which points out a shift in the model of justice, and Herrup's analysis of the interrelations between the different players (accusers, grand jurors, trial jurors, magistrates, judges) in the criminal proceeding and how the decisions reached by the participants in the legal system were grounded in moral concepts of criminality; Herrup, *The Common Peace*; Cynthia B. Herrup, 'Law and Morality in Seventeenth-Century England', *Past and Present*, no. 106 (1985); Norma Landau, *The Justices of the Peace, 1679–1760* (Berkeley: University of California Press, 1984); Langbein, *Origins*.

[46]   Baker, Cockburn, Sharpe, Macfarlane and Beattie and others are among the authors in J.S. Cockburn (ed.), *Crime in England, 1550–1800* (Princeton, NJ: Princeton University Press, 1977). A notable example is Gaskill's work on the changing mentalities of the English people, 1550–1750. By studying the crimes of witchcraft, coining and murder, Gaskill showed how ordinary people perceived their lives and society and how these perceptions changed over time; Malcolm Gaskill, *Crime and Mentalities in Early Modern England* (Cambridge: Cambridge University Press, 2000).

[47]   John Hamilton Baker, *The Law's Two Bodies: Some Evidential Problems in English Legal History* (Oxford: Oxford University Press, 2001).

plea bargaining or magisterial absenteeism from the sessions of the assizes, they claim, are not matters of law per se, but of the manner of the administration of the law, which is shaped by social, cultural and political considerations. All these researchers explore the relationship between the structure of the legal system and the content of its decisions, the gap between the practice and the theory of law, and thus expose basic legal concepts.

Another current of recent research belongs to the intellectual history tradition and examines the interrelation of law and other disciplines. The best example of this line of study is the work of Barbara Shapiro.[48] Shapiro examined the interrelations between law, history, philosophy, natural science, religion, language, literature and witchcraft, and traced as well the formation of basic concepts such as fact, probability and certainty, and evidentiary standards such as 'beyond reasonable doubt'. However, Shapiro's perspective was that of the history of ideas rather than legal history. Like Shapiro, I examine different disciplinary discourses, but my analysis relates the ideas and beliefs to the social positions of the speakers (and specifically their professional affiliations, social class and positions along the centre/periphery axis). Moreover, I explicate how disciplinary discourses were used to materialize further the diverse interests of the actors participating in the witchcraft debate.

These currents of recent legal history research help to reveal the basic cultural and intellectual presuppositions on which the legal system is founded. Substantive criminal law, criminal procedure and criminal evidence law are shown to be social constructions and not independent legal entities. My study also demonstrates that law is shaped and transformed by the practice and interests of actual players in the socio-cultural field and that it has a dialectical relationship with other intellectual and cultural disciplines. It shows that ways of proof were not merely an independent, objective and formal body of law of evidence.

It has been pointed out that although much has been written about the judicial administration of the witch trials, the evidentiary aspect of the crime was neglected, though 'no social, economic, religious or cultural factor shaped the history of English witchcraft more'.[49] Shapiro is one of the few scholars who discuss

---

[48]   Barbara J. Shapiro, *'Beyond Reasonable Doubt' and 'Probable Cause': Historical Perspectives on the Anglo-American Law of Evidence* (Berkeley: University of California Press, 1991); Barbara J. Shapiro, *A Culture of Fact: England, 1550–1720* (Ithaca, NY: Cornell University Press, 2000); Barbara J. Shapiro, *Probability and Certainty in Seventeenth-Century England: A Study of the Relationships between Natural Science, Religion, History, Law, and Literature* (Princeton, NJ: Princeton University Press, 1983).

[49]   Gaskill, 'Witchcraft and Evidence in Early Modern England', p. 38. See also Levack, 'Crime and the Law', pp. 150, 153.

evidence and procedure in the specific context of witchcraft cases. However, in her discussion she did not presume to portray the full criminal procedure or evidence law in witchcraft trials, but to illustrate basic epistemological concepts related to her argument. Unsworth, in examining the relationship between the law and witchcraft beliefs, claimed that, on the one hand, law created the crime of witchcraft by using the procedure and evidentiary techniques to reaffirm the reality of witchcraft and generate knowledge about the nature of witchcraft practices and, on the other hand, the legal process contributed to scepticism and eventually to the decline of witch trials.[50] Gaskill noted another paradoxical aspect of evidence in the English witch trials of 1645 to 1647. He described how the witch finders attacked the crime with extreme testimonies and evidence of diabolic perversion. This heavy-handedness eventually resulted in changing evidentiary standards and hastened the decline of the prosecution.

It is important to remember that the question posed in this research is *not* how one actually proved witchcraft in the courts of early modern England, but rather what the contemporaries' attitudes, dispositions, opinions and beliefs regarding the proof of witchcraft were. What methods were considered sufficient, just and religiously correct? What evidentiary techniques were viewed as illegal, immoral and inadequate? The array of the official evidentiary techniques and procedures and the socio-cultural and intellectual notions of proof overlapped only to a limited extent. As the perspective of this research is broader than a strictly legal one, I draw heavily on historical studies of witchcraft. This study joins the recent scholarship that does not condemn witchcraft beliefs and practices as past superstitions and atrocities, but rather tries to explore the social and cultural uses of witchcraft and how it made sense in the world of the contemporaries.[51]

---

[50]   C.R. Unsworth, 'Witchcraft Beliefs and Criminal Procedure in Early Modern England', in Thomas G. Watkin (ed.), *Legal Record and Historical Reality: Proceedings of the Eighth British Legal History Conference, Cardiff, 1987* (London: The Hambledon Press, 1989), pp. 71–98.

[51]   The earlier monographs belong to a rational, or Enlightenment, approach, which considered the witchcraft beliefs to be superstition and delusion. Ewen, *Witch Hunting and Witch Trials*, p. 113; George Lyman Kittredge, *Witchcraft in Old and New England* (Cambridge, MA: Harvard University Press, 1929), p. 5; Notestein, *A History of Witchcraft in England from 1558 to 1718*, pp. 309–10. It was only during the early 1970s, with the seminal work of Thomas and Macfarlane, that the popular beliefs were not dismissed as mere delusion. Thomas and Macfarlane, drawing on sociological and anthropological theories, demonstrated the social role, or function, of the witchcraft beliefs. Macfarlane, *Witchcraft in Tudor and Stuart England*; Keith Thomas, *Religion and the Decline of Magic* (New York: Charles Scribner's Sons, 1971).

Witchcraft and witch trials have attracted considerable research attention.[52] Keith Thomas stated that 'much nonsense has been written on this subject and the general reader needs to pick his way with caution'.[53] The vast body of literature treats the witch trials from diverse theoretical perspectives and studies different geographic locations.[54] Most scholars currently agree that there is no single explanation for early modern European witchcraft prosecution and beliefs.[55] Single-factor explanations reduce the complexity of the witchcraft phenomenon and are not convincing. My analysis relies mostly on works written from the perspectives of social history and the history of ideas. Both scholarly currents examine witchcraft and witch trials in a wider intellectual and social context.

Thomas and Macfarlane's groundbreaking works attempted to explore the socio-economic rationales behind witchcraft prosecution. Thomas endeavoured to explain it through a tri-tier approach: 'a *psychological* explanation of the motives of the participants in the drama of witchcraft accusation, a *sociological* analysis of the situation in which such accusations tended to occur, and an

---

[52]   A good overview of European witchcraft history is to be found in Levack, *The Witch-Hunt in Early Modern Europe*. Two other European historiographies are Geoffrey Robert Quaife, *Godly Zeal and Furious Rage: The Witch in Early Modern Europe* (New York: St. Martin's Press, 1987), and Geoffrey Scarre, *Witchcraft and Magic in Sixteenth- and Seventeenth-Century Europe*, Studies in European History (Atlantic Highlands, NJ: Humanities Press International, 1987). All of England is the subject of five renowned monographs: Ewen, *Witch Hunting and Witch Trials*; Kittredge, *Witchcraft in Old and New England*; Notestein, *A History of Witchcraft in England from 1558 to 1718*; Sharpe, *Instruments of Darkness*; and Thomas, *Religion and the Decline of Magic*. An example of regional research is Alan Macfarlane's work on Essex. Some researchers limit their scope to a single episode or witch hunt, for example, Richard Deacon's book on the series of trials orchestrated in Essex by the notorious witch hunter Matthew Hopkins, or even a single trial, for example, Geis and Bunn's research on the 1662 trial of Rose Cullender and Amy Denny at the Bury St Edmunds assizes, or Sharpe's research on the case of Anne Gunter. Richard Deacon, *Matthew Hopkins: Witch Finder General* (London: F. Muller, 1976); Geis and Bunn, *A Trial of Witches*; Macfarlane, *Witchcraft in Tudor and Stuart England*; J.A. Sharpe, *The Bewitching of Anne Gunter: A Horrible and True Story of Deception, Witchcraft, Murder, and the King of England* (New York: Routledge, 2000). About the difference between single-case and broad-based studies, see Geis and Bunn, *A Trial of Witches*, p. 109.

[53]   Thomas, *Religion and the Decline of Magic*, p. 435, bibliographical note.

[54]   Historians of witchcraft have been assisted by many other disciplines, including 'social-anthropological functionalism, labelling theories of deviance, revolutionary feminism, acculturation theory, the sociology of state-building, the Gramscian notion of hegemony, Freudian and Kleinian psychoanalysis, theories of collective psychological trauma and psychosis, and psychosomatology and the science of hallucinogens', Clark, 'Introduction', p. 3.

[55]   Briggs, 'Many Reasons Why: Witchcraft and the Problem of Multiple Explanation', p. 51; Gaskill, 'Early Modern Kent', p. 285.

intellectual explanation of the concepts which made such accusations possible'.[56] Macfarlane regarded the socio-economic change as an important factor in encouraging prosecution.[57]

Thomas and Macfarlane pointed to guilt feelings as a significant motivation in making witchcraft accusations (an approach that is often called the charity-being-denied model). The typical scenario they described was of a poor old woman who came to the door to beg and was refused by her better-off neighbours. An inexplicable misfortune that subsequently befell the neighbour was attributed to witchcraft. Blaming the misfortune on the begging neighbour eased guilt feelings and served as a *post factum* proof justifying the initial refusal of charity. The model was criticized as being partial and exaggerated.[58] Yet, it is clear that despite the shortcomings of the charity-being-denied model, Thomas made an enormous contribution by examining the accusations in the wide social and intellectual contexts that made them possible.[59]

Whereas Macfarlane's functionalist approach was limited in accounting for social change, the intellectual history approach examined the change of ideas over time. An original and comprehensive work in that vein is Clark's *Thinking with Demons*, in which he recommended that before setting out to explain the demise of ideas, one must make a serious attempt to say what they were.[60] He demonstrated how witchcraft was part of a larger intellectual environment, influenced by and influencing other concepts. Clark's pretext in the study of beliefs in witchcraft was 'to look at how they worked while they survived, rather

---

[56] Thomas, *Religion and the Decline of Magic*, p. 469. However, Barry points out that despite this ordering, it is significant that Thomas began with the intellectual environment (Barry, 'Introduction', p. 3.

[57] The deepening gap between richer and poorer villagers caused social tensions, which could be relieved by witchcraft accusations. Macfarlane claimed that the prosecution era between 1560 and 1650 was contemporaneous with the weakening of poor-aiding institutions such as church relief, the manorial organization and the networks of kinship and neighbours. He adds that witchcraft prosecution declined once an alternative assistance for the poor became institutionalized. Macfarlane, *Witchcraft in Tudor and Stuart England*, pp. 205–6.

[58] Barry, 'Introduction', p. 37; Gibson, *Reading Witchcraft*, ch. 3; Jim Sharpe, 'The Devil in East Anglia', in Jonathan Barry, Marianne Hester and Gareth Roberts (eds), *Witchcraft in Early Modern Europe* (Cambridge, UK: Cambridge University Press, 1996), p. 242.

[59] Barry, 'Introduction', pp. 26, 42. Thomas was not the first to examine the issue of witchcraft in its social context (for example, H.R. Trevor-Roper, *The European Witch-Craze of the Sixteenth and Seventeenth Centuries, and Other Essays* (New York: Harper & Row, 1969)), but his work was the most comprehensive.

[60] Stuart Clark, *Thinking with Demons: The Idea of Witchcraft in Early Modern Europe* (Oxford: Oxford University Press, 1997), p. 683.

than at how they emerged or declined'.[61] He examined the fields of language, science, history, religion and politics but reckoned that other important categories, not included in his book, are law and jurisprudence.[62] Shapiro took a latitudinal approach by examining the interrelations between law, witchcraft and other early modern intellectual currents such as natural philosophy, experimental science, religion, history and language. Witchcraft, though not the focus of Shapiro's work and not treated in great detail, served Shapiro as a significant component in a system of congruent intellectual fields.[63] Sharpe's *Instruments of Darkness* examined witchcraft in relation to English politics, religion, legal system, elite versus popular concepts and concepts of gender.

Current research views witchcraft as a cultural phenomenon and resource 'which allowed the early moderns to express emotions, pursue strategies and define identities'.[64] In line with that scholarly work, my book aims to transcend the descriptive level of legal and prosecutorial patterns on the one hand, and to refrain from an inventory of witchcraft narratives or social stereotypes on the other hand. This book grounds the intellectual and academic debate about the ways of proof in a specific socio-historical context.

Main Themes

The anti-witchcraft legislation did not set forth any witchcraft-specific procedure or ways of proof. The general criminal procedure was therefore applicable to witchcraft cases as well, although witchcraft-specific modes of proof and procedure existed in addition to the general criminal procedure. To understand how the early modern English thought about proving witchcraft, it is important to be acquainted not only with the details of the pre-trial and trial criminal procedure in such cases, but also with non-official and sometimes illegal procedures that were common during that era (Chapters 1 and 2).

---

[61]   Ibid.

[62]   '[H]ow witches should be legally apprehended, examined, and punished'. Ibid., p. x.

[63]   Shapiro, *A Culture of Fact*; Shapiro, *Probability and Certainty*.

[64]   Alison Rowlands, 'Telling Witchcraft Stories: New Perspectives on Witchcraft and Witches in the Early Modern Period', *Gender & History* 10, no. 2 (1998): p. 301. Other works are Diane Purkiss, *The Witch in History: Early Modern and Twentieth-Century Representations* (New York, NY: Routledge, 1996); Lyndal Roper, *Oedipus and the Devil: Witchcraft, Sexuality, and Religion in Early Modern Europe* (London: Routledge, 1994); Peter Rushton, 'Texts of Authority: Witchcraft Accusations and the Demonstration of Truth in Early Modern England', in Stuart Clark (ed.), *Languages of Witchcraft: Narrative, Ideology, and Meaning in Early Modern Culture* (New York: St. Martin's Press, 2001). Gibson, *Reading Witchcraft* is devoted to reading witchcraft texts as narratives.

My findings demonstrate that in early modern England there was a heated debate over the proof of witchcraft. Underlying the debate were two consensual presuppositions – the first, that witches existed, and the second, that witchcraft was indeed a hard-to-prove crime. The techniques of evidence were tools employed by the participants as part of their general strategies to handle the dilemma of proof. Decisive proof, of course, could ensure that no innocent was condemned and that no guilty escaped, thus solving the dilemma. The early modern English, indeed, were aiming for the 'sure ground, and infallible proofe',[65] or at least 'some very shrewd signes, probable reason, frequent Experience'.[66] But what was that strong, solid, sure and infallible proof? While most authors agreed that good and strong evidence is the solution to the dilemma of the serious but hard-to-prove crime, there were wide disagreements as to what constituted such evidence.

My analysis concentrates on major evidential categories: circumstantial evidence and physical evidence, which is a sub-category of circumstantial evidence (Chapters 3–6), supernatural signs (Chapters 7–9), and the evaluation of the truthfulness of narratives (Chapters 10–12). Various evidential categories are supported by different rationales. Yet, my findings point to the social embeddedness of *all* these categories. The evidentiary methods were shaped in the process of the debate between the different groups and participants, and they are as much a social and cultural construct as a legal solution.

The period under study, 1542 to 1736, is situated between the jurisprudential paradigms of the ordeals and modern evidence rules. In fact, some of my findings reflect the transition from the ordeal to the modern trial. For example, they point to the prominence of the 'experiment' beginning at the end of the sixteenth century and lasting to the beginning of the eighteenth century – well before the rise of so-called modern science. The experiments, which flourished at the pre-trial stage and met with judicial approval at the official proceedings, consisted of methodical, rational and carefully constructed procedures employed in the discovery of facts. Shapiro argued that the concept of fact was created in the legal discourse, especially in the context of trials by lay jurors, and transmitted to other fields.[67] My findings suggest that the establishment of facts by experiments

---

[65]   George Gifford, *A Dialogue Concerning Witches and Witchcraftes* (London: Tobie Cooke and Mihil, 1593), H4.

[66]   John Gaule, *Select Cases of Conscience Touching Vvitches and Vvitchcrafts* (London: Richard Clutterbuck, 1646), pp. 85–7.

[67]   Shapiro, *A Culture of Fact*. Cf. Walter Stephens, *Demon Lovers: Witchcraft, Sex, and the Crisis of Belief* (Chicago: University of Chicago Press, 2002), p. 35. Stephens maintains: 'Legal proof has become subservient to metaphysical proof. In fact, legal proof has *become* scientific proof.'

was initiated mostly by non-lawyers, notably by members of affluent provincial families, and often already at the pre-trial stage. The evidential experiments were used to discover supernatural facts such as witchcraft, often by the reconstruction of ancient supernatural signs (such as the swimming of witches) as experiments. This mixture of the rational and the supernatural reflects a changing mode of proof that was rooted in wider intellectual and social transformation.

The social variable of profession is strongly affiliated with the attitude toward proof of witchcraft. The members of three professional groups – law, medicine and the clergy – were especially active in the witchcraft debate. My findings point out that they used the evidence of witchcraft as a resource to bolster their social and political standing. The physicians strove to position themselves as experts in the diagnosis of bewitchments or possessions. As their practice was the diagnosis of natural symptoms, they regarded themselves as the experts in the field of distinguishing natural from unnatural symptoms. Medical authors tended to favour natural explanations for diseases and resorted to unnatural explanations only after ruling out the former. The learned physicians' claim to unique expertise was directed at other disciplines as well as at other types of medical practitioners. The clerics also tried to use their learning and moral authority to influence the choice and interpretation of proof techniques. However, the clergy were less successful than the physicians in establishing an indispensable position. Finally, the members of the legal profession used evidentiary techniques and strategies not as mere ad hoc solutions for individual cases, but also as part of wider strategies aimed to achieve legitimization for the justice system. Those strategies enhanced flexibility, enabling convictions in individual cases while constructing a sense of prudent and just methods of adjudication. Men of law were also successful in building a sense of professional expertise, while at the same time shifting much of the burden of the dilemma of proof of the crime to others (transferring determination to lay jurors and stressing the importance of expert testimony and confession). The prism of professional affiliation reveals that neither the choice nor the interpretation of evidentiary methods was guided exclusively by truth-finding considerations.

Professional affiliation is, of course, just one of the components of social identity. A physician could still be a deeply religious person. A theologian could be a member of the Royal Society or write a guidebook for jurors.[68] Members of the same profession could also have disagreements among themselves. Thus, none of the social groups was utterly homogeneous. Although professionals had much in common, they varied in economic status, social background and even

---

[68]   Joseph Glanvill is an example of the former and Richard Bernard an example of the latter.

in training and education. Not all those who lived in the countryside belonged to the same social stratum, and there were great differences in lifestyle among the gentry.[69] What guided me in assigning a speaker to a certain profession, other than biographical information derived from secondary sources, was the type of discourse in which he was engaged. For example, if the speaker was the author of a medical book, I associated him with the physicians, no matter whether he was merely an apothecary and not a licensed member of the Royal College of Physicians.[70]

A fuller comprehension of the dispositions of the participants in the witchcraft debate toward the issue of proof must take into account other elements of their social identity. In my analysis I further explore the factors of social class and position along the centre/periphery axis. Elite speakers distinguished themselves as refined through the condemnation of popular proof techniques of those they called the 'vulgar' and the 'superstitious'. Members of the lower strata continued to favour supernatural proof methods, some of which (such as the swimming of witches) were fiercely denounced by elite writers as illegal and immoral. This book examines whether the discourse on proof techniques was indeed polarized along social class. My analysis further endeavours to determine to what degree the poles of high/low or learned/popular correlated with the opposition of centre/periphery.

The findings clearly suggest that the social construction of proof techniques cannot be attributed to a single factor and that sticking to the sharp dichotomies of high/low, learned/popular or above/below leads to over-simplification. Thus, some of the most influential developments in the shaping of evidentiary methods occurred at the intersection of provincial setting and middling social position. Popular and learned notions blended effectively under the leadership of the provincial elite. The members of affluent provincial families acted as social brokers who disseminated new modes of proof and reconstructed the old supernatural signs as new rational evidentiary techniques. For example, in the case of the experiment, provincial families of the 'middling sort' and the petty gentry mitigated between the elite and lower circles of society, translating the beliefs and cultural concepts of one social group to the other and affecting both.

It should be remembered that in addition to profession, social class and locale of residence, social identity is comprised of many other elements such as gender, religious faction, political affiliation, economic status and more. Some

---

[69]   J.A. Sharpe, *Early Modern England: A Social History 1550–1750*, 2nd edn (London: Arnold, 1997), chs 6–8.

[70]   Such was the case of William Drage.

of these variables have been widely researched.[71] Different studies pose different questions and stem from diverse intellectual traditions. The perspective of the serious but hard-to-prove crime and the primary sources in my corpus led me to social class, locale of residence and professional affiliation as factors having significant affinity to evidentiary dispositions. However, I do not claim that these are the exclusive factors in the shaping of evidentiary methods. No single factor per se could explain the formation of evidence law, just as the truth-seeking rationale cannot fully account for it. Instead, my findings point to a complex interplay between a broad collection of variables through which evidentiary methods are constructed. Despite the diversity in the categories of professional affiliation, social class and locale of residence, clear generalizations can still be made about the affinity between each social category and the evidential dispositions of its members. This fact lends support to the centrality of these categories as significant factors in the shaping of evidential dispositions.

---

[71]   About Christian denomination and witchcraft, see Clark, *Thinking with Demons*, and Levack, *The Witch-Hunt in Early Modern Europe*, pp. 100, 104, 112. It seems that although current researchers are reluctant to rely on religious conflict as a dominant explanation, they do link it to witchcraft prosecution, though not in a simple cause and effect manner. About witchcraft and Reformation, see Barry, 'Introduction', p. 34; Larner, *Witchcraft and Religion*, p. 98; Brian P. Levack, 'State-Building and Witch Hunting', in Jonathan Barry, Marianne Hester and Gareth Roberts (eds), *Witchcraft in Early Modern Europe* (Cambridge, UK: Cambridge University Press, 1996), p. 23; Sharpe, 'Introduction', pp. 6–7; Thomas, *Religion and the Decline of Magic*, pp. 454, 493, 498. Politics and witchcraft are discussed in Ian Bostridge, *Witchcraft and Its Transformations, c.1650–c.1750*, Oxford Historical Monographs (Oxford; New York: Clarendon Press, 1997). Gender and witchcraft are considered in Robin Briggs, 'Women as Victims? Witches, Judges, and the Community', *French History* 5 (1991), pp. 438–50; Clark, *Thinking with Demons*, pp. 108, 110, 119–33; Marianne Hester, *Lewd Women and Wicked Witches: A Study of the Dynamics of Male Domination* (London: Routledge, 1992); Marianne Hester, 'Patriarchal Reconstruction', in Jonathan Barry, Marianne Hester and Gareth Roberts (eds), *Witchcraft in Early Modern Europe* (Cambridge, UK: Cambridge University Press, 1996); Clive Holmes, 'Women: Witnesses and Witches', *Past and Present*, no. 140 (1993); Larner, *Enemies of God: The Witch-Hunt in Scotland*, pp. 3, 92; Macfarlane, *Witchcraft in Tudor and Stuart England*, p. 160; Lyndal Roper, 'Early Modern Germany', in Jonathan Barry, Marianne Hester and Gareth Roberts (eds), *Witchcraft in Early Modern Europe* (Cambridge, UK: Cambridge University Press, 1996); Roper, *Oedipus and the Devil: Witchcraft, Sexuality, and Religion in Early Modern Europe*; Thomas, *Religion and the Decline of Magic*, pp. 562, 568; Deborah Willis, *Malevolent Nurture: Witch-Hunting and Maternal Power in Early Modern England* (Ithaca, NY: Cornell University Press, 1995).

Figure 1.1 Three witches riding a pig. From the title page of
*The Witches of Northampton-Shire: Agnes Browne. Ioane Vaughan.
Arthur Bill. Hellen Ienkenson. Mary Barber. Witches. Who Were All Executed at Northampton
the 22. Of Iuly Last* (London: Arthur Iohnson, 1612). [Shelfmark: Tanner 251 (4)]
Courtesy of the Bodleian Library, University of Oxford.

Chapter 1
Pre-trial Procedure

Legal Background

The crime of witchcraft was created by statute in the middle of the sixteenth century, but proving this crime, which was committed through the use of indiscernible devilish powers, posed a grave problem. The application of the anti-witchcraft legislation was intertwined with, and shaped by, significant and simultaneous developments in criminal procedure and evidence law. Shapiro even suggested that the development of standards of proof eventually brought about the disappearance of the crime of witchcraft.[1] The prosecution of witches decreased in the last decades of the seventeenth century, while the rules of evidence became increasingly articulated and widespread around that time.

The procedure for witchcraft cases was the same as the general criminal procedure, with the exception of a few witchcraft-specific presumptions. The use of illegal tests (such as swimming or pricking) by villagers was also typical of witchcraft cases, but these were not part of the official proof system. Yet, much of the procedural and evidentiary transformation of English criminal law developed in the context of the witch trials. Having no divine guidance through the ordeals, and deprived of the confession-inducing mechanism of torture, the English had to seek a way to discover witches. Discovering true witches necessitated consideration and moulding of procedural and evidentiary tools: What was a good proof for witchcraft? What level of certainty was required for a conviction? How could innocent people be protected from false accusations?

The 200 years from the mid-sixteenth to the mid-eighteenth century spanned the period between medieval criminal law, which had not yet fully recovered from the abandonment of the ordeals, and a legal system of human

---

[1] *A True and Impartial Relation ...* (London: Freeman Collins, 1682), pp. 34, 36; Barbara J. Shapiro, *Probability and Certainty in Seventeenth-Century England: A Study of the Relationships between Natural Science, Religion, History, Law, and Literature* (Princeton, NJ: Princeton University Press, 1983), pp. 197, 206. Cf. Shapiro, *Probability and Certainty*, p. 195. See also C.R. Unsworth, 'Witchcraft Beliefs and Criminal Procedure in Early Modern England', in Thomas G. Watkin (ed.), *Legal Record and Historical Reality: Proceedings of the Eighth British Legal History Conference, Cardiff, 1987* (London: The Hambledon Press, 1989), p. 72.

adjudication. It was an era of transformation from criminal prosecution at the will of individuals to the establishment of a state-run prosecution apparatus. The law of evidence, non-existent at the beginning of the period, crystallized toward the end of that era into a set of rules whose basic principles are still applicable today. The standard of proof beyond reasonable doubt was emerging. The defendant's considerable procedural inferiority was ameliorated by the birth of the rights to be represented by counsel, to get a copy of the indictment and investigatory materials, to testify under oath and to call defence witnesses. Lawyer-free altercation between the accused and the accuser was replaced by the adversary criminal trial around the 1730s.[2] Beginning with the last decades of the seventeenth century, the newly introduced involvement of lawyers and their various objections to different kinds of evidence, and the manner of their arguments and examinations in turn, contributed to the development of standards of procedure and evidence rules.[3] The most influential role of defence attorneys was the cross-examination (commonly dubbed 'art' by lawyers) of the prosecution witnesses, which aimed to discover their biases and perceptual deficiencies.[4] The defence infused the notion that not all the evidence submitted by the prosecution must be given weight. Consequently, in the eighteenth century, mechanisms of exclusionary rules intended to shield the defendant from prejudicial or immaterial evidence began to take form.[5] Jurors, grand or petty, no longer served in a testimonial role, and they no longer needed to be acquainted with the accused or reside in close vicinity to the crime, but rather received the evidence from the prosecution.[6]

Passing criminal adjudication into human hands is the best explanation for these transformations. The development, however, was slow and gradual. Tracing the turning points in the process by which existing legal notions became articulated through formulae of exclusionary rules is illusive. On the Continent, the Roman-Canon law developed an intricate and elaborate system of proof standards in which professional judges resembled mathematicians setting variables into a formula. In England, the already existing institution of

---

[2]   John H. Langbein, *The Origins of Adversary Criminal Trial*, Oxford Studies in Modern Legal History (Oxford: Oxford University Press, 2003), ch. 5, esp. p. 253.

[3]   John Hamilton Baker, 'Criminal Courts and Procedure at Common Law 1550–1800', in J.S. Cockburn (ed.), *Crime in England 1550–1800* (Princeton, NJ: Princeton University Press, 1977), p. 37; J.M. Beattie, *Crime and the Courts in England, 1660–1800* (Princeton, NJ: Princeton University Press, 1986), p. 363; Langbein, *Origins*, pp. 243, 251.

[4]   Beattie, *Crime and the Courts*, pp. 361–2.

[5]   Ibid., p. 363.

[6]   Thomas Andrew Green, *Verdict According to Conscience: Perspectives on the English Criminal Trial Jury, 1200–1800* (Chicago: University of Chicago Press, 1985), p. 112.

the inquest, or jury, expanded to fill the vacuum left by forsaking the ordeals, and fact-finding was shifted to lay judges and the jury.[7] God is omniscient, but human adjudication required convincing proof, a need that generated the development of standards of evidence. Human adjudication depends on information; therefore, crimes need to be investigated. The Marian laws, enacted in 1554 and 1555, created a unified pre-trial procedure of investigation for all serious crimes, including witchcraft. A state-run apparatus of investigation and prosecution also contributed to the creation of standardized methods of investigation and proof.[8] The established system of travelling assize judges, who tried practically all the serious crimes, reinforced unified standards of procedure and proof.

At three stages of the criminal procedure it was necessary to determine the guilt of the witchcraft suspect, and each stage required a consideration of proof. Different participants controlled the determination at each stage. The justice of the peace (JP), on the basis of accusations and testimonies brought before him, was the first to determine whether the evidence was sufficient for the case to proceed. If he decided affirmatively, he committed the suspect to jail or released her on bail. In such cases, the JP conducted a pre-trial investigation that included an examination of the suspect. At the second stage, the grand jurors decided whether the evidence supported the bill of indictment that was normally drafted by the court clerks and included the formal charges against the accused. If they found the bill to be 'true' (a *billa vera*), it became an indictment, and the case proceeded to trial. The petty jurors decided the outcome of the last stage. They determined whether the defendant was to be convicted or acquitted on the basis of the evidence presented at trial. The anti-witchcraft laws listed forbidden acts but did not specify how to prove them. The practices of evidence and criminal procedure filled the statutes with content. Acquaintance with the procedural stages is essential for understanding how the contemporaries struggled with the problem of proof.

Steps of the Pre-trial Stage

The 'Bringing': An Initial Arrest by a Constable or Neighbours

The initiation of a criminal proceeding against a defendant required legal tools to secure the physical presence of the suspect for investigation and trial. The

---

[7]   The first criminal jury trial presumably took place at Westminster in 1220. George Fisher, 'The Jury's Rise as Lie Detector', *The Yale Law Journal*, no. 107 (1997): p. 585.

[8]   John H. Langbein, *Prosecuting Crime in the Renaissance: England, Germany, France*, Studies in Legal History (Cambridge, MA: Harvard University Press, 1974), p. 105.

Marian statutes set the procedure for bail or committal by the JP, who was usually not a lawyer,[9] and laid the ground for a pre-trial examination. Langbein noted how the phrasing of those laws presupposed that the suspect was 'brought' before the JP by 'them'[10] or 'those'[11] 'that bring him'.[12] The bringers might be the constable, neighbours who assisted him in case the suspect opposed the arrest, complainants or witnesses. The constables,[13] as Sir Thomas Smith lamented, 'were at the first in greater reputation than they bee nowe'.[14] In the past, Smith added, the constables had enjoyed a prestige similar to JPs. However, that had changed by his time, 'for so much as every little Village hath commonly two Constables, and many times artificers, labourers, and men of small abilitie be chosen unto that office, who haue no great experience, nor knowledge, nor authoritie'. The judicial proceeding, therefore, was launched after the suspected witch was brought before the JP.

In the early days of the common law, the authority to arrest was inherent not only in constables, but in private persons as well. Judge Hale opined that a private person *must* commit an arrest in three situations: (1) on witnessing another commit a felony, (2) on 'hue-and-cry'[15] and (3) in aid of an officer acting under a warrant.[16] A private person, according to Hale, *could* arrest another on 'probable cause' on suspicion of a felony or accompany a public officer, even if the latter

---

[9]   John H. Langbein, *Torture and the Law of Proof: Europe and England in the Ancien Regime* (Chicago: University of Chicago Press, 1977), p. 79.

[10]   1 & 2 Philip & Mary c. 13 (1554–55).

[11]   2 & 3 Philip & Mary c. 10 (1555).

[12]   Langbein, *Prosecuting Crime in the Renaissance*, pp. 11–12.

[13]   According to Smith, the word 'constable' is derived from the 'old English word *Kinning*, which is *Kinningstable*, as ye would say, a man established by the king'. Sir Thomas Smith, *De Republica Anglorum* (1st edn) (London: Printed by Henrie Midleton for Gregorie Seton, 1583), p. 75; Smith's first edition was published in 1583 but written around 1565. Langbein, *Origins*, p. 13, fn. 17.

[14]   Smith, *De Republica Anglorum*, p.74.

[15]   The 'hue-and-cry', as the term implies, was a verbal outcry, upon which all the adult males of the community had to join the constable in pursuit of the felon. Cynthia B. Herrup, *The Common Peace: Participation and the Criminal Law in Seventeenth-Century England*, Cambridge Studies in Early Modern British History (Cambridge, UK: Cambridge University Press, 1987), p. 70.

[16]   Sir Matthew Hale, *Pleas of the Crown* (London: William Shrewsbery and Juon Leigh, 1678), pp. 89–91. The JP could have granted or denied such a warrant according to his discretion. For example, in a case where the mother of two supposedly bewitched children rode to the JP to request the apprehension of the two suspects, John Hutton, a cunning old man, and Mrs Swinow, an upper-class woman, Justice Foster ordered the arrest of only the lower-class cunning man, declined to arrest Mrs Swinow, and even gave her a copy of Hutton's examination. *Wonderfull News from the North ...* (London: T.H., 1650), p. 10.

had no warrant.[17] A constable could also arrest a person if he had reasonable grounds to suspect that the person had committed a felony, no matter whether such felony had been committed. Smith affirmed that 'everie English man is a Sargiant to take the theefe'.[18]

By the mid-sixteenth century, the established concept of the breach of peace buttressed the authority of law enforcement officials to arrest. Lambarde, a lawyer trained at Lincoln's Inn and the author of significant legal treatises,[19] explained that whenever a person was suspect in a breach of peace, the officers could 'carry' them before the JP and be assisted by neighbours to compel the suspect to come.[20] Subsequently, if a suspect ignored a JP's warrant to provide a surety for keeping the peace, then 'the Officer may (upon that Warrant) arrest and carry him to the Gaole'.[21]

Thomas Greenwel, in *A Full and True Account of the Discovering, Apprehending and Taking of a Notorious Witch*, described the apprehension of Sarah Griffeth, a witchcraft suspect, and the manner of bringing her before Justice Bateman in 1704.[22] Sarah Griffeth 'was long time suspected for a bad woman, but nothing could be prov'd against her, that the law might take hold of her'. That was the case until one day, following an incident with 'a good jolly fellow', the apprentice of one Mr John, the latter,

> fearing some further mischief, takes a constable and goes to her lodging where
> he finds the old woman, and charges the constable with her. She made many

---

[17]   Hale, *Pleas of the Crown*, pp. 91–2. A private person who tried to arrest a suspect without sufficient cause could have experienced a similar frustration to that of Richard Galis. Galis believed that Mother Dutton had sent to his room, in the middle of the night, a cat that mysteriously vanished. On meeting her, he took her by the hand to the jailor, who refused to lock her up without a magistrate's warrant. Mr Galis subsequently brought the suspect before the mayor of Windsor, only to be commanded to release her at once. Galis's further actions against the suspects brought on his own arrest. Richard Galis, 'A Brief Treatise' (1579), in Marion Gibson (ed.), *Early Modern Witches: Witchcraft Cases in Contemporary Writing* (London: Routledge, 2000), pp. 55, 57.

[18]   Smith, *De Republica Anglorum*, p. 71.

[19]   For biographical references, see Langbein, *Prosecuting Crime in the Renaissance*, p. 41, fn. 41.

[20]   William Lambarde, *The Duties of Constables* ... (London: Rafe Newberie and Henrie Middleton, 1583), p. 12.

[21]   William Lambarde, *Eirenarcha* (London: Ra: Newbery and H. Bynneman, 1581), p. 102. 'Arrest' is defined by Lambard (ibid.) as: 'An Arrest is a certaine restraint of a mans person, depriuing it of his own wil and libertie, and binding it to become obedient to the will of the Lawe: and it may bee called the beginning of the Imprisonment.'

[22]   Thomas Greenwel, *A Full and True Account* ... (London: H. Hills, 1704).

attempts to escape, but the Devil who owed her ashame had now left her, and she was apprehended. As she was conducted towards the Justices house she tried to leap over the wall, and had done it had not the constable knocked her down. In this manner she was carried before the Justice.

The apprentice, the alleged victim, was also accompanying the group, for the pamphleteer mentioned that on their arrival he gave testimony before Justice Bateman. The initiative in the description came from a private person, the complainant's employer, who located the suspect, brought the constable and accompanied them to the JP's house. Relying on the same Mr John's complaint, the constable apprehended the suspect without a warrant or a need to apply for one prior to the apprehension. Sarah Griffeth 'made many attempts to escape', including a leap over the wall on reaching the JP's home. It is obvious that she was brought forcibly, until eventually the constable 'knocked her down' and she was physically carried into the JP's house. The authority to apprehend suspects included the use of physical force, as it is likely that many suspected offenders would not have come before the JP of their own free will. It may even well be that the use of arms was allowed for that purpose.[23] In any case, the frequent use of the verb 'to carry' denotes the forceful apprehension of unwilling suspects.[24]

The JP, to whose home the suspect was carried or brought, then had to determine the subsequent treatment of the case. Therefore, the initial stage of witch prosecution was the bringing before the JP.[25]

---

[23] The Assize of Arms, issued in 1181, obligated every citizen to have certain arms and to provide the authorities with assistance on request. The Statute of Winchester ordered, among other things, that each man would have arms, according to the Assize of Arms, to keep peace. These enactments were not in use by the middle of the sixteenth century; however, the authority to arrest, including the implied use of force, continued to exist under common law. For discussion of these enactments, see Sir James Fitzjames Stephen, *A History of the Criminal Law of England* (London: Macmillan, 1883), pp. 186–9.

[24] In this pamphlet, Mr Hicks, on hearing from his nine-year-old daughter that her mother taught her the art of witchcraft, 'caused' their carrying to the JP. This involuntary bringing of the two was probably performed through the help of others and most likely by a constable. *The Whole Trial and Examination of Mrs Mary Hicks ...* (London: W. Matthews, 1716), p. 7.

[25] There were also incidents of forceful apprehension by neighbours, outside the scope of a legal proceeding, to conduct illegal tests. Mother Sutton, for example, refused to submit to the questioning of Mr Enger, who suspected her of bewitching his servant. On her refusal to come with him, Mr Enger caused the unwilling woman to be violently brought to his house on horseback. *Vvitches Apprehended ...* (London: Edward Marchant, 1613), B4v-C. Only after being swum twice and searched for teats did the complainant carry her to a justice (ibid., C3). In the Warboys case, Mother Samuel was brought against her will to the

Appearance before the Justice of the Peace and the Examination

The proceeding following the apprehension took place at the JP's house. During the hearing, the JP heard the allegations and was authorized to issue pre-trial orders to ensure the gathering and preservation of evidence for the upcoming proceeding before the assize judges. Many times, the JP tried to arbitrate the dispute and help the parties reach a settlement.[26] He decided whether bail was sufficient or whether committal of the suspect to prison was required to ensure appearance at trial. He also gave orders regarding the appearance of witnesses, including sureties, and could order additional investigation, such as conducting a search or questioning more witnesses. In case the evidence was insufficient, the JP could order that the suspect be arrested for further examination for three more days, during which investigation could advance.[27] For the JP to commit the suspect to prison, 'a fewe lines signed with his hande is ynough'.[28]

The JP's input and determination were critical to the development of the case.[29] Failure to ensure suspects' and witnesses' appearance often frustrated the possibility of any future conviction by the assize judges, who held hearings only during their semi-annual visits. It is obvious why suspects would shun criminal prosecution (especially considering the mandatory hanging in felony cases). However, complainants and witnesses were also prone to change their mind regarding the pursuit of the case. The time lapse between the initial complaint and the assize session allowed angry complainants to cool off and consider

---

Throckmortons' house by a group of people. The uncle of the supposedly bewitched girls made sure that she would not have the opportunity to converse with the other suspects. *The Most Strange and Admirable Discouerie of the Three Witches of Warboys* (London: Thomas Man and Iohn Winington, 1593), Bv. Some believed that the bringing or even a mere threat of legal proceedings could have served as a remedy for witchcraft. See Richard Bernard, *A Guide to Grand-Iury Men* (London: Ed. Blackmore, 1627), pp. 195–6.

[26] Beattie, *Crime and the Courts*, p. 268; Herrup, *The Common Peace*, p. 85; Gwenda Morgan and Peter Rushton, 'The Magistrate, the Community and the Maintenance of an Orderly Society in Eighteenth-Century England', *Historical Research* 76, no. 191 (2003): p. 58. In a case of 1702, a witness testified that the JP persuaded the accusers not to trouble the suspect and persuaded the suspect to move elsewhere and not to prosecute her accuser for attacking her, indicating that in case she failed to prove her claim, she would be spending a great deal of money for no purpose. *The Tryal of Richard Hathaway* (London: Isaac Cleave, 1702), pp. 11–12.

[27] Beattie, *Crime and the Courts*, p. 270.

[28] Smith, *De Republica Anglorum*, p. 68.

[29] James A. Sharpe, 'Introduction: The Lancashire Witches in Historical Context', in Robert Poole (ed.), *The Lancashire Witches: Histories and Stories* (Manchester: Manchester University Press, 2002), p. 8.

the consequences – significant costs (court fees and witnesses' expenses) and the mandatory punishment for felonies. Cooperating witnesses could also reconsider the trouble and expense that their appearance entailed.

To assess the need for bail or committal to jail, the JP interrogated the suspect and the witnesses. In fact, the Marian laws required examination. The statutes were enacted to overcome overly generous, or corrupt, bailing practices of the JPs. The preamble of the first Marian law, the bail statute, explained how JPs took little notice of a 1487 law[30] that required bailment in appropriate cases by at least two JPs, one of whom had to be 'of quorum' (commissioned to sit in the quarter sessions or hear and determine out of sessions). The preamble further denounced the practice of the JPs to set the offenders free and frustrate the possibility of their conviction.[31]

The bail statute provided that in serious cases, manslaughter or felony,[32] no suspect should be released on bail by the JPs unless several conditions were met. As under the 1487 statute, non-complying JPs were susceptible to fines, one of the justices had to be of quorum, and the justices needed to certify the bonds by their signature and submit them to the judges of the next gaol delivery. The bail statute further determined that bailment had to be conducted by two justices sitting ensemble. This provision meant to rectify the existing practice of JPs' bailing suspects single-handedly by using the name of another necessary JP without his knowledge or permission.[33] The most significant novelty, however, was the adoption of the procedure of examination. The JPs,

> when any suche Prysoner ys brought before them for any Manslaughter or Felonye, before any Bailement or Maineprise, shall take thexaminacon of the said Prysoner and informacon of them that bringes him, of the facte and circumstances there of, and the same, or asmuche therof as shalbee materiall to prove the felonye, shall put in writing before they make the same Bailemt, which said examinacon together with the said Bailemt, the said Justices shall certefie at the next generall Gaole Deliverye to bee holden within the lymytes of their commission.

---

[30]   3 Hen. VII c. 3 (1487).

[31]   1 & 2 Philip & Mary c. 13 (1554–55); Langbein, *Prosecuting Crime in the Renaissance*, pp. 6, 9.

[32]   It reiterates the Act of Westminster, 3 Edw. I c. 15 (1275), and relates to manslaughter and felony suspects as well. For the categories of bailable and non-bailable suspects under the Act of Westminster, see Stephen, *A History of the Criminal Law of England*, I, p. 234.

[33]   This judicial malpractice was technically possible, as the 1487 statute did not specify whether the justices should act contemporaneously or not. Langbein, *Prosecuting Crime in the Renaissance*, pp. 8–9.

As this excerpt makes clear, JPs were allowed to bail suspects in cases of manslaughter and felony only if they had previously examined both the suspects and their bringers. Two justices were required for the issuance of a bail, but one JP was sufficient to conduct the examination.[34]

The second Marian act,[35] the committal statute, broadened the range of mandatory examinations. It further stated that examination should also be undertaken when the suspect was committed to jail. There was no quorum requirement, so, as in jail committal, a single JP sufficed. After an examination the JP had no authority to discharge the suspect without bail, even if he believed the suspect was innocent.[36]

Neither statute required the examination of the suspects or witnesses under oath. The lack of an explicit statutory arrangement was the subject of disagreement among the contemporary justices.[37] The oath advocates, such as Lambarde, argued that the use of an oath would allow admitting the examination into evidence in case one of the witnesses died before the trial.[38] This was one of the claims that supported Langbein's argument that the examination had no evidential value in the trial itself. Some courts admitted depositions of dead or absent witnesses, provided that they had been examined under oath and that the JP or his clerk was sworn to the truth thereof.[39] Dalton also supported the oath and emphasized the value of warning witnesses to testify truthfully.[40] Yet, Dalton maintained that only incriminating evidence could be taken under oath.[41]

It appears that there was no established practice with regard to the oath and that some justices did question suspects under oath. For example, in the examination of John Walsh in 1566, who was suspected of sorcery, 'He sayth by the othe that he hath taken' that he never hurt anyone's body or goods.[42]

The first part of the examination was the oral inquiry. Unlike the procedure on the Continent, there was no rigid paradigm of inquiry. The JP heard the

---

[34] Ibid., p. 11.

[35] 2 & 3 Philip & Mary c. 10 (1555).

[36] J.S. Cockburn, 'Introduction', in J.S. Cockburn (ed.), *Calendar of Assize Records*, 11 vols (London: Her Majesty's Stationery Office, 1985), p. 94.

[37] Langbein, *Prosecuting Crime in the Renaissance*, pp. 26–7.

[38] Lambarde, *Eirenarcha*, p. 210.

[39] William Nelson, *The Law of Evidence* (London: B. Gosling, 1735), p. 284.

[40] Michael Dalton, *The Countrey Iustice* (London: Societie of Stationers, 1618), p. 264.

[41] Ibid., p. 268.

[42] *The Examination of John Walsh* (London: Iohn Awdely, 1566), last page. Oath taking in this case may have been influenced by the fact that the examiner was an ecclesiastical official, who may have been used to the compurgation technique.

complaints and allegations of the bringers, be they the victim, witnesses or second-hand informants. The suspect was under no legal obligation to articulate a statement and could be uncooperative if he or she wished (the lack of a plausible explanation, however, could diminish the chances of being released). There were no rules of evidence or any required order of questioning. In fact, anything could be brought up before the justice – hearsay information, speculations, indications of reputation and even gossip.[43] Elizabeth Stile, for example, was arrested after being brought before the JP and arrested as a witchcraft suspect after 'honest neighbours' reported her to be a 'leude, malitious, and hurtfull woman'.[44]

The wording of both Marian laws left the scope of the investigation to be determined at the JP's discretion: 'The facte and circumstances there of, and the same, or asmuche therof as shalbee materiall to prove the felonye.' The Marian laws entrusted the JPs with a mission that is prosecutorial in nature, the gathering and documentation of evidence toward the trial. However, neither law obliged the JPs to look for other witnesses, but allocated to them a somewhat passive role – just to question those who came to them – or, in Herrup's words, they were 'stay-at-home investigators'.[45]

The manner and scope of the examination, therefore, depended on the JP's character, capabilities and inclinations. Some were more sceptical, some were more credulous, some merely documented the statements made before them, some took a more active role in the investigation and some even tried to trick the suspects they interrogated.[46]

Sometimes a single justice would use various questioning techniques to extract the desired self-incrimination from the suspect. A detailed example is *A True and Iust Recorde*, which contains examinations of witchcraft suspects at S. Oses, Essex county, in 1582 by Brian Darcey. Darcey's carefully documented rhetoric swung between temptation and intimidation, deceitful promises of favour for a confession and threats (including by illegal burning) for denial.[47]

Typically, the examinations started out with guilt-assuming questions such as 'How did you become a witch?'; 'From whom did you learn your witchcraft?'; 'When was the first time you saw the Devil?'; or 'How long have you practised

---

[43]   Marion Gibson, *Reading Witchcraft: Stories of Early English Witches* (London: Routledge, 1999), p. 23; Herrup, *The Common Peace*, p. 86.

[44]   *A Rehearsall Both Straung and True ...* (London: J. Kingston, 1579), p. 3.

[45]   Herrup, *The Common Peace*, p. 86.

[46]   Ibid., p. 88.

[47]   W.W., *A True and Iust Recorde ...* (London: Thomas Dawson, 1582), unnumbered, would have been A7v, the 19th page of the pamphlet; B5v; B6v. For an analysis of his examination, see also Gibson, *Reading Witchcraft*, p. 131.

witchcraft?'[48] Contemporary writers of legal treatises and manuals offered points to be considered by the JP when conducting an examination. In Michael Dalton's *The Countrey Iustice*,[49] a popular book that was reprinted in many editions, the author listed issues for the justices' consideration.[50] The clarity and breadth justify this rather long excerpt:

> Now vpon the examination of Felons, & other like offendors, these circumstances following, are to be considered:
>
> 1. His Name; sc. If he be not called by diuerse names.
>
> 2. Quality
>
> His parents, if they were wicked, and giuen to the same kind of fault.
>
> His abilitie of body; sc. If strong & swift, or weake or sickly not like to doe the Act.
>
> His nature; if ciuill or hastie, wittie and subtill, a quarreller, pilferer, or bloudie minded, &c.
>
> His meanes; if he hath whereon to liue, or not.
>
> His trade; for if a man liueth idly or vagarant (*nullam exercens artem nec laborem*)[51] it is a good cause to arrest him vpon suspition, if there haue beene any felony committed.
>
> His companie; if Ruffians, suspected persons, or his being in companie with any of the offendors.
>
> His course of life; sc. If a common Alehouse-hanter, or ryottous in dyet, play, or apparell.
>
> Whether he be of euill fame, or report.
>
> Whether hee hath committed the like offence before; or if he hath had a pardon; or had beene acquited, for felonie before; *Nam qui semel est malus, semper presumitur esse malus, in eodem genere mali.*[52]
>
> 3. Markes or Signes
>
> If he hath any bloud about him.
>
> If any of the goods stollen be in his possession.
>
> The change of his countenance, his blushing, looking downewards, silence, trembling.
>
> His answers doubtfull, or repugnant.
>
> If he offered agrement or composition.

---

[48] Gibson, *Reading Witchcraft*, pp. 14–16. See also *A True and Impartial Relation ...*, pp. 34, 36.

[49] Dalton incorporated Lambarde's *Eirenarcha* into his book. See Langbein, *Prosecuting Crime in the Renaissance*, p. 42.

[50] Dalton, *The Countrey Iustice*, pp. 266–7.

[51] Exercising neither art nor labour.

[52] For he who is bad once is always presumed to be bad in the same type of badness.

The measure of his foote, or horse foote.

The bleeding of the dead bodie in his presence.

If, being charged with the felony, or called theese, he saith nothing, f. Cor. 24.

If he bleede; *fatetur facinus, qui Iudicium fugit.*[53]

Place; sc. If conuenient for such act, as in a house, in a wood, Dale, &c.

4. The fact

Time; the yeare, day, houre, early or late.

Where the offendor was at the time of fact, and where the day or night before, his

businesse, and companie there, and witnesse to proue all these.

Manner; if willingly, by chance, or necessitie.

5. The cause

If former malice.

If to his benefite, or what hope of gaine.

If for the eschuing of any hurt, or danger.

The persons

Agens; if Principall or Accessarie, Enfant, Lunatique, &c.

Patiens; if against the King, Common-wealth, Magistrate, Mr. &c.

The two Marian laws differ as to the timing of producing the transcript. The bail statute decreed that the JPs 'shall put [the examination] in writing before they make the same Bailem[en]t'. The JP who wanted to set bail should have documented the examination beforehand. The transcription did not need to be complete or simultaneous, as implied by the phrasing of the act, which required transcribing only 'asmuche therof as shalbee materiall to prove the felonye'. Thus, only the incriminating facts were to be documented.[54] In Beattie's words, 'in the Marian procedure the magistrate was more a policeman than a judge'.[55]

The editorial role of the transcriber was even broader under the second Marian statute, which also provided that the justice would document the examination within two days. This delay called for inaccuracies and partiality. The transcription took place only *after* the JP had already committed the suspect to jail; thus, the content would tend to support that decision.

The next step was the certification of the documented examinations. The examinations, like all the other bonds and orders issued at the hearing, needed to be certified by the JPs and delivered to the assize judges. To have them ready in advance of sessions, the examinations were transferred to the clerk, who handled

---

[53]   He who escapes judgment confesses a crime.

[54]   Cockburn, 'Introduction', p. 96.

[55]   Beattie, *Crime and the Courts*, p. 271.

them afterwards. If the case was to be tried at the assizes, they would have to be sent to the clerk of the assizes, and if it was to be tried at the Quarter Sessions, they would have to be delivered to the clerk of the peace.[56] As a rule, witchcraft cases were heard before the assizes.[57]

The examinations were delivered to the assize judges to assure better supervision of the JPs' conduct and may have helped the judges and clerks to get a better picture of the scope and nature of the cases and to assist in the preparation of the indictment.[58] However, it appears that they had no evidential value in the trial itself, except for refreshing the memory of a faltering prosecution witness.[59] The examinations were not admitted as evidence, not even in cases where they contained the accused's admission of guilt. There were several reasons for the low evidential value of the examinations. As they were not conducted under oath, and they were transcribed in delay, their content was not approved by the deponent's signature.

The procedure of the examination had existed in England even before the Marian laws. Langbein listed 31 pre-Marian statutes that provided for examination in cases of specific offences.[60] Bellamy described how the examination was imposed by different statutes (mainly misdemeanours pertaining to labour, livery, poaching or vagabonds) up to a century before the Marian laws.[61] However, the main difference between the Marian laws and the other statutes was that the examination under the former was an addition to the regular proceeding, whereas, under the latter, the examination was an alternative to presentment and took the place of a trial.

The Marian statutes might have had the limited objective of correcting judicial malpractices; nevertheless, the introduction of the examination into the legal system had a far-reaching effect: it was the origin of the preliminary inquiry, a most significant procedural feature.[62] In fact, the examination signalled the birth of an organized production of prosecutorial evidence. The outcome of the Marian statutes was a structural change in the English legal system – the

---

[56]   Stephen, *A History of the Criminal Law of England*, vol. 2, p. 237. However, the royal judges could delegate criminal cases to the JPs. See Langbein, *Prosecuting Crime in the Renaissance*, p. 107.

[57]   Herrup, *The Common Peace*, p. 45; Unsworth, *Witchcraft Beliefs*, p. 90.

[58]   John G. Bellamy, *The Criminal Trial in Later Medieval England: Felony before the Courts from Edward I to the Sixteenth Century* (Thrupp, Stroud, Gloucestershire: Sutton, 1998), p. 25.

[59]   Langbein, *Prosecuting Crime in the Renaissance*, pp. 28–9.

[60]   Ibid., p. 67.

[61]   Bellamy, *The Criminal Trial in Later Medieval England*, pp. 25–6.

[62]   Stephen, *A History of the Criminal Law of England*, vol. 1, p. 237.

investigative and the determinative functions were separated, so the jury no longer needed to be self-informed, and the basis for the formation of a law of evidence was established.[63]

Search

Among his other powers, the justice had the authority to issue search warrants,[64] and some JPs who were not satisfied by the testimonies presented to them took a more active position and ordered a search. Some searches were conducted by the constable even before the arrival at the JP's home. Herrup referred to cases where the search was conducted by the constable, sometimes accompanied by others.[65] It seems that citizens were permitted to search only on an explicit warrant or an official instruction. Some laws granted citizens search power that was to be exercised only on judicial order. For example, an act controlling tile manufacturing[66] empowered a special jury of tile experts to search the suspect's premises.[67] The search was normally to be conducted in the suspect's presence, and clandestine searches required a specific statute. For example, in the case of gaming, an act of the parliament[68] authorized 'a diligent & a secrete serche'.[69]

The search could be either a search of the body or a search of the suspect's premises. According to Herrup, the search often began at the suspect's residence.[70] The premises were searched for artefacts or tools used for the art of witchcraft. Searches were not limited to a specific item and could be for anything out of the ordinary,[71] any incriminating proof. Such was the case of 'Iohane Harrison ... condemned for witchcraft on August 4, 1606'. According to the pamphlet, the suspect 'was apprehended, and her house according to the true courte of justice, being searcht'. That is, her house was searched under a previously issued warrant. During the search a chest was opened, and incriminating evidence was discovered – bones and hair and, most incriminating of all, 'in y midst of this pechmat was coloured ... a heart

---

63   Langbein, *Prosecuting Crime in the Renaissance*, pp. 119, 123.
64   Lambarde, *Eirenarcha*, p. 185.
65   Herrup, *The Common Peace*, pp. 74–8.
66   17 Edw. IV c. 4 (1477–78).
67   Langbein, *Prosecuting Crime in the Renaissance*, p. 70.
68   19 Hen. VII c. 12 (1503–04).
69   Langbein, *Prosecuting Crime in the Renaissance*, p. 72.
70   Herrup, *The Common Peace*, p. 75.
71   Ibid., p. 77.

proportionable to the hart of man'.[72] Figures or images of the human body were considered tools of witchcraft, as it was believed that witches could inflict harm by molesting the bodily parts represented.

Occasionally, the search and its findings were reported to the JP during the appearance before him and became another subject for inquiry.[73] In our example, the suspect, Harrison, was confronted with the findings, after which she confessed to practising witchcraft with the help of the objects. This pamphlet emphasized the importance of the findings. The suspect was 'of long time having been suspected for witchcraft', but no evidence had been found against her thus far. Without the items seized at the search, 'there have been no other proofe nor evidence against her'.[74]

Additional Pre-trial Investigations

Though the ordeal was outlawed in 1215, ordeal-like methods continued to proliferate in England as part of witchcraft cases, mostly 'outside, or on the fringes, of legal process'.[75] Investigation by methods such as the scratching or the swimming test also persisted up to the eighteenth century. The tests, in most cases, were applied by complainants or neighbours, and the complainants knew that if they wanted to present a better case, they should come to the JP's house with more than mere suspicions and allegations.[76] This 'fringe adjudication' continued to exist for hundreds of years, despite its illegality and the judicial condemnation of its practices.

Not only were private people forbidden to use force in order to discover witches or obtain a confession, but the investigating officials were prohibited from doing so as well. According to Smith,

---

[72]   *Most Damnable Practises of One Iohane Harrison* ... (London: William Firebrand and Iohn Wright, 1606), C2v–C3. This pamphlet contained two cases. The title, *The Most Crvell and Bloody Mvrther* ..., related to the first, which was not a witchcraft case.

[73]   Herrup, *The Common Peace*, p. 87.

[74]   *Most Damnable Practises of One Iohane Harrison* ..., C2.

[75]   James A. Sharpe, *Instruments of Darkness: Witchcraft in England 1550–1750* (London: Hamish Hamilton, 1996), p. 218.

[76]   For example, in the case of the supposed bewitchment of the boy Thomas Darling, his acquaintances suspected Alice Goodridge, but 'yet making conscience to accuse her till it appeared vpon sure proofe, sent for her into the Towne to talke with her priuately'. This 'private' inquiry was conducted in the presence of many townspeople and included questioning, scratching and the Lord's Prayer test. After the boy's fits persisted, they decide to bring the matter before the JP. I.D., *The Most Wonderfull and True Storie* ... (London: I.O., 1597), pp. 5, 7.

> There is an olde lawe of England, that if any gaoler shall put any prisoner being
> in his custodie to any torment, to the intent to make him an approuer, that is to
> say, an accuser, or Index of his complices, the Gaoler shall die therfore as a felon.[77]

An overzealous jailor who used torture against a suspect to extort incrimination of the accomplices committed a felony punishable by death.

The swimming test gained popularity only after James I endorsed it in his *Daemonologie*, first printed in 1597. James I believed that the swimming test and the witch's mark were the best means to discover a witch. Illegal swimming tests were cause for both civil and criminal suits.[78] Joan Bibb, of Rushock in Worcestershire, who sued Mr Shaw, the parson, for being tied and thrown into a pool as a witch, recovered £10 damages on 8 March 1661.[79]

In 1751, at Tring in Hertfordshire, an angry mob broke into the workhouse of a poor old woman, Ruth Osborne, and her husband, tied the couple and subjected them to a swimming test at a nearby stream. Ruth Osborne consequently died. Three men were prosecuted, and one of them, Thomas Colley, a chimney sweep, was convicted of Ruth Osborne's murder and executed by hanging. His body remained hanging for years at the place of the execution.[80]

Despite the criminal and civil sanctions, the tests were often used, and not only by the common and ignorant, but also by some JPs. Officials who used the swimming test were rarely sanctioned. John Goodere, alias Dinely, a Hertfordshire JP, was removed from office after behaving improperly in a swimming test of a witch in 1716. After subjecting a woman who testified against him in a civil case to the swimming test under the false pretext of her being a witch, he stripped, swam naked on his back in front of the men and women who were present, and made obscene gestures and proposals to some of the women in the crowd. Had it not been for his extremely unhinged behaviour, it is doubtful that this JP would have been removed from office for merely conducting the swimming test. Landau even questioned if the removal would have occurred had the JP been a Whig rather than a Tory.[81]

Another illegal test was the scratching. The victim needed to scratch the witch and draw blood from her body. If the victim subsequently recovered, the suspicion of witchcraft was confirmed. Many times scratching took place

---

[77]   Smith, *De Republica Anglorum*, p. 86.

[78]   Langbein, *Torture and the Law of Proof*, p. 78.

[79]   Ibid., pp. 210–11, fn. 49.

[80]   Ibid.; Brian P. Levack, *The Witch-Hunt in Early Modern Europe*, 2nd edn (New York: Longman, 1995), p. 252.

[81]   Norma Landau, *The Justices of the Peace, 1679–1760* (Berkeley: University of California Press, 1984), p. 91.

with the authorization and encouragement of the JPs. For example, when Mr Avery and his sister, Mrs Belcher, the alleged victims of bewitchment, desired to scratch the suspects, Joane Vaugham and her mother, Agnes Browne, they went to see the suspects at the jail, where they were awaiting their trial.[82] Such a visit required the knowledge and consent of the officials who held them.

Many, of course, were aware that the swimming test and the scratching were illegal and did not want to use them, even on the consent of the suspect.[83] Although officially illegal and subject to sanctions, such methods persisted alongside the official judicial proceedings. These tests were not employed by the assize judges who tried the accused, but entrusting the pre-trial investigation to the JPs made the persistence of the tests possible. A few hundred years after the abolition of the ordeal, the supernatural tests were applied to overcome the lack of substantial proof rather than in adherence to a religious custom.

The Question of Proof

The JP's decision about bail or committal was the first of three procedural crossroads that required assessment of the evidence and determination of the suspect's guilt. In theory, the required level of persuasion was lower than that needed for endorsement of indictment by the grand jury or conviction by the petty jury. Contemporary writers sorted the kinds of evidence by their level of strength. Gaule divided the 'Signes and Markes of a Witch' into unwarrantable, probable and infallible.[84] Bernard distinguished between 'presumptions' and 'proofs'.[85] According to Perkins, some evidence was too weak for conviction but was sufficient to warrant an examination, for example, when the injury occurred subsequent to the suspect's cursing.[86] Yet, in practice, there were no mathematical calculations of the demono-legal degrees of proof. It is possible that certain sceptical JPs were harder to convince than some credulous jurors. Perkins

---

[82]   *The Witches of Northampton-Shire* (London: Arthur Iohnson, 1612), B4.

[83]   When Jane Wenham offered to have her body searched for the devil's mark and to be swum, the judges declined. Possibly, the illegality stemmed from the torturing nature of the tests and not from scepticism as to their probative nature. The judges refused Jane Wenham's proposal to undergo the scratching and swimming test, but offered to test her by repeating a prayer. Failure to repeat passages of a prayer was considered proof of a demonic relationship. Francis Bragge, *A Full and Impartial Account ...*, 2nd edn (London: E. Curll, 1712), p. 10.

[84]   John Gaule, *Select Cases of Conscience Touching Vvitches and Vvitchcrafts* (London: Richard Clutterbuck, 1646), p. 75.

[85]   Bernard, *A Guide to Grand-Iury Men*, pp. 204–25.

[86]   William Perkins, *A Discourse of the Damned Art of Witchcraft* (Cambridge, UK: Vniuersitie of Cambridge, 1608), p. 202.

himself conceded that enraged 'ignorant' accusers might deem presumptions as strong proofs and jurors might convict innocent defendants.[87] The decision of the jurors (grand and petty) is unexplained, and it may very well be that some defendants were convicted by insufficient evidence.

The decision of the JP whether to launch an examination demanded less convincing evidence. Many presumptions were insufficient for conviction but warranted an examination and investigation. Once the JP's investigation was complete, the required evidentiary standard was raised. For conviction (and taking the accused's life), mere suspicions and presumptions were not enough; there needed to be a proof. This proof question was reconsidered at the following stages of the proceedings. Once the JP had examined the suspect, he had to send the transcribed depositions to the clerk of the assizes, and the proceeding marched on. The Marian statutes might have intended only to correct magistrates' malpractices, but they resulted in creating an evidence-gathering apparatus and the formation of evidentiary standards.

---

[87]   Ibid., p. 210.

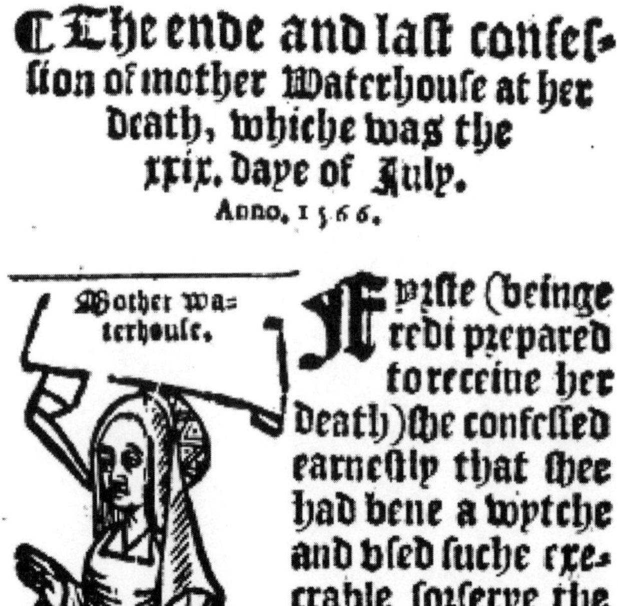

¶ The ende and last confession of mother Waterhouse at her
death, whiche was the
xxix. daye of July.
Anno. 1566.

Mother Wa-
terhouse.

IF yrste (beinge
redi prepared
to receiue her
death) she confessed
earnestly that shee
had bene a wytche
and vsed suche exe-
crable sorserye the
space of. xv. yeres,
and had don many
abhominable dede,
the which she repe-
ted earnestly & vn-
faynedly, and desy-
red almyghty God
forgeuenes in that
she had abused hys
most holy name by

A   her

Figure 2.1 Mother Waterhouse. From *The Examination and Confession of Certaine Wytches* ... (London: Willyam Powell, 1566) (A, Biii). Courtesy of the Trustees of Lambeth Palace Library. [Call # (ZZ) 1587.12.03]

Chapter 2
Trial Procedure

The question of whether the guilt of the accused had been adequately proved was considered twice during the progress of a trial, first by grand and then by petty jurors. Procedural development, and especially the Marian statutes, reshaped the jurors' role. Evidence was gathered in advance and submitted for the jurors' evaluation, and standards of proof began to take form. The enormous difficulty of proving witchcraft led to much discussion about the best evidence and the right procedure to uncover the truth. Important for the trial stages were the roles of the different participants and the interplay between questions of law, fact and procedure.

The Grand Jury and the Indictment

By the mid-sixteenth century, the indictment was the standard measure for criminal prosecution. A private appeal was potentially possible, but the risks involved and the strengthening of the criminal prosecution run by the crown greatly reduced its use. Private appeal was used mainly in situations when it was the only recourse for the victim or the next of kin – acquittal or attaint on indictment in murder cases. By the beginning of the nineteenth century, the private appeal procedure had become obsolete.[1]

A criminal prosecution could also be initiated on the finding of an inquest held before the coroner that a certain individual had murdered the body examined.[2] The Marian statutes granted the coroner duties and powers similar to those of the JP, but this procedure, however, was not typical of witch trials, as they were usually initiated by neighbours' complaints to the JP.[3]

---

[1]   John Hamilton Baker, 'Criminal Courts and Procedure at Common Law 1550–1800', in J.S. Cockburn (ed.), *Crime in England 1550–1800* (Princeton, NJ: Princeton University Press, 1977), p. 18; John Hamilton Baker, *An Introduction to English Legal History*, 3d edn (London: Butterworths, 1990), p. 575.

[2]   Baker, 'Criminal Courts and Procedure at Common Law 1550–1800', p. 19.

[3]   Ewen could not find more than one witchcraft case to be so initiated. Cecil L'Estrange Ewen, *Witchcraft and Demonianism: A Concise Account Derived from Sworn Depositions and Confessions Obtained in the Courts of England and Wales* (London: Heath, 1933), p. 7.

Between 1542 and 1736 a process that had already started became crystallized – the members of the grand jury were transformed from active presenters possessing first-hand knowledge of the case into passive indicters.[4] This change occurred with the transfer of the investigation and prosecution to the state through its JPs and the law enforcement officers of the local government. The grand jurors were no longer required to name the suspects themselves or to submit their own information about the local crimes. Instead, they examined the bills of indictment prepared in advance of the session and the evidence for the crown. The bills were normally prepared by the clerks, though some were prepared by the prosecutors' solicitors.[5] The grand jury's main function was to evaluate the evidence and weed out the cases in which there was a lack of substantial proof. If the prosecution had a prima facie case, the grand jury returned a *billa vera*, the suspect would be indicted and the case would proceed to trial. Otherwise, the grand jury would return an answer of *ignoramus*, 'we do not know'; the suspect would be released, and the case would be dismissed.[6] The endorsement of either a *billa vera* or an *ignoramus* required a majority of twelve votes.[7] The grand jury's answer was pronounced by the clerk, who declared: 'Gentlemen, you find "a true bill", or "no true bill".'[8]

---

[4] Thomas Andrew Green, *Verdict According to Conscience: Perspectives on the English Criminal Trial Jury, 1200–1800* (Chicago: University of Chicago Press, 1985), p. 112; Sir James Fitzjames Stephen, *A History of the Criminal Law of England* (London: Macmillan, 1883), vol. 1, p. 528.

[5] J.M. Beattie, *Crime and the Courts in England, 1660–1800* (Princeton, NJ: Princeton University Press, 1986), p. 334.

[6] J.S. Cockburn, 'Introduction', in J.S. Cockburn (ed.), *Calendar of Assize Records*, 11 vols (London: Her Majesty's Stationery Office, 1985), vol. 1, p. 52; Cynthia B. Herrup, *The Common Peace Participation and the Criminal Law in Seventeenth-Century England*, Cambridge Studies in Early Modern British History (Cambridge, UK: Cambridge University Press, 1987), p. 93; Barbara J. Shapiro, *'Beyond Reasonable Doubt' and 'Probable Cause': Historical Perspectives on the Anglo-American Law of Evidence* (Berkeley: University of California Press, 1991), p. 48; Stephen, *A History of the Criminal Law of England*, vol. 1, p. 274.

[7] Normally, the record contained just the grand jury's final decision. A rare exception is the case against Alice Fuller at the Kent Rochester Assizes, 27 February 1589. The record states: 'billa vera by the judgment of these men whose names are here underwritten: John Manser, Thomas Godden, William Woodden, Thomas Evees, John Rigden, Osmund Norton, Winter Marsh, Edward Willcocks, Thomas Grenstreat, Henry Grenstreat, John Stoakes, Thomas Ladd; ignoramus to the judgment of the rest', in J.S. Cockburn (ed.), *Calendar of Assize Records, Elizabeth I*, 5 vols (London: H.M.S.O., 1975–80), v. 4, case 1760.

[8] Stephen, *A History of the Criminal Law of England*, vol. 1, p. 274.

The panel, previously selected by the sheriff and sworn in, examined the bill of indictment.[9] A foreman, chosen for either his superior social status or legal knowledge, presided over the grand jurors.[10] The number of grand jurors varied from 13 to 23, but at either forum a minimum of twelve jurors needed to vote on the answer.[11]

There were diverse views as to the standard of proof or convincement required for a *billa vera*. The range stretched from a prima facie case (Hale) through a 'meet' or 'fit' case, which called for 'a strong and pregnant presumption', through 'thorough persuasion' (Blackstone) up to the same burden as required by the petty jury.[12] The existence of sufficient proof could be evaluated on the basis of the prosecution's evidence alone. Therefore, the grand jurors heard testimonies of the alleged victims, prosecution witnesses and the examining magistrates, and the written examinations were sometimes read to them. The grand jurors did not hear or receive the defence's evidence.[13] Ideally, the victim, all the prosecution witnesses and the examining JP would appear before the grand jurors, but many times they failed to do so.[14] Their absence at that stage, however, was not fatal to the case.[15] The examinations of the magistrates could be read by somebody else, and the testimony of other witnesses, not necessarily the victim, was sufficient.

The grand jurors were of an inferior social status to the justices. However, they could effectively reject the case that was prepared and submitted by the JP. This division of labour was an inherent source of tension.[16] The grand jurors

---

[9]   Cockburn, 'Introduction', pp. 44–5; Marion Gibson, *Reading Witchcraft: Stories of Early English Witches* (London: Routledge, 1999), p. 54; Shapiro, '*Beyond Reasonable Doubt*', p. 48. The oath they took was: 'You shall diligently inquire and true presentment make all such matters and things as shall be given you in charge. The king's majesty's counsel, your fellows', and your own, you shall well and truly observe and keep secret. You shall present no man for envy, hatred, or malice; neither shall you leave any man unpresented for love, fear, favour, or affection, profit, lucre, gain, or any hope thereof; but in all things you shall present the truth, the whole truth, and nothing but the truth. So help you God' (Baker, 'Criminal Courts and Procedure at Common Law 1550–1800', p. 33.

[10]   Beattie, *Crime and the Courts*, p. 323; Herrup, *The Common Peace*, p. 111.

[11]   Cockburn, 'Introduction', p. 46; Herrup, *The Common Peace*, p. 112; Shapiro, '*Beyond Reasonable Doubt*', p. 48; Stephen, *A History of the Criminal Law of England*, vol. 1, p. 274.

[12]   Baker, 'Criminal Courts and Procedure at Common Law 1550–1800', p. 29; Beattie, *Crime and the Courts*, p. 319.

[13]   Gibson, *Reading Witchcraft*, p. 55; Herrup, *The Common Peace*, p. 112.

[14]   Cockburn, 'Introduction', p. 104.

[15]   Herrup, *The Common Peace*, pp. 62, 120–21. Cockburn estimated the JP's average absenteeism rate at 52 per cent. Cockburn, 'Introduction', p. 101.

[16]   Herrup, *The Common Peace*, p. 96.

were regarded as the voice or conscience of the county, 'the very eyes and spies of the county',[17] a position that became an arena for political power struggles.[18] Although the ideal for grand jurors was of literate gentlemen, freeholders with sufficient income, the reality was that the jurors were of a lower social standing and were often illiterate.[19] Assize judges sometimes tried to improve both the grand and petty juries' quality by drafting constables and even clerks to serve on the panels.[20] The jurors who served at the assizes usually enjoyed a somewhat better status than those who served at the Quarter Sessions and belonged to the lower ranks of the gentry.[21]

The grand jurors sometimes overstepped their authority and attempted to determine guilt or to dismiss a case out of mercy despite its sufficiency, and, as they were part of the community, they were susceptible to social pressures and considerations.[22] Sometimes the assize judges were dissatisfied with grand jurors' excessive leniency.[23] However, it seems that despite the tensions and pressures, they 'seem to have worked from a set of consistent, if informal, evidentiary guidelines that encompassed both the form and substance of accusations. If judged by their decisions, grand jurymen were neither capricious, timid, nor overly concerned with the opinions of the social or legal establishment'.[24] The grand jurors' evaluation was not rigid or technical. To achieve the desired result, they were sometimes willing to ignore technicalities or exploit flaws in the bill of indictment.[25] The criteria for their assessment resembled those used earlier by the magistrate.

Richard Bernard, in *A Guide to Grand-Iury Men*, offered the grand jurors specific guidance regarding witchcraft. His goal was to help the grand jurors differentiate between real and 'counterfeit' witchcraft and to warn them against

---

[17]   Cockburn, cited from C. Read (ed.), *William Lambarde and Local Government* (Ithaca, NY: Cornell University Press, 1962), pp. 73, 93, 112; Cockburn, 'Introduction', p. 51.

[18]   According to Beattie, from the late 1670s until the late 1730s, the Whig and Tory parties battled over supremacy in the grand juries of every county. Beattie, *Crime and the Courts*, p. 332.

[19]   Herrup, *The Common Peace*, p. 103. A sheriff who called 22 grand jurors at Huntigdon Assizes in 1619, mockingly proclaimed the 'gentlemen' 'Mamiliam, King of Tozland', 'Stephen, Pope of Weston' and 'Henry, Prince of Godmanchester'. Cockburn, 'Introduction', p. 47.

[20]   Cockburn, 'Introduction', pp. 47–8.

[21]   Herrup, *The Common Peace*, pp. 98–9, 103; Barbara J. Shapiro, *A Culture of Fact: England, 1550–1720* (Ithaca, NY: Cornell University Press, 2000), p. 24.

[22]   Herrup, *The Common Peace*, pp. 95–6, 127.

[23]   Cockburn, 'Introduction', pp. 51, 53.

[24]   Herrup, *The Common Peace*, p. 113.

[25]   Ibid., p. 119.

believing anyone who claimed to be bewitched.[26] Bernard advised the grand jurors that they should be most careful before returning an answer and that it was better to refrain from indicting when in doubt:

> vnlesse the Witchcraft be very cleere, they may bee much mistaken; and better it were, till the truth appeare, to write an *Ignuramus*, than vpon oath to set down *Billa vera*, and so thrust an intricate case vpon a Iury of simple men, who proceed too often vpon ralations of neere presumptions, and these sometimes very weake ones too, to take away mens liues.[27]

The presumptions that could be adequate to instigate an examination, according to Bernard, were not strong enough evidence to support a finding of guilty in this capital crime.

A finding of a prima facie case resulted in indictment, which needed to contain a commencement, a statement and a conclusion. The commencement was a title that denoted the type of commission and geographical area and defined the court's jurisdiction and venue. The grand jurors came from the area where the crime was committed, even if the trial was conducted at another locale. The statement set forth the details concerning the crime – facts, circumstances and intent that established the offence. Eventually, the indictment needed to conclude whether the offence was a common-law breach of peace or under a statute.[28] Everything needed to be contended in the indictment, and even a slight omission could be fatal to the case.[29] In indictments for witchcraft, the use of force and the names of the witch's imps or familiars were only occasionally mentioned.[30] The indictment against Margery Barnes in 1583 claimed, among other things, that she held three imps in her possession, whom she called 'sperytte', 'le gray Catt' and 'le dundogge'.[31]

---

[26] Richard Bernard, *A Guide to Grand-Iury Men* (London: Ed. Blackmore, 1627).

[27] Ibid., p. 25.

[28] Witchcraft was not a common-law, but a statutory crime.

[29] Stephen, *A History of the Criminal Law of England*, vol. 1, pp. 275–83. The *vi et armis* phrase was sometimes included in the indictment. However, by 37 Hen. VII c. 8 (1546), the omission of these words was ineffectual. Cecil L'Estrange Ewen, *Witch Hunting and Witch Trials: The Indictments for Witchcraft from the Records of 1373 Assizes Held for the Home Circuit A.D. 1559–1736* (New York: Lincoln Mac Veagh: The Dial Press, 1929), p. 76.

[30] Ewen, *Witch Hunting and Witch Trials*, p. 76.

[31] Full text, both in English and Latin, is to be found in Ewen, ibid., pp. 83–4, as well as an abstract (ibid., p. 150).

Initially the indictments were written on parchment in Latin,[32] which was not understood by most witchcraft suspects. Only in 1730 was it enacted that indictments should be in English.[33] Several separate bills against one suspect could be submitted, or one indictment could contain several charges. It was also common to charge several defendants in one indictment.

If the grand jury did not find the case sufficient, the bill was to be destroyed.[34] Only a few *ignoramus* bills survived, possibly because those bills referred to additional defendants, against whom a *billa vera* was found. On return of a *billa vera*, which term needed to be written on the back side of the bill to endorse the indictment, the suspect became an accused and had to answer the charges.[35]

The Arraignment and Plea

On the assize day, the court room was full of people and bustling with activity.[36] At times, the noise was so loud that the accused was unable to hear the prosecution evidence or the judge.[37] In addition to the official participants, the hearings drew a large crowd of parties (civil and criminal), witnesses and spectators. The judicial spectacle had a primary educational value for the public.[38]

All the prisoners were taken to court chained to each other. Following the indictment, they were called, one at a time, to the bar to plead to the charge. The grand jury proceedings were often carried out without the defendant's knowledge. The defendant had as yet no right to receive a copy of the indictment, so the announcement of the charges was, not uncommonly, her first opportunity to hear the full charges.[39] In witch trials, examination was quite frequent, and therefore the accused could get an impression of the nature of the allegations.

---

[32]   Ibid., p. 75. Often with spelling and grammar errors (Cockburn, 'Introduction', pp. 76–7).

[33]   4 Geo. II c. 26 (1730); Stephen, *A History of the Criminal Law of England*, vol. 1, p. 282. During the interregnum, 1651–59, bills of indictment were written in English. Ewen, *Witch Hunting and Witch Trials*, p. 75.

[34]   It needed to be 'rent into peeces immediately' (Sir Thomas Smith, *De Republica Anglorum*, 1st edn (London: Printed by Henrie Midleton for Gregorie Seton, 1583), p. 68).

[35]   Ibid., p. 91.

[36]   Ibid., p. 77.

[37]   Keith Thomas, *Religion and the Decline of Magic* (New York: Charles Scribner's Sons, 1971), p. 459.

[38]   Smith, *De Republica Anglorum*, p. 77.

[39]   Ibid., pp. 77–8.

However, the grand jury sifted the evidence and decided what charges merited indictment, so the actual indictment could be different from the allegations the accused faced at the JP's house.

The possible pleas in a criminal trial were guilty, not guilty, *autrefois acquit* (already acquitted) and *autrefois convict* (already convicted).[40] A plea of guilty was an admission of everything in the indictment. On a pleading of not guilty, the indictment was denied, and the case against the accused needed to be proved by evidence.

An accused who pleaded not guilty was asked, 'Culprit, how will you be tried?' to which the prisoner had to reply, 'By God and my country'.[41] 'By my country' signified consent to a jury trial. 'By God' is reminiscent of the ordeals, which functioned as the medium of divine adjudication. An accused who omitted either phrase was considered to stand mute. If the jury found the incomplete reply to be 'mute by the visitation of God',[42] the trial continued. But if it found him to be 'mute of malice', the plea equalled a refusal of a jury trial.[43] Lack of consent resulted in the infliction of the *peine fort et dure* (pressing), which persisted until its abolishment in 1772.[44]

There is some evidence of a limited plea-bargaining practice, which appeared around 1575, by which the prisoner who maintained his innocence agreed to plead guilty to a lesser or clergiable offence to obtain a reduced penalty.[45]

The Trial by Jury

As the trial proceeded, a different panel, the petty jury, determined whether the accused was guilty of the crime. Jury empanelling began after the arraignment. By the mid-sixteenth century, the jury trial as we know it today was well

---

[40]   Stephen, *A History of the Criminal Law of England*, vol. 1, p. 294.

[41]   Baker, 'Criminal Courts and Procedure at Common Law 1550–1800', p. 34; Stephen, *A History of the Criminal Law of England*, vol. 1, pp. 297–8. Baker claimed that the use of the term 'culprit' did not imply prejudice, but was a distortion of the legal French *culpable: prist*, which signified that the crown was ready to prove the case.

[42]   A clear-cut example was the 'deaf and dumb' defendant. Beattie, *Crime and the Courts*, p. 337.

[43]   Stephen, *A History of the Criminal Law of England*, vol. 1, p. 298.

[44]   By 12 Geo. III c. 20 (Stephen, *A History of the Criminal Law of England*).

[45]   Baker, 'Criminal Courts and Procedure at Common Law 1550–1800', p. 35; Cockburn, 'Introduction', pp. 66, 105. However, Langbein noted how the rapidity of trials, and their being the single opportunity to lay the mitigating circumstances, was a disincentive for plea bargaining (John H. Langbein, *The Origins of Adversary Criminal Trial*, Oxford Studies in Modern Legal History (Oxford: Oxford University Press, 2003), pp. 19–20.

established.[46] In the past, juries had fulfilled the role of witnesses, but by this time, jurors were no longer required to be self-informed, a consequence of the Marian laws and the social and demographical transformations to be discussed later.[47]

No jury was selected if the defendant pleaded guilty.[48] If the defendant pleaded not guilty and replied that he wanted to be tried 'by God and my country', jury empanelling began. The defendant had the right of preemptory challenges (limited to 20 by statute since 1533),[49] which were rarely exhausted,[50] as 'for the most part the prisoner can say nothing against them, for they are chosen but for that day, and are unknowen to him'.[51] The jurors were called and sworn in individually, and if the defendant raised no objection, the next prospective juror was called until the panel was full.[52]

Empanelling presented a practical challenge, as the shortage of jurors became a persistent situation. As the royal court system expanded, more trials were conducted at the assizes, and the need for jurors increased. Many potential jurors, however, recoiled from the service whenever possible. Service on a petty jury was much less prestigious than on a grand jury, and the petty jurors were generally of a lower social status.[53] The official qualifying condition was property worth 40s.[54] The rarely achieved ideal of petty jurors was of:

---

[46]   Stephen, *A History of the Criminal Law of England*, vol.1, p. 263.

[47]   However, jurors were not disqualified for being acquainted with the case. Boulton brought an example of a murder case in which 'a Jury was impannelled ... amongst whom was Dr Zerobabel Endicot, who found the Man bruised to Death, and having Clodders of Blood about his Heart' (Richard Boulton, *A Compleat History of Magick, Sorcery, and Witchcraft* (London: E. Curll, J. Pemberton, and W. Taylor, 1715), vol. 2, p. 40). In such cases the evidentiary rule demanded another oath, as Nelson stated in his evidence-law book: 'A Jury who is a Witness must be also sworn in open Court to give Evidence, if he be call'd for a Witness' (William Nelson, *The Law of Evidence*, 1st edn (London: B. Gosling, 1717), p. 8).

[48]   Cockburn, 'Introduction', p. 65.

[49]   25 Hen VIII c. 3 and additional acts. See Baker, 'Criminal Courts and Procedure at Common Law 1550–1800', p. 36 and fn. 117; Stephen, *A History of the Criminal Law of England*, vol. 1, p. 302.

[50]   Beattie, *Crime and the Courts*, p. 340.

[51]   Smith, *De Republica Anglorum*, p. 79.

[52]   Ibid. The language of the jurors' oath was: 'You shall well and truly try and true deliverance make between our sovereign lord the king and the prisoners at the bar whom you shall have in charge, and true verdict give according to your evidence. So help you God'; Baker, 'Criminal Courts and Procedure at Common Law 1550–1800', p. 36.

[53]   Cockburn, 'Introduction', p. 50.

[54]   2 Hen. V c. 3, 19 Hen. VII c. 13, 23 Hen. VIII c. 13.

substantial yeomen, that dwell about the place, or at the least in the hundred, or neere where the felonie is supposed to be committed, men acquainted with daily labour and travaile, and not with such idle persons as be readie to doe such mischiefes.[55]

The 'substantial yeomen' were less likely to be acquainted or familiar with the social circle of the defendants and were also not enthusiastic about serving on the panel alongside the more common men who were willing to serve as jurors.

Jurors were exposed to pressures exerted by the parties, the grand jurors (who endorsed a bill of indictment and therefore disapproved of acquittals) and the judges. The latter could fine jurors right away and censure them before the Star Chamber. At the Star Chamber the jurors were examined on the reasons for their decisions and were susceptible to punishment.[56]

Only in 1670, in the *Bushell* case, was it ruled that the jurors had a right to return a verdict according to their consciences without being subjected to any subsequent punishments.[57] Bushell was the foreman of the jury in a tumultuous assembly case in which the jury found both defendants not guilty. The judges exhibited little appreciation for that result, fined the jurors and sentenced them to be imprisoned until they paid:

> The Recorder had expressed his admiration for the Spanish Inquisition, and the Mayor had said he would cut Bushell's (the foreman's) throat as soon as he could. The Jury were fined forty marks apiece for their verdict, and sentenced to be imprisoned till they paid it.[58]

After the jurors in *Bushell* had been fined and sent to prison, they managed to obtain a writ of habeas corpus. Ten of the twelve judges who heard their case concurred in a decision that set forth a major constitutional principle – the jury's absolute right to decide the case without being exposed to any questioning or penal consequences.

The modern rule excluding jurors familiar with the parties or the facts did not exist, but the criterion for jury selection was no longer a personal acquaintance with the facts. The jurors were selected from the shire and were not necessarily from the region where the crime was committed. Dislocation was common in early modern times, and the constant demographical changes influenced the

---

[55]   Smith, *De Republica Anglorum*, p. 79.

[56]   Baker, 'Criminal Courts and Procedure at Common Law 1550–1800', p. 23; Cockburn, 'Introduction', p. 70; Herrup, *The Common Peace*, p. 135.

[57]   Stephen, *A History of the Criminal Law of England*, vol. 1, pp. 306, 373–5.

[58]   Ibid., vol. 1, p. 374.

panel structure. A local juror might be a newcomer to the area and therefore as unfamiliar with the defendant or the case as a stranger.[59] The Marian statutes, which shifted the investigatory role to the magistrates, further catalyzed and institutionalized the separation of juries from their previous power base, the regulation of information.[60] No longer self-informant, the jurors were presented with evidence collected by someone else. Because the royal judges who came from outside the shire received the JPs' investigations and were no longer dependent on the jurors for information, their knowledge of the facts sometimes led them to different conclusions than those of the jurors.

The conditions under which the juries conducted their deliberations were not at all attractive. Although the cases were usually decided 'in minutes rather than in hours',[61] jurors were sequestered in prison-like conditions until reaching their decisions:

> And there is a bailife to waite upon them and to see that no man doe speake with them, and that they haue neither bread, drinke, meate, ne fire brought to them, but there to remaine in a chamber together till they agree.[62]

While the hungry jurors were deliberating, the judges and justices went out for dinner and afterwards progressed with civil cases to pass the time until the jurors came back.[63] If the jurors reached no verdict by the end of the session, they could be carried in a cart after the itinerant judges, who continued their journey to the next county.[64]

Juries served in several cases during the sessions and had to decide them all together on the basis of what they could remember after completion of all the sessions.[65] Sometimes the panel had to implore the judge not to encumber them

---

[59]   Herrup, *The Common Peace*, p. 132.

[60]   Ibid., p. 133.

[61]   Ibid., p. 134. In a case of 1659, for example, the jurors acquitted 'in a quarter of an hours time' (James Blackley, *A Lying Wonder Discovered* ... (London: Thomas Simmons, 1659), p. 5).

[62]   Smith, *De Republica Anglorum*, p. 81. Jurors could be fined for having food in their pockets, even if they had not eaten it. Langbein, *Origins*, p. 23. According to Beattie, eighteenth-century jurors deliberated in the public courtroom. This arrangement might have been due to the transfer to a practice of giving a verdict after each case was heard. Cockburn believed that could have been true even for the period of this research (Beattie, *Crime and the Courts*, p. 398; Cockburn, 'Introduction', p. 111).

[63]   Smith, *De Republica Anglorum*, p. 82.

[64]   Cockburn, 'Introduction', p. 71.

[65]   At times they heard up to a dozen cases (Beattie, *Crime and the Courts*, p. 395). In the early decades of the eighteenth century the novelty of deciding a verdict at the conclusion

with additional cases.[66] In practice, juries were allocated more than two or three cases and sometimes determined the verdict for up to 18 prisoners.[67]

Jurors, as a matter of course, were not paid or compensated for their services. As soon as their task was over, they were 'dismissed to goe whither they will, and haue no manner commoditie & profite of their labour and verdict, but onely do seruice to the Prince and commonwealth'.[68]

The result of all those inconveniences and disadvantages was that many tried their best to avoid jury duty. Even constables and grand jurors who were present at court could be drafted to the petty jury.[69] Whoever chanced to be in court as a witness, a spectator or a party risked being snatched up to jury service,[70] a concern that led some victims to refrain from prosecution.[71]

Proving the Crime

The trial began once the empanelling was completed. Under common law the accused had a right to be unshackled during the trial,[72] which was to be conducted in the presence of the accused, who could be removed from the courtroom only in rare circumstances.[73] The trial was no longer a conflict between private parties, but rather between the crown, which was the prosecuting party, and the accused. However, despite its being a party to the criminal proceedings, only rarely was the crown represented by counsel,[74] and the court, with the assistance of the

---

of each case was introduced (ibid., p. 396). In 1738 the jurors' seats in the Old Bailey were rearranged so they could sit together and deliberate at the end of each case (Langbein, *Origins*, p. 21).

[66] Smith, *De Republica Anglorum*, 81.

[67] For statistics of the average number of prisoners arraigned before each jury of the Home Circuit, 1559–1623, see Cockburn, 'Introduction', p. 64.

[68] Smith, *De Republica Anglorum*, p. 86.

[69] Cockburn, 'Introduction', pp. 59–60.

[70] About *de circumstantibus* impanelling, see ibid., p. 60.

[71] Ibid., p. 61.

[72] Baker, 'Criminal Courts and Procedure at Common Law 1550–1800', p. 35.

[73] For example, the accused Elizabeth Device was ordered out of the courtroom 'in the end, when no other meanes would serve' after behaving wildly in trying to prevent her nine-year-old daughter from testifying against her in court (Thomas Potts, *The Vvonderfull Discouerie of Witches in the Countie of Lancaster* (London: Iohn Barnes, 1613), G).

[74] John H. Langbein, *Prosecuting Crime in the Renaissance: England, Germany, France*, Studies in Legal History (Cambridge, MA: Harvard University Press, 1974), p. 77; Langbein, *Origins*, p. 12. The prosecution by counsels developed gradually. At first the government hired lawyers to represent the crown in treason cases, and, beginning in

clerk, managed the proceedings.[75] The JP appeared not as a prosecutor, but 'to give small assist to the assize judge, who coordinated the prosecution at trial, by providing him with a convenient summary of the prosecution case'.[76] The assize judge examined the witnesses and the defendant and thus controlled the flow of evidence to the jury.[77]

The clerk called for the witnesses for the prosecution to come forth by saying: 'If any can giue euidence, or can say any thing against the prisoner, let him come nowe, for he standeth upon his deliuerance.'[78] The absence of the prosecution witnesses was a ground for an acquittal, even in cases where the defendant had previously confessed at the examination. In such cases, those witnesses, who had earlier been bound to appear by the JP, would be required to pay their recognizance.[79]

Because of the probative difficulties in witchcraft cases, confessions were highly desirable. Torture being illegal, however, confessions were not as easy to obtain as on the Continent. Smith expressed a fourfold criticism of the use of torture. First, the value of confessions that were forcibly obtained was doubtful, as the prisoner was likely to admit anything: 'He will confesse rather to haue done any thing, yea, to haue killed his own father.' Second, he condemned the cruelty. Third, the public sentiment might turn against a ruler who forced his subjects to endure such cruelty. And last, there was a practical consideration – torture was futile. As the deposition had no independent probative value, the prisoner could recant in court.[80]

The voluntary confession, according to Michael Dalton in his popular manual *The Country Justice*, 'exceeded all other evidence'.[81] But the English became more and more suspicious regarding the voluntariness of confessions. Later, in the

---

the 1720s, in serious felonies (Beattie, *Crime and the Courts*, pp. 354–6). This account is consistent with Langbein's findings based on the Old Bailey Sessions, tracing a trickle of prosecution counsels starting in the 1710s (Langbein, *Origins*, p. 146).

[75]   Baker, 'Criminal Courts and Procedure at Common Law 1550–1800', p. 16; Langbein, *Prosecuting Crime in the Renaissance*, p. 16. On the importance of the clerk's role, see Cockburn, 'Introduction', pp. 5–6. Langbein saw the role of the English judges as relatively passive and maintained that 'English common law judges were administrators rather than adjudicators' (Langbein, *Origins*, p. 333).

[76]   Langbein, *Prosecuting Crime in the Renaissance*, p. 35.

[77]   Cockburn, 'Introduction', pp. 109, 112.

[78]   Smith, *De Republica Anglorum*, 79.

[79]   Ibid., pp. 79–80.

[80]   Ibid., pp. 85–6. By comparison, Continental jurists, faced with suspects who did not confess under torture, explained their resistance to pain by the use of witchcraft (Esther Cohen, 'The Animated Pain of the Body', *American Historical Review* 105, no. 1 (2000): p. 51).

[81]   Michael Dalton, *The Countrey Iustice* (London: Societie of Stationers, 1618), p. 243.

eighteenth century, out-of-court confessions could be admitted into evidence, but their probative value, or 'weight', depended on the circumstances of the admission of guilt.

Although the results of the pre-trial examination would not independently constitute proof,[82] the examination was used as a road map of the presentation of the case and the content of the prosecution testimonies by the JP.[83] The depositions were not kept on record once the trial was over.[84] However, the reading of the examination and the appearance of the JP did not replace the need to prove the charges by the actual testimony of the witnesses.[85] It might give an impression of the general picture and save time (the witnesses could simply approve their statements to the JP), but without actual testimony, no fact was proven. Afterwards all the prosecution witnesses, beginning with the victim and followed by the constable and all those who participated at the apprehension, were called and sworn in one after the other. The alleged victim ('prosecutor') testified first. The testimony was complemented by the 'altercation', a direct confrontation between the accuser and the defendant.[86] It was a verbal battle between the accused and his accuser and did not take the form of direct and cross-examinations, but was rather a heated exchange of words.[87] In the middle of the sixteenth century the right to be represented by an attorney did not yet exist, and the accused had to struggle with his accuser directly.[88] The accused had no

---

[82]   In Stephen's view it was possible that if the prosecution witnesses did not appear, the accused who confessed before the JP was further examined on the basis of that examination. However, Smith did not say this explicitly in his description. It is important to remember that only defendants who pleaded not guilty reached this stage of the trial; therefore, it seems unlikely that the defendant would be inclined to admit in the absence of the prosecution witnesses (Stephen, *A History of the Criminal Law of England*, p. 348).

[83]   Smith, *De Republica Anglorum*, 80.

[84]   Herrup, *The Common Peace*, p. 67.

[85]   Beattie, *Crime and the Courts*, p. 273. The technique was sometimes to have the witnesses approve their depositions: 'Now at the Assizes, these two Persons again attested the Substance of the same Information, and added ...' (*The Case of the Hertfordshire Witchcraft Consider'd* (London: John Pemberton, 1712), p. 27).

[86]   Smith, *De Republica Anglorum*, p. 80.

[87]   In a case with several defendants, they all argued with the witness. After the testimony of Agnes Brown, both of the accused, Mother Waterhouse and her daughter, exclaimed as follows: 'There thou liest saide Agnes waterhouse ... she saith it is a daggar knif, and I haue none suche in my house, but a greate knyfe, and therein she lieth, yea yea, my lorde, quoth Ione waterhouse she lieth in that she saith that it hadde a face like an ape, for this that came to mee was like a dogge' (*The Examination and Confession of Certaine Wytches at Chensforde in the Countie of Essex* (London: Willyam Powell, 1566), Avii).

[88]   The altercation was the salient feature of what Langbein termed 'the accused speaks' trial of the pre-lawyerization era (Langbein, *Origins*, pp. 2, 13–16). The altercation was

right to receive the indictment or the witnesses' depositions in advance, so there was hardly any chance to prepare. The spontaneity enforced by the deprivation of prior information and the emotional toll contributed to an intense encounter. The anxiety-provoking circumstances could confuse a defendant who was even an experienced barrister[89] and were clearly beyond the coping ability of most defendants, who were poor and uneducated.

The rest of the prosecution witnesses testified after the victim. They included the constable, lay witnesses and, many times in witchcraft cases, expert witnesses. Some cases revolved around the battle between the experts.[90] A common presumption was that illnesses unknown to medical practitioners must originate from witchcraft.[91] Physicians were often called to testify as expert witnesses to prove that, according to existing medical knowledge, the illness could not be attributed to natural causes. It was therefore presumed that witchcraft was behind the illness.

The inferior position of the defendant was manifested in many procedural disadvantages, which hindered the ability to prepare a defence. In felony cases, the defendant was normally imprisoned pending the proceeding, and the indictment and depositions were not revealed to the defendant prior to the trial. There was no right to representation by counsel during the trial or even to assistance by one to prepare. As Baker remarked: 'If counsel were allowed it was pointed out with some alarm in 1602, every prisoner would want it.'[92] The concern was that counsels would complicate and manipulate the trial with fine words and legal trickery.[93] Cockburn discovered that, according to all the available court records of the Home Circuit in the period of Elizabeth I and James I, attorneys were allowed in only three cases.[94] Representation was

---

common in most witch trials. In more celebrated and politically important cases (typically treason cases), the accused would have been examined by a counsel for the crown (Stephen, *A History of the Criminal Law of England*, p. 350). In the above-cited case of Mother Waterhouse in 1566, there was both an altercation and an examination of the suspect by the Queen's Counsel.

[89]   Stephen gave the example of Langhorn, a defendant who was an experienced barrister and who was too distressed and did poorly in his defence (Stephen, *A History of the Criminal Law of England*, vol., 1, p. 398).

[90]   See Stephen for an example of a murder case in which the cause of death, as determined by the experts, was the main issue of the trial (ibid., vol. 1, p. 420).

[91]   Ewen, *Witchcraft and Demonianism*, p. 120.

[92]   Baker, *An Introduction to English Legal History*, p. 582.

[93]   Similar concerns were expressed on the Continent. See Heinrich Kramer and James Sprenger, *Malleus Maleficarum*, trans. Montague Summers (Escondido, CA: Book Tree, 1486; reprint, 2000), p. 217.

[94]   Cockburn, 'Introduction', p. 108.

allowed in misdemeanour cases but forbidden in felony cases. An act in 1696 permitted the assistance of counsel for the pre-trial and trial in treason cases, yet defendants of other serious crimes remained unrepresented.[95] After the 1730s, representation by counsel was commonly permitted as a matter of grace,[96] and in 1836 it became a legal right.[97] Representation was bolstered by deeming the client's disclosures to the attorney to be privileged, about which a defence counsel could not be called to testify – what Gilbert calls 'a Sort of Confidence inviolable'.[98]

Even after the 1730s most defendants were still unrepresented.[99] Only the wealthier defendants were able to afford counsel.[100] The others had to rely on a court's occasional initiative to assign a volunteering counsel who happened to be in court, or try to represent themselves.[101] Yet, despite these deficiencies, the involvement of defence attorneys and the objections they raised generated an elaborate system of evidentiary rules and contributed to shifting the burden of proof to the prosecutor.[102]

It was difficult to oppose the prosecution witnesses. Other than in the altercation with the alleged victim, the defendant had no right to confront the testimonies. Cross-examination did not yet exist. All prosecution witnesses testified under oath.[103] In sharp contrast, defendants could not testify under

---

[95]   7 & 8 Will. III c. 3. For a discussion of the reforms brought about by this act, see Langbein, *Origins*, ch. 2.

[96]   Judges allowed defence counsel to counter the increasing imbalance between the defendants and the prosecution, which was handled more and more by professional lawyers and thieftakers who were rewarded for successful prosecutions and supported by the often-distorted testimony of crown witnesses attempting to save their necks (Langbein, *Origins*, pp. 4, 168).

[97]   Baker, *An Introduction to English Legal History*, p. 583; Langbein, *Origins*, pp. 102, 106–7. The role of the defence lawyer was not clearly defined at first – it was unclear if he himself could cross-examine or just suggest questions to the court, or argue about the facts or questions of law only (Beattie, *Crime and the Courts*, pp. 359–60. However, lawyers often disguised questions of fact as questions of law, thus being able to argue the matter to the jury and developing the criminal evidence in the process. See also Langbein, *Origins*, pp. 27, 216.

[98]   Sir Geoffrey Gilbert, *The Law of Evidence* (London: W. Owen, 1756), pp. 138–9.

[99]   Langbein, *Origins*, pp. 169, 314. Apparently, representation levels at the provincial assizes were higher, as the criminal defence was a training opportunity for young barristers (ibid., pp. 256, 315).

[100]   Ibid., p. 315.

[101]   Ibid., pp. 315–17. One woman, who was convicted in 1757 and sentenced to death, explained: 'I must die because I am poor, I can't help it' (cited by ibid., p. 317.

[102]   Beattie, *Crime and the Courts*, p. 375.

[103]   They were sworn as follows: 'The evidence you shall give to this jury between our sovereign lord the king and the prisoner at the bar shall be the truth, the whole truth,

oath on their own until the middle of the nineteenth century.[104] Testifying under oath was considered advantageous, as the customary view was that if a witness testified under oath, he or she must be believed unless directly contradicted.[105]

Another difficulty for the accused was the barring of defence witnesses.[106] Although Queen Mary I advocated the allowance of defence witnesses, her instruction was often disregarded.[107] The first defence witnesses appeared at the end of the sixteenth century.[108] During the interregnum (1651–59), prisoners could not only cross-examine the prosecution witnesses, but also call their own witnesses.[109] However, the proposal of the Hale Commission to allow defence witnesses to testify under oath was not effectuated.[110] By the mid-seventeenth century, defence witnesses were the normal practice,[111] and, generally, it may be said that the trial procedure from the second half of the seventeenth century had begun to resemble the modern one.[112] Still, when the practice of calling defence witnesses began to be tolerated, they could not testify under oath.[113]

The criminal proceeding was no longer between private parties. Prosecution was in the name of the king, and the prosecution witnesses testified for the

---

and nothing but the truth. So help you God' (Baker, 'Criminal Courts and Procedure at Common Law 1550–1800', p. 38).

[104]   George Fisher, 'The Jury's Rise as Lie Detector,' *The Yale Law Journal*, no. 107 (1997), p. 579; Langbein, *Prosecuting Crime in the Renaissance*, p. 25.

[105]   Stephen, *A History of the Criminal Law of England*, vol. 1, p. 400.

[106]   Langbein explained that there was no evidence rule forbidding defence witnesses; the prohibition was of their testimony on oath (Langbein, *Origins*, pp. 54–6). Of course, without the ability to force the appearance of uncooperative witnesses for the defence, such a right might be meaningless. One of the reforms of the Treason Trials Act was a compulsory process in treason cases (ibid., p. 96).

[107]   Baker, 'Criminal Courts and Procedure at Common Law 1550–1800', p. 38; Fisher, 'The Jury's Rise as Lie Detector', p. 603.

[108]   Gibson, *Reading Witchcraft*, p. 40.

[109]   Stephen, *A History of the Criminal Law of England*, vol. 1, p. 358. Joan Peterson, for example, denied the charges against her and 'delivered a paper of such witnesses as she had to defend her, desiring that they might be called, whereupon Dr Bates, and Dr Colledon Physitians, together with Mr Stamford, and Mr Page Chyrurgians, and divers other persons of good quality' testified on her behalf (*A Declaration in Answer to Several Lying Pamphlets* ... (London: s.n.r., 1652), pp. 6–7).

[110]   Langbein, *Origins*, p. 52.

[111]   Fisher, 'The Jury's Rise as Lie Detector', p. 604.

[112]   Stephen, *A History of the Criminal Law of England*, vol. 1, p. 369.

[113]   Dalton, *The Countrey Iustice*, p. 265.

crown. Courts were reluctant to permit contradition of those witnesses, as it might conceptually injure the interests of the king.[114]

This approach was a remnant of the compurgation method, the wager of oaths. By the oath, the witnesses testified 'under the Solemnities and Obligation of Religion, and the Dangers and Penalties of Perjury'.[115] False testimony was not only perjury, but also heresy, subject to divine sanctions.[116] Conflicting oaths were permitted in civil cases, and even in misdemeanours, the accused was allowed to call defence witnesses to testify under oath. However, such a right was denied to defendants in felony cases.[117] Contradicting oaths in a capital case might suggest the possibility of erroneous execution. By permitting only prosecution witnesses to testify under oath, 'the system assured that a jury's verdict of guilt would seem to bear a divine imprimatur'.[118]

A series of scandalous treason trials during the seventeenth century left a bitter impression of injustice and led to an improvement of defendants' procedural rights. The Treason Trials Act of 1696 mandated that in treason cases the accused should have a copy of the indictment before trial, be allowed representation by counsel and to call witnesses under oath.[119] An act of 1702 gave traitors and other felons the right to call sworn witnesses.[120] An act of 1708 allowed prisoners to have the list of prosecution witnesses ten days before the trial.[121] In 1867 the defence was allowed to depose witnesses in advance of trial

---

[114]   John G. Bellamy, *The Criminal Trial in Later Medieval England: Felony before the Courts from Edward I to the Sixteenth Century* (Thrupp, Stroud, Gloucestershire: Sutton, 1998), p. 48.

[115]   Gilbert, *The Law of Evidence*, p. 4.

[116]   For this reason, explained Gilbert, 'Infidels' could not be witnesses. Also no good for oath were 'Persons Excommunicate', 'Popish Recusants', 'Ideots, Madmen, and Children under the Age of common Knowledge' and 'atheists'. He further explained that Jews were allowed to take an oath as prosecution witnesses in criminal cases 'because they can swear on the Old Testament which is Part of our Belief'. The underlying logic is incoherent, as is evident because he continued to say that Jews were barred from testifying in civil cases under the maxim, 'Judaei et Haeretici contra Orthodoxos produci in Judicio Testes nequeunt' (ibid., pp. 145–6).

[117]   Fisher, 'The Jury's Rise as Lie Detector', pp. 580, 597; Gilbert, *The Law of Evidence*, p. 159.

[118]   Fisher, 'The Jury's Rise as Lie Detector', p. 601.

[119]   Langbein, *Origins*, p. 3.

[120]   1 Anne st. 2 c. 9. Fisher, 'The Jury's Rise as Lie Detector', p. 579; Langbein, *Origins*, p. 52.

[121]   7 Anne c. 27 s. 14. Fisher, 'The Jury's Rise as Lie Detector', pp. 583, 597; Stephen, *A History of the Criminal Law of England*, vol. 1, pp. 416–17.

and to bind their appearance at the trial, thus finally gaining the same rights as the prosecution.[122]

Stephen referred to the defendant's inferiority by using the metaphor of the unfair race, 'in which the King had a long start and the prisoner was heavily weighted'.[123] According to Stephen, it would have made no difference had the prisoner been given a copy of the indictment[124] or been allowed to call witnesses,[125] as the accused was isolated in prison, could not prepare witnesses and had no means of binding their appearance. In addition, the charges were read to the defendants in English at the arraignment,[126] but it is doubtful that most defendants would have been able to read the Latin original. That inferiority, maintained Beattie,[127] was not an accidental disregard of the defendant's rights, but a deliberate policy based on the conviction that the defendant's spontaneous reactions in the court room would help reveal the truth. For the defendant to make an honest defence, it was believed, counsel was superfluous.[128]

Because in the sixteenth century testimony was to be accepted by the merit of oath, defendants' objections were to competency of the witness rather than to credibility,[129] but the competency rules were modified or suspended in witchcraft cases. Children, normally regarded to be incompetent witnesses, were permitted to testify, even against their parents. In the seventeenth century the focus shifted to the quality and veracity of the testimony, rather than the characteristics of the witness. The notions of credibility and weight gained prominence. Alongside the rise of defence witnesses, which brought about the difficulty of dealing with conflicting testimonies, and the search for better truth-finding means because the medieval methods were either illegal or inadequate, the rules of evidence began to form.[130] Facts were ascertained on the basis of the oral testimonies and documents, and it was important to determine which facts could be proven and which facts could not, who might prove them and in what manner. Some principles of evidence law were first developed in civil cases, where counsels were involved, and later extrapolated to criminal cases.[131]

---

[122] Baker, *An Introduction to English Legal History*, p. 583.
[123] Stephen, *A History of the Criminal Law of England*, vol. 1, p. 397.
[124] Ibid., vol. 1, p. 399.
[125] Ibid., vol. 1, p. 350.
[126] Beattie, *Crime and the Courts*, p. 336.
[127] Ibid., p. 271.
[128] Herrup, *The Common Peace*, p. 3; Langbein, *Origins*, pp. 2–3, 34.
[129] Stephen, *A History of the Criminal Law of England*, vol. 1, p. 400.
[130] Ibid., vol. 1, p. 415.
[131] Baker, 'Criminal Courts and Procedure at Common Law 1550–1800', p. 39; Stephen, *A History of the Criminal Law of England*, vol. 1, p. 440.

Defendants' out-of-court confessions were also inspected through the prism of weight. The weight was determined according to the circumstances. If the confession was induced through coercion by threats, violence or promise of favours, its probative value was much weakened.[132] Wigmore assumed that confessions obtained under 'hope of favour' were considered involuntary because of the English class structure, which caused many lower-class defendants to fear that their 'social superiors' would require them to confess.[133] The rule was: 'Confession must be voluntary and without Compulsion.'[134]

Different degrees of probativeness emerged not only from the different personalities and reliability of the witnesses, but from the nature and content of their testimony: Was the evidence detailed? Was it direct or circumstantial? How convincing was the evidence? The early modern standards of evidence were inchoate.[135] From the late fifteenth century onwards, jurors were expected to adhere to the 'satisfied conscience' or the synonymous 'moral certainty' standards, often mentioned together. The term 'beyond reasonable doubt', bearing the same meaning, emerged around the mid-eighteenth century.[136] Its seeds, however, began to sprout much earlier.

Without good evidence, satisfying the conscience or achieving certainty was not an easy task. Therefore, circumstantial evidence played a significant role in the prosecution of hard-to-prove crimes such as rape, poisoning or forgery.[137] Having no direct evidence, the triers of fact had to rely on the next best thing – assumed facts – presumptions that were built on the foundation of circumstantial evidence.

The accused had a right to make a statement at the end of the trial.[138] Failure on the accused's part to respond was interpreted as inability to deny the charges.[139] Without counsel, no one else presented the defendant's case.

---

[132] Beattie, *Crime and the Courts*, p. 365.

[133] Langbein, *Origins*, pp. 229–30; John Henry Wigmore, *Evidence in Trials at Common Law*, 4th edn, 10 vols (Boston: Little, Brown and Company, 1983), vol. 1, § 820, p. 297.

[134] Gilbert, *The Law of Evidence*, p. 140.

[135] Langbein, *Origins*, p. 23.

[136] Shapiro, *A Culture of Fact*, pp. 22–3; Barbara J. Shapiro, *Probability and Certainty in Seventeenth-Century England: A Study of the Relationships between Natural Science, Religion, History, Law, and Literature* (Princeton, NJ: Princeton University Press, 1983), p. 168. Langbein believed it was fully articulated only at the end of the eighteenth century (Langbein, *Origins*, pp. 23, 56).

[137] In addition, the presumption of innocence, which could have hindered conviction solely on circumstantial evidence, was not yet institutionalized (Cockburn, 'Introduction', p. 107).

[138] Stephen, *A History of the Criminal Law of England*, vol. 1, p. 441.

[139] Beattie, *Crime and the Courts*, p. 349.

Trials were short. Many trials lasted just a few minutes and typically not more than 30 minutes from arraignment to verdict.[140] The caseload was between ten and twenty cases a day, sometimes even more.[141] Longer trials were exceptional and a subject of a special remark.[142] After the judge 'hath heard them say inough', he asked the prosecution witnesses if they had anything to add. If they answered negatively, according to Smith, he addressed the jury:

> Good men (saith he) ye of the enquest, ye haue heard what these may say against the prisoner, you haue also heard what the prisoner can say for himselfe, haue an eye to your othe, and to your duetie, & do that which God shall put in your mindes to the discharge of your consciences.[143]

---

[140] Baker, *An Introduction to English Legal History*, p. 582; Beattie, *Crime and the Courts*, pp. 313, 376; Cockburn, 'Introduction', p. 110; Herrup, *The Common Peace*, p. 141; Langbein, *Origins*, pp. 16–17.

[141] Cockburn, 'Introduction', p. 110. On the day Amy Denny and Rose Cullender were tried for witchcraft, nine criminal cases (including murder and theft cases) had been previously heard (Gilbert Geis and Ivan Bunn, *A Trial of Witches: A Seventeenth-Century Witchcraft Prosecution* (London: Routledge, 1997), p. 35).

[142] Langbein, *Origins*, pp. 17–18. For example, see the remark about the five-hour trial in *The Most Strange and Admirable Discouerie of the Three Witches of Warboys* (London: Thomas Man, and Iohn Winington, 1593), O. It was held 'with great patience of the Judge' and 'without intermission or interruption, untill both the Judge, Justices, and Jury said openly that the cause was most apparant: their conscience were well satisfied, that the sayd Witches were guiltie & had deserued death'. In the case against Joan Peterson, 'the business being of great concernment (took up the major part of the day) and indeed very many Witnesses, of good reputation, was examined on both sides' (*The Tryall and Examination of Mrs Joan Peterson* (London: G. Horton, 1652), p. 8). A famous trial presided over by Judge Hale lasted 'from Seven or Eight in the Morning till Seven or Eight at Night, wherein he called to his assistance divers Physitians, and other learned Men' (John Hale, *A Collection of Modern Relations ...* (London: John Harris, 1693), preface, image 4). In the trial of Joan Butts, 'There was in all about Nineteen or Twenty Witnesses against Her. And the Tryal was near three hours long. The Jury having been some time out, returned and gave in their Verdict that she was not Guilty, to the great amazement of some who thought the Evidence sufficient to have found her Guilty; yet others who consider the great difficulty in proving a Witch, thought the Jury could do no less than acquit her' (*An Account of the Tryal and Examination of Joan Buts ...* (London: S. Gardener, 1682), p. 2). In the trial of Richard Hathaway for being an imposter, Lord Chief Justice Holt summarized: 'Gentlemen of the Jury, you have heard a very long and tedious evidence' (*The Tryal of Richard Hathaway* (London: Isaac Cleave, 1702), p. 24).

[143] Smith, *De Republica Anglorum*, pp. 80–81.

In a few cases, the judges summed up the evidence for the jury, and their rhetoric and framing of the evidence could influence the jurors greatly.[144] In most cases, however, the judge's address to the jury was as limited as in Smith's description above.[145]

Other than the indictment, the jurors got no documents for their deliberations and had to rely on their memories. However, when uncertain, they could request further testimony from witnesses who were already sworn.[146] No transcripts were prepared, so there were no written testimonies for the jury to read. The lack of written documents is explained by Smith in a self-laudatory fashion that placed England in a moral position superior to that of her European neighbours:

> This is to be understood, although it will seeme straunge to all nations that doe use the ciuill Lawe of the Romane Emperours, that for life and death there is nothing put in writing but the enditement onely. All the rest is doone openlie in the presence of the Judges, the Justices, the enquest, the prisoner, and so many as will or can come so neare as to heare it, and all depositions and witnesses giuen aloude, that all men may heare from the mouth of the depositors and witnesses what is saide.[147]

In contrast to Smith's perception, the judicial proceeding could be public as well as documented.

The jury's verdict, a terse and unanimous pronunciation of guilty or not guilty, without any rational explanations, could seem as arbitrary as the ordeals.[148] The forming of standards of proof or the jury's degree of persuasion did not have any expression in the verdict. A unanimous verdict was required since 1367.[149] The reason might have been that if not all the jurors, who represented

---

144   Beattie, *Crime and the Courts*, pp. 345, 376.

145   Baker, 'Criminal Courts and Procedure at Common Law 1550–1800', p. 40.

146   Smith, *De Republica Anglorum*, p. 81.

147   Ibid., pp. 81–2.

148   Langbein, *Origins*, p. 340; John H. Langbein, *Torture and the Law of Proof: Europe and England in the Ancien Regime* (Chicago: University of Chicago Press, 1977), p. 77; C.R. Unsworth, 'Witchcraft Beliefs and Criminal Procedure in Early Modern England', in Thomas G. Watkin (ed.), *Legal Record and Historical Reality: Proceedings of the Eighth British Legal History Conference, Cardiff, 1987* (London: The Hambledon Press, 1989), pp. 96–7. English jurors could have convicted based on scant evidence that in Europe would not have sufficed even to order examination by torture.

149   Brian P. Levack, *The Witch-Hunt in Early Modern Europe*, 2nd edn (New York: Longman, 1995), p. 75.

the community's common sense, were certain as to the defendant's guilt, some doubt still remained.

The burden of proof undoubtedly lay on the prosecution (and the Marian statutes placed this onus on the state's shoulders). The concept of the presumption of innocence is ancient and known from classical Roman law (*in dubio pro reo*).[150] However, the formula of the burden of persuasion, 'every man is presumed to be innocent till he is proved guilty beyond reasonable doubt', was first expressed only toward the end of the eighteenth century and became unquestionable only in the nineteenth century. Beattie characterized the earlier era by saying that the prosecution was required to provide evidence to prove the charges. However, it was assumed that an innocent defendant should be able to convince the jury of his innocence by the nature and quality of his reply to the incriminating evidence. Thus, the defendant had to play an active role in the trial.[151]

In some cases the juries found partial verdicts and convicted the accused of some of the charges or of a lesser offence (for example, petty larceny instead of grand larceny). The partial verdicts were on occasion an act of clemency – the offence was reduced to a clergiable crime or to a non-capital crime.[152] In many witchcraft cases, where the original indictment included acts of both felony and misdemeanour, the jury convicted only of the latter.[153] When the jurors were done deliberating, they notified the court by the bailiff, and the prisoners were returned to the courtroom.

Before the empanelling of the jury, the defendant was instructed to 'looke upon them well'.[154] The eye contact assisted the defendant in inspecting his jurors. The second time that the court took care to establish eye contact was at the conclusion of their task. Just before they announced their verdict, the jurors were instructed again by the clerk to look at the prisoner.[155] Unlike for judges, for jurors the trial was a special event – the case was not just another case among many similar cases. The emphasis on eye contact was a reminder to the

---

[150] Langbein, *Origins*, p. 262.

[151] Beattie, *Crime and the Courts*, p. 341.

[152] Baker, 'Criminal Courts and Procedure at Common Law 1550–1800', p. 43; Langbein, *Origins*, p. 58. Juries demonstrated a greater degree of leniency toward the non-clergiable and more serious crimes (Cockburn, 'Introduction', p. 114; Herrup, *The Common Peace*, p. 145).

[153] For a few examples, see Cockburn (ed.), *Calendar of Assize Records, Elizabeth I*, cases no. 652, 750, 1034.

[154] Smith, *De Republica Anglorum*, p. 79.

[155] Herrup, *The Common Peace*, p. 131.

jurors that the issue to be decided was not a theoretical one, but that 'they were deciding upon the life and death of another human being'.[156]

The pause was a dramatic suspension before the peak moment of the trial, the pronouncement of the verdict. The clerk reminded the accused, before knowing the result, that he had consented to be tried by the jury, and then he asked the jury for its decision. The result was a matter of life and death, and it was irreversible.[157] If found not guilty, the accused could leave after paying the jailor his fees. If he was found guilty, the judge moved on to sentencing.

Sentencing

After the conviction, the clerk asked the prisoner about his property so he might forfeit it. Customarily, the convicted would not answer fully, and the sheriff made an inquiry after the trial.[158]

In a pre-sentencing procedure called *allocutus*, after being found guilty, the convicted was called to the bar and asked if there was a reason why he should not suffer the punishment of death. At this stage, the accused could plead for the benefit of clergy. However, witchcraft was not clergiable.[159] Other post-conviction and pre-sentencing motions were a motion in arrest of judgment, a prayer to allow an already granted pardon and a pregnancy plea.[160]

To some extent, judges could manoeuvre around an undesired verdict of the jury. If the judge anticipated a disagreeable verdict, he could stop the trial and transfer the matter to another jury at a later session.[161] Another option was to direct the jury to find a special verdict, that is, to decide only the facts but leave the

---

[156] Considering the rushed nature of the contemporary proceeding, as Herrup explained, the care to ensure eye contact was of great significance (ibid.).

[157] Smith, *De Republica Anglorum*, p. 82.

[158] Ibid.

[159] Stephen, *A History of the Criminal Law of England*, vol. 1, p. 349.

[160] The pregnancy plea was examined, even if it had not always seemed serious. After 80-year-old Mother Samuel was convicted, she answered to the judge, who asked if she had anything to say to prevent her sentencing, 'that shee was with childe: which set all the company on a great laughing, and shee her selfe more than any other'. After the judge failed to convince her to withdraw her plea, he appointed a jury of matrons to examine her (*Witches of Warboys*, O2v). For a description of the judicial administration of the pregnancy plea, see *The Office of the Clerk of Assize* ... (2) (London: Henry Twyford, 1682), pp. 61–2.

[161] Langbein, *Origins*, p. 325. However, Hale explained that this power, of which 'nothing is more ordinary', was limited to cases of insufficient evidence where it seemed to the judge that further inquiry could improve the case (Sir Matthew Hale, *Historia Placitorum Coronae* (London: F. Gyles, T. Woodward, and C. Davis, 1736), vol. 2, p. 295).

question of criminal liability to the court.[162] If the judge believed a convicted felon should not have been found guilty, he could reprieve the accused and sponsor a pardon request,[163] and if he believed an acquittal was unwarranted, he could make the release contingent on a variety of conditions[164] or even impose whipping or imprisonment in jail or in a house of correction.[165] The verdict was normally irreversible; however, when the judge believed the verdict was contrary to the evidence, he could pressure the jurors to redeliberate and return a 'right' verdict.[166]

The various acts of witchcraft were classified into felonies or misdemeanours, depending on their gravity. The standard punishment for a felony was hanging. The death sentence was pronounced by the judge after he put a square black cloth on his wig.[167] All the accomplices were hanged, even if their contribution to the crime was relatively minor: 'euen he that doth but hold the candle to giue light to the murderers'.[168] In some exceptional murder cases, and under a royal instruction, the hanged felon was hanged with chains to rot in the air.[169] The body of Thomas Colley, who was convicted of Ruth Osborne's murder by a swimming test, remained hanging for years at the place of execution.[170]

However, none of the exceptional executions were applicable to witchcraft cases unless petty treason (killing of a husband by his wife) or high treason was committed by means of witchcraft.[171] Mother Lakeland was burned at Ipswich

---

[162]   Langbein, *Origins*, p. 329.

[163]   Ibid., p. 324. For examples of cases in which the woman was reprieved subsequent to her conviction by the jury, see Francis Bragge, *A Full and Impartial Account ...*, 2nd edn (London: E. Curll, 1712), p. 29; John Hale, *A Modest Enquiry into the Nature of Witchcraft* (Boston, NE: Benjamin Eliot, 1702), p. 20.

[164]   Baker, 'Criminal Courts and Procedure at Common Law 1550–1800', p. 40; Herrup, *The Common Peace*, p. 142; Shapiro, *Probability and Certainty*, p. 196. In one case, two allegedly bewitched women vomited pins and other objects before the Yorkshire Assizes judges. The jurors were satisfied with that evidence. The judges, however, were sceptical and gave the jurors 'time for a more deliberate determination'. Henri de Heer, *The Most True and Wonderfull Narration of Two Women Bewitched in Yorkshire* ([S.l.]: Tho. Vere and W. Gilbertson, 1658), p. 4.

[165]   Cockburn, 'Introduction', p. 115.

[166]   Langbein, *Origins*, pp. 326–7.

[167]   Beattie, *Crime and the Courts*, p. 316.

[168]   Smith, *De Republica Anglorum*, p. 85.

[169]   Ibid., p. 84.

[170]   Langbein, *Torture and the Law of Proof*, pp. 210–11, fn. 49; Levack, *The Witch-Hunt in Early Modern Europe*, p. 252.

[171]   A few exceptionally serious crimes merited a more cruel execution. Persons convicted of petty treason were to be drawn on a hurdle to the place of execution. Poisoners were to be boiled. Convicts of high treason were executed in the most horrific manner – after being drawn on a hurdle to the place of execution, they were to be hanged by the neck and cut

in 1645 after being convicted of murdering her husband by witchcraft.[172] If the accused was convicted of felonious witchcraft, hanging was mandatory. Burning was not an option, even if requested by the accused.[173] Yet, the idea of burning witches persisted in the cultural conscience. Examining magistrates threatened suspects with burning,[174] and authors pointed out burning as a possibility.[175] Macfarlane believed that this cultural notion, which lacks practical foundation, might reflect memories of the medieval burning of witches as heretics or of the Continental punishment. In general, the English considered themselves much more humane than their fellow Europeans, who used torture and torment for investigation and punishment.[176]

If the conviction was of misdemeanour witchcraft, a year's imprisonment and four pillory sessions were mandated. The relatively short term of one year, however, was many times equal to a death sentence, as many prisoners did not survive the poor conditions at jail and the 'gaol fever'.[177] In a case in Northampton in 1674, a suspect of witchcraft was chained to a post by the jailors until 'she began to swell in all parts of her Body, that her Skin was ready to burst, which caused her to cry out in a most lamentable manner'. The apparent reason for the chaining was to prevent her from letting the devil suck her.[178] The pillory sessions were used for misdemeanours such as sexual offences, seditious utterances and

---

down alive, their privy members cut off and their bowels taken out of their body, quartered and then disposed of with the head (Baker, 'Criminal Courts and Procedure at Common Law 1550–1800', p. 42; Smith, *De Republica Anglorum*, pp. 84–5).

[172] Jim Sharpe, 'The Devil in East Anglia', in Jonathan Barry, Marianne Hester and Gareth Roberts (eds), *Witchcraft in Early Modern Europe* (Cambridge, UK: Cambridge University Press, 1996), pp. 131, 241.

[173] As described in the case of Ann Foster: 'After Sentence of Death was past upon her, she mightily desired to be Burned, but the Court would give no Ear to that, but that she should be hanged at the Common place of Execution, which accordingly was performed' (*The Full and True Relation of the Tryal, Condemnation, and Execution of Ann Foster* (London: D.M., 1674), p. 8).

[174] W.W., *A True and Iust Recorde ...* (London: Thomas Dawson, 1582), A7v, 19th p.; B5v, B6v.

[175] Gifford said, 'If I had but one fagot in the world, I would carry it a myle upon my shoulders to burne a witch' (cited by Alan Macfarlane, *Witchcraft in Tudor and Stuart England: A Regional and Comparative Study* (New York: Harper & Row, 1970), p. 16.

[176] Langbein, *Origins*, p. 340, fns 408–10.

[177] Beattie, *Crime and the Courts*, pp. 301–7; Langbein, *Origins*, p. 49; Macfarlane, *Witchcraft in Tudor and Stuart England*, pp. 16, 60; Alan Macfarlane, 'Witchcraft in Tudor and Stuart Essex', in J.S. Cockburn (ed.), *Crime in England 1550–1800* (Princeton, NJ: Princeton University Press, 1977), p. 76.

[178] *Tryal, Condemnation, and Execution of Ann Foster*, pp. 6–7.

the lesser degree of witchcraft.[179] The pillory was a humiliation of the morally deviant, who publicly denounced his misdeeds.

Major Legal Developments of Criminal Trials, 1542–1736

In the mid-sixteenth century, there were neither rules of evidence nor evidence textbooks as we know them today. There was a distinction between eyewitnesses and others, but aside from that, the witnesses could testify to almost anything. Hearsay was accepted. Evidence regarding the defendant's bad character was permissible and was submitted to raise a presumption of guilt.[180] When defence witnesses were allowed, they could also testify to fact and to the defendant's character or reputation.[181]

By the mid-eighteenth century, law of evidence was already formulated. Langbein referred to four main rules that were already articulated by then. In addition to the hearsay rule, which coexisted in civil practice, three rules were characteristic of the criminal procedure: the character rule, the corroboration rule and the confession rule.[182] The *hearsay* rule eliminated out-of-court statements made by someone other than the witness and offered to prove the truth. While Wigmore saw the sprouting of hearsay in the mid-seventeenth century and its ripening into a rule by the end of that century, Langbein identified a much later formation, toward the end of the eighteenth century.[183] The *character* rule disallowed presenting evidence of the defendant's bad character and previous crimes unless the defendant opened the door by submitting evidence of good character.[184] That rule took hold around 1715.[185] The *corroboration* rule required that an accomplice's testimony should be supported by additional evidence.[186] Langbein believed that it dates from the 1740s and not from the 1780s, as

---

[179]   Baker, 'Criminal Courts and Procedure at Common Law 1550–1800', p. 44.

[180]   Stephen, *A History of the Criminal Law of England*, vol. 1, p. 368.

[181]   Beattie, *Crime and the Courts*, p. 350; Stephen, *A History of the Criminal Law of England*, vol. 1, p. 449.

[182]   Langbein, *Origins*, ch. 4. The following definitions of the four rules rely on Langbein's summary on p. 179.

[183]   Ibid., pp. 234–5, 245. Findings support the existence of the concept in the mid-seventeenth century (see discussion in chapter 11 of this book).

[184]   For the scope of the rebuttal exception, see ibid., p. 197.

[185]   Ibid., p. 195. Langbein, however, mentioned that Wigmore found cases in 1684 and 1692 using this rule, but in his view, the lapse indicated that the rule was not yet common.

[186]   The rule was softened in 1787 in the leading case of *R. v. Robbins*, so that a caution or recommendation to the jury was sufficient (ibid., pp. 179, 212–17).

Wigmore suggested.[187] The *confession* rule allowed admitting defendants' out-of-court confessions only if they were voluntary. According to Langbein, this rule also dates from the 1740s[188] and was not formulated in the 1770s, as Wigmore wrote. On the basis of the *Old Bailey Session Papers*, Langbein claimed that Wigmore erred in setting the formation of the hearsay and character rules in the seventeenth century (too early) and the corroboration and confession rules in the last decades of the eighteenth century (too late).[189] In 1717 William Nelson published *The Law of Evidence*, which included a chapter on criminal trials. Because of the complexity and multitude of rules, Nelson deemed such a compilation not only 'useful, but also the only Thing necessary'.[190] Sir Geoffrey Gilbert compiled and analysed the then-existing evidence law in *Law of Evidence*, which was first published in England in 1756,[191] three decades after he died. In her book *Probability and Certainty in Seventeenth-Century England*, Shapiro remarked that as the work introduced an already established doctrine, it probably reflected the judicial notions existent in an earlier era.[192]

Witchcraft was surreptitious by nature and often committed by inostensible supernatural means, and the creation of evidentiary standards was particularly complex. The search for ways of proof was closely related to changes in procedure and the structure of the legal system: the development of a prosecutorial apparatus, pre-trial investigation and examinations, the changing roles of grand and petty jurors, the rise of defence witnesses and the growing involvement of attorneys in the process.

Those convergent and interrelated developments shaped the prototype of the common-law criminal trial. The procedure and evidence law and the structure of the legal system, which seem so obvious now, were just coming into being between the years 1550 and 1750. The lifespan of the witchcraft crime overlapped those two centuries of formation. The way in which contemporaries thought about the enforcement of witchcraft laws revolved greatly around procedural and evidentiary matters. Procedures and proof mechanisms were

---

[187]   Ibid., p. 203.

[188]   Langbein even detected peremptory signs in the 1730s. However, he asserted that in the 1740s different judges acted differently in face of involuntary confessions (the options were to exclude, caution or admit without caution), and only by the 1760s was the rule settled as a rule of exclusion.

[189]   Langbein, *Origins*, p. 180.

[190]   William Nelson, *The Law of Evidence* (London: B. Gosling, 1735), vol. 1 (1st edn, 1717).

[191]   I used the second (1756) edition. The first, printed in Ireland, was unavailable.

[192]   Shapiro, *Probability and Certainty*, p. 181. For references to later authors on the subject of evidence, see Beattie, *Crime and the Courts*, p. 363.

not self-evident, but a subject of debate. On the Continent the developments followed a different path. Understanding how contemporaries perceived the proof of witchcraft can help to uncover the basic assumptions behind legal concepts that now seem so natural and obvious.

The developments and transformations were not narrowly contained within the legal system. Shapiro displayed a broad perspective on the contemporary intellectual climate and demonstrated how the emergent law of evidence interrelated with transforming notions of science, religion and philosophy about proof and facts.[193] The participants in the debate about proving witchcraft were not necessarily professional lawyers or judges. Understanding the way in which contemporaries thought about proving this crime requires a consideration of not only the legal sphere, but of a much wider cultural field.

---

[193]   Cf. Stephen, *A History of the Criminal Law of England*, vol. 1, p. 427.

¶Ione Waterhouſe, daughter to the mother Waterhouſe, beings of the age of. xviii. yeres, and examined, cōfeſſeth as foloweth.

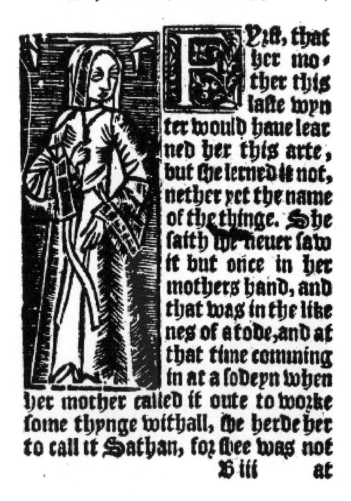

Fyꝛſt, that her mother this laſte wynter would haue learned her this arte, but ſhe lerned it not, nether yet the name of the thinge. Ʃhe ſaith ſhe neuer ſaw it but once in her mothers hand, and that was in the likenes of a tode, and at that time comming in at a ſodeyn when her mother called it oute to woꝛke ſome thynge withall, ſhe herde her to call it Sathan, foꝛ ſhee was not

B iii   at

Figure 3.1 Ione Waterhouse. From *The Examination and Confession of Certaine Wytches* ... (London: Willyam Powell, 1566) (A, Biii). Courtesy of the Trustees of Lambeth Palace Library. [Call # (ZZ) 1587.12.03]

Chapter 3

Circumstantial Evidence

Facing the dilemma of proving witchcraft without eyewitnesses and with scant direct physical evidence, fact-finders had to rely heavily on circumstantial evidence. Circumstantial evidence is not a direct proof of one of the elements that constitute a crime, but an inference of one fact from another – suspicious circumstances that bolster the impression of the suspect's culpability. The archetypal example given in early modern English texts is that of a person seen fleeing a dead man's house holding a bloody sword.[1] Physical evidence (such as fingerprints and DNA evidence today or the devil's mark in early modern England) is a sub-category of circumstantial evidence, as the suspect's guilt is logically inferred from physical traces. Circumstantial evidence can be rebutted with evidence that points to another possible explanation, but in cases without eyewitnesses, suspicious circumstances are extremely powerful. According to Gilbert, the author of one of the first books on evidence law, published in 1756:

> When the fact itself cannot be proved, that which comes nearest to the proof of the fact is, the proof of the circumstances that necessarily and usually attend such facts and are therefore called Presumptions not Proofs for they stand instead of the Proofs of the Fact until the contrary be proved.[2]

For Gilbert, who presumably described the legal reality of the eighteenth century, circumstantial evidence, or 'presumption' in his words, was not a proof, but rather an inferior substitute for actual proof, which stood only as long as nothing was proved to the contrary.

The now-established legal distinctions between presumption of fact and presumption of law,[3] or rebuttable and irrebuttable presumptions, did not as

---

[1] Sir Geoffrey Gilbert, *The Law of Evidence* (London: W. Owen, 1756), p. 160; William Nelson, *The Law of Evidence* (London: B. Gosling, 1717), p. 6. For further discussion, see Barbara J. Shapiro, *'Beyond Reasonable Doubt' and 'Probable Cause': Historical Perspectives on the Anglo-American Law of Evidence* (Berkeley: University of California Press, 1991), pp. 208–9.

[2] Gilbert, *The Law of Evidence*, p. 160.

[3] The former is a deduction of unknown facts from known evidence, and the latter is the application of the same rule of law to a given set of circumstances.

yet exist in early modern English jurisprudence, and the terms 'circumstances', 'presumptions' and 'conjectures' had similar meaning. The sceptic and cynic Reginald Scot (who also attacked the circumstantial as an unsound basis for conviction) equated these terms with impossible and incredible, mocking them as nothing more than mere guesses:

> See first whether the evidence be not frivolous, & whether the proofs brought against them be not incredible, consisting of ghesses, presumptions, & impossibilities contrarie to reason, scripture, and nature.[4]

Under Roman-Canon law, a conviction could be supported only on a full proof, which was either the testimony of two credible eyewitnesses or the confession of the accused. Half proofs, including circumstantial evidence, sufficiently accumulated, could at most allow a judge to order the torture of a suspect. In England the situation was different. Circumstantial evidence had always been allowed in criminal trials under common law. The reason is rooted in the historical development of the jury system. The jury originated as a self-informed panel, familiar with the crimes committed in the local community. The jurors' knowledge included the suspect's reputation, hearsay, rumours and other circumstances surrounding the crime. For this reason, the practice of allowing circumstantial evidence existed long before the intellectual doctrines that justified it.[5] Through a very gradual process, influenced by demographic changes and by the Marian laws, which shifted the function of investigation to the magistrates, the jurors ceased to be self-informed. Circumstantial evidence, nevertheless, continued to be permitted.

The Roman-Canon doctrine, dating at least from the 1150s, which ranked the presumptions in three evidentiary levels, customarily named violent, probable and light, emerged centuries later in early modern England. The tripartite division relates to the levels of circumstantial evidence. The full proof is a separate, fourth, category. A thirteenth-century treatise on the laws of England, ascribed to Bracton, regarded some presumptions (like that of the bloody sword) to be stronger than others.[6] Such instances of overwhelming

---

[4]   Reginald Scot, *The Discouerie of Witchcraft* (London: William Brome, 1584), A6.

[5]   Shapiro, *'Beyond Reasonable Doubt'*, p. 246.

[6]   The work is often referred to as 'Bracton'. Henry Bracton, a judge and clergyman, was probably the last owner of a work that was written to a large extent in the 1220s and 1230s by persons other than Bracton himself. It was edited and updated until the 1250s. Instructing justices to investigate the circumstances with care before waging a duel, Bracton declared that occasionally a proof by duel or by trial was unnecessary, 'when a strong presumption lies against the appelee ... as when he is arrested over the body of the dead man with his knife

presumption required no additional proof. This ranking, first popularized by Bracton, was later made explicit by Sir Edward Coke (who, like Bracton, did not discuss presumptions exclusively in the context of criminal law).[7] Both Bracton and Coke, Shapiro noted, failed to mention their indebtedness to Continental sources on the subject of circumstantial evidence.[8] Both gave the example of a person apprehended with a bloody sword over the body of a dead man as an instance of the strongest level of presumption.[9]

Shapiro believed that witchcraft may have contributed to the development of English criminal law, not because witch trials were common, but because the doctrinal writings on witchcraft contained detailed discussion of circumstantial evidence.[10] The dilemma of the serious but hard-to-prove crime, especially in the context of the debate concerning witchcraft, contributed to sharper definitions and classifications of circumstantial evidence and the creation of an intellectual and epistemological foundation for its admission. The typical witchcraft crime had no eye witnesses, and as torture was not permitted in England, confessions could not be easily obtained. That left the fact-finders in many witchcraft cases with purely circumstantial evidence.

On the Continent, witchcraft was known as a *crimen exceptum*, a doctrine that allowed for the suspension or modification of normal evidentiary rules for conviction in exceptionally serious crimes where normal rules of evidence could not yield convictions. In Continental and Scottish witchcraft cases, this meant a possibility of conviction on circumstantial evidence alone or easier application

---

dripping blood; he cannot deny the death nor is further proof necessary. This is an ancient constitution. Other proof is not necessary.' The treatise, written in Latin, used the term *praesumptio violenta*. Henry Bracton, *De Legibus* (*On the Laws and Customs of England*), trans. and ed. Samuel E. Thorne, 4 vols (Buffalo, NY: W.S. Hein, 1997; reprint, 2005), vol. 2, pp. 386, 404.

[7] 'And Bracton saith there is *probatio duplex, viz. viva.* as by witnesses *viva voce*, and *mortua*, as by deeds, writings, and instruments. And many times Juries together with other matter, are much induced by presumptions, whereof there be three sorts, viz. violent, probable, and light or temararie. *Violenta praesumptio* is many times *plena probatio*, as if one be run thorow the body with a sword in a house whereof he instantly dieth, and a man is seene to come out of that house with a bloody sword, and no other man was at that time in the house. *Praesumptio probabilis* moves little, but, *Praesumptio levis seu temeraria*, moveth not at all.' Sir Edward Coke, *Selected Writings of Sir Edward Coke*, ed. Steve Sheppard, 3 vols (Indianapolis: Liberty Fund, 1608; reprint, 2003), vol. II, p. 622.

[8] Shapiro, *'Beyond Reasonable Doubt'*, pp. 207, 210.

[9] Ibid., p. 208.

[10] Ibid., p. 209. Findings of this research also support such a conclusion. I am much indebted to Shapiro's analysis of circumstantial evidence in general and in the context of witchcraft in particular. Ibid., pp. 200–243.

of torture to extract a confession.[11] Because circumstantial evidence was already permissible in England, application of the doctrine was theoretically unnecessary. Still, the English witchcraft literature is full of traces of the Continental language of *indicia*, signs and half proofs.[12] This borrowing of Continental terms (and the implied possibility of combining different fragments of proof sufficient for conviction) was a resource in proving witchcraft. It facilitated obtaining convictions without having direct evidence; it assisted in creating intellectual justification for the use of circumstantial evidence; and it enabled the classification of circumstantial evidence according to varying degrees of probative strength. The Continental concepts of circumstantial evidence were imported into the English witchcraft debate mostly, but not exclusively, by theologians.

The English theologians maintained that circumstantial evidence could be used in witchcraft cases. Their treatment of circumstantial evidence was another variation of the struggle in proving this crime. The solution offered by William Perkins was to allow circumstantial evidence as a lower-status proof, insufficient for conviction but warranting further investigation. Perkins evaluated 18 signs for the discovery of witches. He adhered to the standards of the Roman-Canon law, which were non-applicable in routine criminal trials in England.[13] It is hard to tell to what extent, if at all, Perkins was aware of the English witchcraft act or the actual procedure in English courtrooms. One should be cautious not to assume knowledge on the part of individuals only because they were members of the elites.[14] The only two signs that Perkins deemed sufficient for conviction were the Continental full proofs – either the testimony of two good witnesses about the suspect's pact with the devil or witchcraft practices, or the confession of the accused.[15] Perkins even seemed to support the use of torture:

> This course hath beene taken in some countries, and may no doubt lawfully and with good conscience be vsed, howbeit not in euery case, but onely vpon strong and great presumptions going before, and when the partie is obstinate.[16]

---

[11]   Ibid., pp. 205, 209; Christina Larner, *Witchcraft and Religion: The Politics of Popular Belief* (New York, NY: Blackwell, 1984), pp. 35–67, esp. p. 44.

[12]   Shapiro, *'Beyond Reasonable Doubt'*, pp. 209–10.

[13]   The principles of the Canon law were applicable in criminal cases held in the Star Chamber and the ecclesiastical courts.

[14]   I thank the anonymous reviewer for stressing this point.

[15]   William Perkins, *A Discourse of the Damned Art of Witchcraft* (Cambridge, UK: Vniuersitie of Cambridge, 1608), pp. 211–14.

[16]   Ibid., p. 204.

Indeed, Perkins mentioned that torture was a practice employed in some countries but made no mention that it was illegal in England. Perkins classified the signs according to their probative value. Testimony of two good witnesses or confession were sufficient for conviction. He deemed supernatural signs (such as the water test or burning the bewitched animal) insufficient. A third category of proofs, which were insufficient for conviction but warranted examination, included a long-standing reputation for witchcraft, suspect family members and friends, avoiding questioning and injury to another following cursing or quarrelling. Perkins called these instances of circumstantial evidence 'presumptions'.

Perkins upheld the difference drawn between full proofs and lower-ranking proofs on the Continent. There, sufficient accumulation of half proofs could warrant torture, a practice that Perkins did not find objectionable. Perkins wrote in the Continental theological tradition. Although he wrote for an English audience, his comments were oblivious to English law.[17] Yet, to his English readers the concept of different levels of proof might have implied two significant notions: first, that circumstantial evidence was classified as less valuable than direct evidence, and, second, that the categorization of evidence as insufficient, sufficient or presumption sufficient to warrant further examination established different standards of proof for the pre-trial investigation and for the conviction in the criminal trial.[18] This type of classification was repeated in subsequent publications by clergymen.

Bernard also ranked three levels of evidence according to a sliding scale of probativeness. Of lower value were:

> *weake coniectures*, which are commonly alledged by the weaker sort, arising out of their owne imaginations, or idle speeches of some others. All of this kinde the wise examiner may draw together, to make so of all, perhaps, a presumption; and in hearing the suspected parties answer to these, may collect matter of more weight.[19]

---

[17] Ady explicitly stated that Perkins' treatise was written in the tradition of Continental authors such as Bodin. The style, however, raised Ady's suspicion that the book was not authored by Perkins himself, but published posthumously to support his widow. Thomas Ady, *A Candle in the Dark* (London: Robert Ibbitson, 1655), pp. 162–3.

[18] Some 'presumptions' were labelled by Perkins as 'good', 'great' or 'strong suspicion', but it is not clear whether Perkins intended to delineate a probative hierarchy of presumptions (for example, when he called injury subsequent to cursing 'sufficient matter of Examination, not of Conuiction', without additional superlatives). Then he moved to injury subsequent to quarrelling and stated 'that also is a great presumption', which means both were 'great', although only the second was specifically so defined. Perkins, *Damned Art*, p. 202.

[19] Richard Bernard, *A Guide to Grand-Iury Men* (London: Ed. Blackmore, 1627), pp. 226–7.

If enough conjectures were accumulated, they might establish at most a presumption, which could lead the examiner to investigate and find weightier proofs. If no such presumption could be formed, these conjectures might have resulted in a more informal 'watchful eye' over the suspect or 'sharpe admonition'.[20] The middle-level evidentiary category was also circumstantial, the 'strong presumptions', which could lead to the suspect's arrest and to conviction in non-capital crimes.[21] Among these presumptions Bernard listed instances of circumstantial evidence such as common report of reputation, injury following cursing and exaggerated interest in the victim's health. It seems that Bernard regarded some presumptions to be more powerful than others. Whereas injury following cursing was a great presumption, being a relative of another witch was a presumption 'vpon very weake grounds'.

Gaule also had three evidentiary levels – unwarrantable, probable but insufficient for conviction, and infallible. Gaule's middle category included instances of circumstantial evidence such as reputation, suspected relatives of friends, some appearance of fact, habitual cursing, 'lewd & naughty' lifestyle and bodily marks.[22] The common feature in the works of these three theologians was the three-level classification of evidence according to its value for proving the crime. The content of their categories did not entirely overlap, but all three had a middle degree characterized as presumption. This category contained various circumstances that were adequate to instigate an examination but did not establish strong enough evidence to send the suspect to the gallows.

The theologians were not the only ones advocating the use of circumstantial evidence in witchcraft cases. John Cotta, for example, the sceptic physician, supported detection of witches by reason, including presumptions and conjectures.[23] Cotta, a firm believer in the power of reason as a way to study the world, supposed that witchcraft, like other phenomena, could be detected by logical inference. Each circumstance may not have been much in itself, but it could lead to other circumstances, and grouped together they made valuable proof.[24] Cotta's discussion, which dealt with the value of the accumulation of circumstances, was influenced by the Continental discourse. Unlike the legal scholars, however, Cotta did not hide the Continental influence. For Cotta, there was no contradiction between reliance on experiments and circumstantial evidence, and *all* human knowledge emerged from 'the sole inseparable

---

[20]   Ibid., p. 227.

[21]   Ibid., pp. 227–8.

[22]   John Gaule, *Select Cases of Conscience Touching Vvitches and Vvitchcrafts* (London: Richard Clutterbuck, 1646), pp. 75–6, 80–81.

[23]   John Cotta, *The Triall of Vvitch-Craft* (London: Samuel Rand, 1616), p. 98.

[24]   Ibid., p. 97.

instruments' of 'right reason' and 'true experience'.[25] In his view, it was possible to infer witchcraft from circumstantial evidence just as a doctor could diagnose a disease with the help of the circumstances.

Bradwell, another physician, agreed that with a sly adversary such as the devil, there was no choice but to rely on circumstantial evidence as proof:

> The Devill is a spirit of darkness, he deales closely, and cuningly, you shall hardly finde any direct proofes in such a case, but by many presumptions and Circumstances, you may gather it.[26]

By the eighteenth century, the triple ladder of presumptions (violent, probable, light), much discussed in the context of witchcraft, became a general evidentiary convention. Nelson cited Coke, who had cited Bracton:

> and many Times Juries together with other Matter are much induced by Presumptions, whereof there be three Sorrts, *viz*. Violent, Probable, Light and Temerary; *Violenta Praesumptio* is many Times *Plana Probatio*; as if one be run thro' the Body with a Sword in a House, whereof he is instantly dieth, and a Man is seen to come out of that House with a bloody Sword, and no other Man was at that Time within the House: *Praesumptio Probabilis* moveth little, but *Praesumptio Levis seu Temeraria* moveth not at all.[27]

Gilbert also described the three levels of evidentiary standards, as well as the bloody sword, as an example of 'violent' presumption.[28] Neither Nelson nor Coke (whose *Institutes* were first published in 1628, two decades after Perkins' *Damned Art*) cited any of the theological witchcraft texts to establish the ranking of presumptions. Yet, as Shapiro claimed, the discussion of presumption in the context of witchcraft helped to develop English criminal law. Coke did not need to cite Perkins, as they both derived the concept of presumption from Canon law. The example of the dripping sword was a standard of medieval

---

[25] John Cotta, *A Short Discoverie of the Vnobserved Dangers* (London: William Iones and Richard Boyle, 1612; reprint, 1972), p. 10.

[26] Michael MacDonald (ed.), *Witchcraft and Hysteria in Elizabethan England: Edward Jorden and the Mary Glover Case*, Tavistock Classics in the History of Psychiatry (London: Tavistock/Routledge, 1991), p. 28. He was quoting Stephen Bradwell, *Marie Glovers Late Woefull Case* (London: 1603), British Library, Sloane MS 831.

[27] Nelson, *The Law of Evidence*, p. 6. For the history of these citations, see Shapiro, *'Beyond Reasonable Doubt'*, pp. 208–9.

[28] Gilbert, *The Law of Evidence*, p. 160.

jurists.[29] However, although Bracton, Coke and Nelson used it as an example of a strong presumption, their discussion related to civil matters as well.[30] In comparison, the theological discussion was specific to the context of criminal law. It was much more detailed and drenched in the terminology of full and half proofs, which revealed its Continental origins. The discussion of presumptions in the context of witchcraft trials imported into the English criminal law a new conceptual basis for the acceptance and evaluation of circumstantial evidence.

Presumptions, or circumstantial inferences, were not unique to witchcraft cases and were used in trials for other crimes, as well as in non-criminal cases. Some presumptions (like that of the bloody sword) relied on common sense, and some on contemporary accepted notions of nature and life experience. One example of a highly regarded presumption in cases of murder (not necessarily by witchcraft) was the bleeding corpse. It was assumed with quite a high degree of probability that the corpse bled freshly in the presence of the murderer. Reginald Scot heard that affirmed by 'credible report, and ... many grave authors'.[31] James VI & I considered it a supernatural sign sent by God to discover a murderer.[32] A pamphlet of 1613 described how the dead body of the victim bled afresh when the suspect in a witchcraft case was brought to it.[33] Michael Dalton relied on this case and included it in his list of evidential rules for the proof of witchcraft, 'if the dead body bleed, vpon the Witches touching it', and so did Bernard.[34] Gaule regarded it as a probable sign, 'yet not so certaine as to serve for the Witches Conviction'.[35] Stearne was aware of that method (although by reading).[36] A dissenting sceptical voice was raised by Ady, whose medical explanation was that all bodies bleed after several days if they have not been buried and that it was 'a common and a natural thing', having nothing to do with the presence of the murderer.[37]

As direct evidence could hardly be found in witchcraft cases, they therefore abounded in presumptions. Some believed witchcraft could not be proved in any other way. Bragge, a minister who wrote pamphlets to convince readers that

---

[29]   Shapiro, *'Beyond Reasonable Doubt'*, p. 319, fn. 363.

[30]   Coke's often quoted paragraph, for example, is found in the section about fee simple.

[31]   Scot, *The Discouerie of Witchcraft*, p. 303.

[32]   James I, *Daemonologie* (Edinburgh: Robert Walde-graue, 1597), p. 80.

[33]   Thomas Potts, *The Vvonderfull Discouerie of Witches in the Countie of Lancaster* (London: Iohn Barnes, 1613), Y3.

[34]   Michael Dalton, *The Countrey Iustice* (London: Societie of Stationers, 1618), p. 243; Bernard, *A Guide to Grand-Iury Men*, pp. 223–4.

[35]   Gaule, *Select Cases of Conscience*, p. 80.

[36]   John Stearne, *A Confirmation and Discovery of Witchcraft* (London: William Wilson, 1648), pp. 55–6.

[37]   Ady, *A Candle in the Dark*, pp. 131–2.

Jane Wenham was guilty of witchcraft, held that witchcraft could be proved only through:

> a Multitude of concurrent Circumstances, all tending to increase and confirm our Suspicions; ... all the World knows that the Evidence must be in a great Measure Circumstantial only; and that we should bring positive Witnesses to a Contract with the Devil, is as unreasonable for others to expect, as it is impossible for us to perform.[38]

Pamphlets and tracts concerning witchcraft time and again contained discussions about signs and presumptions, often grading their probative value. Thus the pamphlet literature allows examining the application of circumstantial inferences in action. While some of the inferences were case-specific, other inferences (such as the bloody sword) became more generalized and institutionalized.[39] A classic example of an established witchcraft presumption is that of an injury following a falling-out or cursing. The work of Thomas and Macfarlane is known for portraying a refusal to give charity as a typical background for witchcraft accusations. The charity-being-denied scenario was of an old woman coming to beg for food and being refused. Being sent away, she cursed or mumbled, and a subsequent misfortune befalling those who denied her charity was attributed to her witchcraft. However, although many cases matched this pattern, there were other instances of conflict and unpleasantness, and therefore a broader framework of offensive interactions was preferable.[40] For similar reasons, although some of the early modern authors considered a falling-out and cursing to be separate presumptions, they can be reviewed jointly. In both instances, the inference traced the misfortune that befell the victim to a previous unpleasant interaction with the suspect. The temporal sequence (misfortune following a conflict) was interpreted as evidence that the suspect bewitched the victim. In 1584 Reginald Scot mockingly described how this circumstantial inference was drawn:

---

[38] Francis Bragge, *A Full and Impartial Account* ..., 2nd edn (London: E. Curll, 1712), preface.

[39] For an eighteenth-century writer advocating the use of circumstantial evidence in witchcraft cases relying on the presumption of the bloody sword, see A.M.G.R., *The Belief of Witchcraft Vindicated* (London: J. Baker, 1712), p. 38.

[40] For discussion of other grounds for conflict and analysis of charity denial and alternative narratives, including examples, see Marion Gibson, *Reading Witchcraft: Stories of Early English Witches* (London: Routledge, 1999), pp. 3–4, 83–109.

See also what persons complaine upon them, whether they be not of the basest, the unwisest, & most faithles kind of people. Also may it please you to waie what accusations and crimes they laie to their charge, namelie: She was at my house of late she would have had a pot of milke, she departed in a chafe because she had it not, she railed, she curssed, she mumbled and whispered, and finallie she said she would be even with me: and soone after my child, my cow, my sow, or my pullet died, or was strangelie taken.[41]

The pamphlet literature abounds in mentions of such injuries. On making an accusation, the complainers often associated a conflict with the suspect. The emphasis was on the conflict, and not on the causes. In many cases it was the accuser who started by being rude, tightfisted or unpleasant. Robert Tayler, for example, deposed that his horse died after he did not allow Elizabeth Gooding to buy cheese from his store on credit.[42] Samuel Pacy testified how his youngest daughter, Deborah, got sick immediately after Amy Denny was denied buying herring from him for the third time and went away grumbling.[43] A pamphlet on the case of Ann Foster describes how a rich grazier refused to share his mutton with the suspect, who went away 'murmerring and grumbling, and told him he had as good have done what she desired, and took her mony'. He took little notice of what she said, until a few days later he found 30 of his sheep in the pasture 'in a condition dead, and in a strange and miserable manner, their Leggs broke in pieces, and their Bones all shattered in their Skins'.[44]

Sometimes it was the accuser, and not the suspect, who used harsh words. Thomas Adams, one of the deponents against Jane Wenham, described the conflictual encounter as follows:

He met Jane Wenham in his Turnip-Field with a few of his Turnips, which she was carrying away, and upon his Threatning her she threw them down; he, this Informant, told her she might keep them, for she should pay Dear for them; then she was very Submissive, and begg'd Pardon, saying, she had no Victuals all that Day, and had no Money to buy any; afterwards they parted, and he saw her not after: But on Christmas-Day Morning One of his best Sheep died without any Signs of Illness.[45]

---

[41]   Scot, *The Discouerie of Witchcraft*, A6–A6v.

[42]   H.F., *A True and Exact Relation* ... (London: Henry Overton and Benj. Allen, 1645), p. 7.

[43]   *A Tryal of Witches* ... (London: William Shrewsbery, 1682), p. 16.

[44]   *The Full and True Relation of the Tryal, Condemnation, and Execution of Ann Foster* (London: D.M., 1674), p. 4.

[45]   Bragge, *Full and Impartial Account*, p. 14.

Thomas Adams had indeed caught Wenham stealing a few turnips from his field. However, the threats and abuse came from him, though this did not prevent him from connecting Wenham and his dead sheep.

The unpleasantness of the interaction was a subjective matter. Sometimes an act of kindness by the suspect was experienced as repulsive, intimidating and an opportunity to offend. Mary Johnson was accused by two mothers of having bewitched their children by offering them a snack. Elizabeth Otley deposed that 'the next day after the said *Mary Johnson* had given this Informants child the Apple, the child was taken with very violent fits, and in the fits (although the Child was but two yeers old) yet this Informant could hardly with all her strength hold it down in the Cradle, and so continued until it died'.[46] Similarly, Anabel Duram deposed that a quarter of an hour after Mary Johnson gave her son a piece of bread with butter, the 'child shricked and cried out it was lame ... the child continued for the space of eight dayes shrieking and tearing it self, and then died'.[47] One witness related the deterioration in her health to being blessed by Temperance Lloyd, who met her on the street and said, 'Mrs *Grace*, I am glad to see you so strong again ... I weep for Joy to see you so well again'. However, 'in that very night she this Informant was taken very ill with sticking and pricking Pains'.[48] An eighteenth-century sceptical author derided such reasoning as follows:

> A poor Woman lies at the point of Death; Jane Wenham, a foul-mouth'd Wretch, comes and Scolds under her Window; The woman dies soon after, therefore this Jane Wenham had bewitch'd her. Very good! But let us go on. Jane Wenham sees a lovely Child in her Neighbour's Lap; she is tempted to stroke and caress the Infant: Soon after the Babe dies stark distracted; and therefore again Jane Wenham had bewitched it. What surprizing Conclusions are these; and what may not one prove by this way of Reasoning? As well might it be said, That it was destroy'd by the Care and Fondness of its own Mother; or that the Sugar'd Milk, or Plumb-cake, were Poyson, which it had eaten the day before.[49]

Immediate injury was a suspicious circumstance. Dorothy Durent, in her deposition against Amy Denny, described how two of her children were afflicted subsequent to tense encounters she had had with the suspect. The deponent had

---

[46] F., *A True and Exact Relation*, p. 18.

[47] Ibid., p. 20.

[48] *A True and Impartial Relation* ... (London: Freeman Collins, 1682), p. 8.

[49] *The Case of the Hertfordshire Witchcraft Consider'd* (London: John Pemberton, 1712), pp. 19–20.

left her son in Denny's care and was critical on her return, on finding that Denny had not obeyed her instructions. In response, she testified, Denny was 'telling her that she had as good to have done otherwise than to have found fault with her, and so departed out of her house; and that very night her son fell into strange fits of swooning, and was held in such terrible manner'.[50] The child did not die, a fact that Durent attributed to a counter-magic technique she used against Denny,[51] who then told her 'she should live to see some of her children dead, and she upon crutches'. About a year later, when her daughter was sick, Durent was upset to find Denny at her home when she returned from the apothecary. Durent testified that in response Denny told her:

> You need not be so angry, for your child will not live long: and this was on a Saturday, and the child died on the Monday following ... that not long after the death of her daughter Elizabeth Durent, she, this deponent, was taken with a lameness in both her legs, from the knees downward, and that she had no other use of them but only to bear a little upon them till she did remove her crutches, and so continued till the time of the assizes that the witch came to be tried, and was there upon her crutches.[52]

Durent's deposition exemplifies how the presumption was applied. The injury was attributed to the suspect even when the child recovered and also when the child was sick before the conflictual interaction but died afterward. The immediacy of the injury was emphasized. Durent's need of crutches was nonetheless attributed to the suspect despite a year's passing from the time of the threat. In both events, Denny tried to help Durent (suckled her son while he was in her care[53] and served water to Durent's sick daughter while the mother was gone). Her help was unwelcome and offensive in Durent's eyes.

According to Bernard's criterion, the injury needed to be immediate. But the requirement of immediacy was not narrowly interpreted.[54] The rich grazier attributed the death of his sheep to the suspect, although a few days had passed

---

[50]   *A Tryal of Witches*, p. 57.

[51]   On the advice of one Dr Jacob from Yarmouth, Durent hung the child's blanket in the chimney corner all day. When she took it to cover the child at night, she found a toad, which she threw into the fire. The next day, Denny's niece told her that Denny was burnt. Ibid., pp. 57–8.

[52]   Ibid., p. 58. See also *A Tryal of Witches*, p. 5.

[53]   According to the deposition, Denny, a menopausal woman by then, suckled the child from her empty breast although warned specifically by Durent not to do it.

[54]   Bernard, *A Guide to Grand-Iury Men*, pp. 204–5.

since their conflict,[55] and Thomas Adam's sheep died about a month after he scolded Jane Wenham.[56] Durent needed crutches about a year after Denny stated she would. One sceptical author suggested that in cases of strange and unaccountable death, the blame could be laid at the door of the usual suspects even if the falling-out had occurred more than 20 years earlier.[57]

The language of the suspects was frequently interpreted as threatening, even if other meanings were equally plausible. After Samuel Pacy caused Amy Denny to be put in stocks, she told two women in the crowd: 'Mr Pacy keeps a great stir about his Child, but let him stay until he hath done as much by his Children, as I have done by mine.' And being further examined about what she had done to her children, she answered 'that she had been pain to open her Child's Mouth with a Tap to give it Victuals'. Two days later, it was deposed, Pacy's eldest daughter fell into a fit 'that they could not open her Mouth to give her breath, to preserve her Live without the help of a Tap which they were enforced to use and the younger Child was in the like manner Afflicted, so that they used the same also for her Relief'.[58] For Hutchinson, writing half a century after the events occurred, this was no logical inference, but a fabrication. He rhetorically asked: 'But who put those Taps into their Mouths? Did any invisible Agents, in a supernatural Way? ... Why did they do it by Taps, rather then by any thing else? Why not by a Quill, a pipe, or any thing else that would have given Breath enough in a Fit? ... What made them voluntarily chuse to lay the Children in such a ridiculous Posture with Taps sticking out of their Mouths?'[59] Hutchinson was suspicious of coincidence that could be manipulated and fabricated by the accusers.

Making a circumstantial inference is an intellectual process dependent on experience and knowledge about the world. It is not too surprising that in a world where devils and witches were perceived as real, unaccountable misfortunes were attributed to the devil and his agents. Yet, in many cases the accuser's behaviour was morally flawed (by refusal to give charity or to sell goods, rudeness or other offensive acts toward the suspect). Nevertheless, the presumption that misfortune following a conflict was due to witchcraft was nevertheless made.[60] Thomas remarked:

---

[55] *Tryal of Ann Foster*, p. 4.

[56] Bragge, *Full and Impartial Account*, p. 14.

[57] *The Case of the Hertfordshire Witchcraft Consider'd*, pp. 19–20.

[58] *A Tryal of Witches*, pp. 18–19.

[59] Francis Hutchinson, *An Historical Essay Concerning Witchcraft* (London: R. Knaplock and D. Midwinter, 1718), pp. 116–17.

[60] Even among the Azande, where witchcraft was ubiquitous, alternative explanations to misfortune were given when the sufferer failed to observe a moral rule, breached a taboo or

It is ironic that such a presumption should have been so readily made. If the curser was provoked by a genuine injury, it is hard to understand why contemporaries should have been so reluctant to see the outcome as a divine judgment. ... The notion that God might avenge the poor by responding to their supplications was one which the church, like society as a whole, seems to have been unwilling to face directly.[61]

And indeed very few early modern writers considered the possibility that the injury was a God-sent punishment for the offensive behaviour of the accuser. Even writers who suggested that the victims should search their own consciences to learn whether they brought the misfortune upon themselves still presumed that witchcraft occurred. Gifford, for example, considered the misfortune to be a punishment that the 'wicked' brought on themselves:

> Where God will strike and plague the wicked by him, he giueth him leaue, it is not the anger of the witch that bringeth it, but their owne wickednes, whereby they haue prouoked God to displeasure, and so giue this enemy power ouer them.[62]

Although Gifford pointed to the accuser's behaviour as the reason for the misfortune, he still believed that the witch was the instrument by which it was brought about (the instruments of darkness, notwithstanding their alliance with the devil, were acting under a providential plan). Only in the eighteenth century did Hutchinson suggest an explanation free of the suspect's involvement. He remarked that the refusal to sell herring to Cullender and Denny was unjustifiable: 'For if others should be so distrustful of God, and unjust, and superstitious, they must of Necessity have perished for want of Food.' He wondered why witchcraft was suspected, when such coincidence had 'a great Appearance of a Divine Providence and Permission, justly punishing ill usage of the Poor, and Superstition'.[63]

The frequently applied witchcraft presumption in cases of injury following an unpleasant encounter enjoyed the theologians' support. Clerical authors, although not considering it a perfect proof, regarded this presumption as a

---

was incompetent. Edward Evans-Pritchard, *Witchcraft, Oracles and Magic among the Azande* (Oxford: Clarendon Press, 1937), ch. iv, esp. p. 64.

[61]   Keith Thomas, *Religion and the Decline of Magic* (New York: Charles Scribner's Sons, 1971), p. 512.

[62]   George Gifford, *A Dialogue Concerning Witches and Witchcraftes* (London: Tobie Cooke and Mihil, 1593), H3v.

[63]   Hutchinson, *An Historical Essay*, p 113.

suspicious circumstance warranting further examination. Perkins considered cursing, quarreling or threatening followed by death or some other mischief to be sufficient grounds to warrant examination but not conviction. He considered it 'a great presumption'.[64] Cooper agreed that an examination could be launched but 'not vpon euery corrupt passion, or sleight ocasion, but vpon *weightie Presumption*'.[65] Among the witchcraft-specific presumptions that Cooper listed were also 'Enmity, *quarreling*, or *threatning*' followed by some mischief or '*the effect of cursing*' on death, which was 'a shrewd token that shee is a Witch'.[66] Bernard agreed and listed it as one of the great presumptions.

> To be much giuen to *cursing* and imprecations, vpon light occasion, and withall to vse threatnings to be reuenged. And presently thereupon euill to happen, and this not once, or twice, to one or two, but often, and to diuers persons.

> This is a great presumption (all these circumstances withall considered) because Satan offers himselfe (as before is shewed) vnto such, and such meanes, wee finde that Witches vse to bewitch men and beasts; yet is this but a presumption, for that many are so bitter spirited, that they will curse & ban, & threaten reuenge, and yet be no Witches.[67]

Bernard, the divine who wrote a guide to grand jurors, set relatively higher standards concerning this presumption. The cursing needed to be habitual, the injury needed to be immediate and there needed to be more than one victim (that is, more than one complainant). Only in the presence of all these conditions might it be found that this was a great presumption. And yet, Bernard reminded, it was 'but a presumption', and the cursing might simply be a symptom of an embittered personality. This reasoning was offered by a defendant who was eventually acquitted, Joan Buts, who defended herself as follows:

> She pleaded, she was innocent, and that those things that were sworn against her, were not true. My Lord asked her, if she did not speak those words: she acknowledged she did: but my Lord, said she, I am a passionate woman, and they having urged me, I spake those words in passion, my Lord, but I intended no such thing.[68]

---

64 Perkins, *Damned Art*, p. 202.
65 Thomas Cooper, *The Mystery of Witch-Craft* (London: Nicholas Okes, 1617), p. 274.
66 Ibid.
67 Bernard, *A Guide to Grand-Iury Men*, pp. 204–5.
68 *An Account of the Tryal and Examination of Joan Buts ...* (London: S. Gardener, 1682), p. 2.

Bernard's analysis was referred to in subsequent legal and clerical writing.[69] Gaule agreed that the 'witches usual cursing & banning' was a probable sign but insufficient for conviction.[70] Gaule repeated that accidents happened and that misfortune did not have to be the result of witchcraft:

> What Conscience then can here bee in common people that are carryed away not onely with suspition but superstition? Every poore and peevish olde Creature (such is their Ignorance and Uncharitablenesse) cannot but fall under their suspition, nay their infamous exprobation, every Accident, (more then ordinary) every disease whereof they neither understand the Cause, not are acquainted with the Symptomes) [sic] must bee suspected for witch-craft. His Cow or his Hog, cannot be strangely taken, but straight it must bee reckoned and rumored for bewitch. And not their ill will to the next neighbouring silly Creature, must peremptorily taxe her ill will (in the worst sense) for the only cause of all.[71]

Whereas, on the Continent, half proofs and presumptions led to torture, which was likely to result in a confession and neatly solve the dilemma of proof, the English remained ambivalent. Cursing was some indication but insufficient for conviction. The suspect might not be a witch, but merely an unpleasant person, and the misfortune could be no more than an accident or a simple coincidence. This ambivalence was highlighted by Filmer, who aimed to contradict Perkins' list of evidentiary means. Filmer, who was trained in law and had experience as a justice, maintained that Perkins himself ruled out the presumption of misfortune following cursing or falling-out as a basis for conviction and that Perkins himself warned that 'ignorant' people might regard these presumptions as strong proofs and convict the innocent.[72]

The fear of use of circumstantial inference by ignorant people was stressed by the sceptic Ady in a comment resonating with Scot's mockery.

> People are now so infected with this damnable Heresie, of ascribing to the power of VVitches, that seldom hath a man the hand of God against him in his estate, or health of body, or any way, but presently he cryeth out of some poor innocent Neighbour, that he, or she hath bewitched him; for saith he, such an old man or woman came lately to my door, and desired some relief,

---

69   *The Lawes against Vvitches, and Conivration* (London: R.W., 1645), p. 4.

70   Gaule, *Select Cases of Conscience*, p. 80.

71   Ibid., pp. 85–6.

72   Sir Robert Filmer, *An Advertisement to the Jury-Men of England, Touching Witches* (London: Richard Royston, 1653), pp. 10, 12.

and I denied it, and God forgive me, my heart did rise against her at that time, my mind gave me she looked like a VVitch, and presently my Child, my VVife, my Self, my Horse, my Cow, my Sheep, my Sow, my Hogge, my Dogge, my Cat, or somewhat was thus and thus handled, in such a strange manner, as I dare swear she is a VVitch, or else how should those things be, or come to pass?[73]

Ady lamented how witchcraft accusations were rashly made, often without any heed to a physician's advice. Furthermore, Ady, possibly a physician himself, criticized the ignorance of some physicians who attributed a disease to witchcraft when consulted.[74] Ady refused to see the denial of charity as convincing grounds for circumstantial inference. If refusal to give charity was to be punished by witchcraft, Ady reasoned, all men of ability in England should have suspected themselves of being bewitched.[75]

Wagstaffe, a sceptical intellectual, also preferred a natural explanation for the sequence of cursing or threatening followed by injury. He explained that in a world full of people and events, such coincidence was likely:

'Tis certain, that poor old people when they are abused by the insulting petulancy of others, being unable to right themselves, either at Law or at Combate, for want of money and strength of body, do often times vent the passion of their discontented souls in threats and curses. 'Tis also certain, that many men troubled with Diseases of the head, or Diseases of the heart, do seem to be in perfect health, and yet fall down dead on a sudden. Now if these two accidents should meet together, I should see nothing but what is natural, nor should I cry out upon the Devil and Witchcraft.[76]

Despite sceptics such as Wagstaffe and Ady, the presumption of injury following cursing or threatening was far from being abolished. Around 1670 it was still fiercely defended. R.T. answered Wagstaffe in a book in 1670 that it was much more conceivable that injuries following cursing were not merely coincidental. Indeed, he admitted: 'Once in a hundred years such a thing may come to pass, as that upon an Old VVomans cursing a man may immediately fall sick, or dye.' However, since this sequence was typical to some more than to others, it was

---

[73] Ady, *A Candle in the Dark*, pp. 114–15.
[74] Ibid., p. 115.
[75] Ibid., p. 129.
[76] John Wagstaffe, *The Question of Witchcraft Debated* ... (London: Edward Millington, 1669), pp. 64–5.

more likely to have been the result of witchcraft.[77] Casaubon, a clergyman who advocated the prosecution of witches, claimed that as long as the testimony about injury following a conflict was credible, it should be accepted:

> What if others, men and women, be convicted by the deposition of sundry creditable witnesses, upon some sudden quarrel, or old grudge; To have cursed, and threatned, thus and thus; men or cattle; and that it hath happened accordingly: Strange deaths, strange diseases, strange unnatural, unusual accidents, have ensued: can all this be, the effects of a depraved fancy?[78]

Casaubon confused two evidentiary concepts, credibility and circumstantial inference. He concluded that if the circumstance in question was credibly proved, the inference should be considered as equally proved. He discussed evidence by 'sundry creditable witnesses', who were not necessarily eyewitnesses, and thus compromised the Continental full proof that required two eyewitnesses. According to Casaubon, if the sequence of conflict followed by an injury was credibly proved, so was witchcraft. The distinction between an eyewitness testifying from direct experience and circumstantial evidence was no longer sharp. As to his rhetorical question whether proximity between a quarrel and an injury might be merely coincidental, a sceptical author writing about 40 years later answered affirmatively, explaining that if 'Two Accidents should meet together, I should see nothing but what is Natural, nor should I cry out upon the *Devil* and *Witchcraft*'.[79]

Participants on both sides of the argument used the language of probability. The essence of the argument of sceptical writers such as Wagstaffe and Ady was that other explanations were *probable*; therefore, circumstantial evidence should be rejected. Those who supported the presumption as a means of proof claimed it was *probable* that the injury appeared in sequence to the unpleasant interaction.[80] During the late seventeenth century the concepts of probability and certainty were explored by English intellectuals in diverse contexts.[81] In the context of law,

---

[77]   R.T., *The Opinion of Witchcraft Vindicated* (London: Francis Haley, 1670), p. 60.

[78]   Meric Casaubon, *Of Credulity and Incredulity in Things Natural, Civil, and Divine* (London: T. Garthwait, 1668), p. 39.

[79]   *The Impossibility of Witchcraft* ... (London: J. Baker, 1712), pp. 25–6.

[80]   In early modern England the term 'probable' had two different, yet related, meanings. It meant 'provable' and also 'likely'. Both meanings related to truthfulness. The usage of probable by the sceptics seems to combine both meanings – they considered alternative explanations that could be supported by proof to be more likely than circumstantial-logical inferences.

[81]   Shapiro, *'Beyond Reasonable Doubt'*, p. 54.

however, the discussion of degrees of probability relied on an ancient tradition.[82] Presumptions were indeed a matter of probability. To reach a verdict of guilty, the jurors needed to achieve moral certainty. The epistemological basis for the admissibility of probabilities was their ability to create moral certainty. What became the accepted standard of moral certainty, proof beyond reasonable doubt, had yet to emerge.[83] However, it seems that in the eighteenth century, coincidence that could be nothing but an 'odd Accident'[84] could no longer be a basis for conviction. In time, circumstantial evidence became a valid foundation for conviction beyond reasonable doubt,[85] and the law made no distinction between the weight given to either direct or circumstantial evidence. Shapiro claimed that once circumstantial evidence became capable of creating a sufficient basis for conviction, the distinction between secret and other crimes was no longer necessary. She referred to the Continental doctrine of *crimen exceptum*, which enabled suspending the normal evidentiary standards in witchcraft cases and convicting on circumstantial evidence.[86] However, because in England circumstantial evidence was always permitted, there was never a real legal need to apply the doctrine of *crimen exceptum*. Once juries ceased to be self-informed and personally acquainted with the defendant and the circumstances, the borrowing of Continental concepts of circumstantial evidence helped to establish a new epistemological basis for allowing the circumstances to serve as evidence.

To sum up, from the accounts contained in the pamphlet literature, it appears that, on a popular level, the presumption of the injury following a conflict enjoyed a high degree of certainty. Alleged victims related the misfortune they experienced to a previous conflict with a suspected witch. The events were interpreted in a way that pointed to the suspect's guilt, even if the conflict was not very recent or in cases where the accuser had initiated the conflict or behaved uncharitably.

The early modern English scholarly writing about circumstantial inferences in witchcraft cases paints a more complex picture and indicates ambivalence. On the one hand, circumstantial evidence was a legitimate manner of proof in witchcraft cases. On the other hand, such evidence was typically regarded as inferior, as it was insufficient for conviction and warranted only an examination by the JP. This ambivalence enhanced flexibility in the struggle to prove witchcraft. Maintaining ambivalence was a strategy that permitted pointing a

---

[82]   Ibid., pp. 114, 116.
[83]   Ibid., pp. 223, 228.
[84]   Hutchinson, *An Historical Essay*, p viii.
[85]   Shapiro, *'Beyond Reasonable Doubt'*, pp. 207, 223.
[86]   Ibid., p. 228.

finger at a suspect who might be guilty, but it did not shed innocent blood by an unjust conviction. Such a strategy enabled keeping witchcraft alive as a serious crime while at the same time demanding higher standards for conviction and actually rendering conviction less likely. Although English law never barred the use of circumstantial evidence, the invocation of the Continental concept of circumstantial evidence as a lesser species of proof was helpful in maintaining this strategy.

Most scholarly writers who advocated the use of circumstantial evidence in witchcraft cases were clerics (with the exception of Cotta, who regarded presumption to be a rational and legitimate way of establishing facts). By clearly defining many conventional accusations as presumptions, these writers emphasized their nature as logical inferences and consequently called for caution. The three-category ranking of circumstantial evidence, and especially the category of evidence sufficient for examination but not for conviction, demanded a higher standard of proof for conviction and buttressed a right not to be examined on mere accusation, but on a minimal and sufficient evidentiary basis.

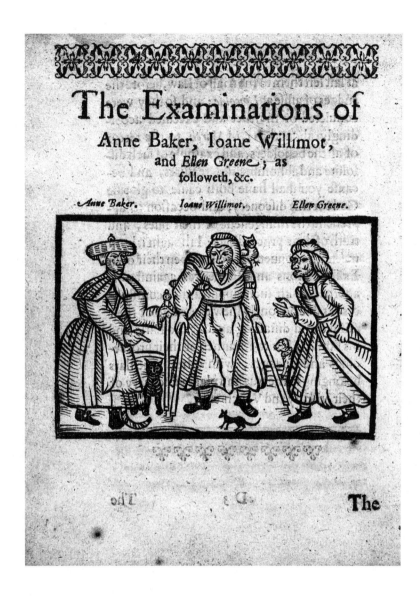

Figure 4.1 Three witches – Anne Baker, Ioane Willimot and Ellen Greene – and their imps. From *The Wonderful Discouerie of the Vvitchcrafts of Margaret and Phillip Flower, Daughters of Ioan Flower* ... (London: Barnes, 1619). Reproduced by permission of the Huntington Library, San Marino, California. [Call # RB 59371]

Chapter 4
Ritual Acts and Artefacts of Witchcraft

Analytically, physical evidence is a sub-category of circumstantial evidence – guilt is logically inferred from the physical traces. Yet, in practice, physical evidence enjoys a preferable status, perhaps because presumably it cannot lie. Proving a crime by direct evidence is seemingly a straightforward, non-problematic issue. This concept is misleading, however, as is demonstrated by the diversity of attitudes toward direct evidence in witchcraft cases. Direct evidence can be either physical evidence or testimony about overt acts that were perceived by the witnesses. A demon captured at the suspect's house and brought to court could have been most significant direct evidence. A reliable witness who had actually seen the suspect flying through the air or transforming her shape into that of a toad would have been valuable. Such evidence, however, was not forthcoming. The vacuum left in the absence of direct evidence was creatively filled by evidentiary techniques that had the facade of physical or direct evidence. A closer look reveals, however, that what was considered physical evidence was hardly as direct as one would expect.

The anti-witchcraft laws of 1542 and 1563 prohibited the invocation and conjuring of spirits but concentrated on *maleficia*. The act of 1604 extended the prohibition to any sort of communication with 'wicked spirits'. Bewitchment could occur without any external means by the power of the mind alone. However, in some cases, malefic rituals were the instruments of bewitchment. The recital of charms, drawing of a circle[1] or use of wax figures were behaviours that could be seen, heard or even smelled.[2] These overt acts, 'witches' deeds', as Bernard named them, constituted the crime, and no further proof was necessary.[3] Artefacts such as 'Figures, Characters, Spells, Ligatures, Circles, Numbers, Barberismes, Images of wax or clay, Crystalls, looking-glasses, Basons of waters,

---

[1] *The Apprehension and Confession of Three Notorious Witches* (London: E. Allde, 1589), A3; Edmund Bower, *Doctor Lamb Revived* ... (London: Richard Best and John Place, 1653), p. 6.

[2] Bernard believed that the feeding place of the imps could be identified by their detestable stench. Richard Bernard, *A Guide to Grand-Iury Men* (London: Ed. Blackmore, 1627), p. 221.

[3] Ibid., pp. 220–21.

herbs, powders, unguents, sawes, knives, pins, needles, Candles, rings, garters, gloves, &C ...'⁴ could be submitted as evidence.

Among those witches' deeds, the most common practice was the destruction, cutting or piercing of images or belongings representing the victim to inflict pain or even kill. Bernard called these images 'pictures' and 'hellish compositions', and considered them proof of the crime.⁵ The first anti-witchcraft law specifically designated as forbidden overt acts of sorcery such as 'dyvers Images and pictures of men women childrene Angelles or develles beastes or fowles'.⁶ However, the Elizabethan and Jacobean laws used more general terms.

Although the use of ritual artefacts was prominent in popular witchcraft belief, it was barely considered by the learned writers of the major legal and theological tracts on the subject of the discovery of witchcraft, Bernard excepted. Medical and theological writers such as Perkins, Gaule, Cotta and Cooper did not elaborate much on ritual artefacts when discussing and evaluating evidentiary techniques. They were evidently aware of the malefic use of figures.⁷ Scot, with whose writing they were all familiar, mentioned the practice as early as 1584.⁸ It is also unlikely that they failed to discuss the evidentiary potential of the images because of their rarity.⁹ They discussed far less known methods of proof such as 'long eyes'¹⁰ or 'sieve and shears'.¹¹ Perhaps the reason for not including sorcery

---

⁴   John Gaule, *Select Cases of Conscience Touching Vvitches and Vvitchcrafts* (London: Richard Clutterbuck, 1646), pp. 113–14.

⁵   Bernard, *A Guide to Grand-Iury Men*, pp. 220–21.

⁶   33 Hen VIII. ch. 8, 1541–2.

⁷   Perkins, when explaining the practice of 'Inchantment' (recital of charms), described the use of figures and categorized it as a non-verbal charm. Gaule specifically listed images of wax and clay among the witchcraft paraphernalia. Cotta referred to Thomas Aquinas on this matter and to an incident of such practice against Elizabeth I. William Perkins, *A Discourse of the Damned Art of Witchcraft* (Cambridge, UK: Vniuersitie of Cambridge, 1608), p. 149; John Cotta, *The Triall of Vvitch-Craft* (London: Samuel Rand, 1616), p. 90; Gaule, *Select Cases of Conscience*, pp. 113–14.

⁸   Reginald Scot, *The Discouerie of Witchcraft* (London: William Brome, 1584), p. 257.

⁹   Thomas believed that the use of image magic was the most common maleficent technique. Keith Thomas, *Religion and the Decline of Magic* (New York: Charles Scribner's Sons, 1971), p. 513. However, no technique was essential for committing the crime of witchcraft.

¹⁰   Gaule remarked that it was a pagan method but did not explain how it was used. Gaule, *Select Cases of Conscience*, p. 76.

¹¹   The sieve was balanced on open shears, and after a meaningless charm was recited (dies, nues, ieschet, benedoefet, donuina, enitemaus), the names of the suspect were called. If the sieve moved, the suspect was guilty. Ibid.; George Lyman Kittredge, *Witchcraft in Old and New England* (Cambridge, MA: Harvard University Press, 1929), pp. 198–200; Bernard, *A Guide to Grand-Iury Men*, p. 213.

artefacts in their lists of evidential techniques was that it was obvious to them that these objects provided direct evidence.[12]

Yet, the notion that possession of ritual artefacts per se constituted witchcraft was not obvious at all. Filmer distinguished between malefic means that caused harm by nature (such as poison) and means that were not inherently injurious but necessitated the devil's assistance (such as wax figures).[13] Filmer further noted that 'the Picture of Wax roasted by the Witch, hath no vertue in the Murdering, but the Devill only. It is necessary in the first place that it be duely proved that the party Murther'd be Murthered by the Devill, for it is a shame to bely the Devill, and it is not possible to be proved if it be *Subtilely done as a spirit*.'[14] A similar insight that such objects carried no inherent harmful power led Perkins, at the beginning of the seventeenth century, to classify the use of figures as a charm.[15] Thus, evidence of wax figures was not in itself sufficient, but required proof of diabolical involvement or of the causal connection between the molestation of the figure and the victim's ensuing death or illness.

Although the writers of learned tracts mostly disregarded the evidential potential of the clay or wax figure practice, voices coming from the lower echelons of society elaborated on it in a series of cases stretching from the sixteenth to the eighteenth centuries.[16] The artefacts in question were burned, boiled, crumbled, torn apart or pricked to achieve the desired effect. In some cases the victim was not represented by an image, but by an item that belonged to him or her,

---

[12] The distinction made by Edward Evans-Prichard in his work about the Azande may be useful in this context. He distinguished between sorcery – learned techniques of magic – and witchcraft – inborn supernatural abilities. Geoffrey Scarre, *Witchcraft and Magic in Sixteenth- and Seventeenth-Century Europe* (Atlantic Highlands, NJ: Humanities Press International, 1987), pp. 3–4.

[13] Sir Robert Filmer, *An Advertisement to the Jury-Men of England, Touching Witches* (London: Richard Royston, 1653), pp. 7–8.

[14] Ibid.

[15] 'For bare picture hath no more power of it selfe to hurt the body represented, then bare words. All that is done commeth by the worke of the devill, who alone by vsing of the picture in that sort, is occasioned so or so, to worke the parties destruction.' Perkins, *Damned Art*, p. 149.

[16] *The Examination of John Walsh* (London: Iohn Awdely, 1566), Avii–Avii; *The Full Tryals, Examination, and Condemnation ...* (London: J.W., 1690), p. 5; Kittredge, *Witchcraft in Old and New England*, pp. 73–86, 139; *The Whole Trial and Examination of Mrs Mary Hicks and her Daughter Elizabeth* (London: W. Matthews, 1716), p. 3; E.G., *A Prodigious & Tragicall History ...* (London: Richard Harper, 1652), p. 6; B. Misodaimon, *The Divels Delvsions ...* (London: Richard Williams Stationer, 1649), p. 4. The list of instances given by Kittredge could easily be extended.

like wool from a mattress, a piece of handkerchief or a pair of gloves.[17] In one instance, pain was allegedly inflicted by pricking a piece of leather.[18]

A case in 1606 exemplifies how villagers of Royston, in the county of Hartford, considered such evidence to be conclusive. Iohane Harrison had been suspected by her fellow villagers for a long time, but other than her ill reputation, no evidence was found against her. Eventually she was apprehended and her house searched under a search warrant. In that search a chest was opened and incriminating objects found, including bones, hair and a parchment with an anatomical sketch.[19] When she was confronted with this evidence, she had no choice but to confess 'her vtmost secret', malevolent use of figures.[20] Both the accusers and the suspect perceived the objects as ultimate proof, which made denial useless.

A very detailed description of the malefic use of figures occurs in the influential pamphlet written by Thomas Potts. Potts, a court clerk, was commissioned by the trial judges to compose the account of a case in 1612 in the Lancaster assizes, in which 19 witches were arraigned.[21] The tone of the pamphlet was legal and factual; however, the rich and detailed description of the use of the figures implied the authenticity of the practice.[22] It is not clear whether it was legally possible to convict solely on evidence of figure witchcraft. Two of the defendants, Anne Whittle, alias Chattox, and her daughter, Anne Redferne, were charged with killing Robert Nutter. One of the other defendants in the case, Old Demdike, implicated both of them – she testified that she had seen Chattox making the clay figures and her daughter kneading the clay beside her.[23] Chattox was found

---

[17]   *The Wonderful Discouerie of the Vvitchcrafts of Margaret and Phillip Flower ...* (London: Barnes, 1619), F3–F4, Gv.

[18]   *A True and Impartial Relation ...* (London: Freeman Collins, 1682), p. 10.

[19]   *Most Damnable Practises of One Iohane Harrison ...* (London: William Firebrand and Iohn Wright, 1606), C2v–C3.

[20]   Ibid., C3.

[21]   Marion Gibson, *Reading Witchcraft: Stories of Early English Witches* (London: Routledge, 1999), p. 1; Marion Gibson (ed.), *Early Modern Witches: Witchcraft Cases in Contemporary Writing* (London: Routledge, 2000), p. 173.

[22]   For example, the suspected witch Elizabeth Demdike confessed that 'the speediest way to take a mans life away by Witchcraft, is to make a Picture of Clay ...' This statement contains idiosyncratic 'expert' knowledge, likely to be possessed by the suspect rather than the investigator. The rich details of the description support that impression. Thomas Potts, *The Vvonderfull Discouerie of Witches in the Countie of Lancaster* (London: Iohn Barnes, 1613), B3v, E–Ev, N4v–O, E4v–F, H3v.

[23]   Ibid., E. Old Demdike also testified that a spirit in the shape of a black cat called Tibb told her they were making the pictures of Christopher Nutter, Robert Nutter and Marie Nutter.

guilty[24] and her daughter acquitted. The author attributed the acquittal of the daughter to the jury's leniency and the weakness of evidence, which was 'not very pregnant' to prove the killing of Robert.[25] This assertion, made by an author who belonged to the legal profession, suggests that figure evidence alone was insufficient to prove the crime. And, indeed, an examination of the depositions shows the existence of additional evidence against the mother.[26] A day after she was acquitted, Anne Redferne was arraigned again, this time for the killing of Christopher Nutter, Robert's father. The evidence was basically the same – Old Demdike's deposition of seeing her and her mother making figures in the image of Christopher and Robert Nutter. This time, however, Anne Redferne was convicted. The additional evidence in her case did not seem to offer much more proof than was presented the day before.[27] It is possible to conclude that there was no rigid rule about the evidentiary power of figure evidence and that it was just a matter of luck, depending on the jurors' leniency. The pamphlet was an edited narrative, and it is quite possible that Potts did not include all the evidence against the defendants.[28] However, while it is doubtful that figure practice alone could have served as the sole legal basis for conviction in court, it is clear that the villagers certainly believed it to be an ultimate proof. Potts added that, in this case, 'all men that know her affirmed, shee was more dangerous then her Mother for shee made all or most of the Pictures of Clay, that were made or found at any time'.[29]

The popular concept of wax and clay figures as significant evidence invaded the writings of scholars once Potts' account was taken as a precedent. Dalton, the author of the popular manual for JPs, stated the legal situation based on

---

[24]   Ibid., K2v.

[25]   Ibid., N3v.

[26]   Chattox confessed to giving her soul to the devil and sending an imp to revenge Robert; James Robinson blamed Chattox for spoiling drinks and testified that he heard Robert Nutter complaining about both her and her daughter; James Device attributed to Chattox use of corpses' parts; Alizon Device reported that her father blamed Chattox for bewitching him, that Chattox threatened Anne Nutter, who later died, and that Chattox had a clay picture, supposedly of one John Moore's child. Ibid., E–F.

[27]   Margaret Crooke, Robert's sister and Christopher's daughter, deposed that Robert died after 'falling-out' with the suspect and that later the father, Christopher, became ill and stated before he died that he was bewitched, though he did not name any suspect. John Nutter deposed that his brother, Robert, blamed Chattox and Anne Redferne for bewitching him but that his father answered: 'Thou art a foolish Ladde, it is not so, it is thy miscarriage.' James Device stated that he had seen Anne Redferne crumbling clay pictures. Ibid., O–O2v.

[28]   Potts stated specifically that there were 'likewise many witnesses examined opon oth *Viva voce*, who charged her with *many strange practices* ...' Ibid., O2. Emphasis added.

[29]   Ibid.

evidence submitted in the Lancaster case, including 'they haue often pictures of clay, or waxe (like a man, &c.) found in their house'.[30] Cotta observed that '[s]ome late Writers haue obserued, that diuers Witches by such pictures, haue caused the persons thereby represented secretly to languish and consume, as was lately proued against some late famous Witches of *Yorke-shire* and *Lancaster*, by the testimonies beyond exception of witnesses, not only present, but Presidents in their tryall and arraignment'.[31] In 1643 an anonymous writer of a treatise about the anti-witchcraft laws relied on Potts when listing the pictures of clay or wax as one of the signs for the discovery of witchcraft.[32]

However, the evidence of figures, which may seem to be excellent proof because the practice of using them in itself constituted witchcraft, did not necessarily prove supernatural powers, and it is doubtful whether such practices could have served as the sole basis for conviction.

Physical objects could have been submitted as subsidiary rather than pivotal evidence, tending to support a wider body of proofs. The objects did not have to be typical to magic (like wax figures or crystal balls), but could be mundane objects such as a dish, a pitcher or a scar. The case against Ales Hunt in 1582 demonstrated this method. *A True and Just Recorde* (1582) was written by 'W.W.', possibly William Lowth, a friend of Bryan Darcy, a JP with an anti-witches inclination, who inspired the account.[33] The eight-year-old Febey Hunt deposed against the defendant, her stepmother, that she had 'seen her mother to have two litle things like horses', which her mother fed with milk 'out of a *blacke trening dishe*'.[34] Thereupon the little girl was carried by the constables to her father's house, where she showed them the feeding corner and the board that covered the creatures. Finally, from all the many dishes in the house, the girl picked out the specific feeding dish.[35]

In her examination, Ales Hunt denied the charges of having imps and plaguing cattle by spirits. Bryan Darcy, the examining JP, ordered that the black dish, which had already been brought by the constable, be presented to

---

[30] Michael Dalton, *The Countrey Iustice* (London: Societie of Stationers, 1618), p. 243.

[31] Cotta, *The Triall of Vvitch-Craft*, p. 90.

[32] *The Lawes against Vvitches, and Coniuration* (London: R.W., 1645), p. 4. The author relied on Bernard as well. He also recommended conducting a search in witchcraft cases for this type of evidence: 'to search also their houses diligently for pictures of clay or wax, &c. haire cut, bones, powders, books of witchcrafts, charms; and for pots or places where their spirits may be kept, the smell of which place will stink detestably.' Ibid., p. 5.

[33] Gibson (ed.), *Early Modern Witches*, p. 72.

[34] W.W., *A True and Iust Recorde* ... (London: Thomas Dawson, 1582), 2A5v–2A6. Emphasis added.

[35] Ibid., 2A6.

her. Ales maintained that she never fed spirits from a dish, that the dish shown was not hers nor had she ever had such a dish in her house.[36] We cannot tell whether Ales' denial was genuine and the black dish was evidence planted by the stepdaughter, the constables or someone else. There were traces of manipulation in the investigation of the case. The young boys of Cysley and Henry Selles also deposed that their parents fed spirits with milk served from a 'black dish'.[37] The repetitive description out of the mouths of very young children raises serious doubts. Ales' eventual confession, as the pamphleteer described, was of having two spirits, and the details of feeding them milk from a black dish were missing. It seems unlikely that Bryan Darcy, considering the details he extracted from other examinees, failed to examine her about details that could have granted reliability to the information against her. It is possible that she was examined about the black dish and her answer was edited. This silence calls for an explanation. The dating of the examinations also seems to have been meddled with. According to the pamphlet, Ales was examined and confessed on 24 February, and her stepdaughter on 25 February. If the child was investigated after the mother had already confessed, the accusers and examiners could not be blamed for the unjustified use of a little girl against her mother, nor could they be accused of influencing her statements, as they only corroborated matters already confessed to by the mother. However, the alleged dating is impossible, because according to the account, the girl first identified the dish and the mother confessed only after that dish was shown to her.[38]

However, Ales' claim that the dish was not hers could have been the result of a total-denial line of defence. In such cases, the corroboration of witchcraft by physical evidence was extremely potent. An object like a black dish had nothing to do with witchcraft and had no probative power in itself. However, if the object was part of a larger witchcraft narrative, proving its existence corroborated the whole story. By producing the trivial and non-essential object that the defendant had denied having in her possession, the whole defence collapsed, and the story of the prosecution witness, including its impossible elements, gained credibility. Using this technique to impeach defendants created an impression that the guilt of the suspect was proved by direct physical evidence.

Similar use of physical evidence in the same case was made against Elizabeth Bennet, who had denied the accusation of keeping spirits in a wool-filled pitcher under the stairs in her house. Nevertheless, when the pot was brought before her,

---

[36]   Ibid., C3v.

[37]   Nine-year-old Henry and John, who was young enough to be described as 'vi years and iii quarters' old. Ibid., Dv, D2v.

[38]   See also Gibson (ed.), *Early Modern Witches*, p. 95, fn. 70.

she admitted that it was hers but denied that the wool therein belonged to her.[39] After further pressure from Bryan Darcy, Bennet made a confession.

The pamphleteer was also careful to note a scar on the leg and the imperfect little toenail of six-and-three-quarter-year-old John Selles, who deposed that a 'black thing' caught his leg at night.[40] The scar did not prove the diabolical elements of his version – that it was made by an imp belonging to his mother – yet, it created an air of credibility. It would therefore be inaccurate to declare that a scar is a scar is a scar.

Glanvill described a case in 1657 of a boy who had a vision of a woman who put two-pence into his pocket, for which the coin was produced as evidence.[41] Nathaniel Crouch, who wrote under the pseudonym of R.B. (Richard Burton), held that the devil:

> Can put Silver and Gold into their hands which afterwards proves but either Counters, Leaves, Shells, or some such like useless matter; These real effects cannot be meer melancholly, for if a man receive any thing into his hand be it what it will there was some body that gave it him, and therefore the Witch receiving some real thing from this or that other shape which appeared unto her, it is an evident sign it was an external thing that she saw, and not a figure only of her melancholly imagination.[42]

According to R.B., not only could a tangible object prove the connection between the devil and the witch, but it also ruled out a common objection to the belief in witchcraft that those who confessed to the crime were 'melancholic', that is, mentally ill. R.B.'s writing was uncritical. He avoided a discussion of theoretical difficulties and merely compiled accounts of witchcraft as a proof of its existence. He did not contemplate whether it would be possible for the melancholic confessors to mistakenly believe that an object they held was given to them by the devil. Twenty-four years later, Francis Bragge, who wrote in defence of the proceedings against Jane Wenham, made a similar argument.[43]

---

[39]   W., *A True and Iust Recorde*, 2A6.

[40]   Ibid., D2v.

[41]   Joseph Glanvill, *A Blow at Modern Sadducism* ... (London: James Collins, 1668), pp. 131–2.

[42]   R.B., *The Kingdom of Darkness* (London: Nath. Crouch, 1688), p. 169.

[43]   'yet, I must needs say, it requires more Credulity to believe, that so many and so clear Circumstances of Fact, as, for Instance, the Conveyance of Pins through the Air into the Hands of a Person when they are ty'd down, or the finding of very curious and artificial Cakes of Feathers in a Pillow but a little before stuff'd with down, and other like strange Things,

Another type of evidence submitted to corroborate accounts of bewitchment was allegedly vomited objects, such as 'Pins, pieces of Walnut-shels, an Ear of Rye, with a Straw to it half a yard long and Rushes of the same Length; which are kept to be shown at the next Assizes for the said County'.[44] Despite quite a few exposures of false bewitchment, in 1712 Francis Bragge described how, during the fits of the alleged victim, Anne Thorn, 'Pins ... were brought to her Hands by Invisible Means ... Mr Chauncy took several from her ... and would have produced in Court, but the Judge did not think it necessary'.[45] This act of the judge, who reprieved Jane Wenham after she had been convicted, was not regarded favourably by Bragge, who tried fiercely to prove Wenham's guilt.

Bragge supported the use of different kinds of physical evidence. However, when his fellows found suspicious feathers, he failed to convince them to preserve them for court use. On searching the bewitched maid's pillow, Bragge and the maid's mistress, Mrs Gardiner, found 'many Cakes of small Feathers, so closely joined together, that an ordinary Force would not pull them asunder'.[46] Thereupon, 'Mr Bragge was very desirous to have some of these Cakes preserved, in order to be produced in Court, but was over-ruled by others, who not without Reason supposing this to be the Charm, would have it all burnt, in hopes the Effects of it might cease. And it is remarkable, that after the burning these Feathers the Maid was better, and had no more Fits till the Assizes.'[47]

One participant in the debate about Jane Wenham's case clearly mocked Bragge regarding this matter:

> I could heartily have wished that some of these Feathers had been preserved; it might have been perhaps more to Mr Bragge's Credit, and I am sure much more to the Satisfaction of others. The Judge wished he could have seen them; and I think his Desire was reasonable: For it was but just, to demand the Feathers to support the Evidence, or else to send the Evidence after the Feathers.[48]

---

to be all but the work of Fancy.' Francis Bragge, *Witchcraft Farther Display'd* ... (London: E. Curll, 1712), pp. 33–4.

[44]   *A True Account of a Strange and Wonderful Relation of John Tonken* ... (London: George Croom, 1686), title page.

[45]   Francis Bragge, *A Full and Impartial Account* ..., 2nd edn (London: E. Curll, 1712), pp. 19, 26.

[46]   Ibid., p. 22.

[47]   Ibid., p. 23.

[48]   *The Case of the Hertfordshire Witchcraft Consider'd* (London: John Pemberton, 1712), p. 40.

Although the anonymous sceptical writer and Bragge were on different sides of the argument about Wenham's case, both seemed to share the belief that the corroborating evidence of physical objects, even in bewitchment cases, could help to prove the charge. Objects such as pins, feathers or dishes were not diabolic per se and could be planted. The 'devil's mark' found on the body of the witch embodied much more effective evidential potential.

Chapter 5

The Devil's Mark

Figure 5.1 A witch feeding her imps. From *A Rehearsall Both Straung and True, of Hainous and Horrible Actes Committed by Elizabeth Stile* ... (London: J. Kingston, 1579). [Shelfmark: C.27.a.11] Courtesy of the British Library.

After Anne Bodenham became a witchcraft suspect in 1653, a panel of women was appointed to search her body.[1] At her trial, these women testified that the 80-year-old defendant 'had ... the marks of an absolute Witch, having a Teat about the length and bignesse of the Nipple of a womans breast, and hollow and soft as a Nipple, with a hole on the top of it, on her left shoulder, and another likewise was found in her secret places, like the former on her shoulder'. A pamphlet describing the case commented on this evidence: 'for which she was arraigned and condemned to be hang'd'.[2]

The search for such marks relied on a mixture of popular and learned theological ideas and was typical of English witchcraft cases. The women who

---

[1] Edmund Bower, *Doctor Lamb Revived* ... (London: Richard Best and John Place, 1653), pp. 27–9.

[2] *Doctor Lambs Darling* (London: G. Horton, 1653), pp. 7–8. This text, aimed at the cheap and popular market, contained plagiarism from the longer and more serious tract by Edmund Bower. Although it cannot be considered an independent historical source on the trial, it reflected the popular sentiment toward the importance of the devil's mark.

examined the body of Anne Bodenham were looking for the 'devil's marks', allegedly imprinted by the devil on the bodies of his human accomplices. The belief was that the devil branded the bodies of witches with symbolic yet concrete corporeal malformations such as marks and growths. The mark was *tangible, ostensible* and also, according to contemporary theory, *insensitive* to pain.[3] These traits made the mark subject to search and pricking, two techniques employed in the quest for physical evidence of witchcraft. The devil's marks were an example of physical evidence that could help 'discover witches', as the contemporary expression put it. Conceivably the early modern forensic equivalent of today's fingerprints, these marks were traces that directly proved the suspect's guilt without depending on possibly untruthful witnesses.

During her trial for witchcraft in 1566, Agnes Waterhouse denied having allowed her cat, Sathan, to suck her blood. Subsequently, her kerchief was removed, exposing visible spots on her face and nose to the judges. Unfavourable conclusions were drawn, and after the queen's attorney had asked Agnes when her blood was last sucked, she incriminated herself by saying 'not this fortnyght'.[4] This court demonstration is an early example of the evidential potential of suspicious 'spots'.

The comprehensive bodily search was a later development. The earliest documentation of such a search relates to a case in 1579, in which a Southampton leet jury demanded that the suspect be searched.[5] At that time the search was not yet used on a regular basis. Other cases from the same year also made use of evidence of suspicious marks. These, however, were not discovered through a search, but confessed to by the suspects.[6] Toward the 1630s the search became quite routine.[7] It was most extensively used during the East Anglia Hopkins trials of 1645–47 and continued to be used after this exceptional episode as well,

---

[3]   Julian Goodare, 'Women and the Witch-Hunt in Scotland', *Social History* 23, no. 3 (1998): p. 302; Thomas Cooper, *The Mystery of Witch-Craft* (London: Nicholas Okes, 1617), p. 88.

[4]   *The Examination and Confession of Certaine Wytches* … (London: Willyam Powell, 1566), Avii verso–Aviii.

[5]   Clive Holmes, 'Women: Witnesses and Witches', *Past and Present*, no. 140 (1993): p. 70; Cecil L'Estrange Ewen, *Witchcraft and Demonianism* (London: Heath, 1933), p. 75. The next documented instance of a search was described in a pamphlet of 1582, where the JP ordered that the two suspects would be searched for marks by a couple of women. W.W., *A True and Iust Recorde* … (London: Thomas Dawson, 1582), C2v–C3, D4.

[6]   *A Rehearsall Both Straung and True* … (London: J. Kingston, 1579), A6; *A Detection of Damnable Driftes* … (London: J. Kingston, 1579), A5.

[7]   See also Holmes, 'Women: Witnesses and Witches', p. 71; Gregory Durston, *Witchcraft and Witch Trials: A History of English Witchcraft and Its Legal Perspectives, 1542 to 1736* (Chichester: Barry Rose Law Publishers, 2000), pp. 317–18.

although the number of documented instances decreased correspondingly with the decline in witchcraft prosecution. The last known search occurred in Jane Wenham's case in 1712, which was also the last known case of conviction of witchcraft.[8]

Learned and Popular Concepts of the Devil's Mark

English writers of the time were familiar with the work of Continental theologians, who were the first to articulate the theory of the devil's mark and the practical guidelines for the search, including search under the eyelids, under the armpits, on the breasts, on the roof of the mouth, in the rectum and on the genitals.[9] And, indeed, primary sources attest that to find the devil's marks, English witchcraft suspects were subjected time and again to an obtrusive bodily search. They were stripped naked and sometimes completely shaved, and every part of their bodies was thoroughly examined. The search superseded the norms of modesty and decency. The suspected men and women, in the words of the sceptical physician, John Webster, 'were so unchristianly, unwomenly, and inhumanely handled, as to be stript stark naked, and to be laid upon Tables and Beds to be searched (nay even in their most privy parts) for these their supposed Witch-marks: so barbarous and cruel acts doth diabolical instigation, working upon ignorance and superstition, produce'.[10]

Although it was not part of official English criminal procedure, the technique became highly elaborated and institutionalized. Almost invariably the search was not an expression of a spontaneous attempt at lynching, but rather a standard element of the pre-trial investigation, ordered by men of authority (mostly JPs, but sometimes the mayor or other figures of authority) and conducted according to customary practice. Around 1645, at the peak of the Hopkins witch scare, East Anglian communities and urban corporations hired witch finders. The search was used extensively, and women searchers (not officially appointed)

---

[8]   Francis Bragge, *A Full and Impartial Account* ..., 2nd edn (London: E. Curll, 1712), p. 11.

[9]   The references to Continental authors such as Bodin, Rémy and Del Rio throughout the early modern treatises demonstrate familiarity despite the lack of translations. Already in 1584 Scot referred to 'Sprenger's fables and Bodin's bables' and criticized the ideas of the *Malleus Maleficarum* throughout his text. Reginald Scot, *The Discouerie of Witchcraft* (London: William Brome, 1584), B5, 9–10.

[10]   John Webster, *The Displaying of Supposed Witchcraft* (London: J.M., 1677), p. 82.

routinely accompanied Hopkins on his journey.[11] However, the practice of the search continued, even after the witch-scare episode of the 1640s, up to the early eighteenth century.

The evidential significance of the devil's mark in early modern England emerged out of two epistemologically inconsistent sources. In high, or learned, theory, which was influenced by Continental theology, the devil often sealed a covenant with the witch by branding her body. The pact with the devil was central to the definition of witchcraft in Continental theology.[12] According to this theory, the mark almost always implied a meeting with Satan himself (rather than his demons), very often involving sexual activity. The mark signified the contractual-like and consensual relationship between the witch and the devil.[13] Although in England the value of the devil's mark was mocked as early as 1584 in Reginald Scot's influential treatise,[14] and English culture emphasized the element of evil-doing (*maleficium*) rather than the pact as the constituent element of witchcraft, significant English writers adopted the Continental theory of the devil's mark.[15]

The other source for the meaning of suspicious bodily features was the popular belief in imps and familiars, which figured prominently in English witch trials up to the early eighteenth century. The English concept of the witch's familiar had no parallel in other European countries.[16] The familiars were devils transformed into animal form that aided the witches in their malevolent missions. It was widely held that witches suckled their imps with their own blood. The indicator of such demonic suckling was either the teat, a nipple-resembling growth, or the appearance of a freshly sucked spot. Marks in strange or animal shapes could also

---

[11]   Malcolm Gaskill, *Witchfinders: A Seventeenth-Century English Tragedy* (Cambridge, MA: Harvard University Press, 2005), pp. 64, 67, 81.

[12]   Although a pact with the devil was a cornerstone of all demonological treatises, some writers stressed the heretical nature of witchcraft, some emphasized the organization of the witches, some called attention to the sexual relationship with demons and still others viewed the sabbath as an essential element.

[13]   Clive Holmes, 'Popular Culture? Witches, Magistrates and Divines in Early Modern England', in S.L. Kaplan (ed.), *Understanding Popular Culture: Europe from the Middle Ages to the Nineteenth Century* (Berlin: Walter de Gruyter & Co., 1984), p. 99; Alexander Roberts, *A Treatise of Witchcraft*, 2nd edn (London: Samuel Man, 1616), pp. 14–15.

[14]   Scot, *The Discouerie of Witchcraft*.

[15]   William Perkins, *A Discourse of the Damned Art of Witchcraft* (Cambridge, UK: Vniuersitie of Cambridge, 1608), p. 203; James I, *Daemonologie* (Edinburgh: Robert Walde-graue, 1597), p. 80; Cooper, *Mystery of Witch-Craft*, p. 88.

[16]   See James Sharpe, 'The Witch's Familiar in Elizabethan England', in G.W. Bernard and S.J. Gunn (eds), *Authority and Consent in Tudor England* (Aldershot: Ashgate, 2002), p. 226.

have diabolical implications. The growths were sometimes squeezed to check whether blood or other fluids could be expressed.[17] Around the 1630s, teats or spots that were believed to be habitually sucked by imps were often searched for in 'shameful' or 'privy' parts and were associated with the suspect's sexuality and carnal relationship with the devil.[18]

Many elements of the English popular belief in familiars challenged Christian dogma. Can the devil, just like God, create life? If the imps were made of spirit (as the theologians, who denied that the devil had the ability to create real life, claimed), why did the witches feed them? Why did they nurse them with blood? If the imps were an embodiment of supernatural spirits, why were they at the command of poor, old and often demented women? The popular English stories about friends or relatives giving familiars to neophyte witches contradicted the Continental demonology that viewed the contract with the devil as an essential step in becoming a witch.[19] Another theologically unsettling element that persisted in the popular view was of enjoyable erotic or sexual contact with imps. Whereas the demonologists emphasized the icy feeling and pain caused by contact with the devil, some English texts embraced testimony of suspects who expressed sensations of pleasure at the devil's touch.[20] The dissonance between theological principles and popular beliefs left room for doubt and scepticism.[21]

---

[17]   John Stearne, *A Confirmation and Discovery of Witchcraft* (London: William Wilson, 1648), pp. 28–9, 43; *A True Relation of the Araignment of Eighteene Vvitches* (London: I.H., 1645), pp. 4–5; Gilbert Geis and Ivan Bunn, *A Trial of Witches: A Seventeenth-Century Witchcraft Prosecution* (London: Routledge, 1997), p. 75; *The Most Strange and Admirable Discouerie of the Three Witches of Warboys* (London: Thomas Man, and Iohn Winington, 1593), O3v–O4; *A Tryal of Witches…* (London: William Shrewsbery, 1682), pp. 35–7.

[18]   Goodare, 'Women and the Witch-Hunt in Scotland', p. 301; Durston, *Witchcraft and Witch Trials*, p. 318; *A True and Impartial Relation…* (London: Freeman Collins, 1682), p. 11; Bower, *Doctor Lamb Revived*, pp. 28–9.

[19]   W., *A True and Iust Recorde*, D5v; John Davenport, *The Witches of Huntingdon* (London: Richard Clutterbuck, 1646), p. 5; *The Apprehension and Confession of Three Notorious Witches* (London: E. Allde, 1589), A4v.

[20]   Jim Sharpe, 'The Devil in East Anglia', in Jonathan Barry, Marianne Hester and Gareth Roberts (eds), *Witchcraft in Early Modern Europe* (Cambridge, UK: Cambridge University Press, 1996), p. 248. Ann Usher felt '2 things like butterflies in her secret p[ar]tes'; *The Examination, Confession, Triall, and Execution, of Joane Williford, Joan Cariden, and Jane Hott* (London: J.G., 1645), p. 4. Jane Holt felt pain when the familiar sucked her at night, but 'when it lay upon her breast she strucke it off with her hand, and that it was soft as a Cat'; ibid., p. 3. Joan Cariden was sucked regularly by the devil, and 'it was no paine to her'; ibid., pp. 3–4.

[21]   James A. Sharpe, *Instruments of Darkness: Witchcraft in England 1550–1750* (London: Hamish Hamilton, 1996), p. 71; Stuart Clark, *Thinking with Demons: The Idea of Witchcraft in Early Modern Europe* (Oxford: Oxford University Press, 1997), p. 451.

Despite the theological difficulties, the widespread search for incriminating marks on the bodies of English witchcraft suspects was supported by a fusion of learned and popular concepts. There was clearly some overlap of the learned concept of the mark and the popular idea of the teat. Both established bodily attributes as manifestation of a diabolical connection, and both enabled their use as physical evidence. It was therefore intellectually feasible to transpose conceptual elements from one domain to the other. A typical narrative in English witchcraft pamphlets was that of the witch who made a contract with the devil, after which she was branded by the devil with a mark through which she later nursed the imp with her blood. Some even held that the first drawing of blood by the devil was for the writing of the covenant.[22] Such a narrative combined the element of the pact with the devil and the suckling of the imps. The conflation of the demonological concept of the devil's mark with the teats and familiars is reflected in the theological reading of English folklore.[23] Locating the familiars in a theological framework alleviated the theological difficulties. The conflated narrative further supported feasible methods of legal proof – the search for bodily marks and testimonies about familiars.

The high and popular origins of the devil's mark are clearly visible in the language. While authors of learned treatises used the term *mark*, which echoed the elite demonological theory of the pact, the searchers for the marks constantly reported to the JPs and judges about finding *teats* and *bigs*, which figured in the English lore of the animal familiar. The different terminology did not necessarily signify distinct traits. In some cases, the same features were deemed probative, although the JPs and gentlemen called them marks, and the searchers said teats. For example, the JPs ordered a group of women to search the body of Alice Goodridge and her mother 'to see if they could finde any such *marks* on them, as are vsually found on witches', but the women reported to have found *teats* and *warts*. Afterward, the searchers exposed the suspicious body parts, demonstrating the evidence to the satisfaction of the JPs.[24] Although the JPs used the term 'marks', they were clearly satisfied with teats as physical evidence of 'good worth'. In the case against Elizabeth Sawyer in 1621, the bench ordered a group of three women to search the defendant's body for any 'vnwonted marke'. When these women testified in court, they described something 'like a Teate the bignesse of the little finger, and the length of halfe a finger, which was branched

---

[22]   B. Misodaimon, *The Divels Delvsions* ... (London: Richard Williams Stationer, 1649), pp. 3–4.

[23]   Holmes, 'Women: Witnesses and Witches', p. 77.

[24]   I.D., *The Most Wonderfull and True Storie* ... (London: I.O., 1597), pp. 8–9.

at the top like a teate, and seemed as though one had suckt it'.[25] In these cases, the differences in terminology were not a cause for conflict. It seems that despite the different terms, there existed a shared meaning of the evidence of the devil's mark, a meaning that emerged in the context of the witchcraft trials and that combined high and popular elements.

The shared meaning became prevalent in later texts, which used the terms marks and teats interchangeably. In 1634, sanctioned by the Privy Council, a group of ten London midwives, headed by William Harvey, reported finding nothing like 'a teate or marke' on the bodies of four women who had been convicted by the Lancaster Assizes.[26] A pamphlet authored by Edmund Bower referred to what was found on the shoulder of Anne Bodenham as 'a certain mark or Teat'.[27] A cheap pamphlet based on Bower's described the 'marks of an absolute Witch' found on Anne Bodenham's body by the women searchers as teats.[28] In 1702 Richard Hathaway was tried for making false witchcraft accusations, inter alia causing Sarah Murdock to be searched for 'any Teats, or other Signs of a Witch'.[29] A decade later, Sir Henry Chauncy ordered a search of the body of Jane Wenham for 'any Teats, or other extraordinary and unusual Marks about her'.[30] The fusion between the high and popular ideas was evident in the writing of Richard Bernard who saw the devil's mark as a seal of the league with the devil. Yet, he also maintained that the mark was the devil's 'sucking place', and that the mark could appear in the shape of a teat.[31]

Theoretically, the early modern English had a simple and direct evidential method to prove witchcraft. However, putting the theory into practice was not trouble-free. The marks were not always easy to discern. It was believed that the devil, a master of deceit and disguise, habitually branded them on hidden body parts. If a mark was found, the discoverer needed to tell the difference between natural growths and marks and diabolical ones. If no mark was found, another kind of difficulty arose. Even those well versed in theology disagreed

---

[25] Henry Goodcole, *The Wonderfull Discouerie of Elizabeth Savvyer a Witch* (London: VVilliam Butler, 1621), B3–B3v.

[26] Multiple convictions at the Lancaster Assizes in 1634 made some doubtful authorities seek a respite of execution, a move that prompted an investigation. Holmes, 'Women: Witnesses and Witches', p. 66.

[27] Bower, *Doctor Lamb Revived*, pp. 28–9.

[28] *Doctor Lambs Darling*, pp. 7–8.

[29] *The Tryal of Richard Hathaway* (London: Isaac Cleave, 1702), p. 5.

[30] Bragge, *Full and Impartial Account*, p. 11.

[31] Richard Bernard, *A Guide to Grand-Iury Men* (London: Ed Blackmore, 1627), pp. 111–12.

on the question of whether all or only some witches were marked.[32] The absence of a mole or growth, therefore, did not necessarily result in the exoneration of witchcraft suspects. It could also be explained by the suspect's cutting the mark off or by some devilish intervention, as these marks, it was believed, could come and go.[33]

Therefore, the potential of the devil's mark as direct physical evidence and its interpretation were not as clear-cut as they might seem. The early modern English differed in their dispositions toward this evidential method. The participants in the debate, which stretched far beyond the boundaries of the legal profession, used diverse arguments to support their positions. They also differed in the degree of their involvement in the search for the mark. In fact, the professional affiliations of the participants shaped their dispositions to a large extent. Clearly, a complex picture of intellectual and practical positions cannot be attributed to a single aspect of the social life. There is no simplistic one-dimensional formulation, but it is possible to shed some light on the affinity between professional affiliation and position on the devil's mark. Those who took an active part in the search for the mark can be characterized, and those who maintained scholarly positions toward the practice can be described.

Participants in the Search

Neighbours and Self-appointed Searchers

Various social actors were involved in the search for the devil's marks. The task was sometimes undertaken by self-appointed suspicious neighbours with no official authority. This attests to a popular belief in the probative power of the devil's mark evidence. Yet, not everyone was certain of the validity of the findings of neighbourly search. And often the neighbours preferred to hire the services of expert searchers, who included professional witch hunters, searchers and prickers.

---

[32]   Geis and Bunn, *A Trial of Witches*, p. 75; Barbara Rosen (ed.), *Witchcraft, Stratford-Upon-Avon Library* (New York: Taplinger, 1972), p. 18.

[33]   Keith Thomas, *Religion and the Decline of Magic* (New York: Charles Scribner's Sons, 1971), p. 551. See also Stearne, *A Confirmation*, pp. 16–17, 19, 44, 46; Davenport, *The Witches of Huntingdon*, p. 15; H.F., *A True and Exact Relation …* (London: Henry Overton and Benj. Allen, 1645), pp. 26, 28.

Professional Searchers

Professional witch hunters, witch searchers or witch prickers were hired to discover the devil's mark more frequently than doctors. This nascent forensic expertise was founded on demonology and experience, and the practising experts claimed to possess special knowledge that enabled them to distinguish between the diabolical marks and normal morbid growths.[34] For the professional searchers, the solid probative value of the devil's mark was a key factor in establishing their professional identity.

The hiring of expert searchers occurred mainly in the exceptional times of 1645 to 1647, proliferating during the Hopkins–Stearne East-Anglia witch scare. During that episode, the technique of searching became much more intricate, with specially trained male and female searchers appointed. The suspects were stripped naked, positioned on a stool in a closed room without food or sleep for up to two days and continuously watched to see if their imps would come and suck them. During this dire time they could be questioned by the professional witch finders.[35]

On their journeys, the infamous witch hunters Hopkins and Stearne were aided by Mary Phillips and Priscilla Briggs, women with years of experience in searching for the devil's marks and who were compensated for their services.[36] Hopkins emphasized both skill and teamwork in contributing to a successful discovery.[37]

Experience and expert knowledge were indeed the major assets of the professional searchers. When they reported their findings to the justices, they explained why they were not natural marks, and why they believed they were devil's marks, on the basis of previous cases where confessions ensued after similar findings.[38]

---

[34] C.R. Unsworth, 'Witchcraft Beliefs and Criminal Procedure in Early Modern England', in Thomas G. Watkin (ed.), *Legal Record and Historical Reality: Proceedings of the Eighth British Legal History Conference, Cardiff, 1987* (London: The Hambledon Press, 1989), p. 93.

[35] *A True Relation of the Araignment of Eighteene Vvitches*, pp. 6–7. That manner of search was later forbidden by the judges. Matthew Hopkins, *The Discovery of Witches* (London: R. Royston, 1647; reprint, 1988), answer 8. See also Sharpe, *Instruments of Darkness*, p. 143.

[36] Gaskill, *Witchfinders*, pp. 64, 67, 80–81.

[37] Hopkins, *The Discovery of Witches*, answer 5.

[38] F., *A True and Exact Relation*, pp. 16, 24.

Even a professional witch hunter like Stearne admitted it was hard to distinguish between natural and diabolical marks.[39] Though he had great confidence in his own ability to discover witches and to distinguish between the marks, Stearne recommended caution 'lest others should unadvisedly and rashly proceed in the discovery of such persons wrongfully, and then fault me for the insight'.[40] Therefore, by his long and tedious description of the marks, and by his call for prudence, Stearne did not cast doubt on the probative value of the devil's mark, but rather established his own claim for privileged expert knowledge. The devil's mark was one of the major tools of the professional witch hunters. Yet, to establish their position as experts, they needed to construct it as a valid evidential method on the one hand, but as one that required special skills and knowledge of detection on the other. This challenge was not always easy to meet, and a notable example is the very first trial of the Hopkins episode, at Chelmsford in July 1645, where six magistrates and a minister, being dissatisfied with the evidence, called for reprieves for nine of the condemned witches.[41]

Prickers

Along with trained witch hunters and searchers, another kind of professional appeared – the pricker. Pricking, a technique to examine the sensitivity of the mark (supposedly rendered insensible by the devil), was carried out by inserting a pin or needle into it. Lack of pain or bleeding was a sign that the suspect was a witch. The suspects could be pricked repeatedly until they confessed.[42]

Pricking was one of the main techniques used to discover witches in Scotland, where, unlike in England, torture was legal.[43] In Scotland, the search

---

[39]   Stearne, *A Confirmation*, p. 16.

[40]   Ibid., p. 46.

[41]   Gaskill, *Witchfinders*, pp. 128–9.

[42]   Brian P. Levack, 'State-Building and Witch Hunting', in Jonathan Barry, Marianne Hester and Gareth Roberts (eds), *Witchcraft in Early Modern Europe* (Cambridge, UK: Cambridge University Press, 1996), pp. 106–7.

[43]   Goodare, 'Women and the Witch-Hunt in Scotland', p. 301. Though investigation under torture was not permitted under the standard English criminal procedure, torture was infrequently warranted by the Privy Council, especially in treason trials. John H. Langbein, *Torture and the Law of Proof: Europe and England in the Ancien Regime* (Chicago: University of Chicago Press, 1977), pp. 73–139; John H Langbein, 'The Legal History of Torture', in Sanford Levinson (ed.), *Torture: A Collection* (Oxford: Oxford University Press, 2004); Elizabeth Hanson, 'Torture and Truth in Renaissance England', *Representations*, no. 34 (1991).

itself could be one of a series of tortures.[44] The idea of the insensitive mark arrived in England from Continental and Scottish demonology.[45] Even though the English materials focused more on the suckling of imps with blood through bodily growths, there are several references to using professional prickers, some of whom were invited from Scotland.[46]

Pricking was distinguished from the practice of scratching the suspect with nails to draw blood and thus relieve the symptoms of the bewitched victim. The prickers were usually men, unlike the juries of matrons that consisted of women who were not compensated for their services.[47]

Jury of Matrons

Bodily search was warranted by the court, which sometimes appointed a jury of matrons for that purpose. These panels, usually consisting of two or three women, were similar to those used to determine pregnancy. The first recorded appointment of a jury of matrons to search for the devil's mark was as early as 1579.[48] The matrons reported the search findings to the court under oath,[49] and their testimony could be crucial.

The women selected for the panel were not necessarily midwives, but could include any respected and mature women, 'honest matrons' or 'women of credit'.[50] Apparently, the women searchers, the matrons, were sought more for their respectability and much less for their medical knowledge. In the Old

---

[44]   *Newes from Scotland, Declaring the Damnable Life and Death of Doctor Fian* (London: E. Allde for William Wright, 1592), B.

[45]   Goodare, 'Women and the Witch-Hunt in Scotland', p. 302; Christina Larner, *Enemies of God: The Witch-Hunt in Scotland* (Baltimore, MD: Johns Hopkins University Press, 1981), p. 110.

[46]   Holmes, 'Popular Culture?' p. 98; E.G., *A Prodigious & Tragicall History ...* (London: Richard Harper, 1652), p. 5; Ralph Gardiner, *England's Grievance Discovered* (London: R. Ibbitson and P. Stent, 1655), pp. 107–10.

[47]   For an instance of pricking by a jury of women, see *Great News from the West of England* (London: T.M., 1689), p. 2. In Scotland it was exposed in 1662 that two of the prickers (Mr Paterson and Mr Dickson) were actually women in disguise. Larner, *Enemies of God*, p. 111.

[48]   Unsworth, 'Witchcraft Beliefs', p. 92.

[49]   R.H. Helmholz, *Marriage Litigation in Medieval England* (London: Cambridge University Press, 1974), pp. 88–9; James C. Oldham, 'On Pleading the Belly: A History of the Jury of Matrons', *Criminal Justice History*, no. 6 (1985); James Oldham, *The Jury of Matrons* (2006), available from <www.law.georgetown.edu/alumni/publications/2006/fall/documents/facultyarticle.pdf>.

[50]   Unsworth, 'Witchcraft Beliefs', p. 92.

Bailey case against Elizabeth Sawyer in 1621, one woman was chosen on the basis of her good reputation, and the other two were respectable-looking women who simply happened to walk down the street when the officer was looking for matrons.[51] According to Henry Goodcole, an ordinary and visitor for the gaol of Newgate from 1620 to 1636, the testimony of these three women influenced the trial jury's decision to convict Elizabeth Sawyer.[52]

Women were excluded from positions of importance or authority in most criminal trials; they could not become legislators, judges, JPs, members of the grand or petty juries or constables. In witchcraft cases, women played a more significant role. It was usually women who were awarded the indispensable yet agonizing role of the defendant. Another disadvantageous role available to women was that of the victim. Most possessed adolescents were girls. Many witchcraft accusations stemmed from tensions between women, a fact that might explain the relatively high number of women witnesses in witchcraft cases.[53] The woman's role as searcher, however, was distinctively powerful. The naked bodies of women were to be searched by other women. It was not only more modest, but women (especially midwives) were more familiar with the female body. It is possible that the unique English characterization of the teat as a grotesque female organ, an extra nipple, might have rendered women appropriate to conduct the search for the devil's mark. The jury of matrons did not determine facts – but their testimony was significant and was hard to rebut.

The active participation of women in the prosecution of witches, it is sometimes argued, contradicts those feminist theories that explain witchcraft prosecution as an attempt of the rising male medical profession to eliminate midwives and gain exclusive control over women's bodies. In England, midwives were not the victims, but the searchers for the devil's mark.[54] This involvement had no parallel on the Continent, where the male executioners or professional prickers carried out the search. The English courts had an established tradition of female jury panels deputized to perform intimate physical examinations to obtain proof. Most widely known are the juries of matrons appointed to ascertain whether

---

[51]   Goodcole, *The Wonderfull Discouerie of Elizabeth Savvyer*, B3.

[52]   Ibid., B3–B3v.

[53]   Jim Sharpe, 'Women, Witchcraft and the Legal Process', in Jennifer Kermode and Garthine Walker (eds), *Women, Crime and the Courts in Early Modern England* (Chapel Hill, NC: University of North Carolina Press, 1994), pp. 116, 120.

[54]   Diane Purkiss, *The Witch in History: Early Modern and Twentieth-Century Representations* (New York, NY: Routledge, 1996), pp. 8, 19; Geoffrey Scarre, *Witchcraft and Magic in Sixteenth- and Seventeenth-Century Europe*, Studies in European History (Atlantic Highlands, NJ: Humanities Press International, 1987), p. 12.

female criminal defendants were 'quick with a child'.[55] It is questionable whether the fact that women were searched by other women could counter claims that witchcraft prosecution was a mechanism for the oppression of women. Thomas and Macfarlane discounted the war between the sexes as a plausible explanation for the prevalence of women among the accused, as complainants and witnesses were as likely to be women as men.[56] Holmes remarked that, nevertheless, it was men who brought the charges and orchestrated the prosecution.[57] Clearly, no other pattern would have been conceivable in early modern Europe, so it is not surprising that it was the male JPs and judges who appointed the matrons and reserved final judgment for themselves in witchcraft cases. Ultimately, it was usually the female body that was scrutinized at the search, being redefined as different and potentially diabolic. Considering the general social patriarchal context, the fact that the searchers were women does not indicate meaningful female power.[58] Having women rather than men as searchers was hardly a comfort to the subjects of the procedure, as was demonstrated in the case of Elizabeth Wright in 1597, who, while they stripped her, 'cursed the daie of her birth, making great outcries, and vsing bitter speeches against all that offered to accuse her'.[59]

Justices and Judges

The appointment of juries of matrons to search the suspects signified a recognition by the justice system of the value of the devil's mark as a method of proof. The JPs, who were not usually lawyers, and the judges of the assizes, who travelled to the counties twice a year to dispense royal justice, differed in their involvement in the search. The JP conducted a pre-trial investigation

[55]   Such special juries were used in civil proceedings as well. For example, in divorce litigation on grounds of impotence, matrons were ordered to inspect the woman's virginity or, most extraordinarily, the man's genitalia to test whether he could be sexually aroused. It was sometimes suggested that 'maleficium could be one of the reasons for male impotence'. Unsworth, *Witchcraft Beliefs*, p. 92.

[56]   Alan Macfarlane, *Witchcraft in Tudor and Stuart England: A Regional and Comparative Study* (New York: Harper & Row, 1970), p. 160; Thomas, *Religion and the Decline of Magic*, p. 568.

[57]   Holmes, 'Women: Witnesses and Witches', p. 76.

[58]   For an analysis of witch hunts as yet another means of social control aimed to uphold patriarchy and to police women's sexuality in a context of social change, see Marianne Hester, 'Patriarchal Reconstruction', in Jonathan Barry, Marianne Hester and Gareth Roberts (eds), *Witchcraft in Early Modern Europe* (Cambridge, UK: Cambridge University Press, 1996), pp. 288–9, 293.

[59]   D., *The Most Wonderfull and True Storie*, p. 13.

that included an examination of the suspect. Theoretically, a judicial search warrant could be issued by the bench of the assizes, but the search was almost invariably ordered at the pre-trial stage by the examining JP.[60] A search ordered by a JP pursuant to receiving complaints about the suspect seems to have been a standard occurrence.[61]

Occasionally, JPs allowed the searchers to prick.[62] It was not uncommon for magistrates to order a search on the basis of intuitive suspicions or evidence that more sceptical contemporaries would have deemed flimsy.[63] In some cases, JPs appointed searchers who were likely to be biased, for example, a woman who was the attendant of the alleged victim for the previous six weeks,[64] the mother of the alleged victim,[65] or searchers hired by the accusers (after the first searchers found no suspicious marks).[66]

In some cases the accusers themselves searched the body of the suspect after she was arrested. The pamphlets did not always mention whether these searches were pursuant to a judicial order. However, it seems that to search the suspect in jail, the cooperation of the authorities was necessary.[67]

Witchcraft cases were generally heard by the travelling assize judges, who tried practically all the serious crimes and reinforced unified standards of procedure and proof. Although the judges did not initiate the search for the devil's mark, which was not a part of any official procedure, they repeatedly heard testimonies about the search.

Surrounding the search for the devil's mark was a lively scholarly discourse about the validity of this proof. A variety of views was expressed by various social actors from different professions. The dominant voices in the debate belonged to members of three professional groups – clerics, lawyers and

---

[60]   One rare instance of a bench-ordered search occurred in the case against Elizabeth Sawyer held at the Old Bailey in 1621. The search, however, was ordered at the insistence of the investigating magistrate, Arthur Robinson. Goodcole, *The Wonderfull Discouerie of Elizabeth Savvyer*, B3–B3v.

[61]   D., *The Most Wonderfull and True Storie*, pp. 8–9; Bernard, *A Guide to Grand-Iury Men*, p. 230; *The Tryal of Richard Hathaway*, p. 5; *Great News from the West of England*, p. 2; *A True and Impartial Relation*, p. 11; F., *A True and Exact Relation*, p. 16; *A Declaration in Answer to Several Lying Pamphlets Concerning the Witch of Wapping* (London: s.n.r, 1652), pp. 5–6.

[62]   *Great News from the West of England*, p. 2.

[63]   For example, one JP ordered that a suspect be searched after seeing the alleged victim, a boy, having a fit in her presence. D., *The Most Wonderfull and True Storie*, p. 8.

[64]   *A True and Impartial Relation*, p. 11.

[65]   *A Tryal of Witches*, pp. 35–7.

[66]   *Answer to Several Lying Pamphlets*, pp. 5–6.

[67]   *The Witches of Northampton-Shire* (London: Arthur Iohnson, 1612), Dv.

physicians. Examination of their discourse demonstrates an affinity between the professional affiliation of the speaker and the perception of the evidential value of the devil's mark. Clearly, there were other relevant social groups. Identity is constructed from many different layers, and the voices cannot always be neatly classified into a single category. For example, a physician might rely on the interpretation of the scriptures, or a demonological tract might contain practical instructions to jurors and examples of particular cases. However, a reading of the texts demonstrates that generalizations can be made on the basis of professional affiliation and that the classification proves analytically useful.

Scholarly Discourse about the Devil's Mark

Physicians

Rarely did a doctor conduct the search for the devil's mark. One famous example was a case in 1634, in which a group of London midwives and surgeons, supervised by William Harvey, who discovered the circulation of the blood and was James I's and later Charles I's physician, examined Lancashire suspects who were found to have marks by the provincial searchers. They cleared the suspects completely.[68]

In the case against Joan Peterson in 1652, the JP ordered a search after the suspect had denied the allegations during examination. The search cleared Peterson, and she was subsequently released on bail.[69] The accusers brought her to another examination and caused her to be searched again, this time by searchers they themselves had hired and who did not fail to find a 'teat of flesh in her secret parts, more then other women usually had'. The JP arrested her on the basis of this finding. The author of a pamphlet who criticized the search as 'unnatural & barbarous' remarked that the day before Peterson's execution, she was searched by physicians who declared the teat natural and that there were grounds for reprieve (pregnancy).[70] Their opinion failed to save Peterson, who was executed. Reprieve was probably denied because Peterson had refused to confess.

---

[68]   Robin Briggs, *Witches and Neighbors: The Social and Cultural Context of European Witchcraft* (New York: Viking, 1996), pp. 280–81; Geoffrey Keynes, *Harvey* (Oxford: Oxford University Press, 1966), pp. 209–10; Holmes, 'Women: Witnesses and Witches', p. 66; Gaskill, *Witchfinders*, p. 46.

[69]   *Answer to Several Lying Pamphlets*, p. 5.

[70]   Ibid., pp. 5–6.

Unlike the professional witch hunters and searchers, the physicians' approach, as it appeared in the texts, treated the devil's mark with reservation. The sceptics Cotta, Ady and Webster all assumed the existence of witches. However, using tools of reason and medical experience, they strove to reform the customary methods of proof. Cotta, whose intellectual method allowed for detection of witches by reason, including presumptions and conjectures, rejected the devil's mark as admissible evidence. He accepted as fact that in some cases the allegedly bewitched victim could specify intimate marks of the suspected witch without ever having seen her body before. 'This is reputed a certain conuiction of a Witch,' he wrote.[71] Yet, such a miraculous event might be the devil's work and could not be a basis for conviction. Cotta made clear that it was entirely illegal to use evidence of 'supernatural illuminations or revelations' as any grounds of just trials. He maintained that judgments based on supernatural evidence were void and ought not to be credited by 'just and righteous men'.[72]

A much harsher criticism of the theory of the devil's mark was voiced by Ady. *All* bodily marks, he argued, could be attributed to natural causes, whether they were congenital or a consequence of disease. He listed many natural reasons for the formation of teats and explained why, in some cases, those growths could issue blood.[73] He questioned the theological theory on which the belief in the devil's mark was supposedly founded.[74] Ady repeated the rhetorical question, 'Where is it written, that the Devill setteth privy marks upon Witches, whereby they should be known or searched out?' He regarded the marks as an invention of Catholic theologians, having no basis in scripture or medicine.[75]

Ady drew a very sharp line between the physicians and the professional witch hunters and searchers. He relied on medical theory and empiricist reasoning rather than on scripture and demonology. He referred to medical books, used Latin and Greek medical terms and distinguished himself from men who 'cavil against Philosophy, and Physick Rules'.[76] Those who sought to discover witches by marks, he called 'witchmongers', 'ignorant people' and 'ignorant Witchmongers', and he severely denounced cases in which such evidence served as a basis for conviction. He asserted that the demonological account of the devil's mark 'is

---

[71]   John Cotta, *The Triall of Vvitch-Craft* (London: Samuel Rand, 1616), p. 114.

[72]   Ibid., pp. 122–3.

[73]   Thomas Ady, *A Candle in the Dark* (London: Robert Ibbitson, 1655), pp. 127–9.

[74]   Sharpe refers to Ady as a physician, although there is no definite proof that he was such. Yet, his prevalent medical perspective justifies classifying him with other authors of medical treatises. Sharpe, *Instruments of Darkness*, p. 68.

[75]   Ady, *A Candle in the Dark*, pp. 99–100.

[76]   Ibid., p. 129.

folly and madness, and to affirm, is a phantastick Lye, invented by the Devil, and the Pope.[77]

A third influential and radical physician's voice was that of John Webster, who explicitly negated the treatises of the cleric writers Casaubon, More and Glanvill with a Royal Society philosophy.[78] Webster's rhetorical means resembled Ady's. He wrote as a physician and man of reason, but spoke in theological terms when denouncing the practices of mark finding not only as 'unChristian', but as diabolical practices in themselves.[79] Webster rejected the idea of suckling the devil through teats. In answer to Glanvill, he proposed to rely not on suppositions, but on observation, and that 'in a thing of this nature, arguments to prove it probable are insufficient'. Webster stressed that such suckling was never observed and should not be believed.[80]

Like Ady, Webster distinguished himself from the witchmongers and especially from the prickers. According to Webster, the practices of the prickers were manifest deceit and directed by greed. The lack of pain could be medically explained by insertion of the needles and pins into warts and 'hollow excrescences', which did not cause pain. Innocent people lost their lives on account of 'wicked means and unchristian practices' of 'wicked Rogues', whose acts were encouraged by 'greater persons', including clerics. The searches were 'barbarous and cruel' and motivated by 'diabolical instigation, working upon ignorance and superstition'. Webster explained that growths had many natural reasons, 'sufficiently known to learned Physicians and experienced Chirurgions', depending on 'Complexion and Constitution ... Age, Sex, and other accidents and circumstances'. Webster made clear that it was against logic to deduce a diabolical contract from insensate warts or excrescences. He asked rhetorically, 'Where is the coherence, connexion, or just consequence?'[81]

An exceptional voice was that of Richard Boulton, an 'obscure figure', as James Sharpe defined him.[82] Boulton, a physician running an unsuccessful practice and a writer of medical treatises[83] who was familiar with up-to-date natural

---

[77] Ibid.

[78] Barbara J. Shapiro, *Probability and Certainty in Seventeenth-Century England: A Study of the Relationships between Natural Science, Religion, History, Law, and Literature* (Princeton, NJ: Princeton University Press, 1983), p. 218.

[79] Webster, *The Displaying of Supposed Witchcraft*, p. 82.

[80] Ibid., p. 81.

[81] Ibid., pp. 82–3.

[82] James A. Sharpe (ed.), *English Witchcraft, 1560–1736*, 6 vols (London: Pickering & Chatto, 2003), vol. 6, p. x.

[83] Some of these were apparently written after Boulton found himself in a financial predicament. Sir Leslie Stephen and Sir Sidney Lee (eds), *The Dictionary of National*

philosophy, strongly advocated belief in witchcraft. He vehemently asserted that the 'surest way' to discover witches, other than by their confessions, was first 'by their Mark, which is insensible; and, secondly, by their swimming'.[84] These were the same two signs which James I had recommended in 1597 while sitting on the Scottish throne and that had been widely criticized since. Boulton's adversary in the debate was the Protestant churchman Francis Hutchinson, a precursor of those who represented the modern approach to witchcraft and who perceived witch beliefs as products of superstition and ignorance. Most writers of medical treatises used a quite radical tone, declaring growths and excrescences to be a medical issue and not a mark of the devil.

Legal Scholars

The tone of legal scholars was very different, a rather conservative perpetuation of the concept that the devil's mark was a valid proof of witchcraft. The writers of legal treatises and manuals took a more descriptive line, which allegedly reflected the existing law. The descriptive approach defined law on the basis of common practices and thus assimilated non-legal elements (such as medical, theological and popular notions) into the legal discourse. The references in the texts of legal scholars demonstrated familiarity with the works of Continental writers but relied mainly on English cases. The starting point of all writers was that witches existed. All legal writers stressed the difficulty of trying the crime of witchcraft and discussed the appropriate evidential standards.

Michael Dalton provided evidential rules based on the Lancaster precedent of 1612, which was documented in detail by the court clerk, Potts. One of the proofs which Dalton listed was the mark allegedly sucked by the familiar.[85] Dalton linked the physical appearance of the mark with the rationale behind it (a trace of diabolical suckling).

The technique of treating the statements of witnesses and confessions of suspects as legal precedents enabled the infiltration of popular beliefs into the body of law. The witnesses reported what they found relevant or important. Their stories contained many popular customs and beliefs, including their conception of the contact between the witch and her imps. The courtroom was the meeting point of official rules and laws and customs – of elite and

---

Biography, 22 vols (London: Oxford University Press, 1963–65), vol. II, p. 917.

[84] Richard Boulton, *A Compleat History of Magick, Sorcery, and Witchcraft* (London: E. Curll, J. Pemberton, and W. Taylor, 1715), p. 23.

[85] Michael Dalton, *The Countrey Iustice* (London: Societie of Stationers, 1618), p. 243; Thomas Potts, *The Vvonderfull Discouerie of Witches in the Countie of Lancaster* (London: Iohn Barnes, 1613).

popular cultural views. The influences were mutual. Laws and procedures were dictated by a central judicial system. Popular concepts were imported through testimonies and depositions, practically implemented by laymen's participation as jurors and JPs, and, sometimes, when adopted as precedents, they became the law. Potts' pamphlet described the relationship of suspects and imps on the basis of statements made by witnesses and defendants. The stories about imps were not denounced as impossible, but their probative power was limited. First, the contact with imps, per se, was not the basis for any of the criminal charges. All the indictments in the Lancaster case concerned malefic acts such as killing or injuring. The indictments did not include charges of communication with spirits or familiars. The relationship of the witches and imps was brought as background or supporting evidence. Second, there was no clear affirmation of the evidential sufficiency of testimonies about imps. On the one hand, the narratives about imps were not denounced, but on the other, the jury's verdict did not reveal the grounds and reasoning. Thus, there was no judgment that specifically formulated a guiding normative statement on the evidential value of the narratives. Third, although imps (in human and animal shapes) were prominent in Potts' pamphlet, the issue of suckling was seldom mentioned.

Therefore, when Dalton treated the suckling of imps as a precedent set forth in the Lancaster case, he assigned to the suckling narrative the authority of a rule of law. In his view, testimony about suckling imps was relevant for proving witchcraft. His book was a guide for JPs and therefore aimed at pre-trial investigation – supposedly not at determining admissibility rules for the trial itself. However, as a popular handbook likely to be referred to in cases of difficulty, Dalton's work must have shaped the opinions of justices, grand jurors and petty jurors about the proof of witchcraft. Pre-trial examinations were later affirmed in court. Therefore, the statements about imps would have been heard in court. In any case, Dalton used the Lancaster case in a way that broadened the possibilities of discovering witches and added popular beliefs (such as suckling of imps) to the repertoire of proofs.[86]

Richard Bernard advocated caution in the prosecution of witches.[87] His work contained demonological aspects, but it also had parts that were drafted as a legal manual. However, the legal characteristics of his work (starting with the title) bore a resemblance to Dalton's. Like Dalton, Bernard saw the mark as a good proof of the crime and based his claim on previous English cases as

---

[86] This is in disagreement with Barbara Shapiro, who listed Dalton as one of the writers whose work brought about the decline of witch prosecution. Shapiro, *Probability and Certainty*, p. 205.

[87] *Oxford Dictionary of National Biography*, s.v. 'Bernard, Richard'; Bernard, *A Guide to Grand-Iury Men*.

precedents. It is illuminating to note that, in a later edition of *The Countrey Justice*, Dalton relied heavily on Bernard's *Guide to Grand-Iury Men* when discussing the probative value of the devil's mark. Dalton quoted Bernard, who had previously quoted him. Repeatedly referring to Bernard's *Guide to Grand-Iury Men*, Dalton's discussion of the mark became much more elaborate, weaving together the elements of folklore and demonology. Dalton then explained that witches ordinarily had a familiar that sucked 'a little teat upon their body'. The devil could also have made other marks on the witches' bodies (such as spots resembling flea bites or 'suncke in and hollow' flesh) and could make them insensible and incapable of bleeding on pricking. These marks were found 'often in their secretest parts, and therefore require diligent and carfull search'.[88]

Legal scholarship is structured by layer upon layer of quotations. Bernard relied on the pamphlets of Potts and others. Later, the anonymous writer of a treatise of 1645 analysing the anti-witchcraft laws and their application relied on the works of Bernard when he declared the mark and the teat to be a valid proof of witchcraft – demonstrating the league and the contact with a familiar.[89] The author followed Bernard's call for 'diligent and careful search'. The timing of the last treatise was significant, around the East Anglia witch hunt of 1645, which was led by the infamous professional witch hunter, Matthew Hopkins.

An Advertisement to the Jury-Men was written by Sir Robert Filmer after the bitter experience of the witch scare of 1645 and an execution of witches in 1652. Filmer, although trained in law and with experience as a justice, had a more radical tone than that of other legal scholars. His rhetoric was more political and philosophical than legal.[90] Filmer stressed that, even according to William Perkins, the renowned Puritan theologian, evidence of the devil's mark was insufficient for conviction.[91] Filmer held royalist and conservative views, and Sharpe noted the irony in the fact that someone so unprogressive in his politics had composed a text hostile to the persecution of witches.[92]

---

[88]   Michael Dalton, *The Countrey Iustice* (London: Miles Flesher, James Haviland, and Robert Young, the assignes of Iohn More Esquire, 1630), p. 273.

[89]   *The Lawes against Vvitches, and Conivration* (London: R.W., 1645), p. 4.

[90]   Ian Bostridge, *Witchcraft and Its Transformations, c.1650–c.1750* (Oxford; New York: Clarendon Press, 1997), pp. 10, 13–20. Other tracts which he wrote dealt with government, politics and related matters. The political and religious debates of the 1640s and 1650s were the backdrop of his discussion of witchcraft, which provided the Arminian Filmer with another stage for attacking Calvinism.

[91]   Sir Robert Filmer, *An Advertisement to the Jury-Men of England, Touching Witches* (London: Richard Royston, 1653), p. 10.

[92]   Sharpe, *Instruments of Darkness*, p. 221.

However, most legal scholars and practitioners did not argue against the probative value of the devil's mark. Indeed, the notion of the devil's mark as sufficient physical evidence made proof of witchcraft much easier. The relative openness of the legal discourse might also be attributed to the structural elements of lay participation in the proceedings (as parties, witnesses, jurors and JPs) and the notion of precedent. Once an issue (contact with imps, for example) had been acknowledged as relevant for the determination of guilt, it became a criterion for determination in subsequent cases. In addition, the fact that the lay jurors did not explain their verdicts might have made it easier to rely on principles that, had they been made explicit, might have created difficulties for the elite legal professionals.

Clergymen

The theory of the devil's mark originated in demonology. Men of the church tried to formulate diagnostic criteria for the mark and to solve the theological difficulties embodied in the popular concept of imps. A vast body of literature tried to distinguish between normal bodily formations and unnatural marks. The distinction was the Achilles' heel of demonological theory. The sceptics claimed that many people had natural bodily marks, warts or growths.[93] The certainty of the marks as proof was mocked as early as 1584 in Reginald Scot's famous treatise.[94] Although the sceptics classified many marks as natural, an opposing intellectual current included even common features as devil's marks. Henry Goodcole, who was convinced of the guilt of Elizabeth Sawyer and obtained a confession from her after her conviction, regarded her paleness, deformed body and rudeness as devil's marks.[95] Proof, for Goodcole, was not a purely legal issue. He kept looking for evidence of Sawyer's guilt and interrogated her after she had already been convicted. Moral certainty was more than a standard of conviction, it was a religious necessity. From this perspective the theological and legal discourses about evidence diverged. Goodcole's readiness to expand the scope of admissible mark-related evidence could be inferred from his willingness to accept rumours about marks as proof. From information given by Elizabeth Sawyer's neighbours, that she had 'a priuate and strange marke on her body', Goodcole concluded that '*their suspition was confirmed against her*'.[96] His credulity became more evident in his relying on the findings of randomly picked

---

[93] Geis and Bunn, *A Trial of Witches*, p. 75.
[94] Scot, *The Discouerie of Witchcraft*, A6v.
[95] Goodcole, *The Wonderfull Discouerie of Elizabeth Savvyer*, A4v–B.
[96] Ibid., B3. Emphasis added.

searchers[97] and in his suggestive questioning of the convicted witch concerning where, when and how the devil sucked her.[98]

Some clergymen, aside from preaching and writing, took an active part in witchcraft cases, trying to influence the result.[99] These were usually local ministers of the lower ranks, and their involvement included taking part in the examination of the case, assisting the magistrates and pressuring the suspect to confess either before or after the conviction. They were usually supporters of witchcraft beliefs and used the justice system and the specific cases as a platform to advance their positions. However, one of the later pamphlets (1702) documented an event in which a local minister, Richard Martin, defended the suspect, Sarah Murdock, against false accusations and assaults launched by the accusers.[100]

An example of the noticeable involvement of clerics is the case against Jane Wenham in 1712. Francis Bragge, the son of a clergyman and himself a Cambridge graduate about to launch his clerical career, wrote several pamphlets in the debate surrounding the case and took an active part in investigating and conducting experiments to prove Wenham's guilt. Two other local clerics, Rev. Mr Strutt and Rev. Mr Gardiner, also participated actively in securing her conviction and were publicly criticized by various writers.[101] Bragge's pamphlet about the case alleged that Wenham voluntarily offered to submit to a search and the swimming test. And, indeed, a search was ordered by the JP the following day.[102] A sceptical anonymous writer remarked about Wenham's offer to be searched that she was 'willing to undergo all those Trials that never fail of discovering a Witch, according to the Country Probations'.[103]

High-ranking clerics were also preoccupied with the mark. It was a subject of profound scholarly treatment in the theological discourse. The most distinguished Puritan theologian, William Perkins, drew a clear line between grounds for suspicion and the evidence used at a trial. In *A Discourse of the Damned Art of Witchcraft*, he listed 18 signs for the discovery of witchcraft. One of the signs, the devil's mark, was, according to Perkins, a *presumption* that

---

[97]   Two of the three happened to walk down the street when the officer came looking for 'matrons'.

[98]   Goodcole, *The Wonderfull Discouerie of Elizabeth Savvyer*, C3–C3v.

[99]   Holmes, 'Popular Culture?' p. 92.

[100]   Peter Elmer, 'Introduction', in Peter Elmer (ed.), *The Later English Trial Pamphlets*, English Witchcraft 1560–1736 (London: Pickering & Chatto, 2003), p. xi; *The Tryal of Richard Hathaway*, pp. 5–8.

[101]   George Lyman Kittredge, *Witchcraft in Old and New England* (Cambridge, MA: Harvard University Press, 1929), pp. 583, 596; Elmer, 'Introduction', p. xiii.

[102]   Bragge, *Full and Impartial Account*, p. 11.

[103]   *A Full Confutation of Witchcraft* ... (London: J. Baker, 1712), p. 17.

warranted examination but was not a sufficient proof in itself. Filmer attacked Perkins' reasoning as incomplete. Suppose that a search did reveal a mark with no evident natural explanation, he argued; its meaning would still have to be proved.[104] Perkins' view was typical of the English Puritans who generally regarded the devil's mark only as a presumption, which was insufficient for conviction.

In early modern English jurisprudence, evidence included documents and testimony, while the circumstances surrounding the case created an entirely distinct evidential category.[105] Presumption was an inference implied by the circumstances, a logical construct used in the absence of perfect evidence. It was an assumption about probable facts that was deduced from known facts or experience. The now-established legal distinction between presumption of fact and presumption of law[106] had not as yet crystallized, but different presumptions were credited with varying degrees of strength.

Perkins regarded the devil's mark as a presumption inferred by 'some',[107] a phrasing that implied that not everybody shared the view that the mark was a significant proof. Considering that James VI & I, who advocated the devil's mark as proof, was among these 'some', we can only surmise the criticism would have been more blatant had this not been the case.[108]

The use of the term presumption in itself demonstrates that in Perkins' view, the devil's mark was not direct physical evidence, but rather an assumption. Perkins' method considerably limited the possibilities of search. A JP might order a search on two cumulative conditions: first, if the mark on the suspect's body was casually observed (not through a deliberate search); and, second, if it could not be explained by any evident natural reason. Thereupon, the magistrate might order a search so 'that the truth may appear'.[109] The mark, for Perkins, was a presumption that warranted an examination by the magistrate but was

---

[104]   Filmer, *An Advertisement to the Jury-Men*, p. 10.

[105]   Barbara J. Shapiro, '"Fact" and the Proof of Fact in Anglo-American Law (c. 1500–1850)', in Austin Sarat, Lawrence Douglas and Martha Merrill Umphrey (eds), *How Law Knows* (Stanford: Stanford University Press, 2007), p. 43.

[106]   The former is a deduction of unknown facts from known evidence, and the latter is the application of the same rule of law to a given set of circumstances.

[107]   Perkins, *Damned Art*, p. 203.

[108]   Perkins died in 1602, when James was still the king of Scotland. The treatise was based on the preaching of Perkins during his lifetime. Perkins was surely aware of both James' demonology and royal position. The treatise was published posthumously, when James ascended the English throne. The publisher did not hesitate to publish this denial of the king's arguments, a fact that may imply that James' image as a zealous witch hunter is incorrect. Kittredge, *Witchcraft in Old and New England*, p. 291.

[109]   Ibid.

definitely not a basis for conviction. Through his discussion of the mark, Perkins imported the Continental concept of varying degrees of probative strength into the English witchcraft debate. He was followed by other theologians.

Thomas Cooper, a witch prosecution enthusiast, borrowed much from Perkins but took a tougher line. If an observed sign had no apparent natural cause, it was 'a shrewd presumption, to examine at least'.[110] The presumption of the devil's mark was a shrewd one, but it was still merely a presumption and not actual evidence.

John Gaule, the Vicar of Great Staughton in Huntingdonshire, published his *Select Cases of Conscience Touching Vvitches and Vvitchcrafts* in the aftermath of the Essex witch hunt.[111] Gaule believed that witches existed but attacked witch hunting, Hopkins' investigation techniques and popular superstitions. For Gaule, unusual bodily marks were a 'probable' sign, yet insufficient for conviction.[112] Gaule maintained that a 'learned Physician' could reach sound conclusions about whether marks were natural, whereas professional witch finders lacked such ability.[113]

Richard Bernard spoke in a different voice. His work, *A Guide to Grand-Iury Men*, cannot be labelled purely theological or legal. Bernard advocated caution in the discovery of witches. The question was not whether witches existed, but rather how to discover them. Nevertheless, the *devil's mark was sufficient proof for conviction*. His confidence was based on previous cases. Judging from his references, Barnard was well versed in Continental literature, but the foundation of his argument was a corpus of English cases in which the devil's mark was presented as a sign of witchcraft.[114] Bernard's discussion maintained the following theses: witches exist; the devil exists; the devil marks the witches; in some cases the devil sucks on the body of the witches; the marks can be in 'very hidden places'.[115] Bernard relied on accumulated experience from actual cases. The technique of treating previous testimonies as precedents is reminiscent of Dalton. Bernard's conclusion was, 'where this marke is, there is a league and a familiar spirit'.[116]

---

[110]　Cooper, *Mystery of Witch-Craft*, p. 275.

[111]　Sharpe, *Instruments of Darkness*, pp. 141–2; Kittredge, *Witchcraft in Old and New England*, p. 25.

[112]　John Gaule, *Select Cases of Conscience Touching Vvitches and Vvitchcrafts* (London: Richard Clutterbuck, 1646), p. 80.

[113]　Ibid., pp. 105–6.

[114]　Bernard, *A Guide to Grand-Iury Men*, p. 112; Kittredge, *Witchcraft in Old and New England*, p. 273; Sharpe, 'The Devil in East Anglia', p. 251.

[115]　Bernard, *A Guide to Grand-Iury Men*, p. 112.

[116]　Ibid., p. 218.

Bernard not only regarded the mark as excellent proof, but he also recommended pricking. He claimed that the mark was insensible and did not bleed when pricked. Pricking was a means of caution, a way to distinguish between natural and devilish marks. In the name of prudence, Bernard suggested pricking the suspect not only in the mark, but in unsuspicious spots as well, for comparison. This tormenting method was proposed for the sake of avoiding conviction of the innocent.[117]

Despite the alleged certainty of the mark, Bernard's text implied doubts. First, it hinted that not all witches had the mark, but that it was branded only 'vpon these baser sort of witches'.[118] Second, in addition to pricking, Bernard used the standard physical description of the mark, thus burdening the readers with a thorny diagnosis.[119] He also held that marks could disappear and grow again, which made negative findings inconclusive.[120] The remedy Bernard offered for this frustrating predicament was procedural – to ensure a thorough and diligent search, the searchers had to be under oath.[121] Bernard's solution was deficient, as even the most diligent search could not detect the disappearing marks. Interestingly, he was in favour of pricking, but objected to scratching.[122]

Bernard guided the JPs to inquire of friends and relatives of the afflicted whether a search for a mark had been conducted.[123] In cases where the accusers had found marks, he suggested asking them how they distinguished them from natural marks. If they had not conducted a search, Bernard guided the JPs 'to command some fittest for the purpose, to make diligent search'.[124] These guidelines legitimized private searches committed by interested accusers acting under no warrant.

Bernard cautioned against conviction of the innocent. When there was doubt, he favoured dismissing the bill of indictment (*ignoramus*) rather than returning it as a true bill (*billa vera*). Nonetheless, the same author vehemently supported the value of the devil's mark as a sign and the procedures of searching and pricking. On a practical level, it seems that for Bernard the mark was physical evidence that cleared away all doubt. However, his *Guide to Grand-Iury Men*

---

[117] Ibid., p. 219.

[118] Ibid., p. 218.

[119] 'its somtimes like a little *teate*, somtimes but a *blewish spot*, sometimes *red spots* like a fleabiting, somtimes the *flesh is sunke* in and hollow'. Ibid., p. 219. Footnote omitted.

[120] Ibid.

[121] Ibid., p. 220.

[122] Ibid., pp. 191–3, 218–20.

[123] Ibid., pp. 229–30.

[124] Ibid., p. 230.

implied that even after a most diligent search, the diagnosis remained knotty and doubt still lurked.

Bernard died before the witch hunt of 1645–48. One can only wonder whether the attitude of this generally cautious writer toward the devil's mark would have been more reserved had he been writing in the aftermath of this mass prosecution. In any case, not all clergymen were reserved. Years before the publication of his *Guide to Grand-Iury Men*, when he was still a minister in Worksop, Bernard took an active part in exorcizing the allegedly possessed John Fox of Nottingham.[125] Generally speaking, although the central religious scholars were reserved, the peripheral clergy were more supportive of witch persecution.

The theory of the devil's mark as a sign of the covenant with the devil originated in demonology. Therefore, it is ironic that although legal scholars (with the exception of Filmer) upheld the mark as valid proof of witchcraft, clerical writers were more reserved in their judgment.

In early modern England, the cultural association between the mark and witchcraft was not the result of a unified theory, but rather a combination of different, sometimes inconsistent or even competing concepts, and the product of a social struggle among various social players. The different social players and groups employed evidential strategies as a resource to realize their distinct goals.

Social identity is multifaceted – composed of social class, gender, profession, religious affiliation and more – and the full picture of the intellectual currents and professional dispositions regarding the proof of witchcraft by the devil's mark is understandably complex. Yet, some generalizations can be made about the connection between the social attributes of the participants in the debate and the nature of their discourse and evidential dispositions. Notable differences have been demonstrated between physicians, professional witch hunters, clergymen and legal scholars in their approach to the devil's mark as proof. The evidential inclinations were closely related to the interests or structural elements of the profession. Thus, the scepticism of the physicians was expressed through rhetoric that was meant to enhance professional jurisdiction. Medical expertise was constructed by physicians as requisite to making legal decisions.

The most intriguing difference was the one between legal scholars and the divines. The legal scholars were less bothered by theological challenges than the clerics, and their writings reflected easier assimilation of imp narratives. Legal scholars upheld the probative value of the devil's mark by treating testimonies in previous cases as precedents. The notion of the mark as sufficient

---

[125]   *Dictionary of National Biography*, s.v. 'Bernard, Richard'; *Broadside Story Concerning a Man Who Became Possessed by an Evil Spirit* (Glasgow: T. Duncan, [probable period 1810–30]).

physical evidence made the judicial struggle of proving the crime much easier. Paradoxically, high-ranking clerics, whom we would expect to identify most with demonology, were the ones who were most reserved about the devil's mark and regarded it as a *mere presumption*. The explanation may be that they, most of all, were aware that the devil's mark was a (theo)logical construct and not concrete direct evidence. It is also possible that the legal profession was structurally more prone to assimilation of popular ideas and other types of discourse. The relative openness of the legal discourse might be attributed to the structural elements of lay participation in the proceedings and the notion of precedent. Once an issue (for instance, contact with imps) had been acknowledged as relevant for the determination of guilt, it became a criterion for determination in subsequent cases. In addition, the fact that the lay jurors did not explain their verdicts might have made it easier to rely on principles that, had they been made explicit, could have created difficulties for the elite legal professionals.

Members of the clergy and the legal profession seemed to be divided in their dispositions along the centre/periphery axis. Local JPs and parish ministers took an active part in the search for proof in the preparation of cases for court and tended to be more tolerant of the popular frame of mind regarding the devil's mark. This fact is not surprising, considering their embeddedness in the local community and their obligation to cooperate with varied local interests. The judges of the assizes and high-ranking churchmen, by contrast, treated the devil's mark with more suspicion.

Attention should be given to the rhetoric meant to enhance professional jurisdiction. It is interesting to see that, despite their opposing views regarding the validity of the mark as proof, both the generally sceptical physicians and professional witch searchers bolstered their arguments by claims of unique professional expertise. The heated debate over witchcraft and ways of proof provided a valuable foundation for achieving much wider goals, such as greater professional autonomy and public recognition of worth. Physicians were the most radical critics of the body search. It is possible that their success in reinforcing their professional position through the witch trials contributed to the decline in prosecution.

The debate about the probative value of the devil's mark also demonstrated the connection between social class and ideology, and the interaction between the different ideas and practices. Popular beliefs of suckling imps and learned demonological concepts infiltrated and spread into other social circles through the criminal proceeding. Peter Burke remarked that 'one of most striking instances of interaction between the learned and the popular traditions is that of the witch ... the image of the witch current in the sixteenth and seventeenth centuries involved both popular elements, like the belief that some people had the power to fly through the air or do their neighbours harm by supernatural means, and learned elements, notably the idea of a pact with the devil'.[126] The English perception of the mark that combined the learned element of the pact with the imps narrative is indeed a striking example of the interaction and blending of the learned and popular processes of thinking.

In theory, the probative value of the devil's mark was no different if found on a male or female body. Yet, most documented instances concerned suspicious marks found on women. In practice, it was mostly the female body that was subjected to observation and search. The search for the devil's mark reflected and reasserted the asymmetrical power structure, where the men orchestrated and ordered the searches and the women complied with their orders, either in the vulnerable position of suspects or in the more empowered role of female searchers.

Supposedly the mark was direct physical evidence that made it possible to prove witchcraft. However, the case of the devil's mark demonstrates that even items of physical evidence – concrete objects that presumably speak for themselves and not through human witnesses whose honesty and reliability need to be assessed – are not necessarily direct traces of the crime. The significance of physical evidence is determined through a culturally influenced mental process of inference. Fingerprints or DNA evidence are now frequently considered to create an immediate and direct link between the suspect and the crime. Yet, such evidence relies on a socially acceptable body of knowledge that needs to be interpreted and explained to the court by expert witnesses. Similarly, the link between physical evidence such as marks and witchcraft was socially and culturally constructed and relied on contemporary theories and assumptions. In addition, the epistemology underlying the evidential logic of the devil's mark was the result of diverse interests and conflicting social influences. The debate over the validity of the devil's mark as proof demonstrates the important role of the socio-cultural context in shaping and directing the trajectories of evidence law.

---

[126]   Peter Burke, *Popular Culture in Early Modern Europe* (Aldershot, England: Scholar Press, 1987; reprint, 1994), p. 62.

A Detection
of damnable driftes, practi-
zed by three VVitches arraigned at
Chelmiffo2de in Effex, at the
laſte Aſſiſes there holden, whiche
were executed in Ap2ill.
1 5 7 9.

Set fo2the to diſcouer the Ambuſhementes of
Sathan, whereby he would ſurp2iſe vs
lulled in ſecuritie, and hardened
with contempte of Gods
. vengeance th2eatened
fo2 our offences.

Imprinted at London for Edward White,
at the little North-dore of Paules.

Figure 6.1   An imp. From *A Detection of Damnable Driftes, Practized by Three Vvitches*
Arraigned at Chelmisforde in Essex, at the Laste Assises There Holden, Whiche Were
Executed in Aprill. 1579 ... (London, J. Kingston, 1579). [Shelfmark: C.27.a.8]
Courtesy of the British Library. [Call # 59439]

Chapter 6

Imps

English witchcraft literature abounds with narratives of imps or familiars, devils or demons in animal form who assist the witch in evildoings. The evil spirits could be transformed into domestic animals such as cats[1] and dogs,[2] other animals such as toads,[3] rats[4] and ferrets,[5] and even insects such as bees or flies.[6] Documented

---

[1] *The Examination and Confession of Certaine Wytches* (London: Willyam Powell, 1566), unnumbered, Avi by order; *The Witch of Wapping* ... (London: Th. Spring, 1652), pp. 6–7; *The Wonderful Discouerie of the Vvitchcrafts of Margaret and Phillip Flower* ... (London: Barnes, 1619), Fv; W.W., *A True and Iust Recorde* ... (London: Thomas Dawson, 1582), 2A3v; *A Rehearsall Both Straung and True* ... (London: J. Kingston, 1579), A5v.

[2] W., *A True and Iust Recorde*, B3, B7; H.F., *A True and Exact Relation* ... (London: Henry Overton and Benj. Allen, 1645), p. 10; John Stearne, *A Confirmation and Discovery of Witchcraft* (London: William Wilson, 1648), p. 31; *The Examination, Confession, Triall, and Execution, of Joane Williford, Joan Cariden, and Jane Hott* (London: J.G., 1645), pp. 1, 3; *Vvitchcrafts of Margaret and Phillip Flower*; Thomas Potts, *The Vvonderfull Discouerie of Witches in the Countie of Lancaster* (London: Iohn Barnes, 1613), B4v, C2, E3, F4, G2, H3v, H4v; I.D., *The Most Wonderfull and True Storie* ... (London: I.O., 1597), p. 26.

[3] Gilbert Geis and Ivan Bunn, *A Trial of Witches: A Seventeenth-Century Witchcraft Prosecution* (London: Routledge, 1997), pp. 50–51; Alexander Roberts, *A Treatise of Witchcraft*, 2nd edn (London: Samuel Man, 1616), p. 58; *The Apprehension and Confession of Three Notorious Witches* (London: E. Allde, 1589), A4v; *A Rehearsall Both Straung and True*, A5v; *A Detection of Damnable Driftes* ... (London: J. Kingston, 1579), A6 by order.

[4] *A Rehearsall Both Straung and True*, A6; John Davenport, *The Witches of Huntingdon* (London: Richard Clutterbuck, 1646), p. 9; *Vvitchcrafts of Margaret and Phillip Flower*, F4v; W.W., *A True and Iust Recorde*, 2A3v.

[5] *The Apprehension*, B–Bv.

[6] Geis and Bunn, *A Trial of Witches*, p. 75; William Drage, *A Physical Nosonomy* (London: J. Dover, 1664), p. 15; Stearne, *A Confirmation*, p. 26. There are also references to bears, Potts, *The Vvonderfull Discouerie of Witches*, E3v; Davenport, *The Witches of Huntingdon*, p. 3.; a hare, Potts, *The Vvonderfull Discouerie of Witches*, H3; an owl, *Vvitchcrafts of Margaret and Phillip Flower*, E4v–F; birds, *Vvitchcrafts of Margaret and Phillip Flower*, F4v; *A True and Impartial Relation* ... (London: Freeman Collins, 1682), pp. 11–12; an ape, *Vvitchcrafts of Margaret and Phillip Flower*, G; a mole, *The Lawes against Vvitches, and Conivration* (London: R.W., 1645), p. 7. On the various shapes of the devil's appearance, see also Roberts, *A Treatise of Witchcraft*, pp. 31–2; Stearne, *A Confirmation*, pp. 15, 26; *A True Relation of the Araignment of Eighteene Vvitches* (London: I.H., 1645), pp. 4–5; *Vvitchcrafts of Margaret and Phillip Flower*, B3–B3v.

instances of belief in animal-shaped demons date as early as the fourteenth century, yet the origins of the familiar folklore remain vague.[7] Witches often treated their animal accomplices as pets, naming them,[8] feeding them[9] and padding their sleeping spot.[10] Less often, the evil spirits took the shape of boys[11] or men (usually described as black).[12] In the likeness of a man, the devil was sometimes ugly[13] and sometimes an elegant gentleman[14] who appeared even 'in the likeness of a lawyer' or 'in the perfect shape of a Bishop'.[15] The human appearance was not always perfect, and sometimes the devilish identity was revealed by a pair of horns on the head,[16]

---

[7]   James Sharpe, 'The Witch's Familiar in Elizabethan England', in G.W. Bernard and S.J. Gunn (eds), *Authority and Consent in Tudor England* (Aldershot: Ashgate, 2002), pp. 227–9.

[8]   Some names expressed the evil nature of the imps, such as 'Sathan', 'Tormentor', 'Beelzebub' or 'Lucifer', *Certaine Wytches*, unnumbered, Avi by order; Edmund Bower, *Doctor Lamb Revived ...* (London: Richard Best and John Place, 1653), p. 6; Richard Bernard, *A Guide to Grand-Iury Men* (London: Ed. Blackmore, 1627), p. 113. Some imps had ordinary pets' names, such as 'Gille', 'Ginnie', *A Rehearsall Both Straung and True*, A5v, A6; 'Tyffin', 'Pygine', 'Iacke', W., *A True and Iust Recorde*, 2A3v; 'Robin', 'Iack', 'William', 'Puppet', W., *A True and Iust Recorde*, D5v; 'Iack' *and* 'Iyll', *The Apprehension*, A3; 'Pluck', 'Blew', 'Catch', 'White', 'Callico' and 'Hrdname', *The Most Strange and Admirable Discouerie of the Three Witches of Warboys* (London: Thomas Man, and Iohn Winington, 1593), M; 'Dicke' and 'Jude', W., *A True and Iust Recorde*, Cv.

[9]   W., *A True and Iust Recorde*, 2A5v–2A6, D6v.

[10]   George Gifford, *A Discourse of the Subtill Practises of Deuilles by Vvitches and Sorcerers* (London: Toby Cooke, 1587), G3.

[11]   Demdike was initiated into witchcraft by a spirit named Tibb in the shape of a boy with a half-brown and half-black coat. Potts, *The Vvonderfull Discouerie of Witches*, B2v.

[12]   Ibid., B4; *The Snare of the Devill Discovered ...* (London: Edward Thomas, 1658), p. 4; F., *A True and Exact Relation*, p. 11; Stearne, *A Confirmation*, p. 30; Davenport, *The Witches of Huntingdon*, A3; Roberts, *A Treatise of Witchcraft*, p. 46. There are two accounts of spirits in the appearance of women. One only did good. See *Vvitchcrafts of Margaret and Phillip Flower*, E3v–E4. The other was 'in the likenesse of a woman called *Jezabell*'. B. Misodaimon, *The Divels Delvsions ...* (London: Richard Williams Stationer, 1649), pp. 3–4.

[13]   Davenport, *The Witches of Huntingdon*, p. 13. A man 'in a ragged sute'. F., *A True and Exact Relation*, p. 33.

[14]   One of Hopkins' examinees described the devil 'like a tall, proper, black haired gentleman, a properer man then your selfe'. Stearne, *A Confirmation*, p. 15. According to another account, the suspect confessed that this proper gentleman wanted to have sex with her. F., *A True and Exact Relation*, p. 2. See also *A True and Impartial Relation*, p. 36.

[15]   *The Tryall and Examination of Mrs Joan Peterson* (London: G. Horton, 1652), title page, 5.

[16]   Roberts, *A Treatise of Witchcraft*, p. 47.

'whorce'[17] or 'hollow voice',[18] chilling touch[19] or cloven feet.[20] Pico della Mirandola observed that 'the Devil can create a nearly perfect facsimile of the human body but never can get the feet to come out right: God makes the feet come out *inversos et praeposteros* so that the people will know that they are human'.[21]

The intimacy between the witch and the imp was sometimes manifested by suckling of blood[22] or sexual contact.[23] The imps attended the witches on evil errands, executing their malefic plans, harming cattle[24] and even injuring and killing neighbours.[25] The imps were a distinct English cultural concept. Although it was also believed that spirits could assume human shape, and there are some accounts of sexual contact between the witch and her imps, the dominant cultural image of the imps was of demonic animal companions. This was very different from the Continental perception that concentrated on *incubi* and *succubi*, devils that assumed the shape of men and women, seduced humans and copulated with them as part of their initiation into witchcraft.[26]

---

[17]   Stearne, *A Confirmation*, p. 26.

[18]   *A True Relation of the Araignment of Eighteene Vvitches*, p. 7; Davenport, *The Witches of Huntingdon*, p. 13.

[19]   Bower, *Doctor Lamb Revived*, p. 10.

[20]   Roberts, *A Treatise of Witchcraft*, p. 57. One account describes a black man with 'ugly feet'. Davenport, *The Witches of Huntingdon*, p. 13. These ugly feet turned to cloven feet in the description of the witch hunter Stearne. Stearne, *A Confirmation*, p. 13.

[21]   Walter Stephens, *Demon Lovers: Witchcraft, Sex, and the Crisis of Belief* (Chicago: University of Chicago Press, 2002), pp. 87–8, 95.

[22]   *Certaine Wytches*, unnumbered, Avii by order; Drage, *A Physical Nosonomy*, p. 16; Stearne, *A Confirmation*, p. 26; Davenport, *The Witches of Huntingdon*, pp. 4, 10; *The Examination, Confession, Triall, and Execution, of Joane Williford*, pp. 3, 5; *Vvitchcrafts of Margaret and Phillip Flower*, F3, G; *Witches of Warboys*, Hv, H2; W.W., *A True and Iust Recorde*, 2A3v; *A Rehearsall Both Straung and True*, A5v, A6.

[23]   Stearne, *A Confirmation*, p. 15; *A True and Impartial Relation*, p. 36. The sucking is often described in erotic terms. One suspect confessed that something like a hedgehog sucked her regularly, 'and when it lay upon her breast she strucke it off with her hand, and that it was soft as a Cat'. *The Examination, Confession, Triall, and Execution, of Joane Williford*, p. 4. There are also reports of sucking of the suspects' 'private parts'. F., *A True and Exact Relation*, pp. 9, 18, 32.

[24]   W., *A True and Iust Recorde*, 2A8, B3; Potts, *The Vvonderfull Discouerie of Witches*, E3.

[25]   W., *A True and Iust Recorde*, B3, Cv; F., *A True and Exact Relation*, pp. 17, 33; *The Examination, Confession, Triall, and Execution, of Joane Williford*, pp. 3, 5; *The Lawes against Vvitches*, p. 8; *Vvitchcrafts of Margaret and Phillip Flower*, F2; Potts, *The Vvonderfull Discouerie of Witches*, F4, Gv, H3v, H4, Iv, I2.

[26]   Heinrich Kramer and James Sprenger, *Malleus Maleficarum*, trans. Montague Summers (Escondido, CA: Book Tree, 1486; reprint, 2000), pp. 21–31, 109–14.

By the act of 1604, to 'consult covenant with entertaine employ feed or rewarde any evill and wicked Spirit to or for any intent or purpose' was prohibited. The evil spirits, the English widely believed, were transformed into concrete physical forms. Presenting the demons in court as direct physical evidence could have been conclusive,[27] but there is no explanation why these hellish pets were never produced. On the Continent, during the same era of witch trials, trials against animals were conducted under both secular and ecclesiastical jurisdiction.[28] Despite the affinity between the animal trials and demonism, familiars were not brought to court as evidence in witch trials. The centrality of the imps in the English belief system notwithstanding, and despite the availability of the Continental model of trials of animals, imp narratives were delivered through testimonies only. Rosen noted that their beds and feeding dishes were solemnly produced, but the animals themselves always 'vanished away'.[29]

It was their elusive quality, Stephens suggested, that made the existence of imps irrefutable. Production of imps in court carried the risk of sceptical scorn and denial of any differences between them and regular animals, whereas 'any absence could be proposed as proof that a demon had *once* been present'.[30] Stephens' explanation, however, disregarded the fact that the devil's mark, evidence with similar probative difficulty, was widely used. Therefore, the question of why imps were not used as evidence remains. Perhaps the reason lay in a theological predicament. Had a real animal been brought to court, it would have implied that the devil had the power to create life, a power equal to that of God. Such a blasphemous insinuation was an intolerable contradiction of the Christian faith.[31] Therefore, considering the familiars to be mere illusory displays was theologically convenient. The author of a pamphlet published in 1612 emphasized:

> Deuils in their owne nature haue no bodily shape nor visible forme, it is moreouer against the Truth and against Piety to beléeue, that Deuils can create, or make bodies or change one body into another, for those things are proper to God.

---

[27]   In some accounts the dogs even spoke English! Potts, *The Vvonderfull Discouerie of Witches*, R4.

[28]   Esther Cohen, 'Law, Folklore and Animal Lore', *Past and Present*, no. 110 (1986): p. 17 and other locations.

[29]   Barbara Rosen (ed.), *Witchcraft, Stratford-Upon-Avon Library* (New York: Taplinger, 1972), p. 26.

[30]   Stephens, *Demon Lovers*, p. 104.

[31]   According to the *Malleus Maleficarum*, the devil had no power to create life or turn people into animals, but animals could be possessed by devils. Kramer and Sprenger, *Malleus Maleficarum*, pp. 28, 61, 65.

It followeth therefore that whensoeuer they appear in a visible form, it is no more but an apparition and counterfeit sh[o]w of a body, vnlesse a body be at any time lent them.[32]

In 1645 a pamphleteer explained that the imps were pure spirits, and, as such, 'cannot be seen by any bodily eye, or be deprehended by any outward sense'. However, 'as they do mix themselues with bodily substances', they can be perceived by the senses.[33]

Sometimes, it was believed, the spirits never assumed bodies, but remained formless entities. Such was the case of one suspect who, fearing a capital sentence, heard the voice of her spirit encouraging her to commit suicide, until 'at last she made good the Deuils word, and to preuent the Iustice of the Law, and to saue the hangman a labour, cut her owne throat'.[34]

The imps' spiritual composition enabled them to become invisible, to penetrate walls and to pay visits to their owner witches when they were being held in jail. In 1597 Alice Goodridge confessed that her familiar dog visited her at Darby jail.[35] Belief in the power of familiars to penetrate walls was also at the basis of the search method employed during the 1640s, when naked suspects were positioned on stools in a closed room in expectation of their familiars. Despite the intervals of invisibility, the familiars could generally be observed, heard and touched – not just by the witch or the victim, but by any bystander. These possibilities rendered the evidence of familiars a direct and concrete link to the crime. In this respect, evidence of familiars was distinguished from spectral evidence, visions of the witch experienced by the victims either in their fits or in their dreams. Such apparitions could not be observed by other witnesses or verified. Their evidential value was therefore problematic, and even those who approved of the use of spectral evidence did not regard it as sufficient basis for conviction, but merely grounds for suspicion.[36]

Because the imps could allegedly be seen by all, in a few cases, suspects were instructed to summon their spirits. Elizabeth Clarke, one of Hopkins' examinees,

---

[32] *The Witches of Northampton-Shire* (London: Arthur Iohnson, 1612), C3v.

[33] F., *A True and Exact Relation*, p. 4.

[34] *The Witches of Northampton-Shire*, C3.

[35] D., *The Most Wonderfull and True Storie*, p. 26; Stearne, *A Confirmation*.

[36] Stearne, *A Confirmation*, p. 39; Bernard, *A Guide to Grand-Iury Men*, pp. 207–8. The Salem trials are commonly known for an extensive use of spectral evidence, supposedly in reliance on the contemporary English law. However, it has been suggested that this is a much exaggerated myth and that suspects charged merely with spectral evidence were not even tried. Wendel D. Craker, 'Spectral Evidence, Non-Spectral Acts of Witchcraft, and Confession at Salem 1692', *The Historical Journal* 40, no. 2 (1997).

was asked to call her imps, and within half an hour there appeared 'a white thing in the likeness of a Cat'.[37] When Margaret Moone was asked to call her imps, she asked for bread and beer, put these in a circle and called her imps. After none appeared, she blamed her 'Devillish Daughters' for taking them.[38] Thus, relying on the cooperation of the suspect did not produce the desired evidence of imps. In some cases, prosecutors even offered to free the accused if they could cause the familiar to appear in court, either in corporeal form or by some supernatural sign.[39] The Queen's Attorney in the case against Agnes Waterhouse in 1566 challenged her to make her familiar appear immediately and, in return, she would be released from prison. But Agnes declined, stating that she had no power over him.[40] The offer to release the suspect if she could command her imps to appear was probably a trap to cause the suspect to further incriminate herself. It can only be surmised whether the Queen's Attorney would have made such a suggestion had he genuinely believed that an imp might have been fetched.

The imps raised the same stumbling block as the devil's mark – even if produced as evidence, it would have been impossible to accept them as proof unless a few theoretical presuppositions were accepted as well. To regard a dog as a demon, it would have to be assumed that demons could be transformed into dogs and that they could commit maleficence in the service of witches.

The literature about the distinction between natural and devil's marks, as the previous chapter illustrated, is vast. In comparison, there are very few references to the distinction between imps and natural animals. There are a few references to killing the imps as a diagnostic method. Flesh-and-blood animals could be killed, whereas imps could not. In the trial against Anne West, the court heard testimony about a man who passed her house around four in the morning and saw four little 'things' in the shape of black rabbits leaping and skipping about him. Having a good stick in his hand, he struck at them, intending to kill them but failed. He then resorted to wringing the neck of one of them, but the animal managed to escape. As he knew of a spring not far off, he tried to drown it, holding it quite a while under water to no avail, as 'it sprung out of the water up into the aire'.[41] This testimony was not delivered by the man himself, but as secondhand hearsay by Sir Thomas Bowes, who affirmed in court that he had heard the story from a 'very honest man ... whom he knew would not speake an untruth'.[42] Bowes' testimony demonstrated that belief in imps did not belong exclusively to the lower classes.

---

[37]   F., *A True and Exact Relation*, p. 3.

[38]   Ibid., p. 24.

[39]   Stephens, *Demon Lovers*, p. 100.

[40]   *Certaine Wytches*, Avii–Avii verso.

[41]   F., *A True and Exact Relation*, pp. 35–6.

[42]   Ibid., p. 35.

Gaule believed in witchcraft but attacked popular beliefs, including the test of trying to kill the imp, as superstitious and contradictory to the Gospel,[43] but further complicated the theory behind the test of killing the imp. He agreed that it was impossible to kill imps, as they were spirits made of air. However, he maintained that real animals, which were killable, could also be possessed by the spirit of the devil. Gaule supported the argument by saying that he heard witches confess that their dog or cat committed mischief against its will.[44]

Gaule was critical of the practices of witch hunters and suggested that, concerning imps, they should consider the following questions:

> Whether all Witches have their Imps or deale with Familiars? Whether a visible Impe be given upon an Invisible Compact? Whether the Impe workes as the Witches, or at the Devills Command or Instigation? How can a Familiar or Impe be discerned, if it never did any thing, but what (by nature, or Art) a Creature of that same kind, may stand in a Capacity to do? Who can flatly atest w[i]th a good Conscience, that this or that Dog, Rat, Mouse, &c. is the Witches Imp or Familiar?[45]

Gaule's discussion was rather exceptional. Most theologians did not confront the topic of imps directly. Perkins steered away from knotty complications and discussed the validity of 18 signs for the discovery of witchcraft. As already mentioned, he regarded the devil's mark as a presumption that warranted no more than examination. Perkins regarded only two proofs to be valid for conviction. One was the confession of the suspect, and the other was the testimony of two witnesses 'of good and honest report' deposing before the magistrate under oath and from their own knowledge either about known witchcraft practices of the suspect or about a league between the devil and the suspect. Perkins gave three instances of such testimony, including whether the suspect had contact with a familiar spirit in the likeness of a mouse, cat or some other visible creature,[46] and considered it good enough for conviction. He did not explain how this argument was compatible with the caution he showed toward the devil's mark, which was the imps' sucking spot. He also did not address the difficulty of discerning between real animals and imps or the other theological problems mentioned above.

---

[43] John Gaule, *Select Cases of Conscience Touching Vvitches and Vvitchcrafts* (London: Richard Clutterbuck, 1646), pp. 79–80.

[44] Ibid.

[45] Ibid., pp. 106–7.

[46] William Perkins, *A Discourse of the Damned Art of Witchcraft* (Cambridge, UK: Vniuersitie of Cambridge, 1608), pp. 213–14.

Unlike identifying the devil's mark, distinguishing natural from diabolic animals never became accepted expertise in England or on the Continent. Hopkins himself was reputed to own a greyhound.[47] Although he refined the discovery of devil's marks to an intricate skill, he offered no method of distinguishing imps from natural pets.

Without a means of distinguishing imps from natural animals, many things could be considered proof. The 'likeness of a rat' passing the suspect's jail cell in the dead of night was not a sign of bad hygiene, but rather of an imp.[48] The constant muttering of another suspect to herself indicated conversations with familiars and spirits.[49] The tortured postures of suspects stripped naked and positioned on stools for two or three days by Hopkins and Stearne signified that the imps had come to suck them.[50] The sceptical Hutchinson described testimony in a case in 1694 in which the witnesses testified about noticing a black and a white imp when peering through the suspect's window at night: 'the white imp believed to have been a Lock of Wool, taken out of her Basket to spin; and its Shadow, it is supposed, was the black one.'[51] Not bringing imps to court might have been the result of an additional theological misgiving – if these creatures were an embodiment of the devil, how was it possible to trust them as witnesses or evidence? In Hutchinson's words:

> Even good Spirits are no legal Evidence in our Courts. What Credit then can we give to the Devil's Words or Actions; or to the Words or Actions of those that are acted by him?[52]

Beliefs in familiars were popular in England well before anti-witchcraft statutes.[53] Ewen referred to a case in Yorkshire in 1510 in which familiars in the shape of bees sucked blood from John Steward, their owner.[54] Akin to the development of the devil's mark concept, the popular belief in imps was incorporated into the

---

[47] F., *A True and Exact Relation*, p. 3.

[48] *The Full and True Relation of the Tryal, Condemnation, and Execution of Ann Foster* (London: D.M., 1674), pp. 6–7. For another case in which such evidence was presented, see F., *A True and Exact Relation*, p. 21.

[49] *Strange Nevvs from Shadvvell* (London: E. Mallet, 1684), p. 1.

[50] *A True Relation of the Araignment of Eighteene Vvitches*, pp. 6–7.

[51] Francis Hutchinson, *An Historical Essay Concerning Witchcraft* (London: R. Knaplock and D. Midwinter, 1718), p. 44.

[52] Ibid., p. 54.

[53] James A. Sharpe, *Instruments of Darkness: Witchcraft in England 1550–1750* (London: Hamish Hamilton, 1996), p. 250, fn. 237.

[54] Cecil L'Estrange Ewen, *Witchcraft and Demonianism* (London: Heath, 1933), p. 73.

demonological concept, and imps were regarded as creatures given to the witch by the devil on bringing the covenant to a close.[55]

Joan Cunny, under examination, told about the initiation of the covenant with two spirits in the similitude of two black frogs. After she knelt in a circle she had made and said a prayer to invoke Satan, as she had been taught, the spirits (that she later named Jack and Jill) appeared and promised to render any service in return for her soul.[56] Old Demdike confessed that she had given her soul to a spirit in the shape of a boy who promised that in return 'she should have any thing that she would request'.[57] Her granddaughter described how, after many persuasions by her grandmother, she yielded to a covenant with the devil. Thereupon, a 'thing' that resembled a black dog appeared and spoke to her, requesting that she give him her soul and promising to give her the power to do anything she wanted. She was tempted, whereupon the black dog sat her down and sucked her breast.[58]

The services and favours of the familiars were a standard provision in the contract with the devil.[59] Chattox confessed that 'the Devill appeared unto her in the likenes of a Man, about midnight' and persuaded her to become his subject, give her soul to him and let him suck her blood. She also said she overheard another spirit, in the shape of a bitch, promise her friend Demdike 'that she should have Gould, Silver, and worldly Wealth, at her will'. The night ended with a banquet, which was probably as fancy as the poor old villager could imagine.

> And at the same time she saith, there was victuals, viz. Flesh, Butter, Cheese, Bread, and Drinke, and bidde them eate enough. And after their eating, the Devill called Fancie, and the other Spirit calling himselfe Tibbe, carried the remnant away: And she sayeth, that although they did eate, they were never the fuller, nor better for the same; and that at their said Banquet, the said

---

[55]   Clive Holmes, 'Popular Culture? Witches, Magistrates and Divines in Early Modern England', in S.L. Kaplan (ed.), *Understanding Popular Culture: Europe from the Middle Ages to the Nineteenth Century* (Berlin: Walter de Gruyter & Co., 1984), p. 98.

[56]   *The Apprehension*, A3.

[57]   Potts, *The Vvonderfull Discouerie of Witches*, B2v.

[58]   Ibid., R3v–R4.

[59]   *Vvitchcrafts of Margaret and Phillip Flower*, B3–B3v. For more examples of giving the soul to the devil in return for goods or services of the imps, see Potts, *The Vvonderfull Discouerie of Witches*, H3, I4v–K; *A True and Impartial Relation*, p. 36; *The Snare of the Devill Discovered*, p. 4; F., *A True and Exact Relation*, p. 10; Stearne, *A Confirmation*, p. 26; Davenport, *The Witches of Huntingdon*, pp. 9–11; *The Examination, Confession, Triall, and Execution, of Joane Williford*, p. 1; *The Lawes against Vvitches*, p. 7; *Vvitchcrafts of Margaret and Phillip Flower*, F4v; Roberts, *A Treatise of Witchcraft*, p. 46.

Spirits gave them light to see what they did, although they neyther had fire
nor Candle light; and that they were both shee Spirites, and Divels.[60]

The banquet, like the spirits, was not described as real. Viewing the ability of
the devil to create as limited might have been theologically convenient, but the
position that contact with the devil was imaginary was no less disturbing and
made the issue of proof even harder. The concept of the contract was absorbed
into the body of English imp beliefs, but other popular notions, including some
theologically unseemly elements, persisted. One such popular idea was that of
giving familiars to friends or relatives.[61]

Another popular notion was the view of witchcraft as a distorted mirror of
Catholicism, and one pamphlet linked imps with such inversion. James Device,
the grandson of Demdike, long reputed to be a witch, described how she asked
him to go to mass and receive communion, but rather than eating the bread,
deliver it to a 'thing' that would meet him on his way home. He did go but ate
the bread. On his way back, he met a 'thing' in the shape of a hare, who spoke
to him and asked him whether he had brought the bread as his grandmother
had requested. On hearing that he had not, the 'thing' threatened to tear him
to pieces. James said he thereupon crossed himself in a Catholic manner and
the 'thing' vanished.[62] This anecdote reflects the belief that witchcraft was
inimical to Catholicism (Demdike wanted James to get a consecrated Host
to be desecrated) and that Catholic rituals (such as crossing) could be used as
protection against demons. Both concepts were definitely disapproved of by
Puritan divines, but they remained popular.[63]

And indeed, such popular notions were criticized by the mainstream Anglicans.
A fine example is found in the pamphlet by Thomas Potts, which contained
detailed testimonies about encounters with familiars that were brought to prove
the suspects' crimes of witchcraft. One testimony was clearly denounced by Potts
as false. Fourteen-year-old Grace Sowerbutts complained that Jennet Bierley
appeared to her in human shape and then transformed herself into a black dog
that later appeared to her again and carried her to a barn, where she lay senseless.[64]
Potts deplored the testimony and claimed it was coached by a Catholic priest.

---

[60] Potts, *The Vvonderfull Discouerie of Witches*, B4. See also a parallel description, D3–D3v.

[61] W., *A True and Iust Recorde*, D5v; Davenport, *The Witches of Huntingdon*, p. 5; *The Apprehension*, A4v.

[62] Potts, *The Vvonderfull Discouerie of Witches*, H3.

[63] Keith Thomas, *Religion and the Decline of Magic* (New York: Charles Scribner's Sons, 1971), pp. 30, 199.

[64] Potts, *The Vvonderfull Discouerie of Witches*, K4v.

What he found missing from her story was a spirit: 'Yet in this discoverie, the Seminarie forgot to devise a Spirit for them.'[65] A black dog was not enough. The spirit, according to Potts, was therefore a necessary element for proof.

The belief in familiars was scorned by Reverend Henry Goodcole, a Puritan cleric and adamant believer in witchcraft. He opened a pamphlet with 'The Authors Apologie to the Christian Readers', in which he deplored:

> most base and false Ballets, which were sung at the time of our returning from the Witches execution. In them I was ashamed to see and heare such ridiculous fictions of her bewitching Corne on the ground, of a Ferret and an Owle dayly sporting before her, of the bewitched woman brayning her selfe, of the Spirits attending in the Prison: all which I knew to be fitter for an Ale-bench then for a relation of proceeding in Court of Iustice. And thereupon I wonder that such lewde Balletmongers should be suffered to creepe into the Printers presses and peoples eares.[66]

These harsh words were possibly the lip service Goodcole paid to his 'Christian readers'. Further reading reveals that when he himself interrogated Elizabeth Sawyer in jail, he asked her questions such as: 'In what shape would the Diuell come vnto you?' 'In what place of your body did the Diuell sucke of your bloud ... ?' 'Whether did you pull vp your coates or no when the Diuell came to sucke you?' 'How long would the time bee, that the Diuill would continue sucking of you, and whether did you endure any paine, the time that hee was sucking of you?' 'What was the meaning that the Diuell when hee came vnto you, would sometimes speake, and sometimes barke?'[67]

Other popular imp beliefs that thrived despite Puritan disapproval included the transformation of shapes,[68] nocturnal horrors[69] and pagan elements.[70] The imps could cause light or food to appear.[71] Another theologically unsettling element that persisted in popular perception was enjoyable erotic or sexual

---

[65]   Ibid., M3.

[66]   Henry Goodcole, *The Wonderfull Discouerie of Elizabeth Savvyer a Witch* (London: Vvilliam Butler, 1621), A3c.

[67]   Ibid., C2v–C3v.

[68]   From human to dog, see Potts, *The Vvonderfull Discouerie of Witches*, K4v, L.

[69]   Like the appearance of devils at midnight. *Vvitchcrafts of Margaret and Phillip Flower*, G; *The Tryall and Examination of Mrs Joan Peterson*, p. 5.

[70]   Like a familiar that sucked the witch always 'about the change and full of the Moone'. *Vvitchcrafts of Margaret and Phillip Flower*, F2v.

[71]   Potts, *The Vvonderfull Discouerie of Witches*, B4, D3–D3V; *The Tryall and Examination of Mrs Joan Peterson*, p. 5.

contact with imps. Although demonologists emphasized the icy feeling and pain caused by contact with the devil, some English texts mentioned suspects who expressed sensations of pleasure at the devil's touch.[72]

The variety of opinions about imp evidence resembled those surrounding the devil's mark. Physicians led the radical side, completely rejecting imp narratives as evidence. Webster denied the main propositions of the familiars' existence in a crystal-clear paragraph.

> We shall here once again repeat the four Particulars, which we are about to confute, which are these. 1. That the Devil doth not make a visible or corporeal League and Covenant with the supposed Witches. 2. That he doth not suck upon their bodies. 3. That he hath not carnal Copulation with them. 4. That they are not really changed into Cats, Dogs, Wolves, or the like.[73]

Ady continued to attack the scriptural basis of the theories of imps with rhetorical questions.

> Where is it written, that Witches have Imps sucking of their bodies? ... Where is it written, that Witches have biggs for Imps to suck on?[74]

The divines found themselves in an awkward position because of the prominence of imp narratives and the theological difficulties they presented. Many popular elements challenged Christian dogma: Can the devil, just like God, create life? If the imp was made of spirit (as the theologians, who denied that the devil had the ability to create real life, claimed), why did the witches feed them? Why did they nurse them with blood? If the imps were an embodiment of supernatural spirits, what were they doing at the command of poor, old and often demented women? The dissonance between theological principles and popular beliefs left room for doubt and scepticism.[75]

---

[72]   Ann Usher felt '2 things like butterflies in her secret p[ar]tes'. Jim Sharpe, 'The Devil in East Anglia', in Jonathan Barry, Marianne Hester and Gareth Roberts (eds), *Witchcraft in Early Modern Europe* (Cambridge, UK: Cambridge University Press, 1996), p. 248. Jane Holt felt pain when the familiar sucked her at night, but 'when it lay upon her breast she strucke it off with her hand, and that it was soft as a Cat'. *The Examination, Confession, Triall, and Execution, of Joane Williford*, p. 4. Joan Cariden was sucked regularly by the devil, and 'it was no paine to her'. Ibid., p. 3. Neither did Elizabeth Harris nor Elizabeth Sawyer feel any pain. Ibid., p. 5; Goodcole, *The Wonderfull Discouerie of Elizabeth Sawyer*, C3v.

[73]   John Webster, *The Displaying of Supposed Witchcraft* (London: J.M., 1677), p. 63.

[74]   Thomas Ady, *A Candle in the Dark* (London: Robert Ibbitson, 1655), p. 6.

[75]   Sharpe, *Instruments of Darkness*, p. 71; Stuart Clark, *Thinking with Demons: The Idea of Witchcraft in Early Modern Europe* (Oxford: Oxford University Press, 1997), p. 451.

Glanvill, not a Puritan, but a neo-Platonist philosopher, a Fellow of the Royal Society and Chaplain in Ordinary to King Charles II,[76] tried to resolve the dissonance. When discussing the suckling of imps, he said: 'We may conjecture at some things that may render it less *improbable*'.[77] Glanvill tried to prove witchcraft with the then-existing theories about nature. He explained:

> For some have thought that the Genii (whom both the Platonical and Christian Antiquity thought embodied) are recreated by the reeks and vapours of humane bloud and the spirits that derive from them. Which supposal ... is not unlikely, every thing being refresh'd and nourish'd by its like. And that they are not perfectly abstract from all body and matter ... That the Familar doth not onely suck the Witch but in the action infuseth some poisonous ferment into her, which gives her imagination and spirits a magical tincture, whereby they become mischievously influential.[78]

In response to the argument that it was unlikely that the devil would choose to serve silly old women, Glanvill said it was possible and that ''tis not impossible that the *Familiars* of *Witches* are a *servile* kind of *spirits*, of a very *inferiour* constitution and nature, and none of those that were once of the highest *Hierarchy*, now degenerated into the spirits we call *Devils*'.[79]

Gifford, an Essex Protestant clergyman, supported the theory that only God could create real bodies and the invisible devils could only create an illusion of a body.[80] For him, the notion of spirits helped to solve another theological difficulty – how poor old women came to possess supernatural powers. It was not the women who were empowered, but their spirits.[81] Yet, Gifford was well aware of the sceptical argument that belief in familiars was an illusion created by the devil, who strove to lead ignorant people into many grievous sins.[82] Writing more than a hundred years later, Hutchinson, who published his treatise in 1718, no longer felt compelled to bring popular concepts into accord with

---

[76] George Lyman Kittredge, *Witchcraft in Old and New England* (Cambridge, MA: Harvard University Press, 1929), p. 335.

[77] Joseph Glanvill, *A Philosophical Endeavour* (London: James Collins, 1666), p. 17.

[78] Ibid., pp. 17–18.

[79] Ibid., p. 21.

[80] Gifford, *A Discourse of the Subtill Practises of Deuilles*, E.

[81] Ibid., G3.

[82] George Gifford, *A Dialogue Concerning Witches and Witchcraftes* (London: Tobie Cooke and Mihil, 1593), B4v–C.

Christian dogma. Hutchinson's condescending tone toward imp narratives was unmistakable. They were nothing but 'vulgar Opinion'.[83]

Legal scholars were less bothered by theological challenges than clerics, and their writings reflected easier assimilation of imp narratives. It seems that at the local level, JPs examined suspects about familiars early on. Already in our first witchcraft case (1566), John Walsh, the suspect, was asked whether he had a familiar.[84] In 1618 Michael Dalton provided evidential rules based on the Lancaster precedent from 1612, including, first, that witches ordinarily had a familiar or spirit that appeared to them, and, second, that this familiar sucked from a growth or place on their body.[85]

Bernard accepted the concept that Satan awarded the witches at least one familiar spirit on establishing the covenant. Bernard cited various previous cases in which testimonies about imps were heard.[86] The devil's mark was the sign of the covenant with the devil.[87] Bernard asserted that witches had familiars but did not specify how to prove it.[88] His views were repeated by a subsequent legal writer who tried to supplement them with more practical examples (such as evidence of suspects' being heard calling on their spirits, talking to them, offering them to others, or being seen with them or feeding them).[89] These suggestions, however, did not solve the difficulty of distinguishing between a real pet and an imp. There was a huge gap between the volume of the numerous imp narratives, relayed mostly by suspects and accusers in their depositions, and the scanty discussion of the subject by learned scholars. Similar to the devil's mark, the imp narratives could not serve as direct physical evidence. A number of presuppositions were essential. In addition, the narratives posed theological difficulties. The evidence of imps, like the devil's mark, the ritual artefacts and the objects produced in corroboration of the impossible, proved to be merely a misleading facade of direct evidence.

The epistemology underlying the variety of physical evidence was not necessarily cogent. The proofs and the logic behind them varied. Thus, for example, although an intricate system of differentiation between natural and diabolical marks was developed, a method of distinction between imps and real animals was not. However, it is possible to generalize that the evidential dispositions of the social actors were to a great extent affiliated with their social

---

[83]   Hutchinson, *An Historical Essay*, p. 11.

[84]   *The Examination of John Walsh* (London: Iohn Awdely, 1566), Aiiii, Av–verso.

[85]   Michael Dalton, *The Countrey Iustice* (London: Societie of Stationers, 1618), p. 243.

[86]   Bernard, *A Guide to Grand-Iury Men*, pp. 112–13.

[87]   Ibid., pp. 115–16.

[88]   Ibid., p. 217.

[89]   *The Lawes against Vvitches*, p. 4.

identity, and their professional affiliation was a significant factor. Physical evidence is typically characterized as direct, simple and, therefore, highly convincing. But this study concerning the legal conundrums presented by the witchcraft phenomenon illustrates that even physical evidence is neither simple nor direct, but rather socially constructed.

Chapter 7

The Swimming Test

Figure 7.1 The swimming of a witch. Title page from *Vvitches Apprehended, Examined and Executed ...* (London: Edward Marchant, 1613). [Call # 25872] Reproduced by permission of the Huntington Library, San Marino, California.

Lacking direct physical evidence to prove witchcraft, contemporaries had to rely on other methods for the discovery of witches The three main remaining evidential possibilities were supernatural signs, circumstantial evidence and testimonies.

When Judge Hale presented the dilemma before the jury at Bury St Edmunds Assizes, he 'desired them, strictly to observe their Evidence; and desired the great God of Heaven to direct their Hearts in this weighty thing they had in hand'.[1] His statement, of course, should not be interpreted literally as a call for the use of supernatural means, but as an acknowledgment of human inferiority in discovering the truth. In addition to strict observance of the evidence, this experienced judge called on the help of God. Before the ordeals were abolished in 1215, guilt or innocence was proved, so the contemporaries believed, by the hand of God. Although determination of criminal proceedings was transferred to human hands, in cases of witchcraft, unlike other crimes, supernatural signs of guilt were still widely sought, even centuries after the abandonment of the ordeals.

The most famous method was the swimming test of witches, but other supernatural methods or signs were the inability of the witch to shed tears or the causing of the witch to appear by burning an object. The early modern cultural toolbox included magical means and supernatural signs that both cured the bewitched and discovered witchcraft. Scratching of the suspect by the victim, for example, was a technique aimed at seeking relief of the symptoms but also at ascertaining the identity of a witch. Similarly, healing of the victims subsequent to the suspect's arrest or conviction was a reassuring sign. The burning of an allegedly bewitched cow annulled the bewitchment. Since the witch was allegedly compelled to appear if the disease had been caused by bewitchment, it also assisted in finding out whether the cattle were bewitched or naturally sick.

Supernatural signs enjoyed popularity, but they were not part of the official procedure. In some instances, those ways of proof were specifically denounced as illegal, and there was much controversy around their use. The chief supernatural method for the discovery of witches was the swimming test. The ordeal by swimming, *judicium aquae frigidae*, was mentioned in English laws and decrees as early as the tenth century.[2] According to these texts, the swimming test was used in cases of theft, adultery, homicide and witchcraft. The suspects were cast into the water. If they sank, they were innocent, and if they floated, they were guilty. There were formal rules regarding the size of the pond and the manner of tying the suspects before throwing them into the water.[3] In the thirteenth century the ordeals became illegal in England and were abandoned.[4] Despite this fact, the seventeenth century witnessed a resurgence of the swimming test

---

[1]   *A Tryal of Witches* ... (London: William Shrewsbery, 1682), p. 56.

[2]   In the laws of Æthelstan (ca. AD 930) and Æthelred (ca. 1000), laws of William the Conqueror (ca. 1100), the Assize of Clarendon (1166), the Assize of Northampton (1176) and borough charters of 1194 and 1207. George Lyman Kittredge, *Witchcraft in Old and New England* (Cambridge, MA: Harvard University Press, 1929), p. 233.

[3]   Ibid., pp. 233–4.

[4]   Subsequent to the fourth Lateran Council of 1215 and the abolition by Henry III in 1219.

only in witchcraft cases. The revival of the swimming test cannot be accounted for by the enactment of anti-witchcraft legislation, as the re-emergence was subsequent to the statutes of 1542, 1563 and 1604. Despite its illegality and a lack of ecclesiastical backing, the practice gained popularity. It took place at the fringes of the official proceedings at the pre-trial stage and was usually conducted by fellow villagers trying to bolster the case against the suspect.

The test was at the centre of a debate about its validity and its moral and religious adequateness. The approach toward the test was both class- and profession-related. Members of the elite were generally opposed to it, though it was popular with the lower classes, while the middling sort was in a somewhat ambivalent position. The middling sort was active in the reconstruction of the swimming test as an experiment, a strategy that made it easier to cope with the dissonance between the two extreme positions. Professional affiliation shaped the types of arguments the elite used against the test. Physicians emphasized natural explanations, clergymen focused on its religious inadequacy and judges deplored its illegality.

Three early and significant treatises that discussed the test and the theory behind it were Reginald Scot's *Discouerie of Witchcraft*, James I's *Daemonologie* and William Perkins' *A Discourse of the Damned Art of Witchcraft*.[5] The first accounts of actual cases of swimming of witches in early modern England were two pamphlets from 1612 and 1613.[6] It seems that the test was most widely used at the time of the Hopkins witch hunt of the 1640s.[7] The practice persisted, although some of its performers were eventually convicted for assault and even murder (in case the ordeal had ended with the drowning of the suspect). There is evidence that swimming continued even after the repeal of the anti-witchcraft act in 1736 until almost the end of the nineteenth century.[8]

The resurrection of the test in witchcraft cases in seventeenth-century England, about four centuries after the abolition of the ordeal system, has puzzled historians, but no satisfactory explanation has yet been offered. Holmes pointed to the functional aspect of this culturally embedded practice as a tension-

---

[5]   Reginald Scot, *The Discouerie of Witchcraft* (London: William Brome, 1584); James I, *Daemonologie* (Edinburgh: Robert Walde-graue, 1597); William Perkins, *A Discourse of the Damned Art of Witchcraft* (Cambridge, UK: Vniuersitie of Cambridge, 1608).

[6]   *The Witches of Northampton-Shire* (London: Arthur Iohnson, 1612); *Vvitches Apprehended* ... (London: Edward Marchant, 1613).

[7]   Clive Holmes, 'Popular Culture? Witches, Magistrates and Divines in Early Modern England', in S.L. Kaplan (ed.), *Understanding Popular Culture: Europe from the Middle Ages to the Nineteenth Century* (Berlin: Walter de Gruyter & Co., 1984), p. 104.

[8]   Kittredge, *Witchcraft in Old and New England*, p. 236.

relieving device,[9] but it is not clear why tensions were relieved in this particular manner. Continental influence was not ruled out.[10] Rosen and Gaskill suggested that in the latter part of the seventeenth century, as the judicial system became reluctant to prosecute witchcraft cases, private persons found informal violence or the swimming test to be an alternative solution.[11] That may be true, but it does not explain the flourishing of the test in the earlier part of the seventeenth century. Pihlajamäki dedicated a whole paper to the mystery of the ordeal's revival and concluded that it was mostly used to cross the evidential threshold needed for the application of torture. He assumed that swimming was seldom used in England because its legal system avoided torture and let jurors evaluate the evidence.[12] However, although there might have been more swimming tests in Germany, the practice was definitely not rare in England.[13] Clark linked the revival to the nature of witchcraft as an opaque crime and to its theological context. Evidence 'of a supernatural or quasi-miraculous character' matched the nature of the crime.[14] James I's approval of the swimming test was also mentioned as a factor that encouraged actual implementation.[15] In his *Daemonologie*, James valued the test as 'good helpe':[16]

> so it appears that God hath appoynted (for a super-naturall signe of the monstruous impietie of the Witches) that the water shal refuse to receiue them in her bosom, that haue shaken off them the sacred Water of Baptisme, and wilfullie refused the benefite thereof.[17]

---

[9]   Holmes, 'Popular Culture?' p. 105.

[10]   Kittredge, *Witchcraft in Old and New England*, p. 235; Heikki Pihlajamäki, '"Swimming the Witch, Pricking for the Devil's Mark": Ordeals in the Early Modern Witchcraft Trials', *Journal of Legal History* 21, no. 2 (2000): p. 46; James A. Sharpe, *Instruments of Darkness: Witchcraft in England 1550–1750* (London: Hamish Hamilton, 1996), p. 218.

[11]   Barbara Rosen (ed.), *Witchcraft, Stratford-Upon-Avon Library* (New York: Taplinger, 1972), p. 29; Malcolm Gaskill, *Crime and Mentalities in Early Modern England* (Cambridge: Cambridge University Press, 2000), p. 118.

[12]   Pihlajamäki, 'Swimming the Witch', p. 52.

[13]   Sharpe, *Instruments of Darkness*, pp. 218–19.

[14]   Stuart Clark, *Thinking with Demons: The Idea of Witchcraft in Early Modern Europe* (Oxford: Oxford University Press, 1997), pp. 589–90.

[15]   Sharpe, *Instruments of Darkness*, p. 218.

[16]   The other kinds of evidence that James I approved were spectral evidence, reputation and the devil's mark. James I, *Daemonologie*, p. 80.

[17]   Ibid., p. 81.

James wrote *Daemonologie* as James VI of Scotland, before ascending to the English throne in 1603. The book expressed his theological views and clearly did not reflect English law. As the king of England, James I took no steps to encourage the implementation of the test. On the contrary, he was not the witch hunter one might have expected as the author of *Daemonologie*, but a cautious fact-finder and the exposer of a few fabricated bewitchments.

Still, James' words echoed in subsequent pamphlets. The pamphlet of 1612 that gave the first account of swimming described how Arthur Bill, a man with a bad reputation as a witch and who was suspected of killing, was thrown into the pond with his parents:

> The Iustices and other officers (thereby purposing to trie the said Arthur by
> *an experiment that (many thinke) neuer failes*) caused them all to bee bound,
> and their Thumbes and great Toes to bée tied acrosse, and so threw the father,
> mother and sonne, and none of them sunke, but all floated vpon the water.[18]

The author then repeated the arguments of James (without due credit) and declared the swimming test, together with the devil's mark, 'more certaine' signs of witchcraft, although his statements were softened by expressions such as 'mee thinke'. Witches were rejected by the water that signified the holiness of baptism and therefore were discovered with the help of God.

Yet, the logic of the author seemed to be flawed, considering the following events he described:

> These thrée, the Father, Mother and Sonne, beeing thus séene floating vpon the
> water, the suspition that was before not well grounded, was now confirmed:
> Whereupon the said Arthur Bill beeing the principall or (I thinke) the onely
> Actor in this Tragedy, was apprehended and sent to Northampton gaole.[19]

The questions remain that, if all three members of the family floated, why the case was pursued against Arthur Bill alone, and if the parents floated as well, why the author saw Arthur Bill as the principal, and even only, perpetrator. James VI & I's rationale was presented by the author as a hypothesis that could be empirically tested, as 'an experiment that (many thinke) neuer failes'. A sense of dissonance is created because the identical result of the experiment for all three subjects (all three floated) did not lead the author to an identical conclusion (that all three were guilty).

---

[18] *The Witches of Northampton-Shire*, C2. Emphasis added.
[19] Ibid., C2–C2v.

Despite the inconsistency, this case is notable because the supernatural ordeal-type rationale (reliance on divine inscrutable determination) was moulded into a template of an empiricist experiment. It is, in my view, this reframing of the rationale behind the swimming test that contributed to its revival in the seventeenth century. The idea that supernatural presuppositions could be tested empirically was a bridge between old and new concepts of knowledge about the world and justice.

It should be noted that in Bill Arthur's case, it was the justices 'and other officers' who ordered the swimming test. The typical scenario, however, was for neighbours to perform the test before taking the suspect to the JP. Such was the case recorded in *Witches Apprehended*. The full title included the promise '*With a Strange and Most True Triall How to Know Whether a Woman Be a Witch or Not*', and an illustration of the swimming test appeared on the title page.[20] The detailed description of the test made the pamphlet a practical manual for swimming witches.[21] The pamphlet tells the story of Mr Enger, a local gentleman who suspected Mary Sutton and her mother of killing his cattle, bewitching his servant and killing his seven-year-old son. His friend advised him to swim the suspect, saying 'I have seene it often tried in the North countrey'.[22] The friend suggested a three-step procedure. First, swim the suspects, stripped to their undergarments with their arms tied and a rope under their waist so they could be pulled out of the water in case of drowning. Second, if the suspect floats, have her searched by women for the devil's mark. Third, if such marks are found, swim her again, this time with her hands and feet tied diagonally.[23] The friend's advice was followed, and next morning Sutton was forcibly taken by Mr Enger and his men to be swum. She was cast into the water, but 'shee sunke some two foote into the water with a fall, but rose againe, and floated upon the water like a planke'. Afterward she was searched by women that Mr Enger had ready for the task. The women found suspicious signs on her body, and Mary Sutton was thrown to the water again, this time with her thumbs tied to her toes. Unfortunately, she 'sunke not at all, but sitting upon the water, turned round about like a wheele, or as that

---

[20]   *Vvitches Apprehended*, title page. Reproduced by permission of the Huntington Library, San Marino, California.

[21]   Marion Gibson (ed.), *Early Modern Witches: Witchcraft Cases in Contemporary Writing* (London: Routledge, 2000), p. 266.

[22]   *Vvitches Apprehended*, C2v. Gibson remarks, 'How much the "friend" was a real person, and how much a literary construct, is unsure. As in *The Witches of Northamptonshire* (1612) the process of swimming a witch was presented in print in the previous year as occurring in the north Midlands, and there might be a connection here.' Gibson (ed.), *Early Modern Witches*, p. 274, fn. 216.

[23]   W.W., *A True and Iust Recorde ...* (London: Thomas Dawson, 1582), C2–C2v.

which commonly we call a whrilpoole'. The men, who were holding the rope on both sides, persisted in their efforts, 'tossing her up and downe to make her sinke, but could not'.[24] The swimming test was followed by questioning. Only on the suspect's insistence on her innocence was she carried to a justice.[25] It is notable that the swimming test in this leading case was not a spontaneous eruption of mob justice, but seems to be a carefully planned and prearranged experiment composed of orderly and predetermined stages and orchestrated by gentlemen.

The swimming test persisted despite fierce attacks on it by the judiciary and clergy. William Perkins listed the test with other insufficient proofs of witchcraft. He was very clear in his denial of James VI & I's rationale.

> And yet to iustifie the casting of a Witch into the water, it is alledged, that hauing made a couenant with the deuill, shee hath renounced her Baptisme, and hereupon there growes an Antipathie between her, and water.

> Ans. This allegation serues to no purpose: *for all water is not the water of Baptisme*, but that onely which is vsed in the very act of Baptisme, and not before nor after. The element out of the vse of the Scrament, is no Sacrament, but returnes again to his common vse.[26]

The treatise was published posthumously, but it definitely took courage on the part of the publisher to publish it while James still sat on the English throne. The fact that the publication was not censored can perhaps demonstrate that, as a king, James did not try to enforce the opinions he himself had expressed years before in his *Daemonologie*.

Filmer, writing a treatise aimed to refute Perkins and demonstrate the futility of his signs for the discovery of witches, regarded Perkins' discussion of the swimming test as a direct refutation of James. Filmer stressed that Perkins 'condemnes point blanke King James's judgment as favouring of Witch-craft in allowing the triall of a Witch by swimming as a principall proofe'.[27] As Filmer's

---

[24] Ibid., C3.

[25] An example of a very spontaneous swimming test is the case of Sarah Griffeth, who was suspected by one 'good jolly fellow' of bewitching him. Unfortunately for her, she met him down by the river, accompanied by two friends. One friend said: 'Let us toss her into the river, for I have heard that if she swims this a certain sign of a witch.' Indeed, Sarah Griffeth was subsequently swum. Thomas Greenwel, *A Full and True Account* ... (London: H. Hills, 1704).

[26] Perkins, *Damned Art*, p. 208. Emphasis added.

[27] Sir Robert Filmer, *An Advertisement to the Jury-Men of England, Touching Witches* (London: Richard Royston, 1653), p. 11.

treatise was an attack against Perkins, it was rhetorically convenient for him to portray Perkins as critical of the king, although he himself also opposed the swimming test. Filmer quoted Perkins, who considered the swimming test to be among the 'lesse sufficient' proofs: '*so far from being sufficient, that some of them, if not all are after a sort practices of witch-craft, having no power by Gods Ordinance*.'[28] This argument, Filmer contended, should have led Perkins to reject the devil's mark, rather than consider it a certain proof, as it was not ordained by God as well.

Cotta, like Perkins, rejected James VI & I's rationale for the test, but for other reasons. In his view, the practice was vulgar:

> IT is vulgarly credited, that the casting of supposed Witches bound into the water, and the water refusing or not suffering them to sinke within her bosome or bowels, is an infallible detection that such are Witches.[29]

Cotta ruled out the possibility that the water test was a miracle preformed by God.[30] He denied James' rationale that the holy baptism water rejected the witch and rhetorically wondered why, if this reasoning was so sound, bread and wine, being elements in the sacrament of the Eucharist, should not likewise be observed to turn back or fly away from the throats and mouths of witches.[31]

Cotta tried to apply the rationale attributed to a single phenomenon to a number of similar cases to determine whether the same rationale could be found. Such examination of hypotheses characterized the emerging empiricist logic. Cotta concluded that if there had been any miraculous aspects in the swimming test, they were more likely to be the work of the devil than of God.

Cotta explained that swimming was not a natural test, as nature cannot distinguish between good and wicked persons.[32] He denied that it was an empirical experiment that could prove or refute the suspicion of witchcraft, as the laws of nature had standard manifestations. Therefore, the same experiment should always yield the same results. The swimming test was not such an experiment. It sometimes succeeded and occasionally failed in discovering a witch. It was not ordinary, necessary, certain or infallible. These qualities, according to Cotta, characterized experiments of natural facts.[33] The test was not established by divine or human law or reason and therefore could not be

---

28   Ibid.
29   John Cotta, *The Triall of Vvitch-Craft* (London: Samuel Rand, 1616), p. 104.
30   Ibid., pp. 108–10.
31   Ibid., p. 108.
32   Ibid., p. 105.
33   Ibid., p. 106.

relied on as a certain proof. Thus the conclusion was 'in no true iudgement or iustice to bee trusted or credited'.[34] The illegal use of the test by private persons further proved this point:

> How farre our vulgar tryall of Witches, by the supposed miraculous indication and detection of them by the water, is different from this care or respect, this equitie, religion, or humanitie, common practice doth openly declare, when without allowance of any law, or respect of common ciuilitie, euery priuate, rash, and turbulent person, vpon his owne surmise of a Witch, dare barbarously vndertake by vnciuill force, and lawlesse violence, to cast poore people bound into the water, & there deteine them, for their owne vaine and foolish lusts, without sense, or care of the shameful wrong, or iniury, which may befall oft-times innocents thereby.[35]

The illegality and cruelty of private persons taking the law into their own hands was inexcusable, and undoubtedly 'rusticall, barbarous, and rude'.[36]

Such an adamant position against the swimming test was not only taken by Cotta, but was also clearly voiced by members of the clergy. Richard Bernard referred to the swimming of Mary Sutton in *Witches Apprehended* as an example of the erroneous opinion of 'some' that it was legal to try suspects by water. He also agreed with Cotta's arguments about the unlawfulness of the trial.[37] In Bernard's opinion, the test reflected the presumption of 'an adulterous, and vnbeleeuing generation' that demanded miraculous signs from God without warrant.[38]

Even someone like Thomas Cooper, a cleric who propagated rigorous prosecution of witches, came out most clearly against the swimming test. He viewed it as one of the '*deceitfull and Satanicall experiments*, to confirme her former detection of the *Witch*'.[39] Like Cotta, Cooper attributed the test to superstitious people. But unlike Cotta, he believed in the validity of the test and that 'the Bad Witch may bee detected by these meanes'. The reason for his objection was religious – the test was un-Christian, a practice that caused

---

Ibid., p. 107.

[35]   Ibid., p. 111.

[36]   Ibid.

[37]   Richard Bernard, *A Guide to Grand-Iury Men* (London: Ed. Blackmore, 1627), pp. 214–15.

[38]   Ibid., p. 215.

[39]   The others being '*sticking of needles, or bodkins, under the stoole where she sits, burning of the thing bewitched, &c.*'. Thomas Cooper, *The Mystery of Witch-Craft* (London: Nicholas Okes, 1617), p. 272.

its performers to 'deeplier engage their soules vnto the power and malice of Satan'.[40] His conclusion was clear: neither should anyone use the test for the discovery of a witch, nor should any magistrate allow it. He discussed the test in a section titled 'unlawful means'. However, he believed that the illegality of the test was a consequence of its un-Christianity, which was the major reason for eschewing the practice.

There seems to be a contradiction in Cooper's approach. On the one hand, he accepted the validity of the test as a method for the discovery of witches, while on the other, he believed that the devil could frustrate discovery by creating deceitful impressions and thus confirm the wrong conceit of superstitious people.

Gaule[41] attacked the prosecution of witches by 'common people' and the witch hunt led by Hopkins. Gaule clearly rejected the swimming test as 'unwarrantable'.[42] In 1645, Matthew Hopkins and John Stearne used the test extensively during a series of witch trials they led. This practice was put to an end by the assize judges when they took control of the proceedings.[43] Stearne admitted to using the swimming test but justified himself and Hopkins by pointing out that the tests took place during a short period, from March to May, 'at such time of the yeare as when none tooke any harme by it'. He explained that suspects were swum only on finding marks on their bodies. The swimming test was voluntary, 'neither did I ever doe it but upon their owne request', and at the suspects' desire to clear themselves. In addition, Stearne claimed that the tests were not used as evidence against any of the suspects and that the practice came to a halt once Judge Corbolt forbade it in mid-August and the divines determined it to be unlawful.[44] Yet, Stearne clarified that, although he had to relinquish the test once it was pronounced illegal, he still thought it was effective and 'that there is something in swimming (if lawfull)'.[45]

According to a pamphlet from 1645, Joan Willoford and Jane Hott declared their innocence and challenged their examiners with confidence that they would undoubtedly sink should they be thrown into the water.[46] Hott was even willing

---

[40]   Ibid., p. 273.

[41]   Sharpe, *Instruments of Darkness*, pp. 141–2.

[42]   John Gaule, *Select Cases of Conscience Touching Vvitches and Vvitchcrafts* (London: Richard Clutterbuck, 1646), p. 76.

[43]   Sharpe, *Instruments of Darkness*, p. 218.

[44]   John Stearne, *A Confirmation and Discovery of Witchcraft* (London: William Wilson, 1648), p. 18.

[45]   Ibid., pp. 18–19.

[46]   *The Examination, Confession, Triall, and Execution, of Joane Williford, Joan Cariden, and Jane Hott* (London: J.G., 1645), pp. 2, 4.

to lay a bet with one gentleman, 'twenty shillings to one', that she would sink. The texts, of course, are selective, and we cannot know whether the suspects actually initiated their own swimming test or whether coercion or persuasion had preceded it. The emphasis on the voluntary nature of the test was directed at countering the allegations against its sinful and unlawful nature. It shifted moral and legal responsibility from the shoulders of the examiners to those of the suspect, who should be blamed for additional wrongdoing. Such a presentation of the events might have shielded the witch hunters who performed the test from possible legal proceedings for assault or murder.[47]

Trying to justify himself, Stearne gave an example of one swimming case that in his opinion proved its importance, because the suspect was previously searched two or three times but no suspicious marks were found. One of the interesting details was that, before throwing the suspect into the water, 'they had formerly cast a freeman in, tyed after the same manner'.[48] The ducking of an innocent man as a control demonstrated the construction of the test as an experiment (rather than an ordeal calling for a sign from God). Such construction revealed an implicit concurrence with the rational prerequisites for an experiment as set forth by Cotta, namely, that similar conditions and procedure should always lead to the same result. Therefore, when the conditions of the experiment were identical (same pond, both subjects tied in the same manner), but one man clearly innocent, the expectation would be to see the sinking of the innocent one and the floating of a guilty suspect.[49] It is also significant that Stearne and Hopkins, who tried to bolster their image as professional witch finders, chose to construct the swimming test as an experiment. In doing so, they probably sought public legitimization. They were both social agents who disseminated the method during a relatively intense period of prosecution.

Thomas Ady jeered at the idea of the test as an experiment. He wrote that objective appearance was 'a meer Jugling delusion to blinde peoples eyes', as the test could be manipulated in various ways. The men holding the rope under

---

[47] Macfarlane suggested that the voluntary swimming test had a cathartic function. His explanation, however, assumed that the swimming test was indeed voluntary, and not a result of pressures, manipulation or a calculated tactic of defence. Alan Macfarlane, *Witchcraft in Tudor and Stuart England: A Regional and Comparative Study* (New York: Harper & Row, 1970), p. 141. Thomas believed that some suspects could have been eager to prove their innocence. Yet, it would be naive to believe that this was always the case. Keith Thomas, *Religion and the Decline of Magic* (New York: Charles Scribner's Sons, 1971), p. 519. For other descriptions of swimming tests as voluntary, see Christina Hole, *A Mirror of Witchcraft* (London: Chatto & Windus, 1957), pp. 169–70, and Francis Bragge, *A Full and Impartial Account ...*, 2nd edn (London: E. Curll, 1712), p. 10.

[48] Stearne, *A Confirmation*, p. 19.

[49] Interestingly, Stearne did not report the outcome of the test in his account.

the tied suspect could pull or loosen it to fiddle with the subject's position. The manner of tying could affect the subject's ability to move. The angle at which the suspect was thrown into the water could influence the result. The casting of an innocent person into the water was often an additional trick, aimed at deluding the viewers:

> for when they will save any man or woman, they will let loose the string which they hold in their hand, and let their feet sink first, and then all their body will sink, then they cry out to the people, Look you now, and see the difference betwixt an honest man or woman, and a Witch, take her out, she is an honest woman, yea verily, for sometimes she is one of their own confederates.[50]

Ady explained the differences in the degrees of sinking of different persons by the variance of medical and physical conditions such as weight, body build, breath, nutrition and gender.

> The reason of this difference is easie to conceive to men of knowledge; for,

> First; There is difference of constitution in peoples bodies; some are heavie of temper, and they sink most; some again are more light of temper, fuller of vital spirits, and they sink not so much.

> Secondly, we must observe the Systole and Diastole of breathing; some happen to fall into the water when their bodies are full of breath, and they swim most; some happen to fall into the water when their breath is out of their bodies, before they can draw it up again, and they sink most. Some are kept long fasting in watching and torment, and then are cast into the water when their bowels and veins are empty of food and filled with Wind, and these swim more than those that are filled with nourishment; or perhaps they are kept fasting so long that they have scarce any life left, and then they happen to sink most, but if they do, it must not serve their turn, for the cruel Inquisitor will still torment them till he extort confession, if the party live long enough for his cruelty to take place. Some again are Women cast into the water, with their Coates tied close toward their feet, and Men with their apparrel on (and for this they pretend modesty) but who knoweth not that their apparrel will carry them above water for a time? Some again are Women, whose bodies are dilated with bearing of Children, and do always after remain spongiously hollow, more apt to swim than to sink, especially tied hands and

---

[50]   Thomas Ady, *A Candle in the Dark* (London: Robert Ibbitson, 1655), p. 100.

feet together, to bring their bodies into a round and apt fashion to swim. They that are used to the Art of swimming in the water, might easily discover these to be but Delusions and Juglings, if they were not too credulous.[51]

What was a popular supernatural way of proof was, for Ady, a purely natural, physical and factual phenomenon. He used what was then up-to-date medical theory to explain why some subjects sank while others floated. An explanation for the unknown should not be attributed to the supernatural, but should be explored in the realm of nature.

The approaches of Cotta and Ady were typical of a rising rationalistic and empiricist worldview. It was, therefore, quite exceptional that Richard Boulton repeated King James' rationale, which had long been denounced by many writers of importance:

> To conclude: The surest way to discover such as practice this odious Craft, besides their evil Lives and Conversation, is, first, by their Mark, which is insensible; and, secondly, by their swimming upon the Water, God having ordained, that such as had cast off the Water of Baptism should not be received into Water, but swim upon it.[52]

It was Hutchinson, in answer to Boulton in the exchange of texts that might be called the crescendo of the witchcraft debate, who repeated the denunciation of the test and regarded it as popular superstition:

> The credulous Multitude will ever be ready to try their Tricks, and swim the old Women, and wonder at and magnify every unaccountable Symptom and odd Accident.[53]

Hutchinson dismissed the swimming test with ridicule, together with other ordeal-type experiments, as a thing of the past and no more than a cruel childish trick.[54]

The nuances of their attitude were often linked to professional affiliation. Physicians focused on natural, rational and factual explanations. Clergymen rejected the test for religious reasons. Assize judges denounced its illegality and

---

[51] Ibid., pp. 100–101.

[52] Richard Boulton, *A Compleat History of Magick, Sorcery, and Witchcraft* (London: E. Curll, J. Pemberton, and W. Taylor, 1715), p. 23.

[53] Francis Hutchinson, *An Historical Essay Concerning Witchcraft* (London: R. Knaplock and D. Midwinter, 1718), p. viii.

[54] Ibid., pp. 55, 65–6.

even punished its performers.[55] The illegality of the practice was abhorred, not exclusively by judges, but by other members of the elite as well.

Attitudes toward the test were also class-related. Although the swimming test was popular with the lower echelons of society, the writers of the elite, including scholars and judges (with the exception of Boulton), distinguished themselves from the 'vulgar'and 'superstitious' masses and deplored its use.[56] Filmer and Ady even hinted that the test was un-English by pointing to the Continental origin of the practice.[57]

The attitude of the lower gentry and middling sort, however, was not always so decisive. As mentioned, in some instances the tests were initiated by petty gentlemen rather than by an angry mob. The JPs were also in a somewhat ambivalent position, somewhere in the middle. They were members of the lower gentry, usually without legal education, and an integral part of the local social fabric. Although assize judges came out explicitly against the test, and many magistrates agreed that they lacked authority to order it themselves, there were other instances of justices who went along with popular demand.[58]

Semi-official cooperation by magistrates could take the form of ordering illegal procedures such as swimming or scratching, being present at illegal proceedings, or turning a blind eye and simply failing to enforce the legal prohibitions when such a procedure was ordered by other men of authority (a mayor, alderman, minister, and so on)[59] or conducted by the mob. Hole speculated that perhaps such magistrates felt that the law was so far from popular belief that it could not be successfully enforced.[60] The desire to achieve moral certainty of the guilt or innocence of the suspect was a moral and social dilemma far wider than the legal issue. This may explain why the use of evidential methods that were not formally allowed in court was tolerated. A more simple explanation may be that such tests could pressure the suspects into confession.

---

[55]   Sharpe, *Instruments of Darkness*, p. 218; Hole, *A Mirror of Witchcraft*, p. 161; Kittredge, *Witchcraft in Old and New England*, pp. 235–7.

[56]   Clark, *Thinking with Demons*, pp. 589–90.

[57]   Filmer, *An Advertisement to the Jury-Men*, p. 11; Ady, *A Candle in the Dark*, pp. 100–101.

[58]   As in the previously mentioned case of Arthur Bill – *The Witches of Northampton-Shire*. See also Malcolm Gaskill, 'Witchcraft and Evidence in Early Modern England', *Past and Present*, no. 198 (2008): p. 53.

[59]   In 1645, at Rye, Margaret Bruff and Anne Howsell were swum by the direct order of the mayor. Hole, *A Mirror of Witchcraft*, p. 161.

[60]   Ibid.

Some swimming or other illegal tests were conducted by villagers after the suspect's arrest. One pamphlet described a woman who, following her detention by the magistrate, was taken three times to be swum at the river.[61] When suspects were in detention, such tests could not have taken place without either the active or passive cooperation of the authorities.

Some magistrates refused to conduct swimming tests for reasons of illegality, but ordered other ordeal-type tests instead. For example, Bragge maintained that Jane Wenham voluntarily offered to undergo the swimming test and be searched. In response, 'One of the Company reply'd, there was no Occasion for it at present, but only desired her to let him hear the Lord's-Prayer; she made several Attempts to do it, but could not'.[62] The next day, so Bragge wrote, Wenham repeated her offer, but 'Sir *Henry* [the magistrate] would by no Means allow of that Sort of Trial, it being Illegal, and Unjustifiable'.[63] Reluctance to use the swimming test and searching techniques, but willingness to use other supernatural signs as ways of proof, demonstrate a sense of ambivalence.

It should be noted that despite the generalizations made by the elite writers about the popularity of the swimming test with the common and superstitious, there are instances of scepticism among the lower classes as well. It was reported in a case in 1689 that a suspect was swum three times, floating each time. The first ducking was in front of about 20 people, the second was in front of about 200, and an even larger crowd attended the third, 'a Company of People of the Town and Country, and many of them, Persons of Quality, as could not well be Numbred; so that now, there is scarce one Person that doubts of the Truth of this thing'.[64] Paradoxically, the doubts of the crowd led to three swimmings in a row. It should be remembered that the first pamphleteer who recorded a swimming test, in the case against Arthur Bill, described a test that 'many think' never fails. This phrasing may suggest that many did find the test convincing but not all agreed. Despite these voices of scepticism and the ambivalent position of the middling sort and lower gentry, including some magistrates, the elite writers, quite unified in their rejection of the test, clearly regarded it as the exclusive superstition of members of the lower classes. The variation in reasoning was in accord with the professional affiliation of the elite.

---

[61] *Great News from the West of England* (London: T.M., 1689), p. 2.

[62] Bragge, *A Full and Impartial Account*, p. 10.

[63] Ibid., p. 12.

[64] *Great News from the West of England*, p. 2.

Figure 8.1 A witch floating on a plank in the river. Title page from *A Most Certain, Strange, and True Discovery of a Vvitch: Being Taken by Some of the Parliament Forces, as She Was Standing on a Small Planck-Board and Sailing on It over the River of Newbury: Together with the Strange and True Manner of Her Death* ... (London: John Hammond, 1643). [Shelfmark: E.69.(9.)] Courtesy of the British Library.

Chapter 8

Scratching

Scratching was another popular, yet illegal, test to reveal a supernatural sign of witchcraft. The belief was that by scratching the suspect with the nails and drawing her blood, the bewitched victim could enjoy temporary relief of symptoms.[1] Therefore, the victim's relief after scratching a suspect confirmed the suspect's guilt. Scratching was a practice of early origin that persisted in England from the thirteenth until the nineteenth century, but was rare on the Continent.[2] Some supernatural ways of proof, scratching included, acted in the double capacity of both discovering the witch and of curing or countering bewitchment. These techniques, of course, involved the presence or participation of the suspected witch.

The rationale for this supernatural counter-magic practice was not articulated, and no one seems to know exactly how it worked. Rosen speculated that the rationale might have been to make the suspect's body uncomfortable for the dwelling devil or that the blood might have been an offering aimed at appeasing the possessing devil and making him leave the bewitched in peace, at least temporarily.[3] Another explanation may be that, while suffering pain, the witch was not available to hurt others.

Scratching should not be confused with 'pricking', which tested the sensitivity or insensitivity of suspicious bodily marks. The logic behind the pricking was that physical evidence directly proved the compact with the devil. The logic behind scratching was in the realm of the supernatural, as it remained an unexplained sign that proved the crime by miraculous coincidence.

The practice of scratching was portrayed in detail in the famous pamphlet of 1593 about the Warboys witches, an early account of possession cum discovery that served as a precedent and model for later accounts. The conflict between

---

[1]   Barbara Rosen (ed.), *Witchcraft, Stratford-Upon-Avon Library* (New York: Taplinger, 1972), pp. 18–19; Gilbert Geis and Ivan Bunn, *A Trial of Witches: A Seventeenth-Century Witchcraft Prosecution* (London: Routledge, 1997), p. 56.

[2]   Rosen (ed.), *Witchcraft*, p. 18; Clive Holmes, 'Popular Culture? Witches, Magistrates and Divines in Early Modern England', in S.L. Kaplan (ed.), *Understanding Popular Culture: Europe from the Middle Ages to the Nineteenth Century* (Berlin: Walter de Gruyter & Co., 1984), p. 96.

[3]   Rosen (ed.), *Witchcraft*, pp. 18–19.

the Throckmorton family, who were gentry, and poor old Mother Samuel, her daughter and husband was described in a vivid and dramatic fashion. Scratching played a significant role in that account.

The Throckmortons suspected Mother Samuel of bewitching their five daughters, who suffered from fits and other symptoms and seemed to be possessed. To investigate their suspicions and obtain better supervision of Mother Samuel, they brought her to their home several times, although she was unwilling, imprisoned her in their home (without judicial permission) for a few months, and finally chose to prosecute her.

It was clearly stated that the parents, who consulted with clerics about their problem, were explicitly advised not to use scratching, an unlawful and irreligious procedure. When Mother Samuel refused to come to their house, as she 'feared the cōmon practise of scratching would be used on her', the girls' uncle, Mr Pickering, convinced her that 'lesse at that present was intended, for both the parents and the said M. *Pickering* had taken advise of good Divines of the unlawfulnes thereof'.[4] Unfortunately for Mother Samuel, her concern was justified, and the inhibitions soon disappeared. On bringing Mother Samuel to meet one of their girls, Jane, they let the girl (or so the author presented it) initiate scratching, which they repeated in a manner of scientific experimentation.

Mr Pickering, who 'was of that opinion, that scratching was meerely unlawful', was reported to have seen the girl scratching her bedcover and to have lain his hand on hers, 'but the childe feeling his own hand would not scratch it, but fortooke his hand and scratched still on the bedde', while she was lying down on her belly, her face turned down and her eyes shut. Notwithstanding the advice of the divines against scratching, 'the occasion being thus offered by the child, or rather by the spirit in the child, to disclose some secret, whereby the Witches might be by some means or token made manifest and knownen', Mr Pickering went to the hall and took the unwilling Mother Samuel to the child's room, where the girl 'lay scraping with her nailes on the bed couering, saying, Oh that I had her'. Then Mr Pickering demonstrated to Mother Samuel how he put his hand in the child's hand, and so did others who were present, 'but the childe would scarce touch, much lesse scratch any of their hands'. Then Mr Pickering, 'without either malice to the woman, confidence, or opinion in scratching (onely to taste [sic] by this experiment whereto the childes would tend) tooke mother Samuels hand and thrust it to the childes hande, who no sooner felt the same, but presently the childe scratched her, with such vehemencie that her nayles brake into Spilles with the force and earnest desire that she had to reuenge'.[5]

---

[4]   *The Most Strange and Admirable Discouerie of the Three Witches of Warboys* (London: Thomas Man, and Iohn Winington, 1593), B.

[5]   Ibid., B2.

Mr Pickering, described by the author as acting from pure scientific curiosity, modified the experiment by laying his hand on Mother Samuel's hand, which the girl was scratching with 'extraordinarie passion'; however, 'the child would not scratch his hand, but felt too and fro upon the bed for that which she missed, and if by any meanes she coulde come with her hand, or but with one of her fingers to touch Mother Samuels hand, she would scratch that hand onely and none other'. The author stressed that all this time Mother Samuel was 'hidden or withdrawn' from the child, and the girl's eyes were shut and her head turned, and therefore dismissed the possibility that she scratched Mother Samuel upon seeing her.[6] The enthusiastic uncle wished to proceed with the other sisters, but his plan was disrupted by the arrival of the parson, Dr Dorrington, who did not allow further scratching.[7]

This first dramatic encounter between the Throckmortons and Mother Samuel was followed by a series of escalating events and further scratchings, not only of Mother Samuel, but also of her daughter, Agnes Samuel.[8] The alleged bewitchment of the eldest Throckmorton girl reached a stage where she started having conversations with the spirits that instructed her about scratching.[9] The uncles, Thomas and Henry Pickering, played an active role, and the parents' earlier objection to scratching because of religious reasons was no longer mentioned. Apparently, scratching was performed on Mother Samuel even after her arrest. One of the jailors suspected her of the death of his servant and serious illness of his son, who was cured instantly after her scratching. The assizes allowed his testimony at the end of Mother Samuel's trial.[10]

The allowance of testimony about scratching in court was not the only instance of *semi-formal recognition* of this practice. There were cases where men of authority ordered scratching. The first record of scratching was in a pamphlet from 1592, wherein the parson of the town, M. Smith, and Maister Burbridge, of a nearby town, orchestrated the scratching of the suspect by the accuser, who was 'perswading himselfe that was a remedy sufficient under God, that would make him well: neither was it or is it any Capital error, experience testyfies: for since that he hath mended reasonablie, and nowe goeth to the Church'.[11] The narrator

---

[6] Ibid., B2–B2v.

[7] Ibid., B2v–B3. On a later occasion in Dr Dorrington's presence, one of the girls gave up her plan to scratch John Samuel, Mother Samuel's husband. Ibid., Lv–L2.

[8] Ibid., K2, K2v, K4v, Lv–L2, M4.

[9] Ibid., I4v, L4, M3, N–Nv.

[10] Ibid., H2v.

[11] G.B., Master of Art, 'A Most Vvicked Worke of a Wretched Witch …' (London: William Barley, 1592), in Marion Gibson (ed.), *Early Modern Witches: Witchcraft Cases in Contemporary Writing* (London: Routledge, 2000), p. 144.

bothered to justify the scratching both morally and practically; therefore we could learn that it might have been an acceptable solution but one that needed justification. A pamphlet from 1597 described how, after Alice Goodridge refused to admit to the charges, Sir Humphrey Ferrers, referred to in the text as one of 'the justices', ordered the allegedly bewitched boy to scratch her.[12]

Local ministers and magistrates were involved in scratching as late as the eighteenth century. In 1702 Richard Hathaway was indicted for fraudulently accusing Sarah Morduck of bewitching him and for assaulting her together with others. The court received evidence about two scratching events, the first initiated by the minister of the parish, Dr Martin, and the second by a London magistrate. It should be noted that Dr Martin orchestrated the scratching to expose Hathaway's deceit. He caused Hathaway to scratch another woman, thus ridiculing his pretended recovery. Yet, although he obtained the consent of the other women to be scratched (therefore did not commit an assault), the active role of a minister in the theologically dubious practice of scratching was still questionable. The London magistrate, Sir Thomas Lanes, on the contrary, was pressed to order the scratching of Sarah Morduck after 'the Rabble got about her and abused her'.[13] This magistrate later found himself in an unpleasant situation when he needed to testify before the judges of Richard Hathaway and explain his decision. He tried to minimize his responsibility by describing his answer to those who demanded scratching as follows: 'I appeal to them whether I did not refuse it, I said, if I should order this, it would be an assault; but if she will consent you may do it. Says she, if I may be secured for the future, I will let him … she did give her consent, and he scratched her.'[14] The testimony demonstrates conflicting pressures on the magistrate. On the one hand, he was well aware of the illegality of the practice and, on the other, he strove to pacify the angry crowd awaiting his decision. On another occasion, in the presence of the JP who came to take depositions, scratching was prevented by bystanders, who took away the alleged victim who had already sprung to her feet, intending to scratch the suspect.[15] The text is not clear whether scratching was prevented by the JP's order or despite his ambivalent passivity.

Semi-official cooperation with scratching sometimes occurred by allowing the alleged victims to scratch the witch who was already awaiting her trial in jail. Mr Avery brought his sister, Mistris Blecher, to scratch the suspect in jail.[16]

---

[12]   I.D., *The Most Wonderfull and True Storie …* (London: I.O., 1597), p. 9.

[13]   *The Tryal of Richard Hathaway* (London: Isaac Cleave, 1702), p. 2.

[14]   Ibid., p. 23.

[15]   Francis Bragge, *A Full and Impartial Account …*, 2nd edn, 2nd reprint (London: E. Curll, 1712), p. 11.

[16]   *The Witches of Northampton-Shire* (London: Arthur Iohnson, 1612), B4.

The practice was clearly illegal and was not allowed in the assizes courts. These examples demonstrate how local magistrates, ministers and other figures of standing in the community cooperated with this practice.

The texts portrayed a popular belief in the effectiveness of scratching as a cure, though a short-lived one. The recurrent need of the Throckmorton family to scratch Mother Samuel and her daughter Agnes in the Warboys case illustrates this point. The pamphleteer in a case of 1612 described how, once the alleged victims scratched the suspect, they were immediately delivered of their pain, yet once the suspect was out of sight, they were tormented again by even more violent fits.[17] The author was well aware of the popularity of the method and of objections to it as superstitious, and tried to remain neutral. He stated that 'many haue attempted the practising thereof, how successfuely I know not'.[18] It seems that the effectiveness of the method was largely a matter of interpretation.

Another pamphleteer explained the brevity of the relief by the witch's return to her malicious wrongdoing once she was left unobserved. He described an incident of scratching, subsequent to which the victim began to mend and feel well. However, the suspect's tendency to assiduous malevolent practice prevailed, and she could not resist an opportunity to touch the victim's neck with her finger. So soon after she departed, 'he fell into as great or farre worse vexation than he had before'.[19]

Perhaps it was the vague rationale behind the test that allowed for a broad interpretation. Contemporaries who practised scratching regarded the procedure as successful, even if the victim's relief was brief, tardy or followed by a deterioration of health. A pamphlet of 1616 described scratching by a man who suspected his neighbour, Joanne Harrison, of bewitching him. Other neighbours recommended that he scratch her so that 'he should recouer presently'. Next morning he had the suspect 'well scratcht'. His health, however, did not improve instantly, but 'within 3 or 4 daies (as fast as the man could recouer strength) he is vp, & goes abroad'.[20] Despite the delay, the author still deemed the scratching successful, the best result for a man in such a condition.

Inability to scratch was also interpreted as proof of witchcraft, although the scratching did not take place. Thus, the inability of Thomas Darling to scratch Alice Goodridge, whom he blamed for bewitching him, was construed as a sign of her guilt (he was able to lay his hands on other bystanders, but not on her).[21]

---

[17] Ibid.

[18] Ibid.

[19] W.W., *A True and Iust Recorde* ... (London: Thomas Dawson, 1582), B4v–C.

[20] *Most Damnable Practises of One Iohane Harrison* ... (London: William Firebrand and Iohn Wright, 1606), C3v.

[21] D., *The Most Wonderfull and True Storie*, p. 9.

Roberts reported that when Edmund Newton tried to scratch a suspect, 'his nailes turned like feathers, hauing no strength to lay his hands vpon her'.[22]

If no blood was drawn despite the scratching, that was another sign of witchcraft. Jane Wenham was violently scratched by the allegedly bewitched maid in the forehead 'with such Fury and Eagerness, that the Noise of her Nails seemed to all that were present as if she were scratching against a Wainscot, yet no Blood followed ... altho' her Forehead was sadly mangled and torn by the Girl's Nails; of this Difficulty in fetching of Blood of *Jane Wenham* the Reader will have another more remarkable Instance by and by'.[23]

The texts demonstrated the gap between the intellectual position of the learned elite and popular practice. The Warboys case demonstrated the conflict between the minister's condemnation of the practice as a religious sin and the strength of popular beliefs. Dr Dorrington, the minister who at first admonished the Throckmortons against scratching, and was even able to prevent at least one incident of scratching in his presence, was eventually described as watching passively and even helplessly as his wife, who was the girls' aunt, participated in scratching.[24]

From a religious point of view, scratching was criticized. The author of a pamphlet of 1597 denounced scratching, notwithstanding its popularity as a means of both discovery and cure. This author explained that although scratching was a common means of discovering witches, it was a virtueless practice that was witchcraft in itself, and its use in England was 'to the great dishonor of God'.[25] Perkins, in his theological discussion about the discovery of witchcraft, regarded scratching as one of the 'weake and insufficient proofes' and reasoned similarly. The supernatural power of the practice, according to Perkins, was not invoked by God, but by the devil. Therefore, scratching (and all other proofs of its kind) were practices of invoking devilish powers and therefore witchcraft by definition. Following the tradition of Continental demonology, Perkins

---

[22]   Alexander Roberts, *A Treatise of Witchcraft*, 2nd edn (London: Samuel Man, 1616), p. 58. See also the report about the Thomas Spatchet case, where 'Some excited him *to s[...]ratch the Witch* or such like, but he had no disposition to it, his heart was so tender that he durst not do it, though his fits continued'. Samuel Petto, *A Faithful Narrative* ... (London: John Harris, 1693), p. 20.

[23]   Bragge, *Full and Impartial Account*, p. 10. For an explanation of the lack of flowing blood due to natural reasons, see *The Case of the Hertfordshire Witchcraft Consider'd* (London: John Pemberton, 1712), p. 72, and also 'who but a pack of Idiots, should have expected a Turment of Blood, or indeed but a few Drops, from a shrivell'd Old Forehead, which, if squeez'd and collected, would not yeild half an Ounce?' *A Full Confutation of Witchcraft* ... (London: J. Baker, 1712), pp. 16–17.

[24]   *Witches of Warboys*, Lv–L2, M3v.

[25]   D., *The Most Wonderfull and True Storie*, pp. 5–6.

apprehended counter-magic as diabolical. The good witch was more horrible and detestable than the bad witch, attacking the soul rather than just the body.[26] Perkins believed that the scratching of the witch verily cured the bewitched and was a devilish means to lure people into the practice of witchcraft.[27] Alexander Roberts, a preacher at Kings Lynn, similarly regarded scratching itself as an act of witchcraft and asserted that it was 'a foule sinne among Christians to thinke one Witch-craft can driue out another'.[28]

Cotta shared the belief that the devil was behind the supernatural nature of scratching. His philosophy advocated strictly natural evidence as a basis for conviction under the laws of men.[29] He believed in witches and spirits but was opposed to supernatural discovery methods such as scratching, swimming or burning of bewitched cattle. These methods, he argued, were not natural. They were not miracles of God, but rather of the devil.[30] Cotta did not deny that with scratching, the victims 'immediately are deliuered from the present fit or agonie', and even vouched that 'I haue also my selfe seene' such cases.[31] The recovery must have been the result of the supernatural power activated by the witch.[32] Such proof of 'miraculous effect by the Diuell' must not be trusted as a basis for conviction.[33] Cotta's insistence on using solely natural methods of proof relied on a theological basis, the fear of the devil's manipulation. Scratching was another vulgar and useless test, not because it was ineffective, but because it was devilish.

Whereas a physician like Cotta accepted that scratching was effective, a cleric like Cooper, supporting witch prosecution, regarded belief in the power of scratching as a superstition held by the ignorant:

> As, to *Scratch the Witch, to hang Amulets about their necke*, &c., which though some doe ignorantly as thinking some inherent power to be in those meanes to cure diseases: yet doth this by degrees draw them from the vse of law full means, cause them to rest in those that are vnlawfull: and so nourishing them in infidelitie, prouoke them in time to forsake God; and so they are iustly left to the power of Sathan, by him to be ripened to the day of vengeance.[34]

---

[26] William Perkins, *A Discourse of the Damned Art of Witchcraft* (Cambridge, UK: Vniuersitie of Cambridge, 1608), pp. 174–5.

[27] Ibid., pp. 206–7.

[28] Roberts, *A Treatise of Witchcraft*, p. 58.

[29] John Cotta, *The Triall of Vvitch-Craft* (London: Samuel Rand, 1616), pp. 122–3.

[30] Ibid., pp. 113–14.

[31] Ibid., pp. 114–15.

[32] Ibid., p. 117.

[33] Ibid., p. 122.

[34] Thomas Cooper, *The Mystery of Witch-Craft* (London: Nicholas Okes, 1617), p. 70.

Scratching per se, according to Cooper, had no inherent power. He believed that the illegality of the procedure led its practitioners to infidelity and the forsaking of God, thus leaving them more vulnerable to the devil's temptation, and he identified disobedience of the law of the state with un-Christian behaviour.[35] For that reason, scratching, like swimming or other supernatural signs, was a deceitful and satanical practice.[36] Richard Bernard similarly associated the illegal with the un-Christian. His legal guidance was founded on religious, moral, legal and practical grounds, and he had three arguments against the use of scratching. First, relying on precedents, it was not very effective, as the relief was brief, and once the witches were out of sight, the victims suffered even worse fits. Second, scratching was illegal. Private use of violence to obtain revenge was illegitimate in Bernard's view. Third, the practice depended on the devil's wishes and help. Bernard accepted the testimony of the Throckmorton girl that she was instructed by a spirit to scratch the suspect, and he regarded it as a sign of diabolic involvement.[37] He also discussed the *beating* of a witch as a means to relieve the victim's suffering and used similar arguments. He explained that '[e]xcept it bee by the appointment of the Magistrate, it is against the Law of man, and being a priuate reuenge, is against the Law of God'.[38] Private vengeance, which was against the secular law, was also a religious offence.

Similar views were still maintained in the eighteenth century by Hutchinson, doctor of divinity (chaplain to the King from 1715 and Bishop of Down and Connor from 1721).[39] To him, scratching itself constituted witchcraft, as it meant compacting and cooperating with the devil.

> All these are seeking to, and consulting with the Devil, and employing of him, and using the *Vinculum Pacti*, and are within the Reach of the Statute against Witchcraft.[40]

Scratching, like swimming, touching or similar supernatural signs, was to Hutchinson part of a repertoire of 'childish tricks', deserving nothing but scorn.[41]

---

[35]   See also ibid., p. 168.

[36]   Ibid., p. 272.

[37]   Richard Bernard, *A Guide to Grand-Iury Men* (London: Ed. Blackmore, 1627), pp. 191–3.

[38]   Ibid., p. 189.

[39]   Ian Bostridge, *Witchcraft and Its Transformations, c.1650–c.1750* (Oxford; New York: Clarendon Press, 1997), p. 144.

[40]   Francis Hutchinson, *An Historical Essay Concerning Witchcraft* (London: R. Knaplock and D. Midwinter, 1718), p. 48.

[41]   Ibid., p. 55.

Most of the scholarly texts about scratching were written by divines, perhaps because the supernatural was their domain. Interestingly, members of other professional groups did not discuss scratching in depth. Cotta was the exception. He based his objection to scratching on theological grounds, reluctance to rely on the devil's deeds to obtain conviction. It is interesting to note that although Cotta relied on theological suppositions, the theologians emphasized the illegality of the scratching as their basis for objection. Legal scholars did not debate scratching to a great extent. However, the legal system conveyed a very clear message against the use of scratching – it was an illegal use of violence punishable by the courts, and offenders were liable to pay damages.[42] When Richard Hathaway was tried for making fraudulent witchcraft accusations and committing acts of assault against Sarah Morduck, his defence attorney tried to justify his scratching. But even he admitted that 'none should advise' scratching.[43] Despite the legal and clerical prohibition of scratching, the pamphlets reflected the popularity of the practice and belief in its validity.

After Iohane Harrison was 'well scratched' by her neighbour, she then successfully sued him for battery and was granted five shillings as damages.[44] Despite her legal victory, the pamphleteer still perceived her as a witch and remarked that, immediately after he had paid her the fine, the 'honest man fell into his former passion, languishing a while & died'.[45]

A man who suspected that his dying sheep were bewitched, scratched the suspect's hand with a knife and drew her blood. In reaction:

> she little regarding and neglecting to apply any remedy to it, it wrankled and swell'd extreamly, whereupon she came again, and threatned that she would arrest and trouble him for it; and he to avoid any thing of trouble, being a quiet Man, was content to give her twenty shillings towards her cure, which she had no sooner received of him, but she returned these or the like words, that that was the Divils mony, and that now she had power enough to punish him, nor did she delay to execute her Malice.[46]

---

[42] Holmes, 'Popular Culture?' p. 96; Malcolm Gaskill, *Crime and Mentalities in Early Modern England* (Cambridge: Cambridge University Press, 2000), pp. 50–51.

[43] The defence attorney claimed that Morduck gave her consent to the scratching and therefore no offence was committed. *The Tryal of Richard Hathaway*, p. 17.

[44] *Most Damnable Practises of One Iohane Harrison*, C3v.

[45] Ibid.

[46] *The Full and True Relation of the Tryal, Condemnation, and Execution of Ann Foster* (London: D.M., 1674), p. 5.

This man, being threatened with legal proceedings, compensated the woman he scratched (although, the author critically remarked, she could have lessened her damages by applying medicine). Her subsequent words were interpreted by the author as an ultimate proof of her guilt.[47]

A pamphlet of 1643 described a group of soldiers who suspected a woman they believed had been walking on the river water of being a witch. The narrator told how they tried to kill her by shooting and by sword, but in vain – the sword and bullets could not penetrate her body. Therefore, it was suggested that they draw her blood 'from forth the veines that crosse the temples of the head' and thus eliminate her power. On hearing this plan, the narrator told the readers, she 'knew then the Devill had left her and her power was gone, wherefore she began alowd to cry, and roare, tearing her haire, and making pitious moan, which in these words expressed were; And is it come to passe, that I must dye indeed?'[48] The events described in the pamphlet were evidently imaginary, but they seem to reflect a popular belief as to the power of scratching. Neither the sword nor the bullets could destroy the witch, but the mere mention of scratching broke her. The suspect's question about whether she should die was interpreted as proof of the efficiency of scratching rather than the desperate cry of a tortured woman.

Scratching was often introduced in the pamphlets as a potent cure, bringing immediate relief to tortured victims.[49] Sometimes the pamphleteer pointed to low-class neighbours or villagers (such as friends or relatives of the maids) as those who suggested scratching.[50] However, sometimes scratching was performed by the more affluent or socially superior members of the local community. Examples were the cases of the Throckmorton family, the Muschamp family[51] and the Pacy family.[52] The cases of the Throckmortons and Pacys were influential precedents, and it is significant that members of the gentry were the social agents that lent legitimacy to the procedure of scratching.

---

[47]   It is quite possible to interpret her words differently. By saying it was the devil's money, she might have meant to say that scratching was a devilish procedure, and the threats to punish him were possibly a reminder that she still had the legal power to prosecute him.

[48]   *A Most Certain, Strange, and True Discovery of a Vvitch* (London: John Hammond, 1643), p. 7.

[49]   H.F., *A True and Exact Relation* ... (London: Henry Overton and Benj. Allen, 1645), p. 18.

[50]   Edmund Bower, *Doctor Lamb Revived* ... (London: Richard Best and John Place, 1653), p. 20; *Strange and Wonderful News from Yowel in Surry* (London: J. Clarke, 1681), p. 5.

[51]   *Wonderfull News from the North* ... (London: T.H., 1650), pp. 8–10.

[52]   *A Tryal of Witches* ... (London: William Shrewsbery, 1682), pp. 13–14.

As in the case of the swimming test, there seemed to be a gap between popular belief, which was favourable to scratching, and the elite position, which considered scratching to be vulgar superstition.[53] Similarly, we can notice ambivalence toward scratching in the circles of the local gentry, JPs and lower-ranking ministers. The pamphlets described how popular belief in scratching flourished despite clerical condemnation and legal prohibitions.

Swimming and scratching, as they were used in early modern England, differed in two major ways from the ordeals. First, whereas the ordeals were a means of ultimate judgment, early modern swimming and scratching were measures of pre-trial investigation. The ordeals were a means of last resort after personal knowledge of jurors or compurgation could not lead to determination. Swimming and scratching, used in the pre-trial and even pre-magistrate phase of the proceedings, bolstered the case and made it sufficient for indictment. The result, however, could not be used as a basis for conviction. Second, despite the resemblance in format, the underlying epistemology was different. In both eras the supernatural ways of proof relied on a power from above to determine the guilt of the suspect. One prevalent feature of the ordeal, a complete trust in divine guidance, was lacking in the early modern procedures. Because the result was no longer blindly trusted, ordeal-type procedures had to be reconstructed as experiments in accordance with the rising empiricist worldview.

---

[53] It is important to note that condemnation of scratching as vulgar did not necessarily mean disbelief in its efficaciousness, as demonstrated by Cotta's argument above.

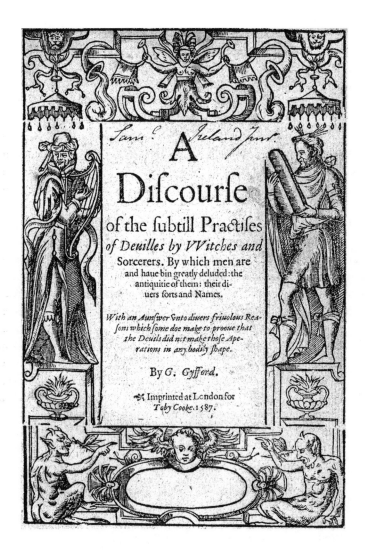

Figure 9.1 Title page from George Gifford, *A Discourse of the Subtill Practises of Deuilles by Vvitches and Sorcerers: By Which Men Are and Haue Bin Greatly Deluded...* (London: Toby Cooke, 1587). [Call # 59291 or 59961] Reproduced by permission of the Huntington Library, San Marino, California.

Chapter 9
Supernatural Evidentiary Techniques as Experiments

Whereas early writers on witchcraft emphasized its scriptural and theological basis, around the mid-seventeenth century the emphasis shifted to the search for factual proofs. The re-shaping of the ordeals as factual and empiricist observations fitted into this frame of thought. This does not imply a simple causal explanation, by which evidentiary techniques were influenced by the emergence of natural philosophy and modern science. The well-documented and influential Warboys case of 1593 provided rich details about the reconstruction of the ordeal as a factual experiment long before the blossoming of natural philosophy in the mid-seventeenth century.

The reconstruction of ordeals as experiments embodied aspirations for controlled conditions through standardization, repetition and use of a control. Controlled conditions were necessary to make sure that the experiments examined the witchcraft variable (whether the subject was a witch) and not other factors. Sometimes the methodical mode of observation was reflected not only in the manner of conducting the experiments, but also in the careful documentation of the observations. The condition of the bewitched victims was observed methodically and routinely, a few times a day, at different hours, and carefully noted down.[1]

The swimming test was standardized to a level where suspects in different cases were tied and cast into the water in a similar manner. Standardization could also be reached in a specific case by repeating the procedure in the same way every time. The first time Mother Samuel was brought to the Throckmortons' house to be scratched, the author emphasized that the girl was in the same position (head turned, eyes shut) every time her uncle let her touch one of the bystanders. The girl scratched only Mother Samuel. The author led the readers to the conclusion that, everything else being equal, Mother Samuel must be a witch.[2] The pamphlet about the Warboys case was abundant with examples of experiments and tests, some of which, like the scratching, were

---

[1]   *The Most Strange and Admirable Discouerie of the Three Witches of Warboys* (London: Thomas Man, and Iohn Winington, 1593), B4v and other locations.

[2]   Ibid., B2–B2v.

culturally established, whereas some were creatively fashioned according to the circumstances of the case. For example, after seven months had passed since one of the girls, Elizabeth Throckmorton, had been sent away from her parents' home to stay with her uncle, and she had not yet recovered, the girl started claiming she would be better only if she was returned to her parents' home at Warboys. There followed a series of experiments examining her condition while she was travelling toward her home. In front of 'many' observers, she was carried, put on horseback, or made to walk for some distance in the direction of Warboys and then made to return toward her uncle's home. The repeated travelling was to examine the influence of the trip on the condition of the girl, who cheered up as they went toward her home and saddened as they turned back each time.[3] Another episode in the Warboys case was the experiment to detect the effect on the girls of Mother Samuel's presence in the house. She was made to enter and exit the house *20 times in one hour* to demonstrate the effect on the girls' fits.[4]

If the repetition of the experiment yielded similar results, both the proof of witchcraft and the validity of the procedure were augmented. In the Warboys case, Bible verses were read to one of the allegedly possessed Throckmorton girls to test the effect of a sacred text on her. The girl was reported to suffer from fits and rage as long as the Bible or any other 'Godly booke' was read to her and to be quiet once the reading stopped. As this 'was a thing very strange, and therefore hardly beleeued', the experiment was repeated despite the torment of the girl, and the same proof was repeatedly obtained.[5] An example from another case (almost a century later, in 1689) is the casting of a suspect into the water three times until enough people were convinced she was a witch.[6]

For an eighteenth-century pamphleteer, not repeating the experiment was grounds for discrediting the proof. In the Jane Wenham case, the accusers set a bottle filled with the victim's urine over the fire to observe whether the suspect would be in pain.[7] Manipulation of the victim's urine (by boiling, burying or otherwise) was considered one of the supernatural ways of discovery. The suspect would suffer great pain, usually from not being able to urinate, and thus be discovered.[8] A sceptical author in 1712 flatly dismissed the urine-boiling test:

---

[3]   Ibid., D.

[4]   Ibid., E2.

[5]   Ibid., B3v.

[6]   *Great News from the West of England* (London: T.M., 1689), p. 2.

[7]   Francis Bragge, *A Full and Impartial Account* ..., 2nd edn (London: E. Curll, 1712), p. 20. This practice should not be confused with uroscopy, a standard early modern medical examination of urine as a means of diagnosing diseases.

[8]   Keith Thomas, *Religion and the Decline of Magic* (New York: Charles Scribner's Sons, 1971), pp. 543–4.

'if they had a mind to have made the World believe, that there was any thing wonderful in this *Experiment*, they ought to have repeated it several times, and to have seen whether or no the same *Effect* always followed. For as the Story stands at present is but one single Instance, and of consequence will prove nothing at all.'[9]

Sometimes an experiment was repeated in variations to negate alternative explanations for the results and to guarantee that the suspect failed the test because she was a witch and not for a different reason. Thus, Jane Wenham was submitted to the test of the Lord's Prayer, one of the supernatural means of obtaining evidence sometimes used in early modern England. The suspect was required to say the prayer, and failure (typically inability to pronounce the sentences 'forgive us our trespasses' or 'lead us not into temptation') was considered proof that the suspect was a witch. Bragge maintained that Wenham made several attempts to recite the prayer but always missed two or three sentences. After Wenham had failed to recite the whole prayer, the experiment was repeated with a slight variation. This time she had to repeat after Mrs Gardiner, who recited it slowly to her, sentence by sentence. Despite repeated attempts, Wenham failed again, 'to the Amazement of all the By-standers. It was observed ... she could not say this Sentence, *Forgive us our Trespasses, as we forgive them that Trespass against us*, nor that, *Lead us not into Temptation*.[10] The next morning, she was again asked to say the Lord's Prayer. She attempted it several times, each time stumbling on the same two problematic sentences. Instead of '*Lead us not into Temptation, but deliver us from Evil*', she proclaimed '*Lead us not into no Temptation and Evil*' or '*Lead us into Temptation and Evil*'. Wenham explained her confusion by saying that she 'was much disturb'd in her Head by the Hurry she was in' and asked for a rest.[11] The test, therefore, resumed the following morning. Reverend Strutt:

> told her ... he hoped she was now in a good Temper, and her Head settled; she answered, yes, and that she had a good Night's Rest. Then Mr *Strutt* reply'd, that he was come according to his Promise, to see whether she could say the Lord's-Prayer; she answer'd she believed she could, for she had try'd several Times in the Night, and she made no doubt but she could say it, and accordingly she essay'd several Times to do it, but could not, making the same Blunders as before.[12]

---

[9]   *The Case of the Hertfordshire Witchcraft Consider'd* (London: John Pemberton, 1712), p. 34.

[10]   Bragge, *Full and Impartial Account*, p. 10.

[11]   Ibid., p. 12.

[12]   Ibid., p. 15.

The repetition with slight variations (sentence by sentence, after a night's rest) proved that Wenham could not say the prayer properly because she was a witch and not because of bad memory, tiredness or confusion.

Sometimes, when the supernatural way failed to prove the suspect's guilt, the experiment was repeated until success was achieved, namely, a result pointing to guilt was obtained. Sarah Morduck, for example, was scratched for a second time, although the first scratching proved the alleged victim, Richard Hathaway, to be an impostor.[13]

Often the experiments were designed to eliminate the effect of possible manipulation by the victim, whose reactions were often observed as part of the experiment. Therefore, the eyes of the allegedly possessed Throckmorton and Pacy girls were blindfolded when they scratched or touched the suspect. Yet, blindfolding the eyes of the alleged victim did not impress all as a sufficient precaution against fabricated symptoms. A sceptical author of 1712 criticized the experiment that confronted Jane Wenham with the allegedly bewitched Anne Thorn while the latter's eyes were closed. According to Bragge's account, Thorn recovered following the confrontation. The writer was not convinced that closed eyes were enough. The victim could still get a hint, recognize a voice or 'peep out a little under her Eye-lids'.[14]

In addition to blindfolding, the neutrality of the experiment was reinforced by using volunteers as a control group. One of the chief supernatural methods of obtaining proof was based on the belief that by the touch of the real witch, the victim would react in some extraordinary fashion.[15] The use of blindfolds and a control group could help discern whether the victim reacted to the presence or touch of the suspect alone or of any passerby.

The cases of the Throckmorton (1589–93) and Pacy (1662) families had many common features. In both cases the allegedly possessed victims were young girls of affluent local families, whereas the chief suspects were marginal and poor

---

[13]   *The Tryal of Richard Hathaway* (London: Isaac Cleave, 1702), p. 11. This repetition recalls the repetitious searches for bodily marks, which could perhaps discover marks that were cut off or disguised by the devil. Samuel Petto, *A Faithful Narrative* ... (London: John Harris, 1693), p. 19.

[14]   *The Case of the Hertfordshire Witchcraft Consider'd*, p. 58.

[15]   For additional cases of confrontation, see Edmund Bower, *Doctor Lamb Revived* ... (London: Richard Best and John Place, 1653), p. 20; John Hale, *A Collection of Modern Relations* ... (London: John Harris, 1693), p. 56; Bragge, *Full and Impartial Account*, pp. 7, 9–11, 24; R.T., *The Opinion of Witchcraft Vindicated* (London: Francis Haley, 1670), p. 6; *Great News from the West of England*, p. 2; W.W., *A True and Iust Recorde* ... (London: Thomas Dawson, 1582), C3, E6; Joseph Glanvill, *A Blow at Modern Sadducism* ... (London: James Collins, 1668), p. 130; M.Y., *The Hartford-Shire Wonder* (London: John Clark, 1669), p. 9.

women, and the supernatural ways of proof were constructed in the format of an experiment. A prominent test in the case of the Pacys was touching. During the trial of Amy Denny and Rose Cullender, accused of bewitching the Pacy girls, 'there were some experiments made with the persons afflicted, by bringing the persons to touch them', and it was observed that the girls opened their clenched fists only when the defendants touched them. Subsequently, 'lest they might privately see when they were touched, they were blinded with their own aprons, and the touching took the same effect as before'.[16] Thereupon, an 'ingenious person' from the crowd objected that:

> there might be a great fallacy in this experiment, and there ought not to be any stress put upon this to Convict the Parties, for the Children might counterfeit this their Distemper, and perceiving what was done to them, they might in such manner suddenly alter the motion and gesture of their Bodies, on purpose to induce persons to believe that they were not natural, but wrought strangely by the touch of the Prisoners.[17]

Heeding this criticism, the judge redesigned the experiment, choosing very respectable persons such as Lord Cornwallis, Sir Edmund Bacon, Serjeant Keeling 'and some other gentlemen there in court' to touch the blindfolded girl in addition to the defendant. This change had a dramatic effect: 'then one other person touched her hand, which produced the same effect as the touch of the witch did in the court. Whereupon the gentlemen returned, openly protesting that they did believe the whole transaction of this business was a mere imposture. This put the court, and all persons into a stand.'[18] Unfortunately for the defendants, Mr Pacy, the father of the afflicted girls, managed to convince the court that since the girl was conscious of the purpose of the experiment, what mattered was her psychological conviction that she was touched by the witch. This meant that the experiment was deemed successful in proving the defendants' guilt after all.[19]

What is notable here is the court's willingness to take an active role in the design of the experiment. This case was presided over by Matthew Hale, one of England's most famous and admired judges. Although assize judges were very clear in their opposition to scratching and swimming tests, they displayed tolerance and ambivalence regarding non-violent supernatural methods of obtaining evidence. In this case, the touching experiment was initiated by the

---

[16]   *A Tryal of Witches* ... (London: William Shrewsbery, 1682), p. 43.

[17]   Ibid., p. 44.

[18]   Ibid., p. 45.

[19]   Ibid., pp. 43–5.

judge himself.[20] The willingness of the judges to modify the experiment in response to a remark from the crowd demonstrated remarkable openness toward novel evidentiary techniques. It is also a clear indication that during the 1660s, the rules of evidence were not yet an institutionalized body of rules and there was a flexible approach to proof.

The Throckmortons and their relatives, ever creative in designing experiments to prove the Samuels' guilt, also enjoyed the cooperation of the court. Judge Fenner, who presided over the case, accepted their invitation to come and see whether Agnes Samuel could stop the fit of one of the Throckmorton daughters by charging the spirit with phrases dictated to her, which were, 'As I am a Witch, and a worse Witch then my mother, and did consent to the death of the Lady Cromwel, so I charge the divel to let mistresse Ioan Throckmorton come out of her fit at this present'.[21] A distinguished control group was assembled, and 'before Agnes Samuel spoke the charge to make some tryall in others of the effect thereof, the Judge himselfe, Doctor Dorington, Master Throckmorton and others, spake the words of the charge, but the said Mistresse Ioan had small ease by their speeches, neither would she come out of her fit'.[22] The girl did not improve even after the prayers said by the judge and the rest of the company, nor after Agnes Samuel was commanded by the judge to pray for her health. The Throckmortons' explanation was that the girl's condition remained poor because Agnes Samuel must have said the words 'God' or 'Jesus Christ'.[23] Next, they modified the text before Agnes Samuel was to charge the spirit, and she was required to make a negative statement: '"as I am no Witch, neither did consent to the death of the Lady Cromwel, so I charge the diuel to let mistris Ioan come out of her fit at this present", but all this was to no purpose.'[24]

Only after experimenting with all these variations was Agnes Samuel finally commanded to say 'the right charge'. The girl's recovery was instantaneous: 'These words were no sooner spoken by the sayd Agnes Samuel, but the said mistresse Ioan Throckmorton wiped her eyes and came out of her fit.' After a few minutes, however, the girl relapsed into a fit again. The judge, 'greatly lamenting the case', ordered her to repeat the charge, and the girl recovered immediately for the second time. After an additional relapse, the judge ordered a charge of different phrasing, and according to the author, that time the girl recovered completely.[25] This experiment included the elements of repetition, a control

---

[20]   *A Tryal of Witches ...*, p. 59.
[21]   *Witches of Warboys*, N4.
[22]   Ibid.
[23]   Ibid., N3v–N4.
[24]   Ibid., N4.
[25]   Ibid., N4v.

group, modification directed to eliminate alternative explanations, verification of the result and the open-minded cooperation of the judge.

Even a much more sceptical judge, Sir John Powell, who presided over the case against Jane Wenham and fiercely objected to her conviction, allowed an experiment of confrontation in the courtroom:

> The first Evidence that was sworn was Anne Thorn, who going to relate what had happened to her, fell into a Fit, being taken Speechless, with violent Convulsions, and was very strong; my Lord said, that he never heard that in any Witches Trial before the Person afflicted fell into a Fit in Court; but for the Satisfaction of the Jury he permitted the Prisoner to be brought near her, and to speak to her, upon which the Girl flew at her with great Fury, as usual.[26]

Judge Powell is reported to have doubted the procedure, yet to have allowed it to appease the jurors.

The cooperation of the court in conducting experiments based on supernatural methods of obtaining proof (except for swimming and scratching) may seem surprising to readers of the twenty-first century. One might ask whether the justices were waiting for supernatural assistance from above or if they were not aware of the theological difficulties inherent in the use of supernatural techniques. These doubts may seem less puzzling if we consider the special character of the English belief in witchcraft, starting around the mid-seventeenth century, as a matter of fact. The learned writers of the seventeenth century shifted from the language of scriptural proofs to factual proofs.[27] Witchcraft became a matter of fact that could be studied by observation. This concept, as well as the justices' openness toward experiments, fit in the framework of human, rather than divine, fact-finding.

Glanvill is probably the quintessential example of the matter-of-fact approach to witchcraft. A Fellow of the Royal Society and Chaplain in Ordinary to Charles II, he collected factual accounts that he considered proofs of witchcraft. He saw no conflict between the supernatural nature of witchcraft and spirits and the ability to prove them:

---

[26] Bragge, *Full and Impartial Account*, p. 24.

[27] In Gibson's words: 'This empirical curiosity wavers towards rejecting divine authority in favour of deductive observation, though rigidly based on given beliefs and hardly "inductive".' Marion Gibson, *Reading Witchcraft: Stories of Early English Witches* (London: Routledge, 1999), p. 175.

the LAND of SPIRITS is a kinde of AMERICA, and not well discover'd
Region; yea, it stands in the Map of humane Science like unknown Tracts,
fill'd up with Mountains, Seas, and Monsters.[28]

Witchcraft could be investigated just like an uncharted land. Glanvill explained
that many phenomena, natural as well as supernatural, had not been deciphered
as yet. He stated: 'We cannot conceive how the *Featus* is form'd in the *womb*, nor
as much as how a *Plant* springs from the *Earth* we tread on; we know not how
our *Souls* move the *Body*.'[29] The invisibility of spirits, claimed Glanvill, did not
make them impossible to prove:

> *matters* of *fact* well proved ought not to be denied, because we cannot *conceive*
> how they can be *perform'd*. Nor is it a reasonable method of inference, first to
> *presume* the thing impossible, and thence to conclude that the *fact* cannot be
> *proved*.[30]

Glanvill criticized the flawed logic in presupposing the impossibility of
witchcraft and therefore concluding that facts of witchcraft could not be proved.
He seemed to believe that by using the right methods, it was possible to prove
witchcraft as a fact:

> many of those matters of Fact, have been since critically inspected and
> examined by several sagacious and deep searches of the ROYAL SOCIETY,
> whom we may suppose as unlikely to be deceived by a contrived Imposture,
> as any persons extant.[31]

Glanvill also hoped that scientific progress would help obtain better proofs of the
world of spirits, for example, by the 'improvement of *microscopical observations* ...
since this little *spot* is so *thickly peopled* in every *Atom* of it'.[32]

Glanvill's focus on witchcraft *knowledge* rather than witchcraft *belief*
was shared by seventeenth-century authors of medical tracts like Cotta and
Drage.[33] Cotta, in particular, established an epistemology and methodology

---

[28] Glanvill, *A Blow at Modern Sadducism*, pp. 93–4.
[29] Joseph Glanvill, *A Philosophical Endeavour* (London: James Collins, 1666), p. 12.
[30] Ibid., p. 13.
[31] Glanvill, *A Blow at Modern Sadducism*, p. 89.
[32] Glanvill, *A Philosophical Endeavour*, p. 9.
[33] Stuart Clark, *Thinking with Demons: The Idea of Witchcraft in Early Modern Europe*
(Oxford: Oxford University Press, 1997), p. 155.

of knowledge of witchcraft (like any other object of investigation) acquired by sense experience and reason.[34]

The perception of spirits and witchcraft as facts that could be proven shed light on the wide use of empiricist experiments in witch trials. Furthermore, the legal arena became the central location for proving the existence of witchcraft. The importance of the legal arena for proving facts was the focus of the analysis by Barbara Shapiro, which demonstrated how science was influenced by the concept of fact already established in law. Other findings suggest that the experiment format began to flourish around the end of the sixteenth century both in and out of the courtroom. The experiments were popular not only in the courtroom, where they enjoyed judicial cooperation, but at the pre-trial stages as well, and often before the case went to the magistrate. As in the times of the ordeals, supernatural indicia were sought after. However, trust, a fundamental feature of the ordeal system, was not blindly given to the signs. On the contrary, supernatural signs had to be repeatedly tested and verified as facts. Part of the experiments' reliability stemmed from their potential to expose counterfeit bewitchments and false accusations, although in practice they were often repeated until they successfully proved guilt.[35]

What seems today to be a contradiction between a scientific format and supernatural content was not experienced as dissonance by the contemporaries. Belief in spirits and witches was, by and large, shared by most members of society. The debate did not focus on the question of whether witchcraft existed, but rather on *how* to prove it. After the withdrawal of clerical sanction and the abolition of the ordeals, new meaning was ascribed to existing cultural tools, the supernatural signs, and they became grounded in a new rational and factual epistemology.

The texts under study illustrate the significant role of the middling sort and lower gentry in this transformation. Affluent families used their influence and resources to subject suspects to a series of supernatural tests carefully

---

[34]   Ibid; George Lyman Kittredge, *Witchcraft in Old and New England* (Cambridge, MA: Harvard University Press, 1929), p. 293; Barbara J. Shapiro, *Probability and Certainty in Seventeenth-Century England: A Study of the Relationships between Natural Science, Religion, History, Law, and Literature* (Princeton, NJ: Princeton University Press, 1983), p. 201.

[35]   Two untypical examples are found in the evidence submitted at the trial against Richard Hathaway, who was charged with counterfeiting bewitchment. In one event, the minister manipulated him into scratching another woman, thus exposing his pretended recovery. In another event, Dr Hamilton locked up the allegedly bewitched victim, Hathaway, to observe whether he fasted for as long a period as he had claimed. Although he did not see Hathaway eating, Hamilton still believed he did. *The Tryal of Richard Hathaway*, pp. 2, 23.

constructed and methodically pre-arranged as experiments. This helped bolster the case against the suspect even before it went to the magistrate. Families' social standing in the community contributed to the dissemination of these methods. In cases that became precedents, the members of these families were even able to convince the assize judges to cooperate in the experiments. The members of the middling sort and lower gentry were powerful agents of social and cultural change that preceded new developments in natural philosophy. The construction of the supernatural tests as factual experiments occurred well before what we today call 'science' came into being.

It may very well be true that the mob storming to swim or scratch a suspect was less interested in establishing rational grounds for the proof of witchcraft. However, it is clear that supernatural signs were used by a wide social spectrum from the lower to higher classes. In addition, the construction of the tests as experiments appealed to those seeking factual and rational methods of proof. Therefore, it would be wrong to characterize the debate on supernatural tests as extreme polarization between the elite and the lower classes or between credulity and scepticism.[36] Still, it is interesting to see that although elite writers and judges vehemently rejected swimming and scratching as vulgar and superstitious, they lent support to other supernatural experiments. It is not clear why scratching and swimming tests were looked on with contempt while other supernatural tests were willingly adopted. The reason cannot possibly be the theological difficulties posed by the use of swimming and scratching, practices which were considered witchcraft in themselves according to some of the divines. The other experiments carried similar theological risks.

A tempting explanation might be related to the physical cruelty of swimming and scratching. Perhaps the scorn poured on swimming and scratching as vulgar and superstitious methods allowed the elite to distinguish themselves as more refined. It should also be remembered that the English prided themselves on the lack of torture in their legal system. However, when considering the support of some elite writers for the procedures of pricking or crude searching for the devil's mark, and the social legitimacy of executions and pillory sessions as punishments, this explanation fails to be entirely convincing. In addition, a non-violent supernatural measure such as comparing the weight of the suspect to the weight of the Bible (believing the Bible outweighed witches) was rare.[37]

---

[36]   These findings support Gaskill's analysis, according to which the decline of witchcraft prosecution should not be explained by a model of polarization between sceptical elite and credulous popular culture. Malcolm Gaskill, *Crime and Mentalities in Early Modern England* (Cambridge: Cambridge University Press, 2000), pp. 95, 118.

[37]   The procedure did not include physical coercion, but involved humiliation by stripping the suspect 'of all her clothes'. Christina Hole, *A Mirror of Witchcraft* (London:

The question of why scratching and swimming were condemned as low-class practices, while the other supernatural methods enjoyed support, still awaits a satisfactory answer.

Co-optation may be a plausible explanation – the incorporation of some elements of alternative methods of obtaining proof that existed outside the formal legal institutions to diffuse the potentially greater threat to the legal establishment. Supernatural signs encompassed a body of procedures and evidentiary techniques that existed as a grassroots alternative to the jurisdiction of the court system. Such a popular alternative posed a threat to the exclusive jurisdiction of the central legal system of the state and to the legitimacy, logic and order of its proceedings. Therefore, inclusion of supernatural procedures as part of the official legal system helped to circumvent these external threats by applying only minor incremental changes. Those threatening external procedures were slightly modified as they were moulded into the format of experiments. This modification neutralized the threat, as it turned the supernatural procedure into rational fact-finding. Moreover, instead of being threatened by alternative modes of proof, the official legal system enjoyed further legitimization by applying rational logic to practices formerly outside its boundaries. Co-optation also prevented the alienation of many people who believed in the validity of supernatural methods. Reconstructed as experiments, supernatural techniques were removed from the realm of vulgar superstition and subjected to the rational and methodological quest for justice and discovery of the truth. As torture was illegal, swimming and scratching, even if they were designed as experiments, could not be imported into the courtroom and could not be embraced along with other supernatural techniques. A side benefit of the co-optation strategy was an addition to the arsenal of courtroom proof techniques that made it easier to cope with proving the crime of witchcraft.

Chatto & Windus, 1957), p. 172. This method secured acquittal, a fact that undoubtedly made the method unpopular. With this method, it was also futile to repeat the experiment until it finally succeeded, that is, until it finally proved guilt.

Chapter 10
Judicial Assessment of Narratives and Statements

Figure 10.1 'Many poor women imprisoned, and hanged for Witches'
From Ralph Gardiner, *Englands Grievance Discovered* ... (London: R. Ibbitson and P. Stent, 1655). [Classmark: M.6.8²²] Courtesy of Cambridge University Library.

As part of the medieval procedure of compurgation, or wager of law, witnesses made a sworn statement affirming the truthfulness of the claims of the party they supported, and their oath was not subjected to cross-examination.[1] The fact-finders in witch trials had to rely almost entirely on narrations. Suspects,

---

[1]   John Hamilton Baker, *An Introduction to English Legal History*, 3rd edn (London: Butterworths, 1990), p. 5.

accusers and witnesses told their stories, and the judiciary faced the tremendous challenge of distinguishing true stories from false ones.

Different narrators had different knowledge, biases, personalities and perceptual limitations. To reach a decision, the fact-finders needed to assess the veracity and importance of the various testimonies. It was important that they consider not only *what* these stories were about, but also *who* told them. The trustworthiness and quality of witnesses were determined both by their individual traits and according to the group of witnesses to which they belonged.

The focus of this analysis, as in other parts of this study, is not on the actual rules of evidence that were used in the courtroom, but on the social attitudes and opinions regarding the question of who should be believed and why. Early modern England saw significant developments of evidentiary rules pertaining to the identity of the witnesses and to the form and content of their testimony. The difficulty of proving witchcraft posed considerable challenges to the assessment of the truthfulness of narratives, and the debate included consideration of evidentiary methods not specific to witchcraft cases (such as credibility, the value of uncorroborated confessions, and so on).

Witness Categories

Because testimony was still to be accepted on oath in the sixteenth century, the defendant's objections could only be to the competency of the witness (to keep categories of potential liars outside the courtroom) rather than to credibility.[2] At first, witnesses were filtered through various competency rules that aimed to exclude the possibly biased witnesses. Categories of incompetent witnesses included defendants in criminal cases, 'spouses of parties, persons with financial interest in the case, convicted felons, irreligious persons', and so on.[3] In Baker's words, it was 'rather a law of witnesses than of evidence'.[4] Later, the focus shifted from competency to credibility.

This chapter is dedicated to three categories of witnesses in witchcraft cases: children (on the basis of age, normally regarded as incompetent because of a lower level of understanding); accomplices (whose competence was challenged

---

[2]   Sir James Fitzjames Stephen, *A History of the Criminal Law of England*, vol. 1 (London: Macmillan, 1883), p. 400.

[3]   George Fisher, 'The Jury's Rise as Lie Detector', *The Yale Law Journal*, no. 107 (1997): p. 624.

[4]   John Hamilton Baker, 'Criminal Courts and Procedure at Common Law 1550–1800', in J.S. Cockburn (ed.), *Crime in England 1550–1800* (Princeton, NJ: Princeton University Press, 1977), p. 39.

by conflicting interests); and expert witnesses (whose knowledge was a source of authority but also a potential threat to judicial superiority). The debate around these three categories demonstrates major considerations in evaluation of testimonies.

Children

Children were normally regarded as incompetent witnesses. The testimony of children under the age of 14 was not generally allowed. Sir Matthew Hale remarked that the testimony of a child between the ages of 9 and 13 might be admitted 'in some cases'.[5] The rationale, Gilbert explained, relying on Hale and a list of court cases, was 'the Want of Skill and Discernment ... *Ideots*, *Madmen*, and *Children* under the Age of common Knowledge ... are perfectly incapable of any Sense of Truth, and therefore are plainly excluded. Children under the Age of 14 are not regularly admitted as Witnesses.'[6]

Yet, in proving witchcraft, the competency rules were bent. The testimony of otherwise incompetent witnesses, such as children under 13, could be admitted to prove crimes like 'rape, buggery, witchcraft and such crimes'.[7] Henry Goodcole, the minister who tried to compel Elizabeth Sawyer to confess, reported that 'some children of a good bignesse, and reasonable vnderstanding' testified in court 'that they had diuers times seene her feed two white ferrets with white bread & milk'.[8] It remains obscure what exactly 'good bignesse' meant. Obviously, Goodcole was trying to justify the reliance on testimonies that led to Sawyer's execution by emphasizing the children's maturity.

The issue of children's testimony was even more problematic in many cases where children were required to give testimony against their own parents. James I maintained that children's testimony was acceptable. One of the characters in his dialogue expressed the dilemma: 'For it is as great a crime ... *To condemne the innocent, as to let the guiltie escape free*.'[9] He therefore concluded that in cases of

---

[5] Sir Matthew Hale, *Pleas of the Crown* (London: William Shrewsbery and Juon Leigh, 1678), p. 224.

[6] Sir Geoffrey Gilbert, *The Law of Evidence* (London: W. Owen, 1756), pp. 146–7.

[7] See Barbara J. Shapiro, *A Culture of Fact: England, 1550–1720* (Ithaca, NY: Cornell University Press, 2000), p. 221, fn. 237.

[8] Henry Goodcole, *The Wonderfull Discouerie of Elizabeth Savvyer a Witch* (London: Vvilliam Butler, 1621), C4.

[9] James I, *Daemonologie* (Edinburgh: Robert Walde-graue, 1597), p. 78, notes omitted.

serious crimes, problematic categories of witnesses (including the children of the accused) should be allowed to testify.[10]

James I believed that the severity of the crime justified admitting evidence otherwise inadmissible, including testimony of children against their parents.[11] Reginald Scot pointed out that Bodin, the renowned French jurist, approved the interrogation of children for statements against their own mothers in cases of witchcraft.[12] Scot, however, believed that youthfulness (among other qualities) reflected negatively on the 'credit' and 'weight and importance' of the testimony. Discussing an account published two years earlier, *A True and Iust Recorde*, Scot considered childhood among other criteria that damaged the value of witnesses.

> Sée whether the witnesses be not single of what credit, sex and age they are; namelie lewd, miserable, and envious poore people; most of them which speake to anie purpose being old women, & children of the age of 4.5.6.7.8. or 9. yeares. And note how and what the witches confesse, and sée of what weight and importance the causes are.[13]

To Scot, the meaning of the terms credit and weight was to a large extent an extrapolation from the category to which the witness belonged. Thus, the veracity of the testimony of children under the age of nine was questionable. Although to some limited extent Scot referred to the individual characteristics of the how and what of the testimony, he had not as yet developed the conceptualization of credit and weight.

Gifford, an eminent preacher of Maldon, in Essex, was also critical of using children against their parents:

> Yea sundry tymes the euidence of children is taken accusing their owne mothers, that they did see them giue milke vnto little thinges which they kept in wooll, The children comming to yeares of discretion confesse they were entised to accuse.[14]

---

[10]   'But in my opinion, since in a mater of treason against the Prince, *barnes* [Offsprings, sons or daughters] or wiues, or neuer so diffamed persons, may of our law serue for sufficient witnesses and proofes. I thinke surely that by a far greater reason, such witnesses may be sufficient in matters of high treason against God: For who but Witches can be prooues, and so witnesses of the doings of Witches.' Emphasis added. Ibid., p. 79.

[11]   Ibid., pp. 78–9.

[12]   Reginald Scot, *The Discouerie of Witchcraft* (London: William Brome, 1584), p. 20.

[13]   Ibid., pp. 542–3.

[14]   George Gifford, *A Discourse of the Subtill Practises of Deuilles by Vvitches and Sorcerers* (London: Toby Cooke, 1587), G4v.

Gifford stressed that children could be easily incited and their testimony against their mothers should be looked on with suspicion. The execution of innocent people on the testimony of their own children was another evil ploy of the devil. The evidentiary effectiveness of children's testimony was a minor concern. The major concern was to resist devilish wickedness.

It is most likely that when Gifford criticized the testimony of children, he had in mind a trial that had been held five years previously in St Osyth, a few miles away.[15] In that case, eight-year-old Thomas Rabbeth, the 'base son' of Ursley Kemp, was made to testify against his mother.[16] Another eight-year-old child, Febey Hunt, deposed against her stepmother, Ales Hunt.[17] Henry Sills, nine years old, deposed that his father scolded his mother 'why thou whore cannot you keepe your impes from my childre~[...] whereat shee presently called it away'. His younger brother, John Sills, under seven, was also examined.[18] Annis Dowsing, the seven-year-old 'base' daughter of Annis Herd, deposed that her mother kept spirits in a box.[19] Clearly, Gifford's opinion did not prevail, and in many cases children's testimony, even against their own parents or grandparents, was permitted.[20] The acceptance of children's testimony continued after the publication of Gifford's book. The ten- and twelve-year-old 'bastard' boys of the 'two lewde Daughters' of Joan Cunny, delivered 'great euidence' against their mother and grandmother.[21] Henry Sutton 'the Bastard of *Mary Sutton*', quoted an incriminating conversation between his mother and grandmother, 'little thinking that his fortune should be to give in evidence to breake the necke of his owne Mother and Grandmother'.[22] According to the pamphlet, the boy also admitted that his mother's 'Spirits in severall shapes as Cats, Moals, &c. used to sucke her'.[23] His mother, Mary Sutton, kept denying the allegations against her, even after she was swum and searched for teats. However, when her accuser told her that 'her owne sonne *Henry* had revealed all ... her heart misgave her, she confessed all, and acknowledged the Divell had

---

[15] I am grateful to Robin Briggs for suggesting this point.

[16] W.W., *A True and Iust Recorde* ... (London: Thomas Dawson, 1582), 2A3v.

[17] Ibid., 2A5v.

[18] Ibid., D, D2.

[19] Ibid., F4.

[20] J.S. Cockburn, *Calendar of Assize Records*, 11 vols (London: Her Majesty's Stationery Office, 1985), vol. 1, p. 106.

[21] *The Apprehension and Confession of Three Notorious Witches* (London: E. Allde, 1589), A4.

[22] W., *A True and Iust Recorde*, Cv.

[23] Ibid., C3.

not left her to that shame that is reward to such as follow him'.[24] Nine-year-old Jennet Device was reported to have testified against her mother and other family members and 'to discover all their Practises, Meetings, consultations, Murthers, Charmes, and Villanies'.[25] The fact that Alizon Device was accused by her own children, Jennet and her older brother James, did not discredit their story, implied Thomas Potts. On the contrary, 'although she were their owne naturall mother, yet they did not spare to accuse her of every particular fact'.[26] Potts regarded the children's testimony, coming from the mouths of infants, as God-sent help:

> such a young witnesse prepeared and instructed to give Evidence against them, that it must be an Act of GOD that must be the means to discover their Practises and Murthers, and by an infant.[27]

Children's testimony was sometimes presented as the breaking point of their mother. Alizon Device was reported to have made 'a very liberall and voluntarie Confession as hereafter shall be given in evidence against her, upon her Arraignment and Triall', after learning that her daughter Jennet had implicated her.[28] It is possible that in some cases the pamphleteers manipulated the dates to avoid the impression of exploiting the children to obtain the mothers' confessions. Sometimes the children's testimony was presented as if they confirmed the mothers' confessions, whereas, in fact, the children were investigated first.[29] In some cases the children's ages are not mentioned.[30] The reason, perhaps, might be the pamphleteer's wish to undermine suspicions of manipulation.

Michael Dalton's popular manual for justices reflected a legal descriptive approach to the subject of children's testimony. Dalton acknowledged the

---

[24]   Ibid., C3–C3v.

[25]   Thomas Potts, *The Vvonderfull Discouerie of Witches in the Countie of Lancaster* (London: Iohn Barnes, 1613), F2v–F3.

[26]   Ibid.

[27]   Ibid., K3v.

[28]   Ibid., F2v–F3.

[29]   Gibson analysed several such instances: the deposition of Henry Sutton against his mother and grandmother, Jennet Device's testimony against her mother and Febey Hunt's deposition against her mother. Marion Gibson (ed.), *Early Modern Witches: Witchcraft Cases in Contemporary Writing* (London: Routledge, 2000), pp. 84, fn. 25; 201, fn. 276; 275, fn. 217.

[30]   For example, in the case of Phillip and Margaret Flower, who testified against their mother. *The Wonderful Discouerie of the Vvitchcrafts of Margaret and Phillip Flower ...* (London: Barnes, 1619), F3–F4.

difficulty of proving witchcraft and provided a list of evidentiary rules based on the Lancaster precedent from 1612, including 'The examination and confession of the children, or seruants of the Witch'.[31] Giving references to the relevant pages in Potts' pamphlet, Dalton cited a few examples of children who deposed against their mothers and later testified in court.[32] Dalton's approach was descriptive, as he aimed to portray the existing legal norm as it was reflected in contemporary cases. However, by uncritically relying on precedents, Dalton supported modification of the general rule against the testimony of young children. By describing the practice of children's testimony in witchcraft cases as the norm, Dalton advocated setting a lower standard of proof for the crime.

In his *Guide to Grand-Iury Men*, Bernard listed possible concerns regarding the credibility of types of witnesses. Children belonged to the category of less credible witnesses:

> some are fearfull, superstitious, or children, or old silly persons, whose testimonies are to be heard, but not easily credited, as being persons in such a case as this is, very much subiect to mistaking.[33]

Like Scot, Bernard associated credit with the category the witness belonged to. Unlike Dalton, he expressed uneasiness about the truthfulness of children.

A later legal author relied on both Potts and Bernard when he provided signs for the discovery of witches, including:

> the examination and confession of the Children (able and fit to answer) or servants of the Witch; especially concerning the first six observations of the party suspected; Her threatnings and cursings of the sick party; her enquiring after the sick party; her boasting or rejoycing at the sick parties trouble: Also whether they have seen her call upon, speak to, or feed any Spirit, or such like; or have heard her foretell of this mishap, or speak of her power to hurt, or of her transportation to this or that place, &c.[34]

Children's testimony was permitted as long as they were 'able and fit to answer'. The topics they could testify to were based on precedents. Their testimony, an aberration of normal procedure, was to be accepted, but with caution.

---

[31]   Michael Dalton, *The Countrey Iustice* (London: Societie of Stationers, 1618), p. 243.

[32]   Ibid., p. 261.

[33]   Richard Bernard, *A Guide to Grand-Iury Men* (London: Ed. Blackmore, 1627), pp. 230–32. Footnote omitted.

[34]   *The Lawes against Vvitches, and Coniuration* (London: R.W., 1645), p. 5.

We can speculate whether the lack of competency limitations in witchcraft cases helped to develop criteria of credibility. If everyone was competent to give evidence, it was necessary to find a method to assess the value of each testimony. The following chapter discusses the concept of credibility as it was developed in the second half of the seventeenth century.

Accomplices

Accomplices were another category of problematic witnesses. Many witchcraft suspects implicated others, saying they had bodily marks and imps in various shapes that they fed and suckled and whose malicious services they enjoyed.[35] The multiple-defendants' cases inspired by Matthew Hopkins involved multiple allegations of witchcraft by the defendants against each other.[36] Suspects in a serious crime who incriminate others through their own confessions might have other interests than the uncovering of the truth.

As objections began to be raised as to credit and weight, the motives and character of accomplices started to be taken into account. At the beginning of the seventeenth century, confessions of accomplices were admitted against each other and even considered as 'specially cogent evidence'.[37] Accomplices' testimony clearly contained a potential bias, especially when it consequently benefited the accomplice by granting immunity. By the middle of the eighteenth century, the testimony of an accomplice who turned king's evidence and incriminated his confederate for immunity or some other benefit could be admitted without corroboration.[38] In contrast, an accomplice's testimony in favour of the prisoner bore little weight.[39]

The crime of witchcraft was committed in secrecy, and the knowledge of the accomplices was invaluable. In his *Daemonologie*, James I included the rhetorical question: 'For who but Witches can be prooues, and so witnesses of the doings

---

[35] For a few examples, see *Vvitchcrafts of Margaret and Phillip Flower*, E4v–F2; *A True and Impartial Relation* ... (London: Freeman Collins, 1682), p. 37; John Davenport, *The Witches of Huntingdon* (London: Richard Clutterbuck, 1646), p. 5.

[36] *The Examination, Confession, Triall, and Execution, of Joane Williford, Joan Cariden, and Jane Hott* (London: J.G., 1645), pp. 2, 5–6; H.F., *A True and Exact Relation* ... (London: Henry Overton and Benj. Allen, 1645), pp. 2–6, 32.

[37] However, in treason it needed to be corroborated, a principle that was frequently disregarded. Stephen, *A History of the Criminal Law of England*, vol. 1, pp. 350, 400–401.

[38] Baker, 'Criminal Courts', p. 40; J.M. Beattie, *Crime and the Courts in England, 1660–1800* (Princeton, NJ: Princeton University Press, 1986), p. 371.

[39] William Nelson, *The Law of Evidence* (London: B. Gosling, 1735), p. 283.

of Witches.'[40] The confederates were the best source of information. This logic led both lawyers and clergymen to support the use of accomplices' testimony.

From a legal point of view, the possibility of proving a case by the accomplice's testimony was legitimate and even applauded. Thomas Potts explained that accomplices' testimony was especially probative in cases of witchcraft.

> Who but Witches can be proofes, and so witnesses of the doings of Witches? Since all their Meetings, Conspiracies, Practises, and Murthers, are the workes of Darknesse.[41]

Potts, who quoted James I without due reference, found his logic convincing. Witchcraft, by nature, was a crime without witnesses. The accomplice was the partner who shared the secret crime and was an excellent source of information.

Bernard, in his *Guide to Grand-Iury Men*, asserted that the testimony of a fellow witch proved the crime. Interestingly, Bernard believed that the statements of cunning men (the 'good witches') ought not to be admitted. Supposedly, the cunning men possessed supernatural powers and could recognize other witches. Bernard did not articulate an explanation to his distinction between good and bad witches. We may speculate that the difference between accomplices and unrelated witches was their possession or lack of direct knowledge of the crime. The accomplices reported to have actually seen the witches:

> with their spirits, or that they haue receiued spirits from them; that they can tell, when they vsed Witcherie tricks to do harme; or that they told to do harme; or that they had done; or that they can shew the marke vpon them; or that they haue bin together in their meetings, and such like, as the Lancashire Witches gaue testimony one against another of these things.[42]

It was not the supernatural capabilities of the accomplices that rendered their testimony sufficient for conviction, but their direct observation of the crime. Bernard also relied on Potts' account as a precedent of legitimate evidentiary use of accomplices' testimony.

A later legal scholar relied on both Potts and Bernard when he included among the signs for discovery of witches:

---

[40]   James I, *Daemonologie*, p. 79.
[41]   Potts, *The Vvonderfull Discouerie of Witches*, P3.
[42]   Bernard, *A Guide to Grand-Iury Men*, pp. 222–3.

the testimony of other Witches, confessing their own Witchcrafts, and witnessing against the suspected, and that they have Spirits, or Markes; that they have been at their meetings: that they have told them what harme they have done, &c.[43]

The testimony of the accomplice was found to be valuable evidence, not only by legal scholars, but also by several clergymen. Cooper, a cleric who advocated severe measures against witches, held:

> The *Accusaion of a fellow Witch*, either at examination, or *at the day of death* is not to bee neglected, because now *Authoritie* hauing seized on hir, though she may *lie* before she be discouered, yet now hauing confessed herselfe, she is an *Instrument of the Lords Iustice, to satisfie Authoritie,* and cleare the innocent, by speaking truth, &c. (though otherwise shee would not) to accuse the delinquent.[44]

For Cooper, the accomplice's testimony was a divine miracle in which the suspect was transformed from an instrument of darkness into an instrument of divine justice leading to the discovery of truth. Gaule, the vicar of Great Staughton, in Huntingdonshire, agreed that testimony from others, 'whom other notorious Witches have impeached to be as ill as themselves', was an 'infallible and certain sign of witchcraft'.[45]

Their confidence was not shared by all. Gifford rejected the statements of those who were already convicted and about to be executed. Even if such statements were sincerely made, the convicted witches might be 'vtterly deluded', that is, under the illusion of having received imps from other women.[46] The devil could 'set a strong fantasie in the mind that is oppressed with melancholie, that such or such a matter was, which indéed was neuer so'.[47] A century later, the prominent New England Puritan clergyman Increase Mather expressed similar ideas in an address given in the aftermath of the Salem trials, and later published as a book in Boston and then in London. Mather argued that suspects who confessed and implicated others in witchcraft were 'not such credible Witnesses, as in a Case of Life and Death is to be desired: It is beyound dispute, that the Devil makes his Witches to dream strange things of themselves and others which are not

---

[43]   *The Lawes against Vvitches*, p. 5.

[44]   Thomas Cooper, *The Mystery of Witch-Craft* (London: Nicholas Okes, 1617), pp. 274–5.

[45]   John Gaule, *Select Cases of Conscience Touching Vvitches and Vvitchcrafts* (London: Richard Clutterbuck, 1646), p. 82.

[46]   George Gifford, *A Dialogue Concerning Witches and Witchcraftes* (London: Tobie Cooke and Mihil, 1593), K2v.

[47]   Ibid., K3.

so.'[48] Mather's disapproval of the accomplice testimony was part of his general criticism of the evidentiary techniques used in witchcraft trials, most famously spectral evidence. The unreliability of accomplices' testimony derived from its spectral nature.

Perkins, the leading English Puritan thinker, ranked accomplices' testimony as a lower-rate proof, a 'presumption' sufficient to warrant an examination, but not enough to support conviction.[49] The testimony of '*a Wisard Witch or cunning Man*' (who were not accomplices) he similarly considered to be of 'lesse sufficient proofe'. Perkins did not want the jurors to rely on a witness who might actually be the devil who 'comes in the likenesse of some knowne man, & tells them the person in question is indeed a Witch, and offers with all to confirme the same by othe'. Under no circumstances, Perkins made clear, could the testimony of a wizard serve as a basis for conviction.[50] Theoretically, similar logic could apply to disqualifying the testimony of the accomplice. The devil might implicate innocent people through allegations made by another witch. However, Perkins did not explain if this was the reason that he considered the accomplice's testimony as a mere presumption, which was insufficient for conviction.

Some legal thinkers also expressed concern about the use of accomplices' testimony. Filmer, who opposed Perkins' evidentiary methods, simply cited Perkins to demonstrate that the testimony of 'a fellow Witch' was not good evidence.[51] Filmer, although he himself disapproved of accomplices' testimony, depicted Perkins as opposing James VI & I, who regarded accomplices' testimony as valuable proof.[52]

A major concern missing from this debate is the emerging practice of crown witnesses (accomplices who became prosecution witnesses in return for receiving benefits). Judge Hale (d. 1676) stated that:

> it would be hard to take away the life of any person upon such a witness, that swears to save his own, and yet confesseth himself guilty of so great a crime, unless

---

[48] At the same time, Increase Mather supported his son, Cotton, who defended the proceedings, refrained from criticism against the judges and, in particular, approved the execution of George Burroughs, a dissenting minister. Increase Mather, *Cases of Conscience Concerning Evil Spirits ...* (London: Dunton, 1693), pp. 35–6; Bernard Rosenthal, *Salem Story* (Cambridge, UK: Cambridge University Press, 1993), pp. 135–7.

[49] William Perkins, *A Discourse of the Damned Art of Witchcraft* (Cambridge, UK: Vniuersitie of Cambridge, 1608), pp. 201–2.

[50] Ibid., p. 209.

[51] Sir Robert Filmer, *An Advertisement to the Jury-Men of England, Touching Witches* (London: Richard Royston, 1653), pp. 9–10.

[52] Ibid., pp. 11–12.

there be also very considerable circumstances, which may give the greater credit to what he swears.[53]

Hale's opinion did not prevail, and the practice of prisoners' avoiding prosecution or pleading to a lesser or clergiable charge continued to develop, eventually resulting in what Langbein called 'the corroboration rule' or 'the accomplice rule'.[54] Under this rule, as it was articulated in the 1740s, an accomplice's testimony was to be excluded unless it was corroborated by other evidence. The rule was mollified in the 1780s, when jurors were requested only to be cautious.[55] The rationale is obvious – the incentive of the accomplice to lie in order to save his neck was an invitation to perjury. Although some evidence suggests that the plea-bargaining practice started to appear around 1575,[56] there is no known evidence that it was employed in any of the witch trials. Some trials ended in the conviction of the defendant of lesser and non-capital charges, but there was no indication that it was the result of plea bargaining (although the possibility of such a practice cannot be ruled out). Witchcraft was, under statute, a non-clergiable offence, which limited the bargaining possibilities.

But even without the option of plea bargaining, suspects in witchcraft cases had motives for falsely implicating others. After Ursley Kemp had confessed on 20 February 1582, she made another confession the next day, in which she tried to shift much of the blame to another woman, Ales Newman. Kemp is reported to have admitted that she had asked Newman to send her imp to a woman with whom she had quarreled. This version cleared her from managing a direct contact with the devil. In addition, Kemp implicated two other women.[57]

Other motivations for falsely implicating others could be the wish of a suspect for revenge or perhaps the attempt of a desperate suspect to expose the unbearable ease with which innocent people were executed for crimes in which innocence was impossible to prove. Such may be the case of 1645 in which Anne Leech, being interrogated, implicated three other women. Two of these women, Elizabeth Clarke and Elizabeth Gooding, whom she blamed for having imps

---

[53]   Sir Matthew Hale, *Historia Placitorum Coronae* (London: F. Gyles, T. Woodward, and C. Davis, 1736), p. 305.

[54]   For a comprehensive discussion about the dangers inherent in accomplices' testimony and the formation of the corroboration rule, see John H. Langbein, *The Origins of Adversary Criminal Trial*, Oxford Studies in Modern Legal History (Oxford: Oxford University Press, 2003), pp. 158–65, 179, 203–17.

[55]   Ibid., pp. 179, 203.

[56]   Baker, 'Criminal Courts', p. 35; Cockburn, *Calendar*, pp. 66, 105.

[57]   W., *A True and Iust Recorde*, B2, B3–B3v; Gibson (ed.), *Early Modern Witches*, p. 85, fn. 30.

and doing harm, were stereotypical witchcraft suspects, and her charges against them did not raise doubts. However, the accusations of Leech against the third woman angered the pamphleteer significantly:

> VVHereas there was a Booke (of the Essex Witches) came forth in print, wherein on Mrs Wayt a Ministers wife was nominiated for one, but it was a palpable mistake, for it is very well knowne that she is a gentlewoman of a very godly and religious life, and a very good conuersations: and this was set on purpose to vindicate her: and lay the fault on the Author, in whom it was a great mistake.[58]

When it came to an accusation against the minister's wife, the author had no doubt it was false. The dangers inherent in the testimony of a fellow witch might have been more visible when the charges were directed against a reputed person.

The value of statements made by suspects against confederates was under debate. The dispute cannot be clearly drawn along lines of professional affiliation (though it seems that, in general, lawyers were more supportive of the use of accomplices' testimony, whereas clerics diverged in their opinions). In practice, however, accusations of suspects against others were often made during the criminal proceeding.

Expert Witnesses

Expert witnesses formed another distinct category in dealing with proof of witchcraft. The involvement of experts in witch trials generated a debate in which three main elite discourses, the medical, the legal and the theological, interacted, sometimes competing with, and sometimes complementing, one another.

Overall, the physicians were most successful in positioning themselves as experts in witch trials. Some cases even turned into a battle of experts in which physicians testified for both parties. In some cases a physician was summoned by the bench. Educated physicians strove to distinguish themselves from other contemporary medical practitioners, who included apothecaries, barber-surgeons, uroscopists, herbalists, empirics, midwives, astrologers, tooth-drawers, lithotomists and cunning men and women.[59] Physicians used the arena of the witch trials to advance their professional superiority, although their prominent role in witch trials was not obvious. Presumably, clergymen were the best

---

[58]   *A True Relation of the Araignment of Eighteene Vvitches* (London: I.H., 1645), p. 8.

[59]   Andrew Wear, 'The Popularization of Medicine in Early Modern England', in Roy Porter (ed.), *The Popularization of Medicine, 1650–1850* (London: Routledge, 1992), p. 19.

experts on the subject of witches and devils. Yet, the clerics were unsuccessful in establishing for themselves a pivotal position in the process of criminal adjudication.

Were doctors, judges or divines best suited to determine whether an illness was caused by witchcraft? The physicians' claim to exclusive expertise was received with ambivalence. Some supported the use of expert witnesses – defenders and accusers alike, as well as the judiciary, used experts to reach a determination. Nonetheless, the claim of exclusive ability to diagnose medical symptoms and determine whether they were natural was sometimes disapproved of by judges. They did not want to delegate to the doctors the ultimate power to determine facts and preferred that the testimony of the expert witnesses be just another piece of evidence to be accepted or rejected at the discretion of the fact-finders.

Physicians' advice was often sought in the preliminary stages of the case, well before it reached court, because those who fell ill sought diagnosis and medical help.[60] The magistrate investigating the case sometimes procured the expert opinion of a physician on whether the symptoms were natural or unnatural. The expert's opinion could also be obtained at the trial itself, either at the request of the bench or of one of the parties. The expert witness at the trial was not necessarily the physician who initially treated the patient. The first known witchcraft case that turned into a battle of experts was in 1602, when Elizabeth Jackson was indicted for bewitching Mary Glover.[61] Both the prosecution and defence tried to prove their arguments by summoning medical experts to testify on their behalf. Another notable case was the trial against Rose Cullender and Amy Denny, where the court, presided over by Sir Matthew Hale, used Sir Thomas Browne as an expert witness. Through their role as experts in witchcraft cases, physicians sought not only to determine whether a certain symptom originated from witchcraft, but also to define the boundaries, identity and standards of the medical profession.

It is unclear whether defendants were routinely allowed to call expert witnesses on their behalf. By the mid-seventeenth century, it was common to

---

[60]   Philip Almond, *Demonic Possession and Exorcism in Early Modern England* (Cambridge, UK: Cambridge University Press, 2004), p. 2.

[61]   For a review of the case and its political context, see the introduction in Michael MacDonald (ed.), *Witchcraft and Hysteria in Elizabethan England: Edward Jorden and the Mary Glover Case*, Tavistock Classics in the History of Psychiatry (London: Tavistock/ Routledge, 1991). The book also includes the three pamphlets relating to the case: Stephen Bradwell, *Marie Glovers Late Woefull Case* (London: 1603), British Library, Sloane MS 831; Edward Jorden, *A Briefe Discovrse of a Disease Called the Suffocation of the Mother* (London: Iohn Windet, 1603); John Swan, *A Trve and Breife Report of Mary Glovers Vexation ...* (London: s.n., 1603).

allow defence witnesses, although this was not yet a statutory right.[62] An account of the trial of Joan Peterson, in 1652, who was indicted for killing an 80-year-old woman by witchcraft, listed a few medical experts who testified in her defence:

> And being asked what she had to say for her self? (upon her knees) she took God to witnesse that she never knew the Lady Powel not the house where she dwelt, nor was any wise guilty of her death; and delivered a paper of such witnesses as she had to defend her, desiring that they might be called, whereupon Dr Bates, and Dr Colledon Physitians, together with Mr Stamford, and Mr Page Chyrurgians and divers other persons of good quality, testified the disease, manner of sickness, and the cause of the said Ladies death, which were the Dropsie, the Scurvey, and the yellow Jaundies, and that they wondered how she was able to live so long, having most of those diseases growing on her for many years before.[63]

The thrust of Peterson's defence was a medical argument – the elderly Lady Powell died from illnesses, an argument presented through a battery of experts. The pamphlet included the post mortem report of the late Lady Powell, which predated the trial by six months.[64] Possibly, Peterson heard about this report and asked the court to summon its authors. This case was tried during the interregnum, a historical period during which defendants enjoyed more procedural rights.[65] Thus, we may not confidently conclude that it was a typical case. The physicians were not always able to diagnose or cure the illness of their patients. For example, Dr Feavor, 'a doctor of physic', affirmed in court that he had examined nine-year-old Deborah Pacy but could not find the cause of her illness.[66] In such cases, doubts began to surface. Were the symptoms natural or unnatural? Was the disease caused by witchcraft?

Some patients, unsatisfied with their doctor's failure to determine the cause of their illness, sought the opinion of cunning men.[67] John Crumpt, according to a pamphlet of 1664, tried to get his daughter the best available medical care after she began to suffer from fits. When the local doctor could not cure her, the father arranged for her to be admitted to a London hospital. However, on the day of the admission of 'the afflicted Maid' into the Thomas Hospital in Southwark, the staff there advised the father that the girl was 'fitter for *Bedlam*

---

[62] Fisher, 'The Jury's Rise as Lie Detector', p. 604.

[63] *A Declaration in Answer to Several Lying Pamphlets Concerning the Witch of Wapping* (London: s.n.r., 1652), pp. 6–7.

[64] Ibid., pp. 10–11.

[65] Stephen, *A History of the Criminal Law of England*, vol. I, p. 358.

[66] *A Tryal of Witches ...* (London: William Shrewsbery, 1682), p. 59.

[67] W., *A True and Iust Recorde*, E.

[the notorious asylum for the mentally ill] than to come into an Hospital among sick People'. The aggrieved father consulted a man 'professing some skill in *Astrologie*', who attributed the illness to witchcraft, asked for a five-pound fee, but promised no result. The father turned his offer down and resolved that they should try to help themselves by fasting and prayer.[68]

Some patients sought a second medical opinion. For example, after the first doctor examined the urine of the Throckmorton girl and saw nothing wrong, the parents turned to Doctor Barrow, from Cambridge, who speculated that the girl might suffer from worms. None of the medicines he gave her helped. The third time the parents consulted with him, he speculated 'whether there was no sorcerie or witchcraft suspected in the child: answere was made no. Then sayd he, all surely cannot be well, for it is not possible that the childs bodie should be distempered by any naturall cause'.[69] Next, the parents obtained the advice of a third doctor, Master Butler, who also suspected worms and prescribed the same medicine as Dr Barrow. Thereafter, Mr Throckmorton decided to act on Dr Barrow's opinion that the daughter was bewitched and 'not strive any more therewith by phisick, nor spend any more money about it: for he himselfe sayd, he [the doctor] had some experiëce of the malice of some witches, & he verily thought there was some kind of sorcerie and witchcraft wrought towards his child'.[70]

It was commonly held that the inability to diagnose an illness medically implied that it was caused by witchcraft. In the words of one pamphleteer: 'It remaineth then that if those things were not meerly from a Natural Cause, then they must be Diabolical.'[71] This was not only considered a logical assumption, but also a valid legal conclusion. According to Brinely:

> when Learned Physicians can find no probable reason or Natural Cause for such Grief, Pangs, and violent Vexations as the Patient does endure, it may *lawfully* be Concluded that the Devils Finger is there.[72]

There are many accounts of doctors who advised their patients that they were bewitched. An account of 1678 described the story of a woman who was

---

68   John Barrow, *The Lord's Arm Stretched Ovt* ... (London: s.n., printed 1664), p. 18.

69   *The Most Strange and Admirable Discouerie of the Three Witches of Warboys* (London: Thomas Man, and Iohn Winington, 1593), A3v.

70   Ibid., p. A4. The parents of Faith Corbet also sought the advice of several physicians, locals at first and then a doctor from York. None of the physicians could help them. John Hale, *A Collection of Modern Relations* ... (London: John Harris, 1693), pp. 53–4.

71   Samuel Petto, *A Faithful Narrative* ... (London: John Harris, 1693), preface, image 3.

72   John Brinley, *A Discourse Proving by Scripture & Reason* ... (London: J.M., 1686), p. 60. Emphasis added.

examined by 'Several Physicians', but none could diagnose her 'so many different and unusual Symptoms'. The doctors ruled out the possibility that the woman suffered from any kind of 'Histerical Passions, or Fits of the Mother'. None of their prescriptions seemed to work, not even when they 'doubled their Doses of the most powerful Chymical Preparation'. The doctors' ultimate conclusion was that the woman was 'under an ill Tongue', or (as we commonly express it) 'bewitcht'.[73] When Dorcas Coleman suffered from severe pains, she went to Doctor Beare, and 'upon view of her Body he did say, that it was past his skill to ease her of her said Pains; for he told her that she was Bewitch'd'.[74] Bovet described the case of a respectable widow who became ill, and said that 'The Physicians were all of opinion that the inner parts of her body were wounded by some Diabolical Art, and ordered her to remove her Habitation'.[75]

Some doctors even considered themselves experts on the subject of witchcraft and prescribed counter-magic rather than medicine for their patients. For example, when Dorothy Durent suspected Amy Denny of bewitching her baby, she went to Dr Jacob, from Yarmouth, who 'had the reputation in the country to help children that were bewitched'. Dr Jacob's advice was to hang up the child's blanket in the chimney corner all day and to throw into the fire, without fear, anything she found in it.[76] A pamphlet of 1682, about the trial of Joan Butts, described the testimony of the parents of Mary Palmer, who was supposedly bewitched by the accused. The parents reported that after their daughter had been 'taken ill in an extraordinary and violent manner', their neighbours recommended Dr Bourn to them, who subsequently told them that 'their Child was under an ill Tongue, and advised them to save the Childs water, and put it into a Bottle, stopping it close, and bury it in the Earth, and to burn the Childs Clothes, assuring them, that then the *Witch* which had done her the hurt, would come in; and that accordingly they did so'.[77] In another case that same year, the doctor advised a man who suspected Jane Kent of killing his five-year-old daughter by witchcraft and of bewitching his wife, to boil a mixture of his wife's urine, paired nails and hair. Subsequently, the man heard the suspect screaming by his door 'as if she were

---

[73]   *Strange and Wonderful Nevvs from Goswell-Street* (London: printed for D.M., 1678), pp. 4–5.

[74]   *A True and Impartial Relation*, p. 2.

[75]   Richard Bovet, *Pandaemonium, or, the Devil's Cloyster* (London: J. Walthoe, 1684), p. 192.

[76]   *A Tryal of Witches ...*, pp. 5–6.

[77]   *An Account of the Tryal and Examination of Joan Buts ...* (London: S. Gardener, 1682), p. 1.

Murdered', and the next day she was reported to appear 'much swelled and bloated'.[78]

Judges, magistrates, municipal authorities, clerics, prosecutors and defendants used physicians to support their positions on witchcraft. At the same time, physicians used the context of witchcraft to advance their professional goals and to define the boundaries and the identity of their occupation. Witchcraft was often portrayed as the litmus test that distinguished learned and qualified physicians from the ignorant and the unskilled. Gaule claimed that when common people did not understand the cause of the disease and were not acquainted with its symptoms, they attributed it to witchcraft.[79] Other writers went so far as to suggest that this was also the practice of some of physicians. Scot argued that unskilled and unlearned physicians found it convenient to attribute to witchcraft those diseases they could not diagnose or treat.[80] Ady, writing 70 years after Scot, agreed that ignorant physicians tried to hide their lack of knowledge by accusations of witchcraft: 'the reason is, *Ignorantiae pallium maleficium & incantatio*, a cloak for a Physicians ignorance, when he cannot finde the nature of the Disease, he saith, the Party is bewitched.'[81] Even in the eighteenth century, there were still cases in which physicians who had been unable to cure their patient attributed the disease to witchcraft.[82]

An eighteenth-century pamphleteer criticized the logic behind attributing unidentified symptoms to witchcraft, saying: 'It is a *Negative Proposition*, and what therefore can never be plainly proved, unless its *Positive* can be brought to a flat Contradiction.' According to this author, it would have been more accurate for the doctors to state they had never met such a symptom before in their practice.[83]

---

[78]   *A Full and True Account of the Proceedings* ... (London: Printed for T. Benskin, 1682), p. 4.

[79]   Gaule, *Select Cases of Conscience*, p. 85.

[80]   Scot, *The Discouerie of Witchcraft*, p. 284.

[81]   Thomas Ady, *A Candle in the Dark* (London: Robert Ibbitson, 1655), pp. 114–15. Keith Thomas agreed that this was an accurate picture and referred to a list of cases to prove the point. Keith Thomas, *Religion and the Decline of Magic* (New York: Charles Scribner's Sons, 1971), p. 537, fn. 531. See also Gilbert Geis and Ivan Bunn, *A Trial of Witches: A Seventeenth-Century Witchcraft Prosecution* (London: Routledge, 1997), p. 173. Cf. Alan Macfarlane, 'Witchcraft in Tudor and Stuart Essex', in J.S. Cockburn (ed.), *Crime in England 1550–1800* (Princeton, NJ: Princeton University Press, 1977), p. 182.

[82]   Richard Hathaway, who was eventually convicted for counterfeiting bewitchment, was hospitalized twice, and the doctors, who were unable to cure him, concluded he was bewitched. *The Tryal of Richard Hathaway* (London: Isaac Cleave, 1702), p. 17.

[83]   *The Case of the Hertfordshire Witchcraft Consider'd* (London: John Pemberton, 1712), pp. 75–7.

Although such writers claimed that ignorance was the reason for erroneously diagnosing unknown diseases as witchcraft, this was not the same as saying that all diseases originated from natural causes. Such criticism against ignorant doctors implied that only learned and prestigious doctors should be making such determinations. There are accounts of learned physicians who suggested witchcraft was the cause of illness in certain cases. The Royal College of Physicians of London, the highest professional body, was sometimes willing to approve of witchcraft as an explanation for disease.[84] In 1602 the physicians of the College, including eminent members, were divided over the question of whether Mary Glover was bewitched or naturally ill.[85] In a case in 1623, the College did not rule out witchcraft as an explanation for the strange infirmities of John Palmer.[86]

Even those writers who accepted witchcraft as a possible cause of illness considered the diagnosis in such cases to be a matter of expertise, differentiating between skilled and unskilled physicians. Cotta discussed at length the problem of diagnosing witchcraft-caused diseases. The solution presented by Cotta, who believed instances of witchcraft could be discovered through reason, was the conjecture. The medical diagnosis of ambiguous symptoms could by made by a 'learned, iudicious, prudent, and discreete artificiall coniecture'.[87] The ability to discern mere accidents from instances of witchcraft was a matter for the 'the prudent and iudicious Physicion'.[88]

Cotta's portrait of the learned and judicious physician was a call for including witchcraft diagnosis in the professional jurisdiction of medicine and a claim for exclusive experience and expertise:

> The like the learned Physician may certainely conclude, concerning diseases inflicted or moued by the Diuell ... where true and iudicious discerning is able to finde the infallible, certaine, and vndeceiued stampe of difference. Thus farre hath been briefly declared, how *the Physician properly and by himselfe doth alone enter into the due consideration & examination of diseases* (where is iust occasion of question) *whether naturally or supernaturally inferred. How vnfit it is here to admit euery idiot for a Physician or Counsellor* (as is too common both in these and all other affaires of health) let wise men iudge.[89]

---

[84] Thomas, *Religion and the Decline of Magic*, p. 537.
[85] Ibid.; MacDonald (ed.), *Witchcraft and Hysteria*, pp. xiv–xvi.
[86] Thomas, *Religion and the Decline of Magic*, p. 537.
[87] John Cotta, *The Triall of Vvitch-Craft* (London: Samuel Rand, 1616), p. 10.
[88] Ibid., p. 13.
[89] Ibid., p. 75. Emphasis added.

The claim for exclusivity was double, and it was directed both at other disciplines and at those who wanted to be part of the medical profession.[90] First, the physician was the only professional who could autonomously determine whether a disease was natural or supernatural. Second, at the intra-disciplinary level, not every idiot could call himself a physician.[91] Diagnosis of witchcraft, according to Cotta, required especially high skills, diligence, prudence and experience.[92] The claim to expertise had the potential to empower those belonging to lesser social categories. Cunning men or women were sometimes consulted when suspicions of witchcraft arose. Women gained power and influence when they served in the jury of matrons. At the time of the Hopkins trials, a few women, professional searchers for the devil's mark, were even compensated for their services. In their testimony they emphasized their past experience in similar cases.[93] Physicians, therefore, strove to establish expertise superior to that of other practitioners in the field.

Cotta provided signs for a supernatural illness. Some could be detected by common sense alone, for example, the vomiting of pins and other objects, the speaking of unfamiliar languages while in a fit and the clairvoyant visions of distant people or objects.[94] The obvious strangeness of these symptoms indicated witchcraft. The detection of other symptoms required elaborate medical knowledge.[95]

---

[90]   Yet, the differentiating rhetoric of the medical groups might be exaggerated, and physicians and empirics might have been closer in practice and theory than they cared to admit. Andrew Wear, 'Medical Practice in Late Seventeenth- and Early Eighteenth-Century England: Continuity and Union', in Roger French and Andrew Wear (eds), *The Medical Revolution of the Seventeenth Century* (Cambridge, UK: Cambridge University Press, 1989), pp. 319–20. The fact that physicians published treatises in the vernacular demonstrates that this was not an internal medical dispute, but that the physicians sought to establish their position among the public in a context of medical marketplace. Andrew Wear, *Knowledge and Practice in English Medicine, 1550–1680* (Cambridge, UK: Cambridge University Press, 2000), pp. 40–45.

[91]   Learned physicians used sharp words to distinguish themselves from other medical practitioners. Yet, despite the rhetoric of differentiation, in practice, the professional and lay medical practitioners were often complementary rather than competitive. Roy Porter, 'The Patient in England, c. 1660–c. 1800', in Andrew Wear (ed.), *Medicine in Society* (Cambridge, UK: Cambridge University Press, 1992), pp. 113–14. For background on the various kinds of medical practitioners, see Porter, 'The Patient in England'), pp. 92–4.

[92]   Cotta, *The Triall of Vvitch-Craft*, p. 76.

[93]   F., *A True and Exact Relation*, pp. 16, 24.

[94]   Cotta, *The Triall of Vvitch-Craft*, pp. 76–7.

[95]   The speed with which the disease progressed and whether the patient remained conscious through the fits and convulsions. Ibid., p. 71.

William Drage, an apothecary and the author of medical tracts, also believed doctors could detect witchcraft. He believed that, by knowledge accumulated through experience, it was possible to diagnose correctly. Drage assumed that if accounts of witchcraft were told by different and unrelated people who belonged to different disciplines 'one the Judge, the other the Physician', they should be credited.[96] Drage supposed that the distinction between natural and unnatural symptoms was thorny and demanded expertise, as many were not aware that they were bewitched, while many others thought themselves bewitched, when they only suffered from natural symptoms. Drage provided diagnostic signs for unnatural symptoms, yet he warned that: 'All Diseases that are caused by Nature, may be caused by Witchcraft; But all that are caused by Witchcraft, cannot be caused by Nature.'[97]

The idea that the devil might inflict natural diseases made the detection of witchcraft more complicated, as a diagnosis of a natural cause for the disease did not rule out witchcraft.[98] Cotta, referring to Job as an example, believed that the devil used his knowledge of natural diseases.[99] This view was elaborated in Dr Browne's testimony in the trial against Rose Cullender and Amy Denny in 1662. Mechanistic understanding of *how* the disease evolved did not provide the reason *why* a certain person was afflicted with it.[100] Browne had made this distinction almost three centuries before Evans-Pritchard made a strikingly similar observation in his study on the Azande.[101]

Not only medical professionals held the belief that the inability of the physician to cure the illness indicated witchcraft.[102] In 1602 Dr Jorden testified that Mary Glover was not bewitched, but that her fits were rather a symptom of hysteria, a natural illness. In response to probing by Lord Chief Justice Sir Edmund Anderson, of the Courts of Common Pleas, Jorden indicated that he would not undertake to cure it. Anderson instantly rejected his thesis. If the fits could not be cured, the judge insisted, they could not be naturally caused. Bernard concurred. According to him, the inability of 'learned and skilfull Physicions' to diagnose or cure the disease indicated witchcraft. Bernard relied

---

[96]   William Drage, *A Physical Nosonomy* (London: J. Dover, 1664), p. 4.

[97]   Ibid., p. 10.

[98]   Thomas, *Religion and the Decline of Magic*, p. 537.

[99]   Cotta, *The Triall of Vvitch-Craft*, pp. 59–60.

[100]   Geis and Bunn, *A Trial of Witches*, p. 153.

[101]   Edward Evans-Pritchard, *Witchcraft, Oracles and Magic among the Azande* (Oxford: Clarendon Press, 1937), ch. IV, esp. p. 64. See also an analysis of this observation in Alan Macfarlane, *Witchcraft in Tudor and Stuart England: A Regional and Comparative Study* (New York: Harper & Row, 1970), pp. 193; 251; 207, fn. 110.

[102]   MacDonald (ed.), *Witchcraft and Hysteria*, p. xviii.

on the precedent of the Warboys case, where the doctors were unable to treat the sick Throckmorton children.[103] Such inference from the inability of the doctor to cure was still made in the eighteenth century.

Bernard supported the involvement of medical experts in the legal proceedings. His argument reflected the distinction between the 'judicious physicians' and the inferior category of folk healers, the 'devilish wizards'. Bernard warned that too many people unjustly believed that they were bewitched and called for caution.[104] He asserted that only doctors were to be trusted with diagnosis of the causes of diseases. He also found medical opinion helpful in determining whether a possession was counterfeited.[105] In cases where it was necessary to determine whether the disease was natural or whether the bewitchment was faked, Bernard regarded the testimony of the doctor as *indispensable*.[106]

Bernard recommended using medical opinion from the early stages of the case. He advised the grand jurors to consider whether the illness had an unnatural cause with the assistance of 'some learned Physicians'.[107] As the distinction between natural and unnatural diseases was problematic, the grand jurors needed the guidance of a:

> skilfull Physician to helpe to discerne, and to make a cleere difference betweene the one and the other, that men may proceed iudiciously, and so rightly with comfort of conscience, that they be not guilty of bloud.[108]

For Bernard, medical opinion could solve the dilemma of proof. Relying on the discretion of the doctor, the jurors could rest assured with *'comfort of conscience'*.

The success of physicians in positioning themselves as indispensable to the diagnosis and proof of witchcraft was remarkable. Their endeavour seems even more impressive given the fact that contemporary learned medicine was not intellectually homogeneous.[109] Beginning with the second half of the

---

103   Bernard, *A Guide to Grand-Iury Men*, pp. 168–9.

104   Ibid., p. 23.

105   Ibid., p. 48.

106   Ibid., p. 232.

107   Ibid., p. 24.

108   Ibid., pp. 24–5.

109   During the seventeenth century, Galenic medicine (relying on humoral explanations), and Paracelsian medicine (chemical explanations) became overshadowed by natural philosophy and the mechanical approach. Andrew Wear, 'Making Sense of Health and the Environment in Early Modern England', in Andrew Wear (ed.), *Medicine in Society* (Cambridge, UK: Cambridge University Press, 1992), pp. 120–21.

seventeenth-century, England was becoming more and more 'medicalized'.[110] The difficulty of proving witchcraft was resourcefully used by physicians to bolster their professional status. Medical experts were indeed used in the criminal proceeding. In some witch trials, the testimony of doctors appeared to provide the central and most significant evidence. The role played by Jorden and Browne in the two key cases mentioned above illustrates two conflicting approaches to the testimony of the expert witness as either complementing, or competing with, the bench.

Jorden testified for the defence in the trial of Elizabeth Jackson for the bewitchment of Mary Glover in 1602. Sixty years later, in 1662, Browne was invited by the court to testify in the trial of Rose Cullender and Amy Denny.[111] The testimony of Jorden had been met with hostility from the bench and was rejected by the judge on medical grounds. In contrast, Browne's testimony was embraced by the court and was probably decisive in tilting the scales toward conviction.

Dr Edward Jorden (1569–1632) is commonly referred to by historians of psychiatry as the doctor who developed the concept of hysteria.[112] Jorden was educated at Cambridge (BA, 1583) and at Padua (MD, 1591). He became a Licentiate of the College of Physicians in 1595 and a Fellow in 1597. He was commended in the Annals of the College for excellence in his examinations. After some years in practice, he enjoyed the appreciation of James I, although he never became an official Royal Physician. After moving to Bath, he treated the queen several times on her visits there.

Mary Glover was the 14-year-old daughter of a Puritan merchant family who blamed Elizabeth Jackson for bewitching her. Following a conflict with Jackson, the girl was struck dumb and blind and was reported to be unable to eat for days. She also suffered from fits and seizures that worsened and intensified and appeared to occur when Jackson was present. During the fits, Glover began to say 'hang her', as if the voice were coming from her nostrils.

Quite a few physicians were asked to voice their opinion concerning the fits and symptoms. The family called on Dr Robert Shereman, a Fellow of the College of Physicians, who was assisted by a surgeon. After failing to cure the girl, Shereman suspected the symptoms were supernaturally caused. The family turned to an even more prestigious physician, Dr Thomas Moundeford, who

---

[110]   Porter, 'The Patient in England', esp. p. 101.

[111]   The dating of the pamphlet, 1664, is incorrect. Geis and Bunn, *A Trial of Witches*, p. 36.

[112]   For a criticism of this prevailing view, see MacDonald (ed.), *Witchcraft and Hysteria*, p. vii. The following description draws heavily on MacDonald's introduction and on Geis and Bunn, *A Trial of Witches*, p. 83.

was seven subsequent times the President of the College of Physicians and an expert on melancholy. After two months of surveillance, he ruled out hysteria but concluded that another natural illness might be the cause of the symptoms. As the case began to attract public attention, the city authorities became involved and initiated more experiments of facing Glover with Jackson. Richard Bancroft, the Bishop of London, who sided with the suspect, initiated another series of experiments, conducted by London's chief legal officer, recorder John Croke. The results appeared to support the allegations against Jackson, and she was remanded. Two weeks before her trial, Jackson petitioned the College of Physicians to consider her case, naming Drs Thomas Moundeford, Francis Herring and Stephen Bradwell as her accusers. Moundeford did not appear, but Herring and Bradwell were questioned by a forum of about a dozen fellows and presented their position that Glover was bewitched. The majority, including eminent members of the College, was reported to have sided with Jackson, holding that Glover's disease was natural. The issue was debated at the trial two weeks later. Herring and Dr Spencer testified on behalf of the prosecution, and the two distinguished physicians, Jorden and Dr Argent, testified for the defendant. James Meadowes, DD, a well-known divine, also testified for the defence. The appearance of these defence witnesses was probably orchestrated by Bishop Bancroft. The Anglican authorities launched an attack on Puritan and Catholic exorcists, insisting that the age of miracles was past.

In court, in contrast to the discussion held at the College of Physicians, those taking the position that the fits were supernatural got the upper hand. The essence of Jorden's testimony was that Glover's symptoms were naturally caused by hysteria. Jorden was greatly humiliated by presiding judge Anderson, who cross-examined him fiercely and advised the jurors contrary to his opinion. Anderson made Jorden retract his earlier insinuations that the girl was faking part of her symptoms, and, being pressed by the judge, Jorden stated that he did not believe that the symptoms were faked. Anderson did not let Jorden get away with evasive phrasings, such as the symptoms 'may' be natural, and Jorden was made to commit 'that in his conscience he thought it was altogether naturall'. Anderson further demanded that the witness spell out the precise diagnosis (*passio hysterica*) and made Jorden admit he would not undertake to cure the girl. Anderson instantly dismissed his testimony:

> Then in my conscience, it is not naturall. For if you tell me neither a Natural cause of it, nor a natural remedy, I will tell you that it is not natural.[113]

---

[113]   Bradwell, *Marie Glovers Late Woefull Case*, 37v–38v; MacDonald (ed.), *Witchcraft and Hysteria*, p. 28. Bradwell's manuscript is transcribed in MacDonald's book, and further references will refer to page numbers in Macdonald's transcript.

After a pause, Anderson directed the jury, his words leaving no room for doubt how they should decide:

> The Land is full of Witches; they abound in all places: I have hanged five or sixe
> and twenty of them; There is no man here, can speake more of them then my selfe;
> fewe of them would confesse it, som of them did; against whom the proofes were
> nothing so manifest, as against those that denied it.[114]

Anderson made clear that if someone was an expert on witches, he was the man. He continued to summarize the evidence for the jurors and elucidated how each and every aspect of the evidence incriminated Jackson: she denied her guilt, she had bodily marks, and she was full of curses and threats that actually took effect. In short, this was a case 'where the presumptions are so great and the Circumstances so apparent'. Anderson continued his summation, dismissing Jorden's testimony, as he addressed the physicians:

> You talke of the mother [the contemporary term for hysteria], I pray you, have
> you ever seen or heard of the mother, that kept it [sic] course unchangeably, every
> second day, and never missed; and yet that chaungeth [sic] his course upon the
> presence of some one person; as this doth, at the presence of this woman. Divines,
> Phisitions, I know they are learned and wise, but to say this is naturall, and tell
> me neither the cause, nor the Cure of it, I care not for your Judgement: geve me a
> naturall reason, and a naturall remedy, or a rush for your phisicke.[115]

It is not surprising that after this speech, followed by the summation of the recorder, who also found the case supernatural, the jury found Jackson guilty. Under the applicable law, she was sentenced to a year's imprisonment and pillory sessions. Anderson's speech was remarkable, not only in the extremity of its style, but also because of the explicit juxtaposition it created of the judiciary and the medical expert. It is clear from the judge's summation that he did not feel bound in any sense by Jorden's opinion. Anderson felt entitled to reject it *on medical grounds*. He asserted that hysteria was an incorrect diagnosis in the case of patterned fits occurring in the presence of a particular person. Jorden's theory, which attributed hysteria to a premenstrual girl and granted the brain a significant role in producing the symptoms, was medically innovative.[116] Anderson did not hesitate to make judgment relating to the subject matter

---

[114]   MacDonald (ed.), *Witchcraft and Hysteria*, p. 28.
[115]   Ibid., p. 29.
[116]   Ibid., pp. xxix–xxx.

of the expert witness. For him, Jorden brought another piece of evidence and was just another witness whose validity should be determined by the court. Anderson acknowledged that divines and physicians were 'learned and wise', but this, however, did not give them the authority to replace judicial discretion.[117]

Eventually, Jackson did not serve her sentence, probably because of a royal pardon. Glover continued to suffer from fits and was freed from possession through a Puritan session of fasting and prayer.[118] The debate ensued in an exchange of tracts after the trial. Jorden's *A Briefe Discovrse of a Disease Called the Suffocation of the Mother* was answered by Bradwell's *Marie Glovers Late Woefull Case* and Swan's *A Trve and Breife Report of Mary Glovers Vexation*, all written in 1603.[119]

The court was only one of the arenas in which witchcraft was debated. Glover's fits were examined in court by the College of Physicians in public experiments conducted privately and by the city authorities, and they were debated in an exchange of pamphlets.[120] None of the spheres of the debate was purely theological, medical or legal. The case demonstrated internal debates within these disciplines as well as among them. The alleged possession was used by the Puritans to gain public support (Glover herself linked her possession to the persecutions against the Puritans by saying, at the moment of her deliverance, the same words that her grandfather, a victim of the Marian persecutions, had said when he was burned on the pyre).[121] The conservative Anglican Church showed concern over the case. Richard Bancroft, the Bishop of London, supported Jackson. He used his political influence and was probably the one who motivated Jorden to publish his pamphlet after the conviction.[122]

---

[117]   Interestingly, a few years earlier, the trial of Darrell and More, two celebrated Puritan exorcists, before the High Commission in 1599, was presided over by an anti-Puritan tribunal that included both Anderson and Bancroft. Ibid., pp. xxi–xxii.

[118]   Ibid., p. xix.

[119]   Bradwell's manuscript remained unpublished, which is a likely indication of the official Anglican objection to Puritan exorcisms.

[120]   The strategies of using a socially contested issue as a resource to bolster a professional group changed from one historical context to another. Early modern physicians used witchcraft to establish an independent (or even superior) position as medical experts. Nineteenth-century American physicians used abortion by taking a moral (and not a medical) stand and influencing lawmakers, rather than developing an independent role. James C. Mohr, *Abortion in America: The Origins and Evolution of National Policy, 1800–1900* (New York: Oxford University Press, 1978). Lavi demonstrated how nineteenth-century religious, medical and legal discourses diverged in their treatment of euthanasia, another socially disputed issue. Shai J. Lavi, *The Modern Art of Dying* (Princeton, NJ: Princeton University Press, 2005).

[121]   MacDonald (ed.), *Witchcraft and Hysteria*, p. xix.

[122]   Ibid., pp. xiv, xix–xxvi; Geis and Bunn, *A Trial of Witches*, p. 189.

James Meadowes, a noted divine, testified for Jackson in court. The physicians were divided in their opinion about the case and appeared in court on behalf of opposing parties. The court was another arena where symbolic advantages such as professional recognition and prestige could be gained. However, the most dramatic confrontation in the case was between Anderson, the representative of the judiciary, and Jorden, the expert witness, the representative of the medical profession.

A much more favourable view of the expert witness by the court, as an aide and partner rather than a threat and competitor, arose from the case of Rose Cullender and Amy Denny in 1662. In this case the court appointed the expert following a disagreement between the judges:

> *At the hearing this evidence,* there were divers known persons, as Mr Serjeant Keeling, Mr Serjeant Earl, and Mr Sergeant Barnard present. *Mr Serjeant Keeling seemed much unsatisfied with it, and thought it not sufficient to convict the prisoners:* for admitting that the Children were in Truth Bewitched, yet said he, it can never be applyed to the Prisoners, upon the Imagination only of the Parties Afflicted; For if that might be allowed, no person whatsoever can be in safety, for perhaps they might fancy another person, who might altogether be innocent in such matters.

> There was *also Dr Brown of Norwich, a person of great knowledge,* who after this evidence given, and upon view of the three persons in court, *was desired to give his opinion,* what he conceived of them.[123]

Experiments conducted in court raised the suspicion of feigned possession,[124] and the court was divided and embarrassed. Browne came to the rescue. The intra-professional conflict among the judges brought about the reliance on an expert witness from a different profession. Dr Browne (1605–82), 56 years old at the time of the trial, was educated at Oxford and obtained most of his medical education abroad, at Leyden, Montpellier and Padua. He was admitted to practise medicine in England, where he ran a successful medical practice and was a prolific writer.[125] Browne was known for his encyclopaedic knowledge, and his assistance was frequently sought by scholars. He is also remembered for his special use of language, and we can still find in use a few of the words

---

[123]   *A Tryal of Witches,* pp. 40–41. Emphasis added.

[124]   It is not clear whether the experiments preceded Dr Browne's testimony. It is questionable whether the pamphlet described the events in chronological order.

[125]   Geis and Bunn, *A Trial of Witches,* p. 148.

he coined, such as electricity, hallucination, suicide and umbrella.[126] Browne published two famous treatises, *Religio Medici*, the first edition of which was published in 1643,[127] and *Pseudodoxia Epidemica*, often called 'Vulgar Errors', in which he denounced various superstitions. Yet, Browne believed in 'astrology, alchemy, witchcraft, and magic, and he never abandoned the Ptolemaic system of astronomy'.[128]

Browne was not the first doctor to testify in the case against Denny and Cullender. Dr Feavor, who examined the sick girl, affirmed in court that he could not determine the cause of the girl's illness.[129] Inability of the doctor to diagnose the disease was commonly believed to indicate an unnatural cause. Browne, a most distinguished doctor and scholar, brought to the court more than mere medical opinion; he carried with him his reputation and fame. And this was his testimony:

> He was clearly of opinion, that the persons were bewitched; and said, That in Denmark there had been lately a great discovery of witches, who used the very same way of afflicting persons, by conveying pins into them, and crocked as these pins were, with needles and nails. And his opinion was, that the devil in such cases did work upon the bodies of men and women, upon a natural foundation, that is, to stir up and excite such humours super-abounding in their bodies to a great excess, whereby he did in an extraordinary manner afflict them with such Distempers as their Bodies were most subject to, as particularly appeared in these children; for he conceived that these swooning fits were natural, and nothing else but what they call the mother, but only heightened to a great excess by the subtilty of the devil co-operating with the malice of these which we term witches, at whose instance he doth these villainies.[130]

In his testimony, Brown set forth that the children were indeed bewitched. However, he did not point to the defendants as the witches. He did not establish who had bewitched the children. The second significant element of his testimony was that the children suffered from *natural* fits of hysteria, which did not rule out bewitchment. He held that the devil employed natural phenomena to achieve his evil goals. Browne adopted the same diagnosis that had attracted so much criticism of Jorden, hysteria. His analysis, however, negated Jorden's

---

[126]   Ibid., p. 149.

[127]   Two unauthorized editions appeared surreptitiously in 1642. *Dictionary of National Biography*, s.v. 'Browne, Thomas'.

[128]   Ibid., p. 67.

[129]   *A Tryal of Witches*, p. 17.

[130]   *A Tryal of Witches*, pp. 41–2.

conclusion that did not associate hysteria with either the devil or with witchcraft. In contrast, Browne opined that natural disease did not rule out witchcraft.

Browne's claim of expertise rested on wide knowledge of the subject, including acquaintance with the experience of foreign experts, and he referred to Danish cases in support of his argument.[131] He also demonstrated command of contemporary medical concepts and terminology, and explained to the judges, using medical-sounding language, how the devil 'excited humours' and 'afflicted distempers'. Hutchinson wryly remarked:

> This Declaration of Sir Thomas Brown's, could not but much influence the Jury;
> and I count it turned back the Scale, that was otherwise inclining to the Favour of
> the accused Persons. And with Submission, I think it should not have been said:
> For this was a Case of Blood, and surely the King's Subjects ought not to lose their
> Lives upon the Credit of Books from Denmark.[132]

We can speculate whether Browne's testimony won the favour of the court because, unlike Jorden's, his opinion matched the outcome desired by the presiding judge. Browne diagnosed hysteria, which was natural, but added that the devil might have caused it. This significant argument was not medical, but theological. In making this argument, Browne presented medical expertise as limited – the doctor could explain the course of the disease, but he was in no superior standing to explain *why* it was inflicted. Perhaps this less presumptuous approach seemed less threatening to the court. Perhaps such an approach was more to the taste of wider circles that feared that the emergence of the natural sciences posed a threat to religion. The experts formed a distinct category of witnesses. Their professional claim to special and exclusive knowledge formed the basis for the validity of their testimony but also threatened the superiority of the bench. This tension underlay the judicial assessment of the value of their testimony.

---

[131]   Geis and Bunn quoted Jens Christian Johansen, a leading Danish historian of witchcraft, who did not identify relevant Danish cases. They also referred to Knud Bogh, who suggested that Browne probably referred to a case that had taken place in Bergen, Norway, which was then under Danish rule. Geis and Bunn, *A Trial of Witches*, p. 85.

[132]   Francis Hutchinson, *An Historical Essay Concerning Witchcraft* (London: R. Knaplock and D. Midwinter, 1718), p. 118.

Figure 11.1 Matthew Hopkins Witch Finder Generall standing, two witches sitting and their imps. From Matthew Hopkins, *The Discovery of Witches: In Answer to Severall Queries, Lately Delivered to the Judges of Assize for the County of Norfolk* (London: R. Royston, 1647). [Call # 145938] Reproduced by permission of the Huntington Library, San Marino, California.

Chapter 11
Searching for Reliable Testimony

From Competence to Credibility

Typically, the entire evidence in witchcraft cases, or most of it, came from witnesses. Trust in the truthfulness of witnesses was an important factor in proving this crime. Assessing the truthfulness of testimony about supernatural and impossible acts is especially challenging, and it became a much-debated issue in the context of witch trials. It is therefore possible that the discussions influenced emerging evidentiary concepts. Competence and credibility are two legal measures aimed at obtaining truthful testimony. The competence rules define who is legally prohibited from giving testimony against the accused (for example, a spouse, children, and so on). The notion of credibility aims to determine how worthy a certain witness is of belief. While competency determines whether a certain witness may or may not testify, credibility is a matter of degree. A witness who is competent to testify may not necessarily be credible.

By the end of the sixteenth century, keeping liars out of court was facilitated by a system of competence rules that prevented witnesses belonging to undesirable categories from testifying. These exclusionary rules were more lax in cases of witchcraft because of the probative difficulties. In criminal trials there was as yet no right to defence witnesses, and the witnesses for the prosecution all testified under oath and were not subject to cross-examination. It was routinely held that a witness who testified under oath must be believed unless directly contradicted.[1]

The seventeenth century saw a conceptual shift in the domain of evidence. Rather than the quantitative approach of considering the number of witnesses or aggregates of presumptions being of greater importance, the emphasis shifted to rules assessing the quality of the evidence, that is, the validity and the probability of witnesses' testimony. In a chapter titled 'Evidence', Matthew Hale referred

---

[1] The judges preferred to handle contradicting testimonies by careful interpretation and whenever possible, it was better to find that a witness was mistaken rather than a perjurer. Sir Geoffrey Gilbert, *The Law of Evidence* (London: W. Owen, 1756), p. 157; George Fisher, 'The Jury's Rise as Lie Detector', *The Yale Law Journal*, no. 107 (1997): pp. 625–7.

solely to competency rules and substantive law issues.[2] Yet, Hale distinguished between competency and credit: 'for the excellency of the trial by jury is in that they are the triers of the credit of the witnesses as well as the truth of the fact; it is one thing, whether a witness be admissible to be heard, another thing, whether they are to be believed when heard.'[3] There was a shift from evidence as a field of substantive law (what facts support the indictment), a concept that vanished in the nineteenth century, to a system of rules governing proof at trial and excluding immaterial matters.[4] By the eighteenth century, Gilbert already discussed the evaluation of witnesses' credit and weight.[5]

Toward the end of the sixteenth century, doubt began to surface as to whether oath-taking was sufficient to ensure the truthfulness of testimony. One pamphlet of 1585, concerning witchcraft proceedings in the Old Bailey, related how 'by the severall *othes of sundrie honest persons*, these matters were prooved'.[6] The number of witnesses was not the only consideration, but personal qualities such as honesty mattered as well. Still, jurors were perplexed when they faced objectionable testimony that was nonetheless given under oath. Sam, one of the characters in Gifford's *Dialogue*, expressed his distress as a juror in a witchcraft case:

> If she were innocent what could we do lesse? we went according to the euidence of such as were sworne, they swore that they in their conscience tooke her to bee a witch, and that she did those thinges.

Another character, Dan, answered with a question of his own:

> If other take their oath that in their conscience they thinke so, is that sufficient to warrant men vpon mine oath to say it is so?[7]

---

[2] Sir Matthew Hale, *Pleas of the Crown* (London: William Shrewsbery and Juon Leigh, 1678), pp. 262–6.

[3] Sir Matthew Hale, *Historia Placitorum Coronae* (London: F. Gyles, T. Woodward, and C. Davis, 1736), vol. I, p. 635.

[4] John H. Langbein, *The Origins of Adversary Criminal Trial*, Oxford Studies in Modern Legal History (Oxford: Oxford University Press, 2003), pp. 237, 248.

[5] Gilbert, *The Law of Evidence*, p. 158.

[6] 'A Severall Factes of Witch-Crafte', in Marion Gibson (ed.), *Early Modern Witches: Witchcraft Cases in Contemporary Writing* (London: Routledge, 2000), p. 126). Emphasis added.

[7] George Gifford, *A Dialogue Concerning Witches and Witchcraftes* (London: Tobie Cooke and Mihil, 1593), L3v.

Gifford explicitly expressed the worry that sworn testimony was not necessarily true. He wondered what the jurors should do when they suspected the testimony of the witnesses to be perjury but could not prove it.[8] Gifford raised the question but did not provide a full and practical answer. Naming the acceptable proofs in a witchcraft trial, Dan allowed for 'proofe by sufficient witnesses' or the confession of the accused. Yet, he warned that the testimony of the witnesses might be unreliable, being either indirect or manipulated by the devil:

> The testimony be such as may be false, as al that commeth from deuils is to be suspected: or if it be but vpon rumors, and likelihoods, in which there may be exceéding sleights of Satan, as for the most parte there be: how can that Iury answere before God, which vpon their oath are not sure, but that so proceéding they may condemne the innocent, as often it commeth to passe.[9]

Gifford's discussion of the reasons for perjury is hardly exhaustive. He did not even suggest an outright lie, made out of malice, as a possible ground for perjury. He warned the jurors not to accept sworn testimony automatically but did not provide them with means to overcome their distress. Yet, by articulating the doubt, Gifford paved the way for the developing concepts of credibility and weight, and for the shift to a rigorous examination of the content of testimony.

Beginning with the seventeenth century, the texts no longer implied that testimony should be accepted solely by virtue of the oath, and the manner and content of testimony began to be scrutinized. Some authors deduced veracity from the manner of testifying. For example, Thomas Potts was impressed by the manner in which nine-year-old Jennet Device testified. Despite her youth, the great audience in court and the fact that she testified against her own brother, Potts commended 'with what modestie, governement, and understanding, shee delivered this Evidence'.[10] Potts also paid attention to the facial expressions of the witnesses.[11] It is likely that the account of Potts, the clerk of the assize, provides us with a glimpse of the judges' nascent awareness of the body language of witnesses.

---

[8] Ibid., L3v–L4.

[9] Ibid., L.

[10] Thomas Potts, *The Vvonderfull Discouerie of Witches in the Countie of Lancaster* (London: Iohn Barnes, 1613), I.

[11] For example, he noted how the 'countenance' of Grace Sowerbutts changed. Ibid., M3v.

Authors also noted the coherence of testimony. Evasive answers reflected negatively on the witness's truthfulness.[12] Consistency among the testimonies of the different witnesses also signified higher probability of truthfulness. According to Casaubon, if the examination revealed that 'more then one, ten, or twenty' witnesses agreed 'in all points and particulars' and their testimonies were supported 'with notable circumstances', then they were most likely to be true.[13]

The motives and interests of the witnesses also began to be inspected. Cotta believed that, just like facts of nature, witchcraft was a fact that could be observed and learned about from the accounts of the observer. Yet, such observations could be the basis of an indictment only on the fulfilment of two conditions. First, 'the witnesses of the manifest magicall and supernaturall' should have no interests and be 'free from exception of malice, partialitie, distraction, folly'. Second, the testimony had to refer to a matter 'manifest vnto the outward sense'. As it was not always clear whether supernatural matters could be perceived by the senses, Cotta suggested assistance 'by conference and counsell with learned men, religiously and industriously exercised, in iudging in those affaires, there bee iustly deemed no deception of sense, mistaking of reason or imagination'.[14] Cotta believed it was possible to distinguish between imagination 'from within the brain' and matters perceived by 'the outward sense'.[15] Cotta's criteria, the observer's impartiality and perception by the senses, were grounded in an empiricist worldview and required the assistance of experts, such as 'learned men'.

William Drage (1637?–99), a medical writer who practised as an apothecary at Hitchin, Hertfordshire, and a profound believer in astrology and witchcraft,[16] also emphasized the importance of impartiality. According to Drage, it was the impartiality that made accounts of witchcraft credible. Drage argued that if many witnesses reported instances of witchcraft, 'specially they not allured by Gain, or obliged by Interest, or superstitionated by Education, or forced by rigour of Authority', then it must be true.[17] It was the quantity and experience of unconnected witnesses in different countries and different times that proved the existence of witchcraft. Although Drage discussed proving the existence of witchcraft in general, his criteria for impartiality were broad yet applicable to

---

[12]   Potts noted how the judge examined the girl 'who could not for her life make any direct answere'. Thereupon the girl let slip that she had not been coached to answer that question. Ibid.

[13]   Meric Casaubon, *Of Credulity and Incredulity in Things Natural, Civil, and Divine* (London: T. Garthwait, 1668), p. 39.

[14]   John Cotta, *The Triall of Vvitch-Craft* (London: Samuel Rand, 1616), p. 80.

[15]   Ibid., p. 83.

[16]   *Dictionary of National Biography*, s.v. 'Drage, William'.

[17]   William Drage, *A Physical Nosonomy* (London: J. Dover, 1664), p. 4.

individual cases (as within individual cases as well, the coherence between the testimonies of unrelated and impartial witnesses made their accounts credible).

Bernard wrote a thorough account of the consideration of testimony. Like Cotta, he supported pre-trial evaluation of testimony. In his *Guide to Grand-Iury Men* ..., he listed possible concerns regarding the credibility of different types of witnesses and even suggested a questionnaire to be answered by the various witnesses to better assess their qualities as witnesses.[18] Bernard's writing blended concepts of competency and credibility. For example, he supported using 'indifferent neighbours'. Yet, he alerted, some of them were 'fearfull, superstitious, or children, or old silly persons, whose testimonies are to be heard, but not easily credited, as being persons in such a case as this is, very much subiect to mistaking'.[19] In the same sentence, Bernard referred to broad categories (such as children) that did not necessarily bear on the truthfulness of an individual witness and to personal attributes, such as being superstitious. The paramount principle was to find the witnesses worthy of credit. After evaluating *who* should be believed, Bernard moved on to determine *what* the testimony should include. For the 'conscionable' neighbours 'of understanding', Bernard composed a list of questions that pertained both to matters of perception (what the witness observed) and opinion (about the parties and authenticity of the bewitchment).[20]

'*Suspected aduersaries*' was the next category of witnesses. These were people who might be motivated by ill will toward one of the parties. Yet, Bernard argued, nosy and inquisitive neighbours might be valuable, as they 'will pry very narrowly into euery thing, to discouer what they desire to finde. Therefore though it bee wisedome to suspect ill will, yet may some things be found out by them, which otherwise may be mistaken, or lye hid.'[21] He similarly made a list of questions to be presented to this type of witness. Another category of witness was 'the *suspected Witches whole family* able and fit to answer'. Many of the questions Bernard prepared for these witnesses related to matters perceived by their senses, such as seeing the suspect's witchcraft acts and artefacts; hearing the suspect's

---

[18]   Richard Bernard, *A Guide to Grand-Iury Men* (London: Ed. Blackmore, 1627), pp. 230–32.

[19]   Ibid., p. 230.

[20]   The questions for 'indifferent neighbours' were: '1. Whether they haue seen the party or parties in their fits, and how often? 2. What the life and course of such hath been? 3. What they thinke of the disease, whether natural, or by the diuel, or whether the party doth not counterfeit, and their reasons euery way? 4. What they think of the suspected party, his or her life and conuersation? 5. If they suspect any, then vpon what grounds? And heere inquire of them the presumptious, and the more euident proofes.' Ibid., pp. 230–31.

[21]   Ibid., pp. 231–2.

curses, recital of charms or admission; and even smelling 'noysome and stinking smell'.[22] Overall, Bernard's two main considerations in assessing testimony were the qualities of the witness and the type of information the witness could provide. Both Bernard and Cotta aimed to determine the genuineness of the testimony at the pre-trial stage. According to their arguments, the grand jurors should have been able to evaluate the witnesses before deciding whether the case should proceed to trial.

From the 1670s on, authors of witchcraft pamphlets routinely hailed the credibility and reliability of their informants, usually at the beginning of the text. A pamphleteer opened with the following statement in 1671:

> These Particulars, with many others omitted, I received from eye Witnesses of unquestionable credit, and reputation, and you may no more doubt the truth of them, than distrust the affection of
> Sir.
> Your most humble Servant.
> *I.A.*
> Hereford 1 March 1670[23]

A pamphleteer declared in 1678 that the following account 'being matter of certain truth, deserves to be inserted in a Chronicle, rather than a Penny Pamphlet'. He added that despite the 'strangeness' of the events, there were 'multitudes of ... Neighbours ready to attest it'.[24] An author in 1681 began with a warning: 'Let not the Incredulous question the verity of the Sequel, since divers ocular and auricular witnesses can and will upon occasion, testifie the truth of what shall be hereafter asserted.'[25] These praises signify the increasing need to establish the credibility of the individual witness.

The reliability of witnesses was used by English theologians to counter scepticism. Bovet, a Puritan theologian, denounced the sceptics who rejected:

> the most unquestionable Testimonies, of persons of the greatest Integrity and Generosity, ... persons of that caution and candour, that any disinterested and ingenous man could not possibly imagine to have any design to impose

---

[22]   Ibid., pp. 234–7.
[23]   I.A., *The Daemon of Burton* ... (London: C.W., 1671), p. 5.
[24]   *Strange and Wonderful Nevvs from Goswell-Street* (London: Printed for D.M., 1678), pp. 3–4.
[25]   *Strange and Wonderful News from Yowel in Surry* (London: J. Clarke, 1681), p. 1.

upon others, what themselves had not with the greatest investigation of circumstances, been convinced to be beyond a possibility of Doubting.[26]

In the preface to the accounts appearing in the second part of his book, Bovet repeated that these were testimonies, 'the Truth of which will be averred from Persons of unquestionable Reputation now alive'. Bovet added that because the events happened in the course of the past few years, those who wanted to do so could verify the integrity of the witnesses.[27] He also accounted for the credit of his various informants, describing them as 'a Gentleman of good Ingenuity and Reputation, an Inhabitant of the City aforesaid'; 'a worthy friend'; 'woman ... of honest Reputation among the neighbours ... who lived about that Town'; a 'Gentleman ... so well known to many worthy Persons, Merchants and others upon the exchange in London, that there can be no need of my justifying for the Integrity of the relation; I will only say thus much, that I have heard him very solemnly affirm the truth of what is here related'.[28]

Richard Baxter, a dissenting divine, lamented that many in London doubted witchcraft and ascribed such accounts to 'Error, Deceit, and easie Credulity: For the sake of such, I have recited many *Credible Instances* in this Book.' The abundance of such reports, claimed Baxter, necessarily implied that at least some of them were true, a conclusion 'past all reasonable cause of doubting'.[29] Like Bovet, before unfolding the account, Baxter first attested to the credibility of its source. The recurrent need to vouch for the source demonstrates that credibility was no longer taken for granted or implied from the authority of the author (as a divine, in this instance). Credibility needed to be explicitly established for each narrator and to reach a high level of certainty. The phrasing of 'past all reasonable cause of doubting' points to a nascent standardized level of certainty and veracity.

Strong emphasis on the reliability of witnesses is found in the writings of New England Puritans that were published in England toward the end of the seventeenth century. John Hale noted that, although he had the narrative 'but at second hand', he heard it from 'a competent Realtor, who had the first Relation from an ancient credible Person, who was then a Scholar in Oxford, when the Tryal was, and I doubt not but related truly what he received

---

[26] Richard Bovet, *Pandaemonium, or, the Devil's Cloyster* (London: J. Walthoe, 1684), p. 60.

[27] Ibid., pp. 163–4.

[28] Ibid., pp. 96, 164, 172, 175.

[29] Richard Baxter, *The Certainty of the Worlds of Spirits and, Consequently, of the Immortality of Souls* (London: T. Parkhurst and J. Salisbury, 1691), pp. 17–18.

concerning the particulars here remembred, as followeth'.[30] Two other cases, Hale stated, he had received from:

> a Person of Quality, of good Ability, and of unquestionable Credit, who was present at both the Tryals, and wrote them in his presence, and afterwards read them to him; and he assured me they were very true in all the Particulars, as they were given in Evidence.[31]

Increase Mather argued that the self-interest of accomplices rendered their testimony not credible.[32]

The amplified awareness of the issue of credibility toward the end of the seventeenth century coincided with the improvement in defendants' rights through the emergence of representation by counsel and defence witnesses. Defendants could dispute the credibility of the prosecution witnesses by calling their own witnesses (Gilbert's treatise on evidence implied that by the eighteenth century this was a common practice)[33] and by their attorneys' making objections and cross-examining prosecution witnesses. A pamphlet from 1702, describing the trial of Richard Hathaway, who was accused of faking his bewitchment, contained a very detailed transcript of the proceeding. It is possible to see that the defence attorney, Mr Jenner, made quite a few objections and that he cross-examined some of the witnesses. The judges in this case also took an active role in questioning the witnesses. Since Hathaway was charged as an impostor, his credibility (in the trial against him and in the former trial, in which he testified against Sarah Murdock) was a central issue.

By the eighteenth century, credibility was a major consideration, and an oath was definitely no longer a sufficient guarantee of truthfulness. Credibility was fiercely contested, and sometimes the argument continued, after the trial was over, in an exchange of heated arguments in pamphlets. For example, the participants in the debate concerning Jane Wenham's case continued to argue about the credibility of the prosecution witnesses. Bragge, who vehemently defended Wenham's conviction, acclaimed 'The Number and Credit of the Witnesses who were sworn, the exact Harmony between 'em and also their impartiality and disinterestedness. It made no sense for them to give false

---

[30] John Hale, *A Collection of Modern Relations ...* (London: John Harris, 1693), p. 48.

[31] Ibid., p. 52. See also his analysis of factors that rendered a confession credible. John Hale, *A Modest Enquiry into the Nature of Witchcraft* (Boston, NE: Benjamin Eliot, 1702), p. 25.

[32] Increase Mather, *Cases of Conscience Concerning Evil Spirits ...* (London: Dunton, 1693), pp. 35–6.

[33] Gilbert, *The Law of Evidence*, p. 157.

evidence.'[34] Another pamphleteer who believed in Wenham's guilt concurred that it was unlikely that the witnesses conspired to have Wenham executed and added that there was no reason to question their honesty.[35] Jane Wenham's supporters attacked some of the witnesses against her, saying two of the accusers were 'evidently very much *disturbed in their Imaginations* ... and for that Reason, I think, there can but little Credit be given to what they say, especially to what they relate as done whilst their *Fits*'.[36] It seems that, although this sceptical pamphleteer agreed that compatibility with other testimony strengthened the witnesses' credit, he observed discrepancies in the testimony.[37] In addition, the inner logic of the testimony was sometimes flawed, and significant material facts were suspiciously missing from Bragge's account.[38] The character of a key witness, Anne Thorne, the alleged victim, was also under attack, and she was reported as subsequently having been caught in great lies. Her reputation served 'to invalidate the Credibility of every thing that depends on her Testimony. For altho' it does not necessarily follow, that a Person has always been a Lyar, because he is now one; yet it has *been* a Piece of Justice always paid to such sort of People, *never to be believed*.'[39]

Credibility became a leading concept, but competency was not altogether forsaken. Rules pertaining to witnesses' competence exist in Anglo-American law until today. Gilbert, in his famous treatise about evidence that was published in 1756, three decades after his death, was not as yet free from the mechanistic concepts of accepting testimony by the merit of oath and in accordance with the number of witnesses. The credit of witnesses, according to Gilbert's rules, was to be examined only when the number of parties on each side was equal in the conflict of sworn testimonies.[40] Gilbert held that 'The Credit of a Witness is to be judged from his State and Dignity in the World'. More affluent witnesses were more credible, as 'Men of easy Circumstances are supposed more hardly induced to commit a manifest Perjury'. Likewise, complete indifference to the dispute was preferable. In addition, 'Men atheistical and loose to Oaths are not of the

---

[34] Francis Bragge, *A Full and Impartial Account* ..., 2nd edn (London: E. Curll, 1712), preface.

[35] A.M.G.R., *The Belief of Witchcraft Vindicated* (London: J. Baker, 1712), pp. 10–11.

[36] *The Case of the Hertfordshire Witchcraft Consider'd* (London: John Pemberton, 1712), p. 3.

[37] Ibid., p. 4.

[38] Ibid., p. 6.

[39] Ibid., p. 78.

[40] Gilbert, *The Law of Evidence*, p. 157.

same Credit as Men of good Manners and clear Conversation'.[41] In this last criterion, Gilbert still adhered to the oath as an assurance of truth-telling. Yet, his reasoning was not entirely mechanical, but related to the different value an oath had for non-believers. When 'Witnesses are equal in Number and Credit', the fact-finders needed to prefer the witnesses who were more knowledgeable and possessed better memory of the details. A similar conceptual mixture existed in the six criteria set by John Locke (1632–1704) for evaluating testimony: 'the number of witnesses, their integrity, their skill at presenting the evidence, their purpose, the internal consistency of the evidence and its agreement with circumstances, and lastly the presence or absence of contrary testimony'.[42]

It is clear that, starting from the last decades of the seventeenth century, lawyers, doctors and divines alike began to use the language of credibility. Because of the religious significance of the oath, we might have expected the divines to demonstrate some difficulty in abandoning the epistemology of oaths and shifting to credibility. This did not happen, and the epistemology of credibility of witnesses was also adopted by clergymen. In 1718 Hutchinson even regarded credibility to be the epistemological basis of the events described in the scriptures. When he compared the relations in the scriptures to those of witnesses in witchcraft cases, he found reliability to depend 'upon the Credit of very different Witnesses ... The Scripture Relations are witnessed by *Prophets* and *Apostles*, that are venerable for a Divine Goodness and Virtue; The gross Part of our Stories of the Devil, are grounded upon the Confessions of Brainsick People.'[43] The scriptures were true not because the text was holy, but because the narrators were credible.

Perhaps the fact that the practice of swearing on oath was not discarded, but rather gradually supplemented by additional requirements, prevented clergymen from experiencing any sense of religious conflict. In addition, the need for credible evidence was not only a legal, but also a religious, imperative. As the prosecution in the case against Richard Hathaway maintained, it was 'the Duty of all Persons, that are concerned for Religion in general, to endeavour to detect such Practices which weaken one of its most solid Foundations'.[44] Making sure that the innocent would not be unjustly convicted was not merely a legal difficulty, but also a religious and moral dilemma.

---

[41]   Ibid. For a speculation whether the religion of the witness had a bearing on credibility, see Gibson (ed.), *Early Modern Witches*, p. 225, fn. 148.

[42]   G. Henry Van Leeuwen, *The Problem of Certainty in English Thought, 1630–1690* (The Hague: Martinus Nijhoff, 1970), p. 132.

[43]   Francis Hutchinson, *An Historical Essay Concerning Witchcraft* (London: R. Knaplock and D. Midwinter, 1718), p. 11.

[44]   *The Tryal of Richard Hathaway* (London: Isaac Cleave, 1702), p. 3.

Hearsay

As discussed above, one of the elements constituting credibility is the ability of the witness to testify about things perceived directly through his or her senses. The rise of the concept of hearsay is related to this feature of credibility. In the sixteenth century there was no rule barring witnesses from testifying about statements they had heard from others. The rule of hearsay, shared with civil practice, began to develop in the second half of the seventeenth century.[45] Hearsay statements were not necessarily excluded from admission, but by the mid-eighteenth century, the courts were sensitive to their limited probativeness, and they were mostly used merely for corroboration. By the end of the century, out-of-court statements could not be admitted unless the deponent could be cross-examined under oath.[46]

The greater focus on credibility that began in the second half of the seventeenth century brought about the inspection of three dimensions: *who* the witness was (identity), *how* the witness testified (manner), and *what* the witness testified to (content). The emerging characteristics of credible content included coherence, compatibility with other testimony, level of detail, plausibility, and first-hand knowledge. The rule of hearsay was one of the related and significant developments accompanying the growing emphasis on direct perception of the events by the senses of the witness.

There are many instances of hearsay in witchcraft cases, but just a few examples should suffice to characterize them. A pamphlet of 1582 described how the girl Ales Hunt testified that she had heard her mother (one of the defendants) say that Joan Pechey (another defendant) was 'skilfull and cunning in witcherie' and that she could perceive what was said or done in any of the houses in town.[47] One of the witnesses in the Warboys case, the vicar Robert Poulter, testified about what one of his parishioners had told him he had overheard said one day by Mother Samuel.[48] Sometimes witnesses testified about statements they had heard many years earlier. Potts described in his pamphlet the testimony of

---

[45]   J.M. Beattie, *Crime and the Courts in England, 1660–1800* (Princeton, NJ: Princeton University Press, 1986), p. 273; John Hamilton Baker, 'Criminal Courts and Procedure at Common Law 1550–1800', in J.S. Cockburn (ed.), *Crime in England 1550–1800* (Princeton, NJ: Princeton University Press, 1977), p. 39; Langbein, *Origins*, p. 233.

[46]   Beattie, *Crime and the Courts*, p. 364; Langbein, *Origins*, p. 234. The current rationale for the hearsay rule (ability to cross-examine the deponent) was not formulated until the nineteenth century. Langbein, *Origins*, p. 233.

[47]   W.W., *A True and Iust Recorde ...* (London: Thomas Dawson, 1582), 2A4v.

[48]   *The Most Strange and Admirable Discouerie of the Three Witches of Warboys* (London: Thomas Man, and Iohn Winington, 1593), O2.

James Robinson that, 'about some eighteene yeares agoe', Robert Nutter, who had fallen sick, told him he was bewitched by Chattox and Anne Redferne.[49] Margaret Crooke and John Nutter, the sister and brother of Robert Nutter, also deposed about hearing Robert's statements 18 or 19 years previously. Margaret also described similar statements made by their father before he died years before.[50] These are just a few of the many examples of cases where the court allowed witnesses to testify about things they *heard from others*. Witnesses were not limited to testifying only about matters they perceived through their own senses. There are also relations of witnesses who described matters told to them by an imp. Joan Willimot testified that her spirit told her that 'there was a bad woman at *Deeping* who had giuen her soule to the Diuell'.[51]

Only around the mid-seventeenth century was the term hearsay occasionally used as a label for inferior evidence. For example, in 1652 a pamphleteer showed his disrespect for the prosecution witnesses by stating that: 'Many other witnesses were produced, but could only swear to generallities, *hear-says*, and most absurd and rediculous impertinences.'[52]

Wigmore claimed that awareness of the deficiency of hearsay appeared in the mid-seventeenth century and turned into an exclusionary rule by the end of the century. Langbein identified a much later formation toward the end of the eighteenth century.[53] Wigmore's assertion is supported by a case of 1702, in which hearsay clearly functioned as an exclusionary rule. In this case, Dr Martin, a witness for the prosecution, described how he was verbally abused by Hathaway's supporters after testifying in favour of Sarah Murdock at the assizes, where she was acquitted. Mr Jenner, Hathaway's defence attorney, fiercely objected to this testimony. His claim was that other people's acts should not implicate his client. Jenner stated: 'I object to what the Doctor says by hearsay only.'[54] Judge Holt replied that the testimony should be permitted, as the purpose of the testimony was to relay what Hathaway *did* (leading others to believe he was bewitched). Although Lord Chief Justice Holt disagreed with Jenner on whether this particular statement should be allowed, they both shared an agreement that hearsay should not (Holt just believed that, in this instance,

---

49   Potts, *The Vvonderfull Discouerie of Witches*, E2.

50   Ibid., Ov. For other instances of hearsay in the pamphlet, see ibid., E4v–F, S.

51   *The Wonderful Discouerie of the Vvitchcrafts of Margaret and Phillip Flower* ... (London: Barnes, 1619), E2v–E3.

52   *A Declaration in Answer to Several Lying Pamphlets Concerning the Witch of Wapping* (London: s.n.r., 1652), pp. 7–8. Emphasis added.

53   Langbein, *Origins*, pp. 234–5, 245.

54   *The Tryal of Richard Hathaway*, p. 9.

the testimony was not hearsay). Despite the judge's opinion, when addressing the jury, Hathaway's defence attorney stated:

> The Doctor has taken a great deal of pains ... but that which he does tell you by *hearsay*, what other Persons told him, *is not such Evidence as you are to take any notice of ... tho it may be true, is not to come under your Consideration.*[55]

It seems that in this case, the prosecutor, Mr Conjers, also shared the notion that witnesses could testify only about what they had personally perceived, and not about what they heard from others. Conjers called Mr Shipps to testify that Hathaway pretended to be fasting for an extended period. Judge Holt was interested in knowing what Hathaway said about his fasting at the trial of Sarah Murdock, whom he accused of bewitching him:

> L.C.J. *Holt.* What did he say at the Assizes about his Fasting?
> M. *Shipps.* I was not at the Assizes.
> Mr *Coniers.* Then we must leave it here.[56]

It was obvious to the prosecutor that he was not able to ask the witness about matters he did not witness himself. This case presented hearsay as evidence that should be ignored, even if it was true. However, since the trial was not for witchcraft, but for counterfeiting witchcraft, it is hard to know for sure whether the hearsay rule was also applicable in witchcraft cases. As already demonstrated, the rules of evidence were sometimes more lenient in witchcraft cases. However, at least in this early eighteenth-century case, hearsay was already formulated as an exclusionary rule. The emerging notion that events not directly perceived by the senses of the witness were less credible no doubt contributed to the formation of the hearsay rule.

The need to rely mostly on witnesses to prove witchcraft necessitated the creation of mechanisms to ensure their trustworthiness. On the one hand, witnesses not routinely regarded as competent (such as children) were allowed to testify in witch trials. On the other hand, it was the credibility of the witnesses rather than their competence that began to matter. The credibility of the witnesses and their ability to describe events perceived directly enhanced the probative value of their testimony. Criteria for assessing testimony began to be articulated, and exclusionary concepts of evidence began to form. As the standard competency rules were bent in witchcraft trials, an alternative

---

[55]   Ibid., p. 16. Emphasis added.
[56]   Ibid.

method to distinguish between liars and truthful witnesses had to be found. It is worthwhile therefore, to consider the contribution of the witchcraft debate to the rise of the general legal concept of credibility and the diminishing significance of competence.

Figure 12.1 The hanging of three witches. Title page from *The Apprehension and Confession of Three Notorious Witches* ... (London: E. Allde, 1589). (1597.15.3) Courtesy of the Trustees of Lambeth Palace Library. [Call # (ZZ) 1597.15.03]

Chapter 12

Confession

Confession was a pre-trial statement made by the suspect in which he or she admitted guilt (wholly or partly, implicitly or explicitly). The confession was made either to the examining JP or to other persons. Technically, the confession could be submitted into evidence after the suspect had pleaded not guilty (as no evidence was required in the case of a guilty plea). Thomas Potts, the clerk of the assizes, described the events after Elizabeth Device had pleaded not guilty at her arraignment.

> Whereupon there was openly read, and given in evidence against her, for the Kings Majestie, her owne voluntarie Confession and Examination, when shee was apprehended, taken, and committed to the Castle of Lancaster by M. *Nowel*, and M. *Bannester*, two of his Mejesties Justices of Peace in the same Countie, *viz.*[1]

There was a debate about whether confession sufficed for conviction in witchcraft cases, but it is clear that a confession was enough to arrest the suspect pending trial. In 1674, when Ann Foster was brought before the JP on suspicion of bewitching the victim's sheep and causing fire in his barn, 'she freely confessed all, and boasted that she would make many more die as well as her self'. Upon which confession, the JP committed her to Northampton Goal, where she was to remain until the next assizes.[2]

For many, confession was the most elegant solution to the dilemma of proving the crime. Bernard considered the confession to be a good proof of the witches' relationship with the devil. To those who doubted that any sane person could freely admit crimes that would necessarily lead him or her to the gallows, Bernard answered that it was a fact that witches did confess their evil deeds, and he listed precedents to support this claim.[3] Potts, the author of one of the accounts which Bernard relied on, was careful to portray the confessions

---

[1] Thomas Potts, *The Vvonderfull Discouerie of Witches in the Countie of Lancaster* (London: Iohn Barnes, 1613), F4.

[2] *The Full and True Relation of the Tryal, Condemnation, and Execution of Ann Foster* (London: D.M., 1674), p. 6.

[3] Richard Bernard, *A Guide to Grand-Iury Men* (London: Ed. Blackmore, 1627), pp. 224–5.

as voluntary. Potts remarked about the confession of Chattox, one of the chief defendants in the case of 1612, that she murdered the young Robert Nutter:

> Since *the voluntarie confession and examination of a Witch, doth exceede all other evidence*, I spare to trouble you with a multitude of Examinations, or Depositions of any other witnesses.[4]

Relying on this case, Michael Dalton provided evidentiary rules for the discovery of witches and repeated that the voluntary confession of witches 'exceeds all other evidence'.[5] An author of a legal tract in 1643 repeated this statement and clarified that the confession was effective in proving both the maleficia and the alliance with the devil:

> Their own voluntary confession (which exceeds all other evidences) of the hurt they have done, or of the giving of their soules to the Devil, and of the Spirits which they have, how many, how they call them, and how they came by them.[6]

The idea that confessions were decisive also appeared in the pamphlet literature, which emphasized instances of confessions and their value. A confession, one of the authors expressed, was 'unquestionable, it being confessed by the Witch her self'.[7]

Confessions were highly desired, and suspects' statements were often liberally interpreted. Confession could have been implicit as well as explicit. Mother Samuel's words as Lady Cromwell cut a lock of her hair, 'I never did you any harme as yet', were retroactively interpreted as proof of Mother Samuel's being a witch.[8] In a dramatic moment of the Warboys affair, when Mother Samuel fell on her knees and asked Mr Throckmorton for forgiveness, this was interpreted as proof of her guilt.[9]

Bernard, who regarded the explicit confession as a good proof, considered the implicit confession to be a 'great presumption' that warranted an examination (not conviction). Bernard cited examples from previous cases, which he used as precedents, such as, 'You should haue let me alone then', or 'I will promise you

---

[4]   Potts, *The Vvonderfull Discouerie of Witches*, E2. Emphasis added.
[5]   Michael Dalton, *The Countrey Iustice* (London: Societie of Stationers, 1618), p. 243.
[6]   *The Lawes against Vvitches, and Coniuration* (London: R.W., 1645), p. 5.
[7]   Samuel Petto, *A Faithful Narrative* ... (London: John Harris, 1693), preface.
[8]   *The Most Strange and Admirable Discouerie of the Three Witches of Warboys* (London: Thomas Man, and Iohn Winington, 1593), D4.
[9]   Ibid., G2v–G3.

that I will doe you no hurt, vpon this or that condition'.[10] In addition, Bernard claimed that the pact with the devil could be inferred from 'Witches words', such as calling upon familiars, threatening to hurt people or cattle, or discussing other witchcraft-related matters.[11] Bernard's analysis of the implicit confession was cited in subsequent legal writing.[12]

Yet, some of the contemporaries doubted whether confession was indeed superior evidence. What did 'voluntary' mean? Should the confession be corroborated with additional evidence? Was it possible to accept a confession about improbable events? Could the confession be an illusion created by a mentally ill mind? Could an out-of-court confession be submitted as evidence after the defendant had recanted in court? And, if so, in what manner? Such concerns were already addressed in 1584 by Reginald Scot, who explained that confessions about inflicting damage by natural means (such as poisoning) should be accepted:

> If they confesse that, which hath béene indéed committed by them, as poisoning, or anie other kind of murther, which falleth into the power of such persons to accomplish; I stand not to defend their cause.

Yet, Scot maintained, it was necessary to reject confessions relating to impossible or unnatural acts. Confessions about killing with a look, a word or a touch of the bare hand, are unacceptable by any standard, and if 'examined by divinitie, philosophie, physicke, lawe or conscience', they would be found false and insufficient.[13]

Scot also denied the validity of confessions made by mentally ill suspects. Such confessions 'may be untrulie made, though it tend to the destruction of the confessor; and that melancholie may moove imaginations to that effect'.[14] Mental illness, called 'melancholy' by the early modern English, could lead the suspects to confess to crimes they had never committed, even though it led to their execution. It was because of their melancholy, Scot believed, that some persons genuinely, but erroneously, believed themselves to have perpetrated acts of witchcraft. He gave an example he was familiar with, a 'Kentish storie of a late accident' about the couple Ade and Simon Davie. The wife, who became

---

[10]   Bernard, *A Guide to Grand-Iury Men*, pp. 205–6.

[11]   Ibid., pp. 220–21.

[12]   *The Lawes against Vvitches*, pp. 4–5.

[13]   Reginald Scot, *The Discouerie of Witchcraft* (London: William Brome, 1584), p. 50. Footnotes omitted.

[14]   Ibid., p. 55.

depressed and withdrawn, confessed to her husband that she had 'bargained and given hir soule to the divell'. The husband immediately replied:

> Wife, be of good cheere, this the bargaine is void and of none effect: for thou hast sold that which is none of thine to sell; sith it belongeth to Christ, who hath bought it, and déerelie paid for it, even with his bloud, which he shed upon the crosse; so as the divell hath no interest in thée.

Having heard his answer, the women failed to be consoled and continued to confess in penitent tears that she had bewitched him and their children. The husband stayed calm and assured his wife: 'Be content ... by the grace of God, Jesus Christ shall unwitch us: for none evil can happen to them that feare God.' The husband then made his repentant wife read psalms and pray for God's mercy. And, indeed, the same day at midnight, when they heard a great rumbling under the window, they realized it was the devil below, but too weak to come in 'because of their fervent praiers'. Scot clarified that the woman had clearly committed no crime and bewitched none, but being depressed, was 'pressed downe with the weight of this humor', and believed herself to be a witch. Scot had no doubt that, had this woman been tried by Bodin, or by other witchmongers, she would have been executed.[15] The moral of the story, Scot explained, is that in cases of the mentally ill, confession could not be considered true or voluntary, since 'this melancholike humor (as the best physicians affirme) is the cause of all their strange, impossible, and incredible confessions'.[16]

Scot's conclusion was general and applied not only to mentally ill suspects. In fact, he stated that confession alone was insufficient to prove witchcraft. In capital cases, proofs 'must be brought more cleare than the light it selfe'.[17] Scot addressed those who claimed that confession was the only way to prove witchcraft. His answer was that confessions about unnatural acts were 'not worthie of credit', and if the suspects confessed to 'a fact performed but in opinion, they are to be reputed among the number of fooles'.[18]

Scot had used the term 'voluntarie confession', which denoted mostly internal motives, such as melancholy, which induced suspects to deliver false confessions.[19] Perkins referred to a 'free and voluntarie confession',[20] a phrase still

---

[15]   Ibid., pp. 56–7. Footnotes omitted.

[16]   Ibid., p. 57.

[17]   Ibid., p. 69.

[18]   Ibid.

[19]   Ibid., p. 55.

[20]   William Perkins, *A Discourse of the Damned Art of Witchcraft* (Cambridge, UK: Vniuersitie of Cambridge, 1608), pp. 211–12.

used today. By adding the term free, Perkins emphasized freedom from external coercion. He also retained the term voluntary to denote internal freedom. By voluntary, Perkins demanded that statements be undistorted by delusions or mental illness. Pamphleteers often described the confessions of suspects as voluntary.[21] The requirement that confessions be free and voluntary had also been adopted in the American colonies. Increase Mather, an influential Puritan leader in the Massachusetts Bay Colony writing in the aftermath of the Salem witch trials, stated that 'a free and voluntary Confession of the Crime made by the Person suspected and accused after Examination, is a sufficient Ground of Conviction'. Mather declared, 'nothing can be more clear' than confessions made by 'any Persons out of Remorse of Conscience, or from a Touch of God on their Spirits'. And as for those who made false confession, Mather felt no qualms and asserted that 'they ought to dye for their Wickedness, and their Blood will be upon their own Heads; the Jury, the Judges, and the Land is clear'.[22] By confessing to crimes they never committed, Mather said, the suspects ensnared the jurors and judges into wrongful conviction, and for that they ought to die anyway.[23]

Perkins considered confession to be one of the two proofs sufficient for conviction (the other being testimony by two credible witnesses). He explained that 'all men both Diuines, and Lawyers' considered the confession to be a sufficient basis for conviction, as 'For what needs more witnes, or further enquirie, when a man from the touch of his own conscience acknowledgeth the fault'.[24] Since the confession was against the suspect's self-interest, it must be true. In the words of an eighteenth-century pamphleteer, 'we may Suspect the Truth of a Malefactor, who asserts his Innocence to the Last Moment; yet surely never any question'd the Truth of a Criminal's Confession'.[25] Perkins, however, was not so naive as to believe that every self-damaging confession must be true. In answer to those he called 'the patrons and aduocates of Witches', who claimed that an

---

[21]   One example is: 'She ... offered to give Testimony of many things ... as of her *free and Volunta*[...] *Confessing*, that She had a Familiar Spirit, and that She had been the Death of some &c'. Petto, *A Faithful Narrative*, p. 19. Francis Bragge described how Jane Wenham's confession was 'free and unconstrain'd, no Force having been us'd to bring her to it'. Francis Bragge, *Witchcraft Farther Display'd* ... (London: E. Curll, 1712), p. 37.

[22]   Increase Mather, *Cases of Conscience Concerning Evil Spirits* ... (London: Dunton, 1693), p. 34.

[23]   Another justification for the execution of possibly innocent suspects was offered by Hobbes and Selden, who argued that a malicious intent to cause evil by witchcraft warranted capital punishment even if the suspect had no real power. See the discussion in Keith Thomas, *Religion and the Decline of Magic* (New York: Charles Scribner's Sons, 1971), p. 523.

[24]   Perkins, *Damned Art*, p. 211.

[25]   A.M.G.R., *The Belief of Witchcraft Vindicated* (London: J. Baker, 1712), p. 38.

untrue confession could be obtained through fear, threats or other pressures, Perkins clarified that a 'bare confession' was not enough. Conviction could rest only on 'a confession after due examination taken vpon pregnant presumptions' and 'vpon good probabilities'.[26] Without such corroborating circumstances, the confession could not be relied on.

Although he regarded confession to be superior evidence, Dalton was more cautious and believed that the confession in examination was not sufficient for conviction even in witchcraft cases. He argued that in witchcraft cases, as well as in other hard-to-prove crimes, the confession of the accused in the examination, something he considered a 'half proof', ought to be admitted into evidence:

> And yet the confession of the offendor, vpon his examination before the Iustice of Peace shall be no conuiction of the offendor, except he shall after confesse the same againe vpon his tryall or arraignment, or be found guiltie by verdict of twelue men, &c.

> Also in cases of secret murthers, and in cases of poysoning, witchcraft, and the like secret offences, where open and euident proofes are seldome to be had, ther (it seemeth) halfe proofes are to be allowed, and are good causes of suspition.[27]

Dalton's contention was that in witchcraft cases, the confession in examination was a good cause of suspicion, but it needed corroboration to achieve conviction. Although Perkins declared confession to be sufficient proof and Dalton regarded it only as half proof, the difference is more semantic, and the essence of their views is the same – to be accepted as valid and true, the confession had to be freely made and should have been corroborated by other evidence.

Gaule, a clergyman, agreed with Perkins that a bare confession was a probable sign but insufficient for conviction.[28] Although in Gaule's view the witch's 'free confession' was one of the 'more infallible and certaine signes', he insisted it should be corroborated, '*For Confession without Fact, may be a meer delusio; & Fact without Confession, may be but a meer accidet*'.[29] Gaule recommended that the witch hunter consider the following factors when evaluating a confession:

> if the party confessing bee of right mind: and not diabolically deluded to confesse not improbabilities only, but impossibilities: if it be not forced, but a free

---

26   Perkins, *Damned Art*, pp. 211–12.

27   Dalton, *The Countrey Iustice*, p. 268.

28   John Gaule, *Select Cases of Conscience Touching Vvitches and Vvitchcrafts* (London: Richard Clutterbuck, 1646), p. 80.

29   Ibid., p. 81. Emphasis added.

confession. If Melancholy Humors work not too fond and false self-perswasions. If they may not be some seeds of superstition disposing to witchcraft only; whereof the Conscience convicted and distracted, errs confusedly in apprehending and acknowledging all the Completion thereof.[30]

Corroboration of the confession with additional evidence seems to have been the practice in English courts of the early seventeenth century. Thomas Potts emphasized that although James Device's confession was legally sufficient proof, Judge Bromley insisted on having the other witnesses testify and on examining the suspect in court:

> This *voluntary Confession* and Examination of his owne, containing in it selfe matter sufficient in Law to charge him, and to prove his offences, contained in the two severall Indictments, *was sufficient to satisfie the Gentlemen of the Jury* of Life and Death, that he is guiltie of them, and either of them: *yet my Lord Bromley commanded, for their better satisfaction, that the Witnesses present* in Court against any of the Prisoners, *should be examined openly, viva voce,* that the Prisoner might both heare and answere to every particular point of their Evidence; notwithstanding any of their Examinations taken before any of his Majesties Justices of Peace within the same Countie.[31]

Although technically a mere confession would have sufficed, Judge Bromley felt more comfortable after hearing the witnesses.

Not everyone agreed that corroboration was a satisfactory precaution. Filmer, the author of a treatise of 1653 attacking the ways of proof offered by Perkins, did not neglect to oppose the confession, one of the two proofs Perkins considered sufficient. Filmer contested the use of confession for a few theoretical reasons. First, he agreed with Perkins that some suspects might be induced to admit crimes they did not commit. Second, Filmer claimed that corroborating confessions by presumption, as Perkins had suggested, did not solve the problem, as the presumptions are indeed insufficient. Third, Filmer did not accept Perkins' argument that the witches were sober when they made the covenant but might

---

[30]   Ibid., pp. 101–2.

[31]   Potts, *The Vvonderfull Discouerie of Witches*, H4. Emphasis added. A 1674 account relates how Ann Foster confessed before the JP, then pleaded not guilty at her arraignment and confessed again after all the evidence against her had been laid out at her trial. *Tryal of Ann Foster*, p. 7.

be unreasonable and deluded afterward. Filmer held that if a person was deluded when making the confession, such confession was invalid in any case.[32]

Suspects in witchcraft cases confessed to having committed acts normally considered impossible or unnatural. They confessed to having imps or spirits, sending them to kill or injure other people or to destroy their property.[33] Some suspects confessed to having sexual relations with devils and imps.[34] We do not know what caused suspects to make a confession of impossible acts, which was often the most significant evidence leading to their execution.[35] Coercion is the first explanation that comes to mind. Although torture was not permitted in the investigation of witchcraft cases, milder means could be no less effective.

The witch hunter Stearne, Matthew Hopkins' assistant, acknowledged that some suspects were deprived of sleep for up to four days. However, he claimed, he did not 'use violence, or extremity to force them to confesse, but made an observation necessary for the detection of imps'.[36] Stearne also claimed that suspects could be led to confess 'without extremity', if after being instructed by divines or other 'godly' people about their sins, they wished to call on God's mercy.[37]

---

[32]   Sir Robert Filmer, *An Advertisement to the Jury-Men of England, Touching Witches* (London: Richard Royston, 1653), pp. 12–13. Perkins answered those who claimed that persons who confessed to acts such as passing through keyholes or flying in the air were insane or deluded and explained that such weakness of mind could follow a soberly made contract with the devil. Perkins, *Damned Art*, pp. 194–6.

[33]   Just a few examples are *The Apprehension and Confession of Three Notorious Witches* (London: E. Allde, 1589), A3–A4, B2; John Davenport, *The Witches of Huntingdon* (London: Richard Clutterbuck, 1646), A3; H.F., *A True and Exact Relation ...* (London: Henry Overton and Benj. Allen, 1645), pp. 29–31, 34–5; I.D., *The Most Wonderfull and True Storie ...* (London: I.O., 1597), p. 26.

[34]   An extreme example is Temperance Lloyd, who confessed to killing men and cattle but also drowning ships, having a carnal relationship with the devil and nursing him (which was his way to sexually seduce her). *The Tryal, Condemnation, and Execution of Three Vvitches* (London: J. Deacon, 1682), pp. 4–5. A far less juicy description of her confession is found in *A True and Impartial Relation ...* (London: Freeman Collins, 1682), pp. 13–19. Another interesting example is a woman who confessed to flying in the air at night to her sister's bedroom to kill her baby. John Hale, *A Collection of Modern Relations ...* (London: John Harris, 1693), p. 49.

[35]   This problem is still relevant today. For an example of research that concentrates on psychological reasons for false confessions, see Elizabeth Loftus, 'The Devil in Confessions', *Psychological Science in the Public Interest* 5, no. 2 (2005).

[36]   John Stearne, *A Confirmation and Discovery of Witchcraft* (London: William Wilson, 1648), p. 13.

[37]   Ibid., p. 14.

Coercion by various measures cannot be the single explanation of confessions. Whether suspects confessed to crimes that they had never committed also depended greatly on their personalities. In some cases with multiple defendants, some of the suspects confessed while others denied the charges.[38] The poor, old and 'silly' were considered more prone to being manipulated into giving false confessions. As one sceptical author observed, 'the Wisest Men in the World may be brought by Imprisonment and Torture, to confess any thing, whether it be True or False'. It is not surprising, therefore, that 'many Miserable Creatures' and 'some poor, silly, melancholly *Wretches*' confessed to being witches.[39]

The only partial influence of coercion might be inferred from some cases where the suspects admitted to some of the facts but denied others. John Walsh, in 1566, denied being maleficient but acknowledged using techniques of witchcraft.[40] Joan Cunny confessed to having spirits hurt some people but denied sending spirits to hurt others.[41] Joan Prentice confessed to sending the ferret to 'nippe' a girl, but claimed it killed her against her instructions.[42] Partial confessions might mean that coercion and pressures could be resisted to some degree. They could, however, have other explanations, such as suspects who were convinced that they might be guilty of some of the charges[43] or desperate suspects trying to implicate others, hoping it might save their own necks. Some suspects initially denied the charges but broke down and confessed as the

---

[38]   For example, out of a group of suspects investigated in 1645 during a witch hunt orchestrated by the notorious Hopkins and Stearne, a few confessed to maleficia and having imps, while others denied the charges. Elizabeth Clarke *confessed* to being a witch and having imps sucking her; Anne Leech *confessed* that together with Elizabeth Gooding, she sent imps to kill Mr Edwards' cows and child, Elizabeth Kirk and the daughter of widow Rawlyns; Rose Hallybread *confessed* to having imps and to maleficia; Joyce Boansed *confessed* to suckling imps and maleficia; Susan Cock *confessed* to sending imps on evil errands; Rebecca Jones *confessed* to having imps and killing a sow and people; Johan Cooper *confessed* to having imps and to maleficia, as did Anne Cate. F., *A True and Exact Relation*, pp. 6, 8, 9, 29–31, 33–5. The other suspects, Elizabeth Gooding, Helen Clark, Mary Johnson, Margaret Moone and Sarah Hasting *denied* the charges against them. F., *A True and Exact Relation*, pp. 7, 10, 18, 25, 29. In comparison, a month later, in another episode in the Hopkins' witch scare, all 18 defendants confessed. Additional suspects who were arrested but not tried had also confessed. *A True Relation of the Araignment of Eighteene Vvitches* (London: I.H., 1645), pp. 3–5.

[39]   *The Impossibility of Witchcraft* ... (London: J. Baker, 1712), p. 26.

[40]   *The Examination of John Walsh* (London: Iohn Awdely, 1566).

[41]   *The Apprehension*, A3–A4.

[42]   Ibid., B2.

[43]   For example, Margaret Landishe admitted to the possibility of an imp sucking her but denied all other charges. It sounds as though she was persuaded to doubt her innocence. F., *A True and Exact Relation*, p. 32.

interrogation progressed. Mary Sutton denied all allegations at first (obstinately, as the pamphleteer noted), even after being swum twice. However, she broke down after learning that her son had deposed against her, implicating her mother as well.[44]

Whereas legal scholars and clerics tended to allow confession as a valid proof, albeit with corroboration, physicians displayed scepticism toward the evidentiary value of confession. Thomas Ady deplored the practice of coercing suspects to confess to 'Lyes and Impossibilities'.[45] Interestingly, the means of coercion which he denounced were not those of extreme torture (in comparison to the Continental strappado or thumbscrews),[46] but methods such as deprivation of sleep for 'many nights and dayes, thereby to distemper their brains and hurt their fancies, at length to extort confession from them', or psychologically pressuring the suspects through an investigation of their children in an attempt to have them accuse their parents – 'this trick will tame any wilde Beast'.[47] Sleep deprivation, the *tormentum insomniae*, was a very effective method of extracting confessions of witchcraft, as very few could endure it.[48] Ady blamed the 'Popish writers' and 'Popish darkness' for using cruel methods to obtain impossible confessions as the last resort to prove unreasonable theories. For Ady, the swimming tests and the bodily search for the devil's mark were cruelties used to force the innocent to confess.[49]

Wagstaffe, a sceptical intellectual, was not a physician himself but supported the use of medical knowledge to address allegations. He believed witchcraft allegations stemmed from 'want of knowledge in the Art of Physick', which made men (including physicians 'laboured in Anatomy and Chymistry') attribute diseases to spirits.[50] He explained that 'the wisest men in the world' could be induced to confess anything by torture and imprisonment and did

---

[44]   W.W., *A True and Iust Recorde ...* (London: Thomas Dawson, 1582), C3–C3v.

[45]   Some editions were titled *A Candle in the Dark*.

[46]   Geoffrey Scarre, *Witchcraft and Magic in Sixteenth- and Seventeenth-Century Europe*, Studies in European History (Atlantic Highlands, NJ: Humanities Press International, 1987), p. 27.

[47]   Thomas Ady, *A Candle in the Dark* (London: Robert Ibbitson, 1655), p. 99. Sleep deprivation was a highly effective method of obtaining confessions. 'Mathew Hopkins, "the great witch finder" of 1645–46 sometimes obtained confessions by keeping suspects from sleeping for several days.' John H. Langbein, *Torture and the Law of Proof: Europe and England in the Ancien Regime* (Chicago: University of Chicago Press, 1977), p. 210, fn. 249.

[48]   Brian P. Levack, *The Witch-Hunt in Early Modern Europe*, 2nd edn (New York: Longman, 1995), p. 81.

[49]   Ady, *A Candle in the Dark*, pp. 101, 104–5.

[50]   John Wagstaffe, *The Question of Witchcraft Debated ...* (London: Edward Millington, 1669), p. 66.

not doubt that 'some poor, silly, melancholick old wretches' genuinely believed themselves to be witches. False confessions could be a result of 'the strange effects of melancholly, especially if it hath been heightened by poverty, or want of good diet, by ignorance, solitariness, and old age'.[51] An author debating with Wagstaffe provided three arguments against his position. First, there was no torture in England. Second, it was impossible that all those who confessed were 'silly Old Women overgrown with melancholy and dotage'. Third, as it was 'not onely the Old man or woman, but the Judge, the Jury, and the whole Assize' who accepted such confessions, could it be that they were all fools? Could it be that 'all the Christian world' erred in establishing laws against a non-existent crime?[52]

Joseph Glanvill, a man of the Church and a Fellow of the Royal Society, objected to the kind of argument suggested by Wagstaffe that those who confessed were 'commonly *poor* and *miserable old women*, who are overgrown with *discontent* and *melancholy*, which are very *imaginative*'.[53] It made perfect sense for the devil, Glanvill explained, to use 'the weak and the ignorant' for his wicked plans.[54]

Webster, a practising physician (and previously a priest) was adamantly against accepting the confessions of suspects in witchcraft cases, which he regarded as null, impossible and false, and that therefore 'no credit at all ought to be given unto them'.[55] Webster's opinion was that confessions of suspects in witchcraft cases:

> are no sufficient evidence, nor worthy of any credit; because there is neither Reason, Law, nor Equity that allows the testimony or confession of an Idiot, Lunatick, mad or doting person, because they are not of a right and sound understanding, and are not to be accounted as *compotes mentis*, nor governed by rationability ... nor ought to be credited ... Because the things they confess are not attested by any other persons of integrity and sound ... Because they confess things that are impossible ... There is no good end wherefore they make these Confessions, neither do they receive any benefit by them, either spiritual or temporal, internal nor external. And this doth sufficiently shew, that they are deluded, melancholy, and mad persons, and so their Confessions of no credit, truth, or validity.[56]

---

[51] Ibid., pp. 65–6.
[52] R.T., *The Opinion of Witchcraft Vindicated* (London: Francis Haley, 1670), pp. 60–62.
[53] Joseph Glanvill, *A Philosophical Endeavour* (London: James Collins, 1666), p. 30.
[54] Ibid., pp. 31–3.
[55] John Webster, *The Displaying of Supposed Witchcraft* (London: J.M., 1677), p. 79.
[56] Ibid., p. 66.

Webster also suggested various reasons for suspects to make false confession, such as the wish 'to escape the present miseries of a poor, wretched, and troublesom life', torture, 'force, waking, craft, and cunning, in hope of pardon and life', indoctrination by the inquisitors, delusions and lies 'contracted by ignorant, unchristian, and superstitious education, which they have suckt in with their milk', impossible act and, naturally, madness and melancholy. In short, there was 'not any jot of truth in these Confessions'.[57] Believing confessions was absurd, as it was not 'possibly credible to a rational and unbiassed judgment' to trust the statements of 'the Slaves and Vassals of the Devil'.[58] Webster also denounced as absurd the argument that confessions ought to be trusted because otherwise many wise and honest judges and jurors who sentenced suspects to death would have to be deemed deceived. It was evident for Webster that 'Our Judges and Juries have no such sinister and corrupt ends, to wrest the Laws, or wring forth and extort feigned and false Confessions'. Judges and jurors could not be held liable for the falsity of witnesses.[59]

The English grew more and more suspicious regarding the voluntariness of confessions, especially in the context of witchcraft. Later, in the eighteenth century, out-of-court confessions could be admitted into evidence, but their probative value, or weight, depended on the circumstances of their acquiescence.[60] Ultimately, the concerns that surrounded confessions ripened into an exclusionary rule rejecting non-voluntary confessions. Of course, whether a confession was voluntary or not was another question. John Langbein argued that the *confession rule*, one of the main rules of criminal evidence, was articulated in the eighteenth century. According to Langbein, the confession rule required that confessions be voluntary. The mature rule excluded confessions

---

[57] Ibid., p. 67–8.

[58] Ibid., p. 71.

[59] Ibid., p. 72.

[60] For that purpose, a confession made to the magistrate *under oath* (which supposedly validated the content) was paradoxically regarded to be contrary to the prosecution's interest. Such confession could not be admitted, being a breach of the rule that suspects may not be compelled to testify against themselves. J.M. Beattie, *Crime and the Courts in England, 1660–1800* (Princeton, NJ: Princeton University Press, 1986), p. 365. Cf. Sir Geoffrey Gilbert, *The Law of Evidence* (London: W. Owen, 1756), p. 140. Langbein traced the origin of the maxim *nemo tenentur prodere seipsum* (no one is obliged to accuse himself) in an ecclesiastical context (the duty to confess was not extended to criminal proceedings). The maxim was later used by those who challenged the ex officio oath and was ultimately perceived as the expression of the privilege against self-incrimination. Langbein noted that in practice, the accused was forbidden to testify under oath even if the person wanted to. John H. Langbein, *The Origins of Adversary Criminal Trial*, Oxford Studies in Modern Legal History (Oxford: Oxford University Press, 2003), pp. 277–8.

induced by hope of favour or out of fear.[61] In the early decades of the eighteenth century, relying on the *Old Bailey Sessions Papers*, Langbein found no indication of 'sensitivity to the dangers of confession evidence'.[62] He traced signs of change beginning with the 1730s to the 1760s, when the confession rule prevailed.[63] Yet, the findings of this research prove otherwise.

These findings clearly demonstrate that in the context of witch trials, there was great awareness of the dangers that lurked in confession evidence, starting with Reginald Scot's *Discouerie of Witchcraft*, which was published as early as 1584. Different writers, whether scholars or pamphleteers, emphasized the importance of confessions being voluntary and free, and discussed at length the meaning of these expressions. The participants in the debate surrounding confession evidence pointed to various circumstances that carried a likely risk of false confessions, including mental illness, delusions, a false sense of guilt, torture, physical abuse, psychological pressures, fear and a desperate hope of being saved on confessing and implicating others. The authors differed in their overall position toward confession. Some rejected it entirely, while others demanded corroborating evidence as well. However, it is clear that, by and large, confession evidence needed to be voluntary and was treated with caution.

The participants in the debate clearly differed in their views regarding the value of confession evidence. Physicians, as in other areas of evidence, were the most radical voice, entirely rejecting confession evidence. Both divines and lawyers found confession a valid and legitimate proof as long as it was supported by corroborating evidence. For lawyers and legal scholars, the confession, despite all its shortcomings, provided an acceptable solution to the dilemma of proof. With the exception of Filmer (who was trained in law and experienced as a justice, but perhaps is better characterized as a political thinker), all legal authors supported the use of confession. Nonetheless, they were all cautious, and none wished to rely solely on confessions.

For clerical writers, confession had additional meaning. The term used in the context of the criminal trial was not 'admission' or 'acknowledgment', but 'confession', carrying many religious connotations. It was one of the sacraments retained by the Anglican Church. Forgiveness was afforded only to the true penitent who confessed. By admitting sins, the suspect could conform to prescriptive religious and social norms. The Protestants had forsaken the sacrament of confession but continued to address the issues of sin and penance.[64]

---

[61] Langbein, *Origins*, p. 179.

[62] Ibid., p. 218.

[63] Ibid., pp. 220–21.

[64] Katharine Jackson Lualdi and Anne T. Thayer (eds), *Penitence in the Age of Reformations* (Aldershot: Ashgate, 2000), p. 2. According to Reis' analysis of the confessions

It should be remembered that in that era the distinction between non-compliance with secular and divine authority was less clear-cut than it is today.[65]

Indeed, clergymen were actively involved in the investigation of many witchcraft cases. A famous example is the case of Jane Wenham, in which three ministers participated in her investigation.[66] Divines were familiar with the theological elements required to establish a charge of covenant with the devil. Some suspects were even made to confess in church. In the Warboys case, after the Throckmorton family had made Mother Samuel confess, they wanted to demonstrate publicly that they had not coerced her. They took her to the church, where, in front of all the neighbours, accusers and the minister, she was made to confirm that her confession was freely made. She then 'desired all her neighbours to pray to God for her, and to forgive her.'[67] The religious aspect of confession as purification of a sinful soul was demonstrated by various instances in which convicted witches confessed before their execution, often publicly, standing at the gallows, hoping to regain God's mercy.[68] Some ministers tried very hard to compel those already convicted to confess, especially if they had maintained

---

made in witchcraft cases by Puritan women in New England, a good Puritan woman confessed her sins and repented, thus confirming society's belief in God and the devil. Elizabeth Reis, *Damned Women: Sinners and Witches in Puritan New England* (Ithaca, NY: Cornell University Press, 1997).

[65]   J.A. Sharpe, '"Last Dying Speeches": Religion, Ideology and Public Execution in Seventeenth-Century England', *Past and Present* 107, no. 1 (1985): p. 16.

[66]   Francis Bragge, *A Full and Impartial Account* ..., 2nd edn (London: E. Curll, 1712), pp. 15–16. The Reverend's questions were described by one sceptical author as manipulative and 'ensnaring'. *A Full Confutation of Witchcraft* ... (London: J. Baker, 1712), pp. 23–4.

[67]   *Witches of Warboys*, G3v.

[68]   Among the witches confessing at their execution were *Mother Samuel*, 1593, ibid., O3–O3v; *Mary Smith*, 1616, Alexander Roberts, *A Treatise of Witchcraft*, 2nd edn (London: Samuel Man, 1616), unpaginated dedication to the reader, 60; *Elizabeth Sawyer*, 'in the hearing of many hundreds at her last breath', Henry Goodcole, *The Wonderfull Discouerie of Elizabeth Sawyer a Witch* (London: Vvilliam Butler, 1621), D2–D2v.; *Joan Williford*, *The Examination, Confession, Triall, and Execution, of Joane Williford, Joan Cariden, and Jane Hott* (London: J.G., 1645), p. 2.; *John Palmer*, B. Misodaimon, *The Divels Delvsions* ... (London: Richard Williams Stationer, 1649), p. 5.; *Anne Bodennam* was pressured to confess by the minister, but when she stood on the ladder, she refused to confess, and when the executioner requested her forgiveness, she replied, '"Forgive thee? A pox on thee, turn me off"; which were the last words she spake', Edmund Bower, *Doctor Lamb Revived* ... (London: Richard Best and John Place, 1653), pp. 33, 41; *Susanne Edwards, Temperance Lloyd* and *Mary Trembles*, who were interrogated at length at their execution, *A True and Impartial Relation*, pp. 37–40; *Mary Hicks* and her nine-year-old daughter confessed, 'Then the Ladder being over-turn'd they were both hang'd', *The Whole Trial and Examination of Mrs Mary Hicks and Her Daughter Elizabeth* (London: W. Matthews, 1716), p. 8.

their innocence throughout the trial. The minister Henry Goodcole stated that he obtained Elizabeth Sawyer's confession after her conviction, 'though with great labour it was extorted from her'.[69] An account from 1652 contained an extreme example of clerical pressure to confess following conviction. The pamphleteer described how, after Joan Peterson was incriminated by false witnesses and wrongfully convicted, the minister attempted nine or ten times to pressure her to confess before her execution. This was obviously exaggerated, and 'the Executioner told the Ordinary, he might be ashamed to trouble a dying woman so much'.[70] The frantic efforts to secure confession, even after the suspect was duly convicted in court, demonstrate that the role of the confession was not merely juridical.

Confessions were a significant factor of legitimization, for the justice system in particular and for society at large. Confirmation that the judges and jurors had convicted the right person and that the result was not the shedding of innocent blood, a grave religious and moral sin, was of great value. Penitential gallows speeches were characteristic of early modern executions in England, and they legitimized not merely the punishment, but the whole secular and religious structure of authority.[71] The pursuit of post-conviction confessions demonstrates that confession was not merely a legal tool and that the dilemma of proof was not merely a legal quandary, but a weighty societal predicament. Confession evidence was, no doubt, much more than a simple legal proof.

The crime of witchcraft, more than other crimes, called attention to the difficulty of relying on the stories of witnesses. Narrations of supernatural and improbable events were hard to believe, even if they came out of the mouths of the suspects themselves. Doubts concerning the possibility and existence of witchcraft necessitated direct confrontation with the issue of the assessment of witchcraft narratives. The techniques of keeping liars outside the courtroom underwent transition during the early modern era. From the gatekeeping rules of competence and the mechanism of oath, focus shifted to techniques that took into consideration the individual characteristics of the witnesses and the content of their stories. The narratives needed to be credible and present first-hand impressions. Credibility became an overriding notion, both in pamphlets and in the learned discourse of the elite. Toward the end of the seventeenth century, lawyers, physicians and churchmen alike demanded that the reports of witnesses

---

[69]   Goodcole, *The Wonderfull Discouerie of Elizabeth Savvyer*, B4.

[70]   *A Declaration in Answer to Several Lying Pamphlets Concerning the Witch of Wapping* (London: s.n.r., 1652), p. 9.

[71]   Sharpe, "'Last Dying Speeches': Religion, Ideology and Public Execution in Seventeenth-Century England', p. 20.

be credible. Although the notion of credibility overshadowed the mechanical concept of the oath, the divines seemed to embrace it as well.

In general, it is possible to say that, although witchcraft was a crime with a considerable religious foundation, and although the divines were supposedly well trained to define it or prove it, the men of the church lost this privileged position as they gave in to general secular notions of proof. If witchcraft was to be proven by credible means, as any other matter of fact, the men of the church no longer held a unique standing in proving it.

Although the differences between lawyers and divines regarding problematic categories of witnesses (such as children or accomplices) were not sharp, and the dispute on this subject cannot be clearly arranged along lines of professional affiliation, it still seems that lawyers were generally supportive of the use of children and accomplices' testimonies, whereas clerics diverged in their opinions. The tone used by lawyers was more descriptive, allegedly limited to reflecting the then-existing law. However, the differences were subtle, and one needs to refrain from over-simplifying generalizations.

It may be the case that the exceptional witchcraft evidentiary arrangements contributed to the rise of the notion of credibility and heightened sensitivity to the disadvantages of hearsay statements. To facilitate the proof of witchcraft, the normal competency rules were abandoned and categories of witnesses who were usually left outside the courtroom, such as children or accomplices, were allowed to testify. Hearsay was traditionally allowed in English courts. Yet, in witchcraft cases, where eyewitnesses were scarce, hearsay statements were especially significant. However, if everyone could testify, and if second- or third-hand testimonies about supernatural events could be heard, new criteria of assessment needed to be developed to distinguish between true and false testimonies. Wigmore found an awareness of the shortcomings of hearsay starting in the mid-seventeenth century and recognized the existence of an exclusionary rule by the end of that century. Langbein concluded that the hearsay rule was formed toward the end of the eighteenth century. Concerning the witchcraft debate, there is a manifest awareness of the dangers posed by hearsay starting in the mid-sixteenth century and a case in 1702 where hearsay functioned as an exclusionary rule.

Legal authors and theologians alike tended to support confession evidence as a valid proof, although typically contingent on sufficient corroboration. The great value they attributed to confessions might have had different motives. Divines seemed to bear in mind the religious significance of confessions and often sought to obtain a post-conviction and pre-execution confession as well. For legal scholars and practitioners, the confession was a good solution to the problem of proof and had great power of legitimization when they faced the dilemma of proving witchcraft.

All agreed that confessions had to be free and voluntary, yet physicians doubted that witchcraft confessions could be so. They demonstrated a great amount of scepticism toward confessions of fantastic and supernatural crimes and elaborated on psychiatric and psychological factors (melancholy, stress, and so on) that rendered such confessions worthless. While churchmen seem to have adopted proof standards beyond their discipline and to lose their prominent standing in witchcraft cases, physicians were much more successful in using the debate as a platform for professional achievement. They created for themselves an indispensable role in the diagnosis of witchcraft, and they used the area of witchcraft to distinguish between learned physicians and inferior medical practitioners.

The most dramatic confrontation between the different professional discourses occurred in the area of expert testimony. Heavy reliance on the testimony of experts, which was another solution to the dilemma, entailed a potential threat to the authority of the judiciary. Judges relied on experts and even summoned them on behalf of the court, yet clarified that their testimony should be assessed just like any other piece of evidence. Physicians as expert witnesses were not always sceptical as to witchcraft allegations. Some celebrated cases presented a battle of experts, in which one physician testified for the defence and one for the prosecution. The result for the physicians, however, was that no matter which party prevailed, the court relied on medical testimony.

Conclusions

Wigmore defined evidence as facts that are offered to persuade 'as to the truth of a proposition'. He assumed that the rules of evidence are consistent with this basic goal: 'The rules of Evidence, as recorded in our law, may be said to be essentially rational. The reason may not always be a good one, in point of policy. But there is always a reason.'[1] Wigmore's ambition was to study the reasons for each rule of evidence. He recognized that different evidentiary rules may have different rationales that, on occasion, may be contradictory.[2] Yet, the deepest underlying rationale is that of evidence as a truth-finding device.[3] In many respects Wigmore's perception reflects the current widespread view of the legal community, which also tends to perceive the rules of evidence as an objective and inherently rational apparatus aimed at discovering the truth.[4] This assumption is taken for granted, so some scholars do not even find it necessary to state it but instead open their treatises on evidence with the rules themselves.[5] What is missing from many existing depictions is the socio-cultural context, which has an important role in shaping and directing the trajectories of evidence law.

This study offers a strikingly different picture of evidence law: the common-law rules of evidence do not necessarily possess a universal or 'real' objective

---

[1] John Henry Wigmore, *Evidence in Trials at Common Law*, 4th edn, 10 vols (Boston: Little, Brown and Company, 1983), vol. 1, p. 8, see also p. 9, fn. 5. Wigmore cited Sir James Stephen, who devoted his work 'to prove the proposition that the English rules of Evidence are *not* a mere collection of arbitrary subtleties which shackle, instead of guiding, natural sagacity'. Wigmore, *Evidence*, p. xx.

[2] David P. Leonard, *The New Wigmore: A Treatise on Evidence*, ed. Richard D. Friedman (Gaithersburg, NY: Aspen Law & Business, 2001), p. lvii.

[3] For a review of works that consider the social policy, moral and economic aspects of evidence law, see William Twining and Alex Stein (eds), *Evidence and Proof*, The International Library of Essays in Law and Legal Theory, ed. Tom D. Campbell (New York: New York University Press, 1992), pp. xxi–xxv. See also Alex Stein, *The Foundations of Evidence Law* (Oxford: Oxford University Press, 2005). Yet these studies still viewed evidentiary techniques as intentional and rational truth-finding tools, designed to enhance a general social good.

[4] For a review of the common assumptions of the rationalistic theories of evidence, see Twining and Stein (eds), *Evidence and Proof*, pp. xvi–xvii.

[5] Sidney L. Phipson, *Phipson on Evidence*, 15th edn (London: Sweet & Maxwell, 2000); Adrian Keane, *The Modern Law of Evidence*, 5th edn (London: Butterworths, 2000).

value, and they are not guided by reason alone. The debate over the early modern crime of witchcraft demonstrates how evidentiary methods were socially constructed through a symbolic struggle between various social and cultural groups. The epistemology underlying the evidentiary logic was the result of diverse and often conflicting social influences. This is true in relation to various evidentiary categories – circumstantial evidence (including items of physical evidence), the criteria for assessment of the veracity of witnesses, and the degree to which extra-judicial proof methods (such as supernatural signs) were tolerated and even adopted by the legal establishment. It is also evident that the usual standards and methods of evidence were modified, bent, liberally interpreted or even abandoned to facilitate proving a serious, but hard-to-prove crime such as witchcraft.

The period between the enactment of the first anti-witchcraft law in 1542 until the repeal of the third, and last, anti-witchcraft statute in 1736 was an era of significant transition in English criminal adjudication. During that era, major structural, procedural and evidentiary developments occurred. The lawyer-free proceedings, where witnesses could testify to almost anything, including hearsay and gossip, and very few procedural privileges were accorded to the defendants, were gradually changing. By the mid-eighteenth century, the law of evidence was already formulated, including the basic rules of hearsay, character, corroboration and confession. Treatises on evidence began to appear. The changes also included the development of a prosecutorial apparatus, pre-trial investigation and examinations, the changing roles of jurors, the growing involvement of lawyers and the rise of defence witnesses.

This book has examined the proof techniques that were in use in early modern English witchcraft cases, their underlying epistemological basis, and how they were shaped by the surrounding social context. Uncovering the hidden assumptions of the contemporaries is important, given the fact that today many of these evidentiary concepts (such as 'credibility', the use of expert witnesses or the prominence of physical evidence) seem natural and obvious. In their formative years, these proof techniques were the focus of a heated debate in which the basic assumptions were laid bare and questioned publicly.

The early modern English mostly agreed that solid and infallible evidence was the solution to the problem of proof. Acquiring an uncompromising ability to discover who was a true witch eliminated the need to choose between convicting the innocent and setting the guilty free. Yet, the appropriate ways of proof were the subject of great disagreement. The debate was not a purely legal dispute held exclusively among evidence-minded jurists. Instead, the discovery of witches invoked social, moral, religious and political tensions as well as a legal difficulty. Analysis of the debate clearly demonstrates that evidentiary methods, many of which were eventually articulated as rules, were cultural products, a multilayered combination of beliefs, practices and dispositions of socially diverse participants. The focus of research was predominately the social context of the position along the centre/periphery axis, social class and professional affiliation.

It is important to note that other factors also affected attitudes toward proof of witchcraft. Religious and political affiliations were significant factors as well. Witchcraft was used by the church and the state to achieve political goals, mainly through strategies of division and union, labelling opponents as witches and trying to unite different factions against a common demonic enemy. This entailed the condemnation of certain evidentiary techniques on a religious basis, for example, as being papist. The religious and political contexts are significant, but as they have been widely discussed in other studies, they were not central to this research, although the clergy as a social and professional group has been widely discussed.

Geographic Context – Position along the Centre/Periphery Axis

Broadly speaking, the position along the centre/periphery axis correlated with inclinations toward elite or popular proof methods.[6] This is not to imply a simple dichotomous model of the social relationships in early modern England.[7] On the contrary, the significant role played by the middling sort in shaping evidentiary methods presents a much more complex and fine-grained picture. Furthermore, lordship and distribution of land were sources of status and authority in early modern England, so elite and periphery were not mutually exclusive. However, the national power structure of the crown and church had a clear centre – the monarch as the figurehead. The English legal and administrative state radiated outward from this centre into the periphery. London was the locus of central political and economic institutions in this power grid. Yet the oppositions centre/periphery, London/rural England or elite/popular are not coterminous. For example, differences along the centre/periphery line can be found even within the boundaries of a single professional community. Thus, the provincial JPs and parish ministers tended to facilitate the use of supernatural proof techniques during the stage of the pre-trial investigation, either by taking an active part or by turning a blind eye

---

[6]   Region-specific conditions may be another geographical variation.

[7]   For an overview of historical works that criticize a simple bipolar model of early modern English society, see Michael J. Braddick and John Walter (eds), *Negotiating Power in Early Modern Society: Order, Hierarchy and Subordination in Britain and Ireland* (Cambridge, UK: Cambridge University Press, 2001), pp. 1–42.

toward neighbours and accusers who prepared their case for court. In contrast, the high-ranking theologians and assize judges who came from Westminster tended to treat supernatural techniques more critically. The degree of exposure to community pressures, no doubt, influenced the practices and dispositions of local elite members. It seems that popular notions percolated more effectively into learned ones where the elite members resided side by side with their social inferiors in the same peripheral community. The blending of the learned and the popular was not merely an intellectual interaction among ideas, but also the consequence of practical considerations generated by shared life.

The English justice system was structured in a way that combined peripheral and central input. The pre-trial stage was handled by the local community, whose members prepared the case for trial. The trial was orchestrated by the assize judges, who travelled from the centre to dispense royal norms. At the end of the trial, however, the verdict was given by the representatives of the community, the jurors. It was not surprising to find differences between the assize judges, outsiders by definition, and the locals. Thus, for example, the swimming of witches, strictly forbidden by the assize judges, nevertheless continued to flourish in many communities. A comparison between the London elite and plain villagers illustrates the range of difference. Yet, understanding the dynamics requires observation of the interaction between concepts and practices of centre and periphery. A significant meeting point was embodied in those who resided in the periphery but were socially and culturally closer than their neighbours to the London outsiders. Those were the members of the peripheral elite, provincial residents who enjoyed elevated local status either as members of the petty gentry or by virtue of their profession or financial affluence.

Members of local elites were not merely passive assimilators of popular practices, but also acted as social agents who disseminated new modes of proof and remoulded ancient ones to adhere to current ideas. The foremost example is that of the experiment. Reconstructed as experiments, supernatural proof techniques were removed from the realm of popular vulgar superstition and became techniques in the rational and methodological quest for justice and discovery of the truth. In a series of celebrated witchcraft cases, affluent provincial families took an active and creative role in this re-shaping. The suspect witches were scratched, swum, confronted with their allegedly bewitched victims and ordered to recite the Lord's Prayer in carefully orchestrated sequences of tests. The tests were designed as experiments repeated under varied and controlled conditions (including a control group consisting of innocent volunteers) to eliminate the effect of possible manipulation by the victim and of interfering variables, and to negate alternative explanations for the results. The formats of the tests were standardized so the experiments were all conducted in the same way. These so-called experiments were typically witnessed by impartial observers and often diligently documented.

At first glance, these tests seem to be a revival of ancient ordeals and popular supernatural methods. A closer look reveals a completely different epistemological distinction. The ancient ordeal was an ultimate proof technique used to attain divine guidance in deciding guilt or innocence in inconclusive cases. In contrast, in early modern times, determination of guilt was already in the hands of humans. When supernatural tests appeared again, they were no longer a divine sign, but rather reconstructed as rational truth-seeking techniques. The format of the ordeals was re-shaped to resemble factual and empiricist observations, and ordeals were used after routine evidentiary methods were exhausted. The experiments were conducted in the course of the criminal trial, but were most popular at the pre-trial stage in preparation of the case for court. Trust in divine guidance, an essential precept of the ordeal, was no longer the foundation for the supernatural procedures. The experiments were constructed to discover facts by means of reason and not through belief.

It is unlikely that the reconstruction of the ordeal as an experiment was due to the emergence of natural philosophy and modern science, as the highly structured supernatural experiments were used in witchcraft cases well before the birth of what we today call science. It is also doubtful that the provincial gentry, who had an important role in structuring the experiments, were well versed in the latest discoveries of the Royal Society. In the 1593 Warboys case, the methodical scratching of Mother Samuel by the Throckmorton family did not rely on any established scientific doctrine or declared principles of natural philosophy. To observers today it may seem paradoxical that the experiments, techniques of disenchantment of the world in the Weberian sense, were used to revive supernatural methods. Yet it is important to bear in mind that for the contemporaries, supernatural phenomena were a legitimate subject of study and observation.

Barbara Shapiro demonstrated how various legal concepts of proof and facts had first crystallized in the legal arena and subsequently migrated to the sphere of science.[8] When we look at the factual experiments that began to flourish around the end of the sixteenth century, both in and out of the courtroom, we can see that some of these concepts (such as probability and impartiality) have even deeper popular roots. Experiments enjoyed their greatest popularity at the pre-trial stage, at which point they were conducted by the accusers of the witch and other members of the provincial local community. Beginning at the end of

---

[8] Barbara J. Shapiro, *A Culture of Fact: England, 1550–1720* (Ithaca, NY: Cornell University Press, 2000).

the sixteenth century and continuing well into the beginning of the eighteenth century, courts heard testimonies about pre-trial experiments. Requests to conduct such experiments in the courtroom were often met with judicial open-mindedness. Judges granted the requests of parties, and even people from the crowd, to conduct experiments and agreeably cooperated in designing and modifying the experiment as it developed. The experiments were made more sophisticated and elaborate by the leadership of a few influential local families who believed their children to be bewitched and used their influence and resources to submit the suspects to a series of rational and highly structured tests in the search for facts. The peripheral elite, because of their liminal social status, played a significant role in carrying out the cultural process of translating popular notions into elite concepts. As a result, the peripheral elite transformed both popular and elite dispositions.

Historians tend to rule out a simple causal connection between the decline of witchcraft and the rise of science.[9] Contemporaries saw no contradiction between belief in witchcraft and factual and empiricist modes of investigation. During the era in which witchcraft flourished, it was often discovered in a 'scientific' way – through a series of methodical experiments aimed to establish 'facts'. Peter Burke claimed that the early modern European intellectual revolutions were 'no more than the surfacing into visibility' of pre-existing types of popular or practical knowledge newly legitimized by some academic establishments.[10] The reconstruction of supernatural tests as experiments well before the emergence of the so-called Scientific Revolution is definitely a case in point.

Class Context

Social class was another significant factor determining the choice and interpretation of legal proof techniques. Texts written by members of the social elite were abundant with condemnations of popular proof methods (mainly the supernatural signs frequently sought after in witchcraft cases) as superstitious, the realm of the ignorant and vulgar. Clearly, the condescending tone of elite writers toward popular proof methods of witchcraft was aimed at creating a social distinction, a sense of a more sophisticated, refined, educated and superior social stratum. Yet, ideas and people of different classes interacted, and it would

---

    [9]   Peter Elmer, 'Science, Medicine and Witchcraft', in Jonathan Barry and Owen Davies (eds), *Witchcraft Historiography*, Palgrave Advances (Houndmills, UK: Palgrave Macmillan, 2007).

    [10]   Peter Burke, *A Social History of Knowledge: From Gutenberg to Diderot* (Cambridge, UK: Polity Press, 2000), pp. 14–15.

be an over-simplification to sort all concepts by sharp dichotomies of high/low, learned/popular or above/below.

The case of the devil's mark, one of the best-known methods of proof, exemplifies this point. Devil's marks, certain marks or growths on the suspect's body, supposedly proved she was a witch. The English concept of the devil's mark demonstrates how learned and popular concepts mutually shaped the interpretation of this kind of evidence. Even items of physical evidence, concrete objects that presumably spoke for themselves, and not through human witnesses whose honesty and reliability needed to be assessed, were not necessarily direct traces of the crime. Physical evidence is a sub-category of circumstantial evidence, and its significance is determined through a culturally mitigated mental process of inference. Fingerprints or DNA evidence are frequently considered to create an immediate and direct link between the suspect and the crime. Yet, such evidence relies on a socially acceptable body of knowledge that needs to be interpreted and explained to the court by expert witnesses. Similarly, the link between physical evidence such as wax figures or bodily marks and the crime of witchcraft was socially and culturally constructed and relied on contemporary theories and assumptions. These underlying currents of ideology and belief were the product of a social struggle between various social players.

The devil's marks were presumably direct physical traces left by the devil on the body of his subject witches. Yet, the cultural association between the mark and witchcraft was not the result of a unified theory, but rather a combination of different, sometimes inconsistent or even competing concepts. This meaning of the devil's mark relied on a mixture of high and learned demonological theory, which viewed the mark as a symbol imprinted by the devil to seal the covenant, and of popular English beliefs about imps fed by witches. Although the imp narratives were not part of the traditional demonology, the English version depicted the devil's mark as a suckling device designed to feed animal-shaped demons. Thus, the widespread search for the devil's marks on the suspect witch was supported by a fusion of learned and popular concepts.

The choice and content of evidentiary techniques were influenced by the social context. The ability of the participants in the debate to disseminate proof techniques was an outcome of their social position. Social class, of course, was a significant factor. Continuing with the example of the experiment, it is clear that the reconstruction of the ordeal by the peripheral elite combined effectively peripheral or popular beliefs with reasoning and the cultural capital of the elite. The combination of the middling social stratum and peripheral locale seems most influential. Those who were in the lead in using the supernatural proof methods and long-forsaken ordeals, refurbishing them with new epistemological foundations and reconstructing them anew as experiments, were provincial gentlemen and the middling sort. Not only did these gentlemen set an example for the members of lower social strata (some of these cases even turned into legal precedents), but they also influenced the elite assize judges, who heard evidence about such supernatural experiments and cooperated in conducting such cases in the courtroom. Even an eighteenth-century highly sceptical assize judge such as Sir John Powell permitted, 'for the satisfaction of the jury', an experiment to inspect the reaction of the allegedly bewitched victim to the presence of the defendant, Jane Wenham.[11] By resisting altogether popular pressures to use supernatural methods, the assize judges might have risked loss of popular support. Acquiescing to the format of the experiment, the judges could dodge external pressures and threats. They continued to attack the torture-inducing (and therefore illegal) experiments of swimming and scratching as vulgar and superstitious, but employed an array of supernatural proof techniques as long as they were conducted in the format of experiments. Slightly modified to match the notions of higher social strata, the supernatural ordeal-type methods underwent co-optation that incorporated them into the justice system, defused the danger of alternative popular proof mechanisms and enhanced flexibility in accepting proof.

Class was a significant factor in shaping evidentiary techniques. However, no single factor can fully explain the intricate nature of the social construction of legal techniques. When one delves into the significance of the professional context, the picture of a symbolic struggle between various social actors with diverse interests over the choice and meaning of evidentiary techniques seems far more complex.

Professional Context

One of the main focuses of this study is the manner in which different professional groups used evidence of witchcraft as a social resource designed to bolster their standing. The analysis gives special attention to the professions of law and medicine and to the clergy, whose members were particularly active in the witchcraft debate. The attitude of physicians exemplifies this point. Physicians, it is possible to generalize, sounded the most radical and sceptical voice. Medical writers held that many of the purportedly supernatural phenomena ascribed to witchcraft actually originated from natural causes. Physicians advocated the use of medical knowledge, observation and reason in detecting unnatural

---

[11]   Francis Bragge, *A Full and Impartial Account* ..., 2nd edn (London: E. Curll, 1712), p. 24.

phenomena. They positioned themselves as experts especially in relation to two major subjects, the devil's mark and bewitchment. They claimed to be able to diagnose whether the marks and growths found on the suspect's body and the symptoms of the allegedly bewitched victim were caused by the devil or by natural processes. Their claim to having exclusive professional knowledge was directed at other disciplines, as well as at other practitioners of medicine and healing. In a brief treatise, Cotta warned the public against various kinds of medical practitioners.[12] One of the chapters of the treatise was dedicated to witchcraft, which was one of the arenas in which physicians strove to establish the boundaries and prestige of their profession. Toward other disciplines, the claim was that only physicians (and not judges, divines or witch hunters) could independently diagnose whether physical symptoms were natural or supernatural. Toward other practitioners of medicine, physicians claimed that diagnosis of witchcraft demanded high skills and experience not possessed, as Cotta put it, by 'every idiot'.[13] They distinguished themselves from other professionals through this double claim for professional superiority and exclusive expertise in the detection of witchcraft. In trials involving a battle of experts, no matter which particular physician prevailed, the medical profession was able to establish itself as a necessary authority on certain questions of fact.

The physicians' claim of expertise was met with ambivalence. On the one hand, physicians provided a convenient solution for proving the crime. Reliance on experts enabled the judiciary to shift the moral burden of fact-finding without losing legitimacy. On the other hand, the claim of superior ability to detect symptoms originating from witchcraft was sometimes found to be threatening to judges. In some cases physicians even held their own hearings at the College of Physicians to determine the cause of alleged bewitchment, thus demonstrating autonomous professional discretion independent of judicial authority.

Physicians were not alone in advocating evidentiary methods that were in accord with the best interests of their profession. Clerics used similar strategies, aimed both at protecting their professional superiority and at advancing the political interests of their religious faction. The religious context was mentioned above, but here the professional angle is examined. By the mid-sixteenth century, the clergy was an established and well-organized professional group, having material assets, political influence and cultural prominence. Although the church had abandoned the ordeals more than three centuries earlier and had no official role in the criminal proceedings, members of the clergy were involved

---

[12]   John Cotta, *A Short Discoverie of the Vnobserved Dangers…* (London: William Iones and Richard Boyle, 1612; reprint, 1972).

[13]   John Cotta, *The Triall of Vvitch-Craft* (London: Samuel Rand, 1616), p. 76.

in many witch trials. For example, they were often active in the investigation of suspects, using their religious authority to obtain confessions.

Unfortunately for the churchmen, they were less successful than the physicians in utilizing witchcraft as a resource to enhance their social position and ended up losing much of their indispensability in witch trials. Presumably, the church started with an advantage. Though witchcraft was the subject of a secular law, it was also a grave sin against Christianity. In addition, in the face of growing scepticism, the church had a strong interest in preserving belief in the existence of devils and witches. If people no longer believed in evil spirits, it was feared, they might begin to disbelieve the existence of good spirits and of God. Supposedly, churchmen were the best experts on issues of devils, witches and evil spirits. Their prominence in the witchcraft debate relied on knowledge of the scriptures and theology, and a standing of moral authority enabling them to determine who was a witch and what proof techniques were permissible. Indeed, up to the mid-seventeenth century their arguments relied to a great extent on religious literature. Writers such as Perkins, Bernard, Gaule and Cooper referred to many of the proof methods (such as swimming, scratching, burning the bewitched animal or the witch's house thatch) as un-Christian, satanic, or even as a sub-species of witchcraft. Clerical writers did not limit their criticism to the religious inadequacy of the evidentiary methods, however. They also evaluated ways of proof according to their sufficiency. Perkins, for example, sorted all the evidentiary techniques according to three degrees of sufficiency: insufficiency, sufficient only to warrant an examination and sufficient for conviction. By sufficiency, Perkins was not necessarily alluding to the definition of the term under secular English law, as he was more influenced by the principles of Canon law. Yet, sufficiency is not a religious term, but a legal and logical standard. Clergymen possess intricate knowledge of religion, but they do not hold a monopoly over logic. When clerical writers chose to analyse ways of proof on the basis of sufficiency, they did not enjoy better standing than others.

Starting around the second half of the seventeenth century, writers on theology who wanted to prove witchcraft relied less on the scriptures and appealed more to reason. The quintessential example is Joseph Glanvill, who argued that witchcraft could be proven as a matter of fact. This shift of focus proved to be a historical mistake from a professional standpoint. It disarmed the clergy of the relative advantage they held in the debate about proving witchcraft, their learning of the scriptures and religious doctrine. This is probably the reason why, although witchcraft-proving techniques were rife with religious connotations, the clergy, unlike the physicians, did not make full use of witchcraft evidence as a resource to bolster their professional standing.

In shifting the focus to members of the legal profession, it is important to remember the diversity of players in the legal arena. There were judges, lawyers, legal scholars, JPs, lay jurors, defendants, accusers, witnesses and the audience in the courtroom. In this context, the legal profession refers only to those who were formally educated and trained to practise law. Because primary sources show very little involvement of lawyers in witch trials, this analysis relates mostly to judges and legal scholars.

For the members of the legal profession in England, the crime of witchcraft posed, first of all, a technical evidentiary difficulty – how to prove a very serious crime without direct witnesses and with scarce, if any, physical evidence. The anti-witchcraft legislation was hardly helpful in this respect, setting forth no statutory guidelines for proof. The problem had weighty moral implications: the courts were entrusted with ultimate responsibility for proving the crime. Any error risked the life of an innocent person. Any error could also create doubts concerning the legitimacy of the justice system and, consequently, of a regime purporting to be just.

The techniques of evidence were tools employed by the participants in the juridical-cultural arena as part of their general strategies to handle proof. Several prominent strategies or modes of reasoning aimed at relieving the dilemma were used in the symbolic struggle over ways of proof. One strategy was the *certification of knowledge*. It comprised validation of testimonies through: the extensive use of experts, professionals who possessed unique knowledge and ability to determine facts; the rise of the concept of credibility, which sought to establish the truthfulness of witnesses; and the notion of precedent, deriving proof from knowledge established in previous cases. A second strategy was *shifting the moral burden of the dilemma* by, for example, entrusting the determination of guilt to lay jurors, relying on experts in making factual findings or emphasizing the importance of confession as a basis for conviction. A third strategy was the adoption of *conviction-enabling mechanisms*, which included built-in procedural devices to facilitate convictions, for example, evidentiary exceptions allowing the normally prohibited testimony of children or an interpretative framework that made convictions possible. A fourth strategy was the *legitimization of the justice system*, through the co-optation of threatening alternative modes of proof and the use of evidentiary techniques as tools for building a strong sense of a just and moral society and justice system.

Analysis of the professional context demonstrates that neither the choice nor the interpretation of the ways of proof was guided by the sole and impartial consideration of truth-seeking. Focus on professional affiliation further reveals that the views and strategies held by the participants in the debate cannot be fully comprehended without taking into account the other elements of their social identity. The example of the devil's mark illustrates this argument.

It was shown that the evidentiary significance of the devil's mark originated from a combination of popular and learned ideas. Yet, examination of the professional affiliations of the participants in the debate exposes further influences on shaping the meaning of this technique. The legal implication of the mark as evidence, whether it was a natural occurrence or supernaturally created by the devil, and whether it was sufficient evidence for conviction, hinged on interpretation. The interpretation was influenced to a large extent by the professional affiliations of the participants in the debate. Thus, professional searchers and witch hunters strongly advocated the use of the devil's mark, which was valuable as a witch-hunting tool. In contrast, physicians displayed a fair degree of scepticism toward the devil's mark as evidence. Interestingly, both groups used witchcraft as a resource for bolstering professional standing and jurisdiction by claiming unique expertise to determine whether the marks were natural.

Legal authors valued the devil's mark as probative physical evidence. Previous witchcraft cases in which evidence of devil's marks was presented were treated as precedents. Whereas the legal minds readily embraced the evidentiary technique of finding the devil's mark, theologians, who might be expected to identify more with demonology, seem to have been more reserved. By treating the devil's mark as a mere presumption, theologians emphasized its circumstantial nature. The term presumption was a reminder that such evidence was an inference and not a physical object that spoke for itself. Likewise, lawyers were more ready to incorporate supernatural proof techniques, whereas the clergy displayed more caution. Perhaps the theologians' familiarity with demonology made them, more than others, aware of the cognitive aspect of the devil's mark as evidence. Lawyers were possibly more prone to assimilate popular concepts because of lay participation in the judicial process and the notion of precedent.

The epistemology underlying the theory of precedent in the common-law system is the preservation of pre-existing norms. By declaring a certain concept to be a precedent, legal writers kept it alive and relevant for the future. The notion of precedent persisted in early modern England despite the fact that the grounds for verdicts were not articulated in a formal judicial decision. English legal authors considered the type of evidence tendered in the trial as precedents. For example, if a witness in a previous witchcraft case testified about seeing the witch feeding her imps, or if there was a search for the devil's mark, these issues were considered by legal authors as precedents. This enabled the production of similar evidence in future cases, although it is not known whether the jury actually based its verdict on this testimony. In other words, these so-called precedents did not necessarily reflect the conservation of proofs already in use in actual criminal proceedings. It is not unlikely that the appearance of the precedent as representing legal continuity has been the facade of innovative manufacturing of new means of conviction and creative incorporation of popular signs of guilt. Pre-established and supposedly pre-approved proof techniques exempted the jurists from experiencing the difficulty of determining guilt to its full extent. By treating certain methods of proof as precedents, lawyers and judges confronted the dilemma equipped with a professional toolbox that lessened doubts and made convictions possible. The notion of precedent also helped to protect the legal system from accusations of wrongful convictions. One of the replies to sceptics' arguments was that if higher standards of proof should be required, that would declare past judges and jurors of convicted witches to be murderers. Treating evidentiary methods such as the devil's mark as precedents shielded the justice system from doubts concerning the propriety of past convictions.

It is evident that neither class, nor profession nor religious faction alone can explain the social construction of the evidentiary technique of the devil's mark. The choice, use and interpretation of this method of proof were all shaped through a complex process of a symbolic struggle between various social actors with diverse social and cultural interests.

Expanded Strategies of Proof

Infallible evidence, the early modern English believed, was a good solution to the question of proof. The disagreement focused on what could constitute such evidence. The debate encompassed the choice, content and interpretation of evidentiary techniques. It is important to remember that evidence is more than a bundle of rules and that modes of proof are embedded in wider judicial strategies. The grave moral and religious implications of establishing proof and the multiple social pressures it entailed were eased by flexibility-enhancing strategies. Increased flexibility in the application of proof methods could facilitate obtaining or avoiding convictions according to the circumstances of individual cases.

The Gap between Procedure and Interpretative Framework

The case of the experiment provides a lucid illustration of this strategy. Behind the facade of the narrow, carefully structured format of the experiments lay a broad interpretative framework for their results. Experiments, often initiated by the accusers or the investigating JP, were frequently interpreted as pointing toward the guilt of the suspect. Experiments were repeated until deemed successful. Results were interpreted as consistent with guilt. If the devil's mark was not found, it could have been cut off or hidden by devilish means. If no imps were found, it was because they could become invisible. If the suspect, who was made to stand naked on a stool for days, moved uncomfortably, it was not because she was physically tortured, but because her body yearned for her imps.[14] If the suspect admitted guilt, she was a witch. But if she denied the accusations, it was the devil that did not allow her to confess.[15] If the victim recovered after the suspect was scratched to bleed, it proved the latter was a witch. However, if the victim's recovery lasted for only a fleeting moment, the suspect was still regarded as a witch, who used her powers to bewitch the victim again.[16] Even if the alleged victim was unable to draw blood from the suspect when scratching her, this was another remarkable sign of witchcraft.[17] If the suspect's marks were insensitive to pricking, then she must be a witch. But if she felt pain, they were probably not pricked in the right way.[18]

One of the most noteworthy instances of broad and flexible interpretation is found in the case of Rose Cullender and Amy Denny, who were accused of bewitching the children of Samuel Pacy. During the course of the trial, experiments were conducted in which it was observed that the clenched fists of the girls, while they were in fits, could be opened only after being touched by the suspects. The same results were observed when the girls were blindfolded during the experiment. Subsequently, following a suggestion from the crowd, and with judicial cooperation, the experiment was to be further controlled. One girl was blindfolded and touched alternately by Amy Denny and by several distinguished gentlemen. The girl's reaction was identical, '[w]hereupon the Gentlemen returned, openly protesting, that they did believe the whole transaction of this business was a meer Imposture'. Presumably, this proved that the girl faked her symptoms and, indeed, 'this put the Court and all persons into a stand'.[19] Nonetheless, the experiment was eventually interpreted as proving the guilt of the defendant. Samuel Pacy, the girl's father, urged the court to regard the results as incriminating. He explained that the girl was in fits but was conscious. Therefore, what mattered was her understanding that she was touched by the

---

[14] *A True Relation of the Araignment of Eighteene Vvitches* (London: I.H., 1645), pp. 6–7.

[15] Keith Thomas, *Religion and the Decline of Magic* (New York: Charles Scribner's Sons, 1971), pp. 523, 551.

[16] W.W., *A True and Iust Recorde* ... (London: Thomas Dawson, 1582), B4v–C.

[17] Bragge, *Full and Impartial Account*, p. 10.

[18] John Stearne, *A Confirmation and Discovery of Witchcraft* (London: William Wilson, 1648), pp. 46–7.

[19] *A Tryal of Witches* ... (London: William Shrewsbery, 1682), p. 45.

defendant. Although modern readers might deem such reasoning as proof of false accusations, the English court, presided over by one of England's greatest legal minds, Sir Matthew Hale, found this interpretation convincing.

The elaborate and methodical pattern of the experiment presented a diligent, meticulous and highly structured course of fact-finding. Such a rational manner of proof granted legitimacy to convictions based on evidence of experiments. Apparently, this narrowly tailored pattern of fact-finding did not limit the interpretation of the results of the experiments. The disparity between the carefully structured plan of the experiment and the broad interpretative framework enhanced flexibility in determining guilt. The early modern English could achieve convictions and at the same time pride themselves on scrutinous fact-finding proceedings.

Different Levels of Proof for Different Procedural Stages

Proving witchcraft necessitated a choice between lesser evidentiary standards, which might render convictions feasible, and higher standards, which would reduce the chance of convicting the innocent. Allocating different evidentiary standards to different procedural stages allowed the enjoyment of the best of both worlds. Demanding lesser evidentiary standards at the pre-trial stage enabled, during the course of the examination, the gathering of otherwise inadmissible evidence such as rumours, hearsay, depositions about private experiments and even reports on illegal procedures such as swimming and scratching.[20] Yet, the meaning of a lower standard was that lesser kinds of evidence warranted investigation and examination but were not a basis for conviction. Of course, since the depositions were read at the trial stage, it is difficult to tell whether juries were influenced by such evidence in practice.

The arbitrary use of circumstantial evidence and presumptions exemplifies the mechanism of this strategy. Although circumstantial evidence has always been permissible in the English court, the Continental concept of circumstantial evidence as inferior was nevertheless embraced. Clerical and English legal writers adopted a tripartite ladder of circumstantial evidence, often termed violent, probable and light presumptions, and advocated that lesser presumptions be insufficient for conviction but warrant examination by the JP. Thus, various writers deemed factors such as the reputation of a witch, suspicious family members, visions of the bewitched, the suspect's curses, the suspect's interest in the victim's health or injury subsequent to a quarrel with the

---

[20]   Another example of such strategy is Francis Bacon's justification of torture: 'It is used for discovery and not for evidence.' Elizabeth Hanson, 'Torture and Truth in Renaissance England', *Representations*, no. 34 (1991): p. 65.

suspect to be insufficient for conviction, but good grounds for an examination by the JP. Setting circumstantial standards that were insufficient for conviction but good enough to warrant keeping an eye on witchcraft suspects enabled the maintenance of witchcraft as a serious crime while demanding a higher standard for convictions. The original Continental doctrine of *crimen exceptum* enabled compromising regular evidentiary standards when adjudicating witchcraft and permitting conviction on the basis of circumstantial evidence, which was normally insufficient for conviction. In England, circumstantial evidence was permissible to begin with. Therefore, the implementation of the *crimen exceptum* doctrine had a contrary effect. By implementing the doctrine, the English relegated the circumstantial evidence to an inferior status and consequently rendered convictions less probable. This ambivalence enhanced flexibility in dealing with witchcraft, as it permitted pointing the finger at a suspect who might be guilty but without shedding innocent blood through an unjust conviction. Such a strategy enabled keeping witchcraft alive as a serious crime while at the same time demanding higher standards for conviction and actually rendering conviction less likely.

The Jury System and Structural Ambiguity

Common-law criminal evidence and procedure, as they were formed in early modern England, developed into an intricate set of rules. The purported rationale for these rules was the advancement of fact-finding, the discovery of the truth. Toward the middle of the eighteenth century, some of the evidentiary rules even began to be articulated as exclusionary rules aimed at preventing the exposure of jurors (who were no longer self-informed) to inappropriate evidence. Yet, at the end of the day, jurors were supposed to hand down a determination consisting only of the words 'guilty' or 'not guilty', without any reasoning or explanations attached. This prevented knowing what pieces of evidence were at the core of their verdict and whether it also relied on impermissible evidence or extra-evidentiary considerations. For example, it was impossible to tell whether an accused was convicted as a witch on the basis of permissible evidence, or because the juries heard that she floated during the course of an illegal swimming test, or simply because she looked like a stereotypical witch.

This structural aspect of the jury system eases the dilemma of proof in two respects. First, it shifts the ultimate moral responsibility from the bench to lay representatives of society, who are less likely to grasp all the evidentiary subtleties. Second, it allows the judiciary to presume to adhere to high evidentiary standards, although, in practice, it is hard to tell how the jurors reached their verdict. This structural peculiarity enhances flexibility, as it allows professing high evidentiary standards while leaving the door open to popular justice.

Final Remarks

The era of anti-witchcraft legislation overlapped the formative phase of common-law evidence law and criminal procedure. Proof of witchcraft, fiercely debated by diverse members of English society, opens a window to some basic presuppositions of the English justice system. Any error in fact-finding, leading either to the acquittal of a true witch or to the execution of an innocent suspect, was considered fatal and a grave moral sin. The fact finders had scant evidence with deficiencies that were difficult to ignore. The dangers of convicting on the basis of hearsay testimony or confessions about unnatural acts, for example, were explicitly debated long before these issues had become a matter of concern in general criminal procedure.

The scarce evidence in witch trials led to the bending of the rules of proof to achieve convictions. For example, witnesses normally considered incompetent, such as children, were allowed to testify against suspects. However, the application of lower evidentiary standards in cases of witchcraft was in itself an evidentiary danger zone, and it sometimes led to a counter-reaction. For example, if everyone was competent to testify in witch trials, then the existing competency rules, which were designed to keep potential liars out of the courtroom, lost their value. Fact finders were presented with the narratives of potentially problematic witnesses, and they needed a tool that allowed them to discern true from false stories. An alternative criterion, credibility, was established to assist fact finders in witchcraft cases.

The dilemma posed by crimes that are difficult to prove in modern times, such as terrorism or sex crimes, is no less agonizing than the one faced by the early modern English. What should be the evidentiary value of the uncorroborated testimony of a child against a sexually abusive parent? Are unusual steps or even torture justified when investigating terror suspects? Should evidence obtained by torture be admissible? Should lesser evidence be required to detain or convict terror suspects? Just as in early modern England, the debate is not limited to jurists, but encompasses socially diverse participants. Similar debates today are no less vigorous. Many arguments echo those made centuries ago in the witchcraft debate. Indeed, what, exactly, guides today's choice of evidentiary methods and standards? Is it any different from the case of the crime of witchcraft? Are there any social players who use the ways of proof as a resource to bolster their social standing and professional power? How do modern courts deal with the dilemma posed by these crimes? All these questions are still relevant today, centuries after the period central to this study.

Legal scholars' emphasis on the rationality of the method of the rules of evidence ignores much of the process of their creation through a socio-cultural struggle. The conclusion we draw here suggests that evidence law is not merely about fact-finding. Behind the facade of rational truth-seeking devices lie multi-dimensional influences and the well-disguised process of the social construction of legal evidence.

Examination of the dynamics of the cultural struggle over the structuration of evidentiary methods in early modern England illuminates the most significant role of the middling sort and petty gentry. Major cultural processes were manifested through those social actors who were culturally able to translate modes of proof of one social group to another, thereby creating compelling new alternatives and influencing both popular and elite circles. The ability to successfully influence other social players seems to be bolstered by some degree of closeness rather than by a sharp distinction between social circles.

Of the three professional elite circles whose discourses were the focus of this analysis, law seems to embrace the popular notions most closely. The increased infiltration of popular beliefs into the legal discourse may have stemmed from structural features of the English legal system, including lay participation and the notion of precedent. Supernatural methods of proof, thriving at the fringes of the official legal system, were reconstructed as rational experiments and then underwent co-optation that neutralized the subversive potential of these means of popular justice. The relative openness to concepts and practices of other social players, and the procedural, evidentiary and structural mechanisms that enhanced flexibility in proving witchcraft, helped to maintain the sense of a just and cautious justice apparatus while rendering convictions possible. These mechanisms contributed not only to the legitimation of the justice system, but also to the legitimation of the ruling regime in general. Such a strong sense of self-satisfaction and self-perceived justice was vividly pronounced by Smith, who declared in 1583 that 'In no place shall you see malefactors go more constantly, more assuredly, & with lesse lamentation to their death, than in England'.[21]

---

[21]   Sir Thomas Smith, *De Republica Anglorum*, 1st edn (London: Printed by Henrie Midleton for Gregorie Seton, 1583), p. 85.

Bibliography

Primary Sources

An Account of the Trial, Confession & Condemnation of Six Witches: At Maidstone, in the County of Kent, at the Assizes Held There July 1652, before Sir Peter Warburton ... : To Which Is Added the Trial, Examination and Execution of Three Witches Executed at Faversham, in the Same County, September 1645 (London: s.n., 1837).

An Account of the Tryal and Examination of Joan Buts, for Being a Common Witch and Inchantress, before the Right Honourable Sir Francis Pemberton, Lord Chief Justice, at the Assizes Holden for the Burrough of Southward and County of Surrey, on Monday, March 27, 1682 (London: S. Gardener, 1682).

The Apprehension and Confession of Three Notorious Witches. Arreigned and by Iustice Condemned and Executed at Chelmes-Forde, in the Countye of Essex, the 5. Day of Iulye, Last Past. 1589: With the Manner of Their Diuelish Practices and Keeping of Their Spirits, Whose Fourmes Are Heerein Truelye Proportioned (London: E. Allde, 1589).

Broadside Story Concerning a Man Who Became Possessed by an Evil Spirit (Glasgow: T. Duncan, [probable period 1810–30]).

The Case of the Hertfordshire Witchcraft Consider'd: Being an Examination of a Book, Entitl'd, a Full and Impartial Account of the Discovery of Sorcery & Witchcraft, Practis'd by Jane Wenham of Walkern, Upon the Bodies of Anne Thorne, Anne Street, &C (London: John Pemberton, 1712).

A Certaine Relation of the Hog-Faced Gentlewoman Called Mistris Tannakin Skinker: Who Was Born at Wirkham, a Neuter Towne Betweene the Emperour and the Hollander, Scituate on the River Rhyne, Who Was Bewitched in Her Mothers Wombe in the Yeare 1618 ... And Can Never Recover Her True Shape Tell She Be Married, &C.: Also Relating the Cause, as It Is since Conceived, How Her Mother Came So Bewitched (London: J.O., 1640).

The Clerk's Manual: Or, an Exact Collection of the Most Approved Forms of Declarations, Pleas, General Issues, Judgments, Demurrers, and Most Kind of Writs Now Used in the Court of Kings Bench with Necessary Instructions to All Clerks, Attorneys, Sollicitors, &C. In the Use of the Same (London: George

Sawbridge, William Rawlins, and Samuel Roycroft, assigns of Edward Atkins Esq, 1678).

A Declaration in Answer to Several Lying Pamphlets Concerning the Witch of Wapping: Being a More Perfect Relation of the Arraignment, Condemnation, and Suffering of Jone Peterson, Who Was Put to Death on Munday the 12 of April, 1652: Shevving the Bloudy Plot and Wicked Conspiracy of One Abraham Vandenbemde, Thomas Crompton, Thoma S Collet, and Others (London: s.n.r., 1652).

A Detection of Damnable Driftes, Practized by Three Vvitches Arraigned at Chelmisforde in Essex, at the Laste Assises There Holden, Whiche Were Executed in Aprill. 1579: Set Forthe to Discouer the Ambushementes of Sathan, Whereby He Would Surprise Vs Lulled in Securitie, and Hardened with Contempte of Gods Vengeance Threatened for Our Offences (London: J. Kingston, 1579).

The Disclosing of a Late Counterfeyted Possession by the Deuyl in Two Maydens within the Citie of London (London: Richard Watkins, 1574).

A Discourse on Witchcraft: Occasioned by a Bill Now Depending in Parliament, to Repeal the Statute Made in the First Year of the Reign of King James I, Intituled, an Act against Conjuration, Witchcraft and Dealing with Evil and Wicked Spirits (London: J. Read, 1736).

Doctor Lambs Darling: Or, Strange and Terrible News from Salisbury: Being a True, Exact, and Perfect Relation, of the Great and Wonderful Contract and Engagement Made between the Devil, and Mistris Anne Bodenham; with the Manner How She Could Transform Her Self into the Shape of a Mastive Dog, a Black Lyon, a White Bear, a Woolf, a Bull, and an Cat; and by Her Charms and Spels, Send Either Man or Woman 40 Miles an Hour in the Ayr. The Tryal, Examination, and Confession of the Said Mistris Bodenham, before the Lord Chief Baron Wild, & the Sentence of Death Pronounc'd against Her, for Bewitching of an Stiles, and Forcing Her to Write Her Name in the Devils Book with Her Own Blood; So That Sometimes the Devil Appearing All in Black without a Head, Renting Her Cloaths, Tearing Her Skin, and Tossing Her up and Down the Chamber, to the Great Astonishment of the Spectators. Appointed to Be Printed and Published, as a Caveat and Warning Piece for England, Scotland, and Ireland. James Bower, Cleric (London: G. Horton, 1653).

The Examination and Confession of Certain Witches at Chelmsford in the County of Essex (1556; reprint, London: s.n., 1864).

The Examination and Confession of Certaine Wytches at Chensforde in the Countie of Essex: Before the Quenes Maiesties Judges, the Xxvi Daye of July, Anno 1566, at the Assise Holden There as Then, and One of Them Put to Death for the Same

Offence, as Their Examination Declareth More at Large (London: Willyam Powell, 1566).

The Examination, Confession, Triall, and Execution, of Joane Williford, Joan Cariden, and Jane Hott: Who Were Executed at Feversham in Kent, for Being Witches, on Munday the 29 of September, 1645: Being a True Copy of Their Evill Lives and Wicked Deeds, Taken by the Major of Feversham and Jurors for the Said Inquest: With the Examination and Confession of Elizabeth Harris, Not yet Executed: All Attested under the Hand of Robert Greenstreet, Major of Feversham (London: J.G., 1645).

The Examination of John Walsh: Before Maister Thomas Williams, Commissary to the Reuerend Father in God William Bishop of Excester, Vpon Certayne Interrogatories Touchyng Wytchcrafte and Sorcerye, in the Presence of Diuers Gentlemen and Others. The .Xxiii. Of August. 1566 (London: Iohn Awdely, 1566).

A Full Confutation of Witchcraft, More Particularly of the Depositions against Jane Wenham, Lately Condemned for a Witch; at Hertford. In Which Modern Notions of Witches Are Overthrown, and the Ill Consequences of Such Doctrines Are Exposed by Arguments; Proving That Witchcraft Is Priestcraft ... In a Letter from a Physician in Hertfordshire to His Friend in London (London: J. Baker, 1712).

A Full and True Account of the Proceedings at the Sessions of Oyer and Terminer, Holden for the City of London, County of Middlesex, and Goal-Delivery of Newgate; Which Began at the Sessions-House in the Old-Bayly, on Thursday, Iune 1st. And Ended on Fryday, Iune 2d. 1682: Wherein Is Contained the Tryal of Many Notorious Malefactors, for Murders, Fellonies, Burglary, and Other Misdemeanours, but More Especially the Tryal of Jane Kent for Witch-Craft. Together, with the Names of Those That Received Sentence of Death, the Number of Those Burn'd in the Hand, Transported, and Vvhip'd. As Likewise Some Proceedings in Relation to the Persons That Violently Took the Lady out of the Coach on Hounslow-Heath (London: Printed for T. Benskin, 1682).

The Full and True Relation of the Tryal, Condemnation, and Execution of Ann Foster: (Who Was Arrained for a Witch) on Saturday the 22th of This Instant August, at the Place of Execution at Northampton: With the Manner How She by Her Malice and Vvitchcraft Set All the Barns and Corn on Fire Belonging to One Joseph Weeden Living in Eastcoat, and Bewitched a Whole Flock of Sheep in a Most Lamentable Manner ... : And Also in What Likeness the Devil Appeared to Her While She Was in Prison, and the Manner of Her Department at Her Tryal (London: D.M., 1674).

The Full Tryals, Examination, and Condemnation of Four Notorious Witches at the Assizes Held at Worcester, on Tuesday the 4th of March: With the Manner,

How They Were Found Guilty of Bewitching Several Children to Death, as Also, Their Confessions, and Last Dying Speeches at the Place of Execution, with Other Amazing Particulars Concerning the Said Witchcraft (London: J.W., 1690).

Great News from the West of England: Being a True Account of Two Young Persons Lately Bewitch'd in the Town of Beckenton in Somerset-Shire, Shewing the Sad Condition They Are in by Vomiting or Throwing out of Their Bodies the Abundance of Pins, Nails, Pewter, Brass, Lead, Iron, and Tin to the Admiration of All Beholders, and of the Old Witch Being Carryed Several Times to a Great River, into Which Her Legs Being Tied, She Was Thrice Thrown in, but Each Time She Swam Like a Cork, Afterwards by Order from a Justice of the Peace She Was Search'd by a Jury of Women and Such Signs and Marks Being Found About Her, Positive Oath Was Given in against Her So That She Is Committed to Jayl until the Next Assizes (London: T.M., 1689).

The Impossibility of Witchcraft Further Demonstrated, Both from Scripture and Reason, Wherein Several Texts of Scripture Relating to Witches Are Prov'd to Be Falsly Translated ... By the Author of the Impossibility of Witchcraft, &C (London: J. Barker, 1712).

The Impossibility of Witchcraft, Plainly Proving, from Scripture and Reason, That There Never Was a Witch; ... In Which the Depositions against Jane Wenham, ... Are Confuted and Expos'd (London: J. Baker, 1712).

The Lawes against Vvitches, and Conivration: And Some Brief Notes and Observations for the Discovery of Witches. Being Very Usefull for These Times, Wherein the Devil Reignes and Prevailes over the Soules of Poore Creatures, in Drawing Them to That Crying Sin of Witch-Craft. Also, the Confession of Mother Lakeland, Who Was Arraigned and Condemned for a Witch, at Ipswich in Suffolke. Published by Authority (London: R.W., 1645).

The Life and Death of Lewis Gaufredy: A Priest of the Church of the Accoules in Marseilles in France, (Who after Hee Had Giuen Him Selfe Soule and Bodie to the Diuell) Committed Many Most Abhominable Sorceries ...: Together with the 53. Articles of His Confession (London: Richard Redmer, 1612).

A Magazine of Scandall, or, a Heape of Wickednesse of Two Infamous Ministers, Consorts, One Named Thomas Fowkes of Earle Soham in Suffolk, Convicted by Law for Killing a Man, and the Other Named Iohn Lowes of Brandeston, Who Hath Beene Arraigned for Witchcraft, and Convicted by Law for a Common Barrettor: Together with the Manner How My Lord of Canterbury Would Put and Keep Them in the Ministery: Not Withstanding the Many Petitions and Certificates from Their Parishioners and Others, Presented to Him, They Being the Head and Most Notorious of the Scandalous Ministers within the County of Suffolke, and Well May Be Said of All England: And against Whom as Chiefe of the Scandalous Ministers the County of Suffolke Have Petitioned to the Parliament: And Desired to Bee Seene by Parliament Because Herein Is Something Mentioned Which Is Conceived, That One of These Scandalous Ministers Have Abused the Authority of the Lords in Parliament (London: R.H., 1642).

A Magical Vision, or, a Perfect Discovery of the Fallacies of Witchcraft as It Was Lately Represented in a Pleasant Sweet Dream (London: Thomas Palmer, 1673).

A Most Certain, Strange, and True Discovery of a Vvitch: Being Taken by Some of the Parliament Forces, as She Was Standing on a Small Planck-Board and Sayling on It over the River of Newbury: Together with the Strange and True Manner of Her Death, with the Propheticall Words and Speeches She Used at the Same Time (London: John Hammond, 1643).

The Most Cruell and Bloody Murther Committed by an Inkeepers Wife, Called Annis Dell, and Her Sonne George Dell, Foure Yeeres Since: On the Bodie of a Childe, Called Anthony Iames in Bishops Hatfield in the Countie of Hartford, and Now Most Miraculously Reuealed by the Sister of the Said Anthony, Who at the Time of the Murther Had Her Tongue Cut out, and Foure Yeeres Remayned Dumme and Speechlesse, and Now Perfectly Speaketh, Reuealing the Murther, Hauing No Tongue to Be Seen. With the Seuerall Vvitch-Crafts, and Most Damnable Practises of One Iohane Harrison and Her Daughter Vpon Seuerall Persons, Men and Women at Royston, Who Were All Executed at Hartford the 4 of August Last Past. 1606 (London: William Firebrand and Iohn Wright, 1606).

The Most Strange and Admirable Discouerie of the Three Witches of Warboys: Arraigned, Conuicted, and Executed at the Last Assises at Huntington, for the Bewitching of the Fiue Daughters of Robert Throckmorton Esquire, and Diuers Other Persons, with Sundrie Diuellish and Grieuous Torments: And Also for the Witching to Death of the Lady Crumwell, the Like Hath Not Been Heard of in This Age (London: Thomas Man, and Iohn Winington, 1593).

Newes from Scotland, Declaring the Damnable Life and Death of Doctor Fian: A Notable Sorcerer, Who Was Burned at Edenbrough in Ianuary Last. 1591. Which Doctor Was Regester to the Diuell That Sundry Times Preached at North Barrick Kirke, to a Number of Notorious Witches. With the True Examination of the Saide Doctor and Witches, as They Vttered Them in the Presence of the Scottish King. Discouering How They Pretended to Bewitch and Drowne His Maiestie in the Sea Comming from Denmarke, with Such Other Wonderfull Matters as the Like Hath Not Been Heard of at Any Time. Published According to the Scottish Coppie (London: E. Allde for William Wright, 1592).

News from Pannier-Alley, or, a True Relation of Some Pranks the Devil Hath Play'd with a Plaster-Pot There (London: Randal Taylor, 1687).

The Office of the Clerk of Assize Containing the Form and Method of the Proceedings at the Assizes and General Gaol-Delivery as Also on the Crown and Nisi Prius Side: Together with the Office of the Clerk of the Peace: Shewing the True Manner and Form of the Proceedings at the Court of General Quarter Sessions of the Peace: With Divers Forms of Presentments and Other Precedents at Assizes and Sessions: With a Table of Fees Thereunto Belonging, 2nd edn (London: Henry Twyford, 1682).

The Power of Vvitchcraft: Being a Most Strange but True Relation of the Most Miraculous and Wonderful Deliverance of One Mr. William Harrison, of Cambden in the County of Glocester, Steward to the Lady Nowel. Who Was Supposed to Have Been Murthered by His Own Servant, and His Servants Mother and Brother: But to the Amazement of All the People That Live near the Said Place, the Truth Is Now Brought to Light; and Mr. Harrison after About Two Years Absence Is Returned into His Own Country and Place of Abode in Cambden. The Manner How He Was Bewitched Away, and the Manner of His Safe Return Back Again into His Own Countrey You Shall Hear in This Following Discourse (London: Charls Tyus, 1662).

A Rehearsall Both Straung and True, of Hainous and Horrible Actes Committed by Elizabeth Stile: Alias Rockingham, Mother Dutten, Mother Deuell, Mother Margaret, Fower Notorious Witches, Apprehended at Winsore in the Countie of Barks. And at Abbington Arraigned, Condemned, and Executed, on the 26 Daye of Februarie Laste Anno. 1579 (London: J. Kingston, 1579).

A Relation of the Deuill Balams Departure out of the Body of the Mother-Prioresse of the Vrsuline Nuns of Loudun: Her Fearefull Motions and Contorsions During the Exorcisme, with the Extract of the Proces Verball, Touching the Exorcismes Wrought at Loudun (London: R. Badger, 1636).

A Sad and Lamentable Account of One Mary Jawson ... Who Wickedly Sold Her Self to the Devil ... To Be Revenged on Her Aunt: ... A Dreadful Story of a Young Maid in Devonshire, Who, for Renouncing Her Contract in Marriage, Had Fearful Judgements Shewn on Her: Also an Account of a Dreadful Judgment on a Rich Man for the Cruel Usage of His Servant ... : To Which Is Added Three Dreadful Examples & Judgments That Hath Befallen Three Notorious Sinners (Glasgow: s.n., 1702).

'A Severall Factes of Witch-Crafte' (1585), in Marion Gibson (ed.), *Early Modern Witches: Witchcraft Cases in Contemporary Writing*, 125–8 (London: Routledge, 2000).

The Shee-Devil of Petticoat-Lane, or, a True and Perfect Relation of a Sad Accident Which Befel Mr. Freeland at the Kings-Head in Petticoat-Lane near White-

Chappel-Bars on Friday Last, Jully 20, 1666: Occasioned (as It Is Supposed) by a Maid Servant Living in the House, Who Upon Cause Thereof Was Searched by the Neighbour Women, and What Was the Effects Thereof (London: Peter Lillicrap, 1666).

Signes and Wonders from Heaven. With a True Relation of a Monster Borne in Ratcliffe Highway, at the Signe of the Three Arrows, Mistris Bullock the Midwife Delivering Here Thereof. Also Shewing How a Cat Kitned a Monster in Lombard Street in London. Likewise a New Discovery of Witches in Stepney Parish. And How 20. Witches More Were Executed in Suffoke This Last Assise. Also How the Divell Came to Soffam to a Farmers House in the Habit of a Gentlewoman on Horse-Backe. With Divers Other Strange Remarkable Passages (London: I.H., 1645).

The Snare of the Devill Discovered, or, a True and Perfect Relation of the Sad and Deplorable Condition of Lydia, the Wife of John Rogers, House-Carpenter: ... How She Wanted Money the Devil Appeared to Her in the Shape of a Man, on Monday Night the 22th of March Last and Broght Her Money, and Caused Her to Cut a Vein in Her Right Hand, and a Contract Was Made between Them: Also Her Examination by Mr. Johnson, the Minister of Wappin, and Her Confession, as Also in What a Sad Condition She Contines, Likewise a Brief Relation of Her Former Life and Conversation (London: Edward Thomas, 1658).

Strange and Dreadful News from the Town of Deptford, in the County of Kent: Being the Full, True, and Sad Relation of One Anne Arthur, Who According to Her Own Report, Had Divers Discourses with the Devil, on the Third of This Instant March 1684/5. Who Offered Her Gold and Silver; Telling Her Many Strange and Wonderful Things; and, in the End, Carried Her in the Air a Quarter of a Furlong, &C. Together, with the Life and Conversation of the Said Party; and Directions to the Place of Her Abode. And a Particular Relation of the Sad Distractions She Fell into, Upon the Occasion; and Divers Other Circumstances Relating Thereto (London: D.W., 1684).

Strange Nevvs from Shadvvell: Being a True and Just Relation of the Death of Alice Fowler, Who Had for Many Years Been Accounted a Witch; Together with the Manner How She Was Found Dead with Both Her Great Toes Ty'd Together, and Laid out on the Floor Having a Blanket Flung over Her. She Being Left Lock'd up Alone by Her Nurse, with a Discovery of What Markes or Teats Were Found About Her, When She Was Searched by the Neighbours (London: E. Mallet, 1684).

A Strange Report of Six Most Notorious Vvitches: Who by Their Diuelish Practises Murdred Aboue the Number of Foure Hundred Small Children: Besides the Great Hurtes They Committed Vpon Diuers Other People: Who for the

Same, and Many Other Like Offences, Were Executed in the Princely Cittie of Manchen in High Germanie The. 29. Of Iuly. 1600. Printed at Nuremberge by Lucas Mayr Ingrauer, Dwelling in Kramergesle: And Now Translated out of Dutch, According to the Same Coppy There Imprinted, translated from German (London: W.W., 1601).

Strange & Terrible Nevves from Cambridge: A True Relation of the Quakers Bewitching of Mary Philips out of the Bed from Her Husband in the Night, and Transformed Her into the Shape of a Bay Mare, Riding Her from Dinton, Towards the University: With the Manner How She Became Visible Again to the People in Her Own Likeness and Shape, with Her Sides All Rent and Torn, as If They Had Been Spur-Gal'd, Her Hands and Feet Worn as Black as a Coal, and Her Mouth Slit with the Bridle Bit: Likewise Her Speech to the Scholars and Countrey-Men, Upon This Great and Wonderful Change, Her Oath before the Judges and Justices, and the Names of the Quakers Brought to Tryal on Friday Last at the Assises Held at Cambridge, with the Judgment of the Court: As Also the Devil's Snatching of One from His Company, and Hoisting of Him up into the Air, with What Hapned Thereupon (London: C. Brooks, 1659).

Strange and Wonderful Nevvs from Goswell-Street: Or, a Victory over the Devil: Being. A True Relation How a Person, Living at the House of Francis Jordan at the Sign of the Hunsman and Hounds, near Mount-Mill in Goswell-Street, Having for Three Years Last Past Lain under an Evil-Tongue and Lamentable Fits, Generally Judged to Proceed from Witchcraft, and Was in a Lamentable Condition, and Her Flesh Was as If It Were Tore Off Her Bones. With the Strange Noises Heard at That Time, and How the Spirit Struck the Man of the House a Grievous Blow on the Head, Which for Some Hours Occasion'd Great Pain to Him, but Now He Is Recovered. The Truth of This Relation Is and Will Be Attested by Francis Jordan at the Sign of the Hunsman and Hounds, near Mount Mill Aforesaid. Susan Shawe. Margaret Flamstead. Rachel Hopkins. Ralph Jordan. And Several Other Persons. With Allowance (London: printed for D.M., 1678).

Strange and Wonderful News from Yowel in Surry: Giving a True and Just Account of One Elizabeth Burgiss, Who Was Most Strangely Bewitched and Tortured at a Sad Rate, Having Several Great Lumps of Clay Pulled Forth from Her Back, Full of Pins and Thorns, Which Pricked So Extreamly That She Cry'd and Roar'd in a Vehement and out-Ragious Manner, to the Great Amazement of All the Beholders: As Also, How Great Stones as Big as a Mans Fist Were Thrown at Her ... And Afer She Came to Her Fathers House, the Throwing of the Pewter-Dishes, Candlesticks, and Other Clattering of Household-Goods at Her, Besides the Displacing of a Musical Instrument, Hanging up Her Grand-Fathers Breeches on the Top of the Sealing: With Many More Strange and Miraculous Things, Filling the Spectators with Wonder and Amazement (London: J. Clarke, 1681).

The Triall of Maist. Dorrell, or a Collection of Defences against Allegations Not yet Suffered to Receiue Convenient Answere: Tending to Cleare Him from the Imputation of Teaching Sommers and Others to Counterfeit Possession of Divells. That the Mist of Pretended Counterfetting Being Dispelled, the Glory of Christ His Royall Power in Casting out Divels (at the Prayer and Fasting of His People) May Evidently Appeare (Middelburg: R. Schilders, 1599).

A True Account of a Strange and Wonderful Relation of John Tonken, of Pensans in Cornwall: Said to Be Bewitched by Some Women, Two of Which on Suspition Are Committed to Prison, He Vomiting up Several Pins, Pieces of Walnut-Shels, an Ear of Rye with a Straw to It Half a Yard Long and Rushes of the Same Length, Which Are Kept to Be Shown at the Next Assizes for the Said County (London: George Croom, 1686).

A True Discourse. Declaring the Damnable Life and Death of One Stubbe Peeter, a Most Wicked Sorcerer: Who in the Likenes of a Woolfe, Committed Many Murders, Continuing This Diuelish Practise 25. Yeeres, Killing and Deuouring Men, Woomen, and Children. Who for the Same Fact Was Taken and Executed the 31. Of October Last Past in the Towne of Bedbur Neer the Cittie of Collin in Germany. Trulye Translated out of the High Duch, According to the Copie Printed in Collin, Brought Ouer into England by George Bores Ordinary Poste, the Xi. Daye of This Present Moneth of Iune 1590. Who Did Both See and Heare the Same, translated from German (London: R.W., 1590).

A True Discourse, Vpon the Matter of Martha Brossier of Romorantin: Pretended to Be Possessed by a Deuill, translated from French (London: Iohn Wolfe, 1599).

A True and Impartial Relation of the Informations against Three Witches, Viz., Temperance Lloyd, Mary Trembles, and Susanna Edwards, Who Were Indicted, Arraigned and Convicted at the Assizes Holden for the County of Devon, at the Castle of Exon, Aug. 14, 1682: With Their Several Confessions, Taken before Thomas Gist, Mayor, and John Davie, Alderman, of Biddiford, in the Said County, Where They Were Inhabitants: As Also, Their Speeches, Confessions and Behaviour at the Time and Place of Execution on the Twenty Fifth of the Said Month (London: Freeman Collins, 1682).

A True Relation of the Araignment of Eighteene Vvitches: That Were Tried, Convicted, and Condemned, at a Sessions Holden at St. Edmunds-Bury in Suffolke, and There by the Iudge and Iustices of the Said Sessions Condemned to Die, and So Were Executed the 27. Day of August 1645. As Also a List of the Names of Those That Were Executed, and Their Severall Confessions before Their Executions. Vvith a True Relation of the Manner How They Find Them

Out. The Names of Those That Were Executed. Mr. Lowes Parson of Branson. Thomas Evered a Cooper with Mary His Wife. Mary Bacon. Anne Alderman. Rebecca Morris. Mary Fuller. Mary Clowes. Margery Sparham Katherine Tooley. Sarah Spinlow. Iane Limstead. Anne Wright. Mary Smith. Iane Rivert. Susan Manners. Mary Skipper. Anne Leech (London: I.H., 1645).

The Tryal, Condemnation, and Execution of Three Vvitches: Viz. Temperace [Sic] Floyd, Mary Floyd, and Susanna Edwards. Who Were Arraigned at Exeter on the 18th. Of August, 1682. And Being Prov'd Guilty of Witch-Craft, Were Condemn'd to Be Hang'd, Which Was Accordingly Executed in the View of Many Spectators, Whose Strange and Much to Be Lamented Impudence, Is Never to Be Forgotten. Also, How They Confessed What Mischiefs They Had Done (London: J. Deacon, 1682).

The Tryall and Examination of Mrs Joan Peterson: Before the Honorable Bench, at the Sessions House in the Old-Bayley, Yesterday; for Her Supposed Witchcraft, and Poysoning of the Lady Powel at Chelsey: Together with Her Confession at the Bar: Also, the Tryal, Examination, and Confession, of Giles Fenderlyn, Who Had Made a Convenant with the Devil for 14 Years (London: G. Horton, 1652).

The Tryal of Richard Hathaway: Upon an Information for Being a Cheat and Imposter, for Endeavouring to Take Away the Life of Sarah Morduck, for Being a Vvitch, at Surry Assizes, Begun and Held in the Burrough of Southwark, March the 24th, 1702 ..., to Which Is Added a Short Account of the Tryal of Richard Hathaway, Thomas Wellyn and Elizabeth His Wife, and Elizabeth Willoughby, Wife of Walter Willoughby, Upon an Information for a Riot and Assault Upon Sarah Morduck, the Pretended Witch, at the Said Assizes (London: Isaac Cleave, 1702).

A Tryal of Witches, at the Assizes Held at Bury St. Edmonds for the County of Suffolk, on the Tenth Day of March, 1664: Before Sir Matthew Hale Kt. Then Lord Chief Baron of His Majesties Court of Exchequer (London: William Shrewsbery, 1682).

Vvitches Apprehended, Examined and Executed, for Notable Villanies by Them Committed Both by Land and Water: With a Strange and Most True Triall How to Know Whether a Woman Be a Witch or Not (London: Edward Marchant, 1613).

The Whole Trial and Examination of Mrs Mary Hicks and Her Daughter Elizabeth: But of Nine Years of Age, Who Were Condemo'd the Last Assizes Held at Huntington for Witchcraft: And There Executed on Saturday the 28th of July, 1716 (London: W. Matthews, 1716).

The Witch of Wapping, or, an Exact and Perfect Relation, of the Life and Devilish Practises of Joan Peterson, Who Dwelt in Spruce Island, near Wapping: Who

Was Condemned for Practising Witch-Craft, and Sentenced to Be Hanged at Tyburn, on Munday the 11th of April, 1652 ...: Together, with the Confession of Prudence Lee, Who Was Burnt in Smithfield on Saturday the 10th of This Instant for the Murthering Her Husband; and Her Admonition and Counsel to All Her Sex in General (London: Th. Spring, 1652).

The Witches of Northampton-Shire: Agnes Browne. Ioane Vaughan. Arthur Bill. Hellen Ienkenson. Mary Barber. Witches. Who Were All Executed at Northampton the 22. Of Iuly Last. 1612 (London: Arthur Iohnson, 1612).

The Wonderful Discouerie of the Vvitchcrafts of Margaret and Phillip Flower, Daughters of Ioan Flower Neere Beuer Castle: Executed at Lincolne, March 11. 1618: Who Were Specially Arraigned and Condemned before Sir Henry Hobart, and Sir Edward Bromley, Iudges of Assise, for Confessing Themselues Actors in the Destruction of Henry L. Rosse, with Their Damnable Practises against Others the Children of the Right Honourable Francis Earle of Rutland. Together with the Seuerall Examinations and Confessions of Anne Baker, Ioan Willimot, and Ellen Greene, Witches in Leicestershire (London: Barnes, 1619).

Wonderfull News from the North, or, a True Relation of the Sad and Grievovs Torments, Inflicted Upon the Bodies of Three Children of Mr. George Muschamp, Late of the County of Northumberland (London: T.H., 1650).

Ady, Thomas, *A Candle in the Dark: Shewing the Divine Cause of the Distractions of the Whole Nation of England and of the Christian World* (London: Robert Ibbitson, 1655).

Barrow, John, *The Lord's Arm Stretched Ovt in an Answer of Prayer, or, a True Relation of the Wonderful Deliverance of James Barrow, the Son of John Barrow of Olaves Southwark, Who Was Possessed with Evil Spirits near Two Years: The Diversity of Means Used, with the Way in Which He Was Delivered* (London: s.n., printed 1664).

Baxter, Richard, *The Certainty of the Worlds of Spirits and, Consequently, of the Immortality of Souls: Of the Malice and Misery of the Devils and the Damned: And of the Blessedness of the Justified, Fully Evinced by the Unquestionable Histories of Apparitions, Operations, Witchcrafts, Voices &C* (London: T. Parkhurst and J. Salisbury, 1691).

Bekker, Balthasar, *The World Turn'd Upside Down, or, a Plain Detection of Errors, in the Common or Vulgar Belief, Relating to Spirits, Spectres or Ghosts, Daemons, Witches, &C.: In a Due and Serious Examination of Their Nature, Power, Administration, and Operation: In What Forms or Shape Incorporeal Spirits Appear to Men, by What Means, and of What Elements They Take to Themselves, and Form Appearances of Bodies, Visible to Mortal Eyes, Why They Appear, and What Frights and Force of Imagination Often Delude Us into the*

Apprehensions of Supposed Phantasms, through the Intimidation of the Mind, &C.: Also What Evil Tongues Have Power to Produce of Hurt to Mankind, or Irational Creatures, and the Effects Men and Women Are Able to Produce by Their Communication with Good or Evil Spirits, &C (London: Eliz. Harris, 1700).

Bernard, Richard, *A Guide to Grand-Iury Men: Diuided into Two Bookes: In the First, Is the Authors Best Aduice to Them What to Doe, before They Bring in a Billa Vera in Cases of Witchcraft, with a Christian Direction to Such as Are Too Much Giuen Vpon Euery Crosse to Thinke Themselues Bewitched. In the Second, Is a Treatise Touching Witches Good and Bad, How They May Be Knowne, Euicted, Condemned, with Many Particulars Tending Thereunto* (London: Ed. Blackmore, 1627).

Blackley, James, *A Lying Wonder Discovered, and the Strange and Terrible News from Cambridge Proved False: Which False News Is Published in a Libel, Concerning a Wicked Slander Cast Upon a Quaker ...: Also ... An Answer to John Bunions Paper Touching the Said Imagined Witchcraft* (London: Thomas Simmons, 1659).

Boulton, Richard, *A Compleat History of Magick, Sorcery, and Witchcraft* (London: E. Curll, J. Pemberton; and W. Taylor, 1715).

——, *The Possibility and Reality of Magick, Sorcery, and Witchcraft, Demostrated* (London: J. Roberts, 1722).

Bovet, Richard, *Pandaemonium, or, the Devil's Cloyster: Being a Further Blow to Modern Sadduceism, Proving the Existence of Witches and Spirits, in a Discourse Deduced from the Fall of the Angels, the Propagation of Satans Kingdom before the Flood, the Idolatry of the Ages after Greatly Advancing Diabolical Confederacies, with an Account of the Lives and Transactions of Several Notorious Witches: Also, a Collection of Several Authentick Relations of Strange Apparitions of Daemons and Spectres, and Fascinations of Witches, Never before Printed* (London: J. Walthoe, 1684).

Bower, Edmund, *Doctor Lamb Revived, or, Vvitchcraft Condemn'd in Anne Bodenham: A Servant of His, Who Was Arraigned and Executed the Lent Assizes Last at Salisbury, before the Right Honourable the Lord Chief Baron Wild, Judge of the Assise: Wherein Is Set Forth Her Strange and Wonderful Diabolical Usage of a Maid, Servant to Mr. Goddard, as Also Her Attempt against His Daughters, but by Providence Delivered: Being Necessary for All Good Christians to Read, as a Caveat to Look to Themselves, That They Be Not Seduced by Such Inticements* (London: Richard Best and John Place, 1653).

Boys, James, *The Case of Witchcraft at Coggeshall, Essex, in the Year, 1699, Being the Narrative of the Rev. J. Boys, Minister of That Parish* (1699; reprint, London: A.R. Smith, 1901).

Bracton, Henry, *De Legibus* (*On the Laws and Customs of England*), trans. and ed. Samuel E. Thorne, 4 vols, vol. 2 (Buffalo, NY: W.S. Hein, 1997; reprint, <hlsl.law.harvard.edu/bracton/index.htm> (2005)).

Bradwell, Stephen, *Marie Glovers Late Woefull Case: Together W Ith Her Joyfull Deliverance Written Upon Occasion of Dr. Jordens Discourse of the Mother ...: With a Defence of the Truthe against D.J. His Scandalous Impugnations* (London: 1603), British Library, Sloane MS 831; in Michael MacDonald (ed.), *Witchcraft and Hysteria in Elizabethan England: Edward Jorden and the Mary Glover Case*, Tavistock Classics in the History of Psychiatry (London: Tavistock/Routledge), 1991.

Bragge, Francis, *A Defense of the Proceedings against Jane Wenham, Wherein the Possibility and Reality of Witchcraft Are Demonstrated from Scripture, and the Concurrent Testimonies of All Ages. In Answer to Two Pamphlets, Entituled, I. The Impossibility of Witchcraft, &C. Ii. A Full Confutation of Witchcraft* (London: E. Curll, 1712).

———, *A Full and Impartial Account of the Discovery of Sorcery and Witchcraft, Practis'd by Jane Wenham of Walkerne*, 2nd edn (London: E. Curll, 1712).

———, *The Witch of Walkerne. Being I. A Full and Impartial Account of the Discovery of Sorcery and Witchcraft, Practis'd by Jane Wenham of Walkerne in Hertfordshire ... With Her Tryal at the Assizes at Hertford ... Where She Was Found Guilty ... And Received Sentence of Death for the Same, March 4, 1711–12. Ii. Witchcraft Farther Display'd. Containing an Account of the Witchcraft Practis'd by Jane Wenham, since Her Condemnation ... The Tryals of Florence Newton ... At the Assizes Held at Cork, 1661; and of Two Witches At ... Bury St. Edmonds ... 1664 ... Who Were Found Guilty, and Executed. Iii. A Defense of the Proceedings against Jane Wenham, Wherein the Possibility and Reality of Witchcraft Are Demonstrated from Scripture, Reason, and the Concurrent Testimonies of All Ages. In Answer to Two Pamphlets, Entitled, 1. The Impossibility of Witchcraft. 2. A Full Confutation of Witchcraft. Iv. A General Preface to the Whole. By Francis Bragge ... Edition: The Fifth Edition* (London: E. Curll, 1712).

———, *Witchcraft Farther Display'd, Containing I. An Account of the Witchcraft Practis'd by Jane Wenham of Walkerne, in Hertfordshire, since Her Condemnation, Upon the Bodies of Anne Thorn and Anne Street, and the Deplorable Condition in Which They Still Remain. Ii. An Answer to the Most General Objections against the Being and Power of Witches: With Some Remarks Upon the Case of Jane Wenham in Particular, and on Mr. Justice Powel's Procedure Therein. To Which Are Added, the Tryals of Florence Newton, a Famous Irish Witch, at the Assizes Held at Cork, Anno 1661; as Also of Two Witches at the Assizes Held at Bury St. Edmonds in Suffolk, Anno*

1664, before Sir Matthew Hale, (Then Lord Chief Baron of the Exchequer) Who Were Found Guilty and Executed (London: E. Curll, 1712).

Brinley, John, *A Discourse Proving by Scripture & Reason and the Best Authors, Ancient and Modern, That There Are Witches: And How Far Their Power Extends to the Doing of Mischief Both to Man and Beast: And Likewise the Use and Abuse of Astrology Laid Open* (London: J.M., 1686).

Bugg, Francis, *The Great Mystery of the Little Whore Unfolded, and Her Witchcrafts (by Which She Hath Deceived Nations) Discovered: Whereby the Quakers Are Once More Set in Their True Light. By Way of Dialogue between First, a Church of England Man. Secondly, a Protestant Dissenter. Thirdly, a Right-Bred Quaker* (London: Tho. Bennet, R. Wilkins, Edw. Evets, and Ralph Smith, 1705).

Burthogge, Richard, *An Essay Upon Reason, and the Nature of Spirits* (London: John Dunton, 1694).

Camfield, Benjamin, *A Theological Discourse of Angels and Their Ministries: Wherein Their Existence, Nature, Number, Order and Offices Are Modestly Treated Of: With the Character of Those for Whose Benefit Especially They Are Commissioned, and Such Practical Inferences Deduced as Are Most Proper to the Premises: Also an Appendix Containing Some Reflections Upon Mr. Webster's Displaying Supposed Witchcraft* (London: R.E., 1678).

Casaubon, Meric, *Of Credulity and Incredulity in Things Natural, Civil, and Divine: Wherein, among Other Things, the Sadducism of These Times, in Denying Spirits, Witches, and Supernatural Operations, by Pregnant Instances and Evidences, Is Fully Confuted: Epicurus His Cause Discussed, and the Jugling and False Dealing, Lately Used to Bring Him and Atheism into Credit, Clearly Discovered: The Use and Necessity of Ancient Learning ... Proved and Asserted* (London: T. Garthwait, 1668).

Clark, G., *Relation of a Memorable Piece of Witchcraft, at Welton, near Daventry, in Northamptonshire ...: Contained in a Letter of Mr. G. Clark to Mr. M.T.* (1658; reprint, Northampton: Printed and published by Taylor & Son, 1867).

Coke, Sir Edward, *Selected Writings of Sir Edward Coke*, ed. Steve Sheppard, 3 vols, vol. II (Indianapolis: Liberty Fund, 1608; reprint, <oll.libertyfund.org/ToC/0462-02.php#toc2> (2003)).

Cooper, Thomas, *The Mystery of Witch-Craft: Discouering, the Truth, Nature, Occasions, Growth and Power Thereof. Together with the Detection and Punishment of the Same. As Also, the Seuerall Stratagems of Sathan, Ensnaring the Poore Soule by This Desperate Practize of Annoying the Bodie: With the Seuerall Vses Therof to the Church of Christ. Very Necessary for the Redeeming of These Atheisticall and Secure Times* (London: Nicholas Okes, 1617).

Cotta, John, *A Short Discoverie of the Vnobserved Dangers of Seuerall Sorts of Ignorant and Vnconsiderate Practisers of Physicke in England: Profitable Not Onely for the Deceiued Multitude, and Easie for Their Meane Capacities, but Raising Reformed and More Aduised Thoughts in the Best Vnderstandings: With Direction for the Safest Election of a Physition in Necessitie* (London: William Iones and Richard Boyle, 1612; reprint, 1972).

——, *The Triall of Vvitch-Craft: Shewing the True and Right Methode of the Discouery: With a Confutation of Erroneous Wayes. By Iohn Cotta, Doctor in Physicke*, in *Early English books online* (London: Samuel Rand, 1616).

Coxe, Francis, *A Short Treatise Declaringe the Detestable Wickednesse, of Magicall Sciences: As Necromancie. Coniurations of Spirites, Curiouse Astrologie and Such Lyke* (London: Ihon Alde, 1561).

D., I., *The Most Wonderfull and True Storie, of a Certaine Witch Named Alse Gooderige of Stapen Hill, Who Was Arraigned and Conuicted at Darbie at the Assises There: As Also a True Report of the Strange Torments of Thomas Darling, a Boy of Thirteene Yeres of Age, That Was Possessed by the Deuill, with His Horrible Fittes and Apparitions by Him Vttered at Burton Vpon Trent in the Countie of Stafford, and of His Maruellous Deliuerance* (London: I.O., 1597).

Daillon, Jacques de, *Daimonologia, or, a Treatise of Spirits: Wherein Several Places of Scripture Are Expounded, against the Vulgar Errors Concerning Witchcraft, Apparitions, &C. To Which Is Added, an Appendix, Containing Some Reflections on Mr. Boulton's Answer to Dr. Hutchinson's Historical Essay; Entitled the Possibility and Reality of Magick, Sorcery and Witchcraft Demonstrated* (London: Printed for the author, 1723).

Dalton, Michael, *The Countrey Iustice: Conteyning the Practise of the Iustices of the Peace out of Their Sessions. Gathered for the Better Helpe of Such Iustices of Peace as Haue Not Beene Much Conuersant in the Studie of the Lawes of This Realme. By Michael Dalton of Lincolnes Inne, Gent* (London: Societie of Stationers, 1618).

Daneau, Lambert, *A Dialogue of Witches, in Foretime Named Lot-Tellers, and Novv Commonly Called Sorcerers: Vvherein Is Declared Breefely and Effectually, Vvhat Soueuer May Be Required, Touching That Argument. A Treatise Very Profitable ... And Right Necessary for Iudges to Vnderstande, Which Sit Vpon Lyfe and Death. Written in Latin by Lambertus Danaus. And Now Translated into English*, translated from Latin (London: R.W., 1575).

Davenport, John, *The Witches of Huntingdon: Their Examinations and Confessions; Exactly Taken by His Majesties Justices of Peace for That County. Whereby Will Appeare Haw Craftily and Dangerously the Devill Tempteth and Seizeth on Poore Soules. The Reader May Make Use Hereof against Hypocrisie,*

Anger, Malice, Swearing, Idolatry, Lust, Covetousnesse, and Other Grievous Sins, Which Occasioned This Their Downfall (London: Richard Clutterbuck, 1646).

Davis, Ralph, of Northampton, *An Account of the Tryals, Examination and Condemnation, of Elinor Shaw and Mary Phillips (Two Notorious Witches): At Northampton Assizes, on Wednesday the 7th of March 1705* (1705; reprint, Northampton: Reprinted by Taylor & Son, 1866).

——, *The Northamptonshire Witches: Being a True and Faithful Account of the Births, Educations, Lives, and Conversations, of Elinor Shaw and Mary Phillips, (the Two Notorious Witches) That Were Executed at Northampton on Saturday, March the 17th, 1705, for Bewitching a Woman and Two Children to Death & C* (1705; reprint, Northampton: Taylor & Son, 1866).

Defoe, Daniel, *The History of the Devil, Ancient and Modern. In Two Parts ... With a Description of the Devil's Dwelling* (London: T. Warner, 1726).

Drage, William, *A New and True Description of the Law of God (Called Nature) in the Body of Man: Confuting by Manifest and Manifold Experiences of Many Learned Men, as Well as the Authors, the Rules and Methods Concerning Sicknesses and Changes in Mans Body, Delivered by the Antient Physicians, and Moderns That Followed Them: Shevving Also What the Order and Method of Nature Is, as Well as What It Is Not: With a Full and Fair Examination of Their Causes, Inwardly Detected* (London: J. Dover, 1664).

——, *A Physical Nosonomy* (London: J. Dover, 1664).

——, *Daimonomageia: A Small Treatise of Sicknesses and Diseases from Witchcraft, and Supernatural Causes: Never before, at Least in This Comprised Order, and General Manner, Was the Like Published: Being Useful to Others Besides Physicians, in That It Confutes Atheistical, Sadducistical, and Sceptical Principles and Imaginations* (London: J. Dover, 1665).

——, *A Relation of Mary Hall of Gadsden, Reputed to Be Possessed of Two Devils, 1664, from 'a Small Treatise of Sicknesses and Diseases from Witchcraft,' Appended to 'Physical Experiments,' by William Drage, London. Printed for Miller at the Star Next the George in Little Britain 1668 with an Introductory by W.B. Gerish* (1668; reprint, Bishop's Stortford: 1912).

Eluthery, Pen neer the Covent of, *A Pleasant Treatise of Witches: Their Imps, and Meetings, Persons Bewitched, Magicians, Necromancers, Incubus, and Succubus's, Familiar Spirits, Goblings, Pharys, Specters, Phantasms, Places Haunted, and Devillish Impostures: With the Difference between Good and Bad Angels, and a True Relation of a Good Genius* (London: C. Wilkinson, Tho. Archer and Tho. Burrell, 1673).

F., H., *A True and Exact Relation of the Severall Informations, Examinations, and Confessions of the Late Witches, Arraigned and Executed in the County of Essex: Who Were Arraigned and Condemned at the Late Sessions, Holden at Chelmesford before the Right Honorable Robert, Earle of Warwicke, and Severall of His Majesties Justices of Peace, the 29 of July, 1645. Wherein the Severall Murthers, and Devillish Witchcrafts, Committed on the Bodies of Men, Women, and Children, and Divers Cattell, Are Fully Discovered. Published by Authoritie* (London: Henry Overton and Benj. Allen, 1645).

Filmer, Sir Robert, *The Free-Holders Grand Inquest Touching Our Sovereign Lord the King and His Parliament* (London: Wing(?), 1648).

——, *An Advertisement to the Jury-Men of England, Touching Witches: Together with a Difference between an English and Hebrew Vvitch* (London: Richard Royston, 1653).

——, *Reflections Concerning the Original of Government: Upon I. Aristotle's Politiques, Ii. Mr. Hobs's Leviathan, Iii. Mr. Milton against Salmasius, Iv. H. Grotius De Jure Belli, V. Mr. Hunton's Treatise of Monarchy, Vi. Another Treatise of Monarchy* (London: s.n., 1679).

——, *Observations Concerning the Original and Various Forms of Government: To Which Is Added the Power of Kings, with Directions for Obedience to Government in Dangerous and Doubtful Times* (London: R.R.C., 1696).

G.B., Master of Art, 'A Most Vvicked Worke of a Wretched Witch (the Like Whereof None Can Record These Manie Yeeres in England. Wrought on the Person of One Richard Burt, Seruant to Maister Edling of Woodhall in the Parrish of Pinner in the Countie of Myddlesex, a Myle Beyond Harrow. Latelie Committed in March Last, An. 1592 and Newly Recognised According to the Truth. By G.B. Maister of Arts' (London: William Barley, 1592), in Marion Gibson (ed.), *Early Modern Witches: Witchcraft Cases in Contemporary Writing*, 138–45 (London: Routledge 2000).

G., E., *A Prodigious & Tragicall History of the Arraignment, Tryall, Confession, and Condemnation of Six Witches at Maidstone, in Kent, at the Assizes There Held in July, Fryday 30. This Present Year. 1652.: Before the Right Honorable, Peter Warburton, One of the Justices of the Common Pleas. Collected from the Observations of E.G. Gent. (a Learned Person, Present at Their Conviction and Condemnation) and Digested by H.F. Gent. To Which Is Added a True Relation of One Mrs. Atkins a Mercers Wife in Warwick, Who Was Strangely Caried Away from Her House in July Last, and Hath Not Been Heard of Since* (London: Richard Harper, 1652).

G.R., A.M., *The Belief of Witchcraft Vindicated: Proving, from Scripture, There Have Been Witches; and from Reason, That There May Be Such Still. In Answer to a Late Pamphlet, Intituled, the Impossibility of Witchcraft: Plainly Proving, from Scripture and Reason, That There Never Was a Witch, &C* (London: J. Baker, 1712).

Galis, Richard, 'A Brief Treatise' (1579), in Marion Gibson (ed.), *Early Modern Witches: Witchcraft Cases in Contemporary Writing*, 50–71 (London: Routledge, 2000).

Gardiner, Ralph, *England's Grievance Discovered, in Relation to the Coal-trade with the Map of the River of Tine, and Situation of the Town and Corporation of Newcastle: The Tyrannical Oppression of those Magistrates, their Charters and Grants, the Several Tryals, Depositions, and Judgements Obtained against Them: With a Breviate of Several Statutes Proving Repugnant to their Actings: With Proposals for Reducing the Excessive Rates of Coals for the Future, and the Rise of their Grants, Appearing in this Book* (London: R. Ibbitson and P. Stent, 1655).

Gaule, John, *Select Cases of Conscience Touching Vvitches and Vvitchcrafts. By Iohn Gaule, Preacher of the Word at Great Staughton in the County of Huntington* (London: Richard Clutterbuck, 1646).

Gifford, George, *A Discourse of the Subtill Practises of Deuilles by Vvitches and Sorcerers: By Which Men Are and Haue Bin Greatly Deluded: The Antiquitie of Them: Their Diuers Sorts and Names. With an Aunswer Vnto Diuers Friuolous Reasons Which Some Doe Make to Prooue That the Deuils Did Not Make Those Aperations in Any Bodily Shape* (London: Toby Cooke, 1587).

——, *A Dialogue Concerning Witches and Witchcraftes: In Which Is Laide Open How Craftely the Diuell Deceiueth Not Onely the Witches but Many Other and So Leadeth Them Awrie into Many Great Errours* (London: Tobie Cooke and Mihil, 1593).

Gilbert, Sir Geoffrey, *The Law of Evidence* (London: W. Owen, 1756).

Glanvill, Joseph, *A Philosophical Endeavour: Towards the Defence of the Being of Vvitches and Apparitions. In a Letter to the Much Honoured, Robert Hunt, Esq; by a Member of the Royal Society* (London: James Collins, 1666).

——, *A Blow at Modern Sadducism in Some Philosophical Considerations About Witchcraft: To Which Is Added the Relation of the Fam'd Disturbance by the Drummer in the House of Mr. John Mompesson, with Some Reflections on Drollery and Atheisme* (London: James Collins, 1668).

——, *Saducismus Triumphatus, or, Full and Plain Evidence Concerning Witches and Apparitions: In Two Parts: The First Treating of Their Possibility, the Second of Their Real Existence* (London: J. Collins and S. Lownds, 1681).

Goodcole, Henry, *The Wonderfull Discouerie of Elizabeth Savvyer a Witch: Late of Edmonton, Her Conuiction and Condemnation and Death: Together with the Relation of the Diuels Accesse to Her, and Their Conference Together* (London: Vvilliam Butler, 1621).

Grainge, William, *Daemonologia: A Discourse on Witchcraft as It Was Acted in the Family of Mr. Edward Fairfax, of Fuyston, in the County of York, in the*

Year 1621; Along with the Only Two Eclogues of the Same Author Known to Be in Existence. With a Biographical Introduction, and Notes Topographical & Illustrative. By William Grainge (1621; reprint, Harrogate: R. Ackrill, Printer and Publisher, Herald Office, 1882).

Greenwel, Thomas, *A Full and True Account of the Discovering, Apprehending and Taking of a Notorious Witch: Who Was Carried before Justice Bateman in Well-Close, on Sunday, July the 23: Together with Her Examination and Commitment to Bridewel, Clerkenwel* (London: H. Hills, 1704).

Hale, John, *A Collection of Modern Relations of Matter of Fact Concerning Witches & Witchcraft Upon the Persons of People: To Which Is Prefixed a Meditation Concerning the Mercy of God in Preserving Us from the Malice and Power of Evil Angels, Written by the Late Lord Chief Justice Hale, Upon Occasion of a Tryal of Several Witches before Him* (London: John Harris, 1693).

——, *A Modest Enquiry into the Nature of Witchcraft: And How Persons Guilty of That Crime May Be Convicted: And the Means Used for Their Discovery Discussed, Both Negatively and Affirmatively, According to Scripture and Experience* (Boston, NE: Benjamin Eliot, 1702).

Hale, Sir Matthew, *Pleas of the Crown* (London: William Shrewsbery and Juon Leigh, 1678).

——, *A Short Treatise Touching Sheriffs Accompts* (London: Will. Shrowsbery, 1683).

——, *Historia Placitorum Coronae* (London: F. Gyles, T. Woodward, and C. Davis, 1736).

Hallywell, Henry, *Melampronoea, or, a Discourse of the Polity and Kingdom of Darkness: Together with a Solution of the Chiefest Objections Brought against the Being of Witches* (London: Walter Kettilby, 1681).

Harsnett, Samuel, *A Discouery of the Fraudulent Practises of Iohn Darrel Bacheler of Artes in His Proceedings Concerning the Pretended Possession and Dispossession of William Somers at Nottingham: Of Thomas Darling, the Boy of Burton at Caldwall: And of Katherine Wright at Mansfield, & Whittington: And of His Dealings with One Mary Couper at Nottingham, Detecting in Some Sort the Deceitfull Trade in These Latter Dayes of Casting out Deuils* (London: Iohn Wolfe, 1599).

Heer, Henri de, *The Most True and Wonderfull Narration of Two Women Bewitched in Yorkshire: Who Coming to the Assizes at York to Give in Evidence against the Witch, after a Most Horrible Noise, to the Terror and Amazement of All the Beholders, Did Vomit Forth before the Judges, Pins, Wool and Hafts of Knives, &C., All Which Was Done (to Make the Wonder More Wonderfull) without the Least Drop of Bloud or Moisture from Their Mouths: Also a Most True Relation of a Young Maid Not Far from Luyck Who Being Bewitched in the Same Manner Did (Most Incredibly) Vomit Forth Wadds of Straw, with Pins a Crosse in Them, Iron Nails, Needles, Points, and Whatsoever She Had Seen in the Basket of the Witch That Did Bewitch Her* ([S.l.]: Tho. Vere and W. Gilbertson, 1658).

Hoadly, Benjamin, *A Plain Account of the Nature and End of the Sacrament of the Lord's-Supper in Which All the Texts in the New Testament, Relating to It, Are Produced and Explained: ... To Which Are Added, Forms of Prayer* (London: printed for James John and Paul Knapton, 1735), microform.

Holland, Henry, *A Treatise against Vvitchcraft: Or a Dialogue, Wherein the Greatest Doubts Concerning That Sinne, Are Briefly Answered: A Sathanicall Operation in the Witchcraft of All Times Is Truly Prooued: The Moste Precious Preseruatiues against Such Euils Are Shewed: Very Needful to Be Knowen of All Men, but Chiefly of the Masters and Fathers of Families, That They May Learn the Best Meanes to Purge Their Houses of All Vnclean Spirits, and Wisely to Auoide the Dreadfull Impieties and Great Daungers Which Come by Such Abhominations. Hereunto Is Also Added a Short Discourse, Containing the Most Certen Meanes Ordained of God, to Discouer, Expell, and to Confound All the Sathanicall Inuentions of Witchcraft and Sorcerie* (Cambridge: Vniuersitie of Cambridge, 1590).

Hopkins, Matthew, *The Discovery of Witches: In Answer to Seuerall Queries, Lately Delivered to the Judges of Assize for the County of Norfolk* (London: R. Royston, 1647; reprint, 1988).

Hutchinson, Francis, *An Historical Essay Concerning Witchcraft: With Observations Upon Matters of Fact, Tending to Clear the Texts of the Sacred Scriptures, and Confute the Vulgar Errors About That Point; and Also Two Sermons, One in Proof of the Christian Religion, the Other Concerning the Good and Evil Angels* (London: R. Knaplock and D. Midwinter, 1718).

I., T., *A Vvorld of Vvonders. A Masse of Murthers. A Couie of Cosonages Containing Many of the Moste Notablest Wonders, Horrible Murthers and Detestable Cosonages That Haue Beene within This Land. Not Imagined Falso to Delight Vaine Heads Ociose, Not Practised Trans Mare to Breed Trueth Cum Ambiguitate, but Commited Euen at Home Re Vera, and May Be Prooued Cum Honestate. A Matter Moste Fit to Be Knowen, Well Wayed and Considered of All Men* (London: William Barley, 1595).

I.A., *The Daemon of Burton, or, a True Relation of Strange Witchcrafts or Incantations Lately Practised at Burton in the Parish of Weobley in Herefordshire: Certified in a Letter from a Person of Credit in Hereford* (London: C.W., 1671).

James I, *Daemonologie: In Forme of a Dialogue, Diuided into Three Bookes* (Edinburgh: Robert Walde-graue, 1597).

Jollie, Thomas, *The Surey Demoniack, or, an Account of Satans Strange and Dreadful Actings, in and About the Body of Richard Dugdale of Surey, near Whalley in Lancashire and How He Was Dispossest by Gods Blessing on the Fastings and Prayers of Divers Ministers and People* ... (London: Jonathan Robinson, 1697).

Jorden, Edward, *A Briefe Discovrse of a Disease Called the Suffocation of the Mother: Written Vppon Occasion Which Hath Beene of Late Taken Thereby, to Suspect Possesion of an Euill Spirit, or Some Such Like Supernaturall Power: Wherin Is Declared That Diuers Strange Actions and Passions of the Body of Man, Which in the Common Opinion, Are Imputed to the Diuell, Haue Their True Naturall Causes, and Do Accompanie This Disease* (London: Iohn Windet, 1603).

Juxon, Joseph, *A Sermon Upon Witchcraft: Occasion'd by a Late Illegal Attempt to Discover Witches by Swimming: Preach'd at Twyford, in the County of Leicester, July 11, 1736* (London: H. Woodfall, 1736).

Keith, George, *A Refutation of Three Opposers of Truth: By Plain Evidence of the Holy Scripture, Viz. I. Of Pardon Tillinghast, Who Pleadeth for Water-Baptism, Its Being a Gospel-Precept, and Opposeth Christ within, as a False Christ. To Which Is Added, Something Concerning the Supper, &C. Ii. Of B. Keech, in His Book Called, a Tutor for Children, Where He Disputeth against the Sufficiency of the Light within, in Order of Salvation; and Calleth Christ in the Heart, a False Christ in the Secret Chamber. Ii. Of Cotton Mather, Who in His Appendix to His Book, Called, Memorable Providences, Relating to Witchcrafts, &C. Doth So Weakly Defend His Father Increase Mather from Being Justly Chargeable with Abusing the Honest People Called Quakers, That He Doth the More Lay Open His Fathers Nakedness; and Beside the Abuses and Injuries That His Father Had Cast Upon That People, C. Mather, the Son, Addeth New Abuses of His Own. And a Few Words of a Letter to John Cotton, Called a Minister, at Plymouth in New England. By George Keith* (Philadelphia: printed and sold by William Bradford, 1690).

Kramer, Heinrich, and James Sprenger, *Malleus Maleficarum*, trans. Montague Summers (Escondido, CA: Book Tree, 1486; reprint, 2000).

Lambarde, William, *Eirenarcha: Or of the Office of the Iustices of Peace: In Two Bookes: Gathered. 1579. And Now Reuised, and Firste Published, in The. 24. Yeare of the Peaceable Reigne of Our Gratious Queene Elizabeth: By William Lambard of Lincolnes Inne Gent* (London: Ra: Newbery and H. Bynneman, 1581).

——, *The Duties of Constables, Borsholders, Tithingmen, and Such Other Lowe Ministers of the Peace: Whereunto Be Also Adioyned the Seuerall Offices of Church-Wardens: Of Surueyors for Amending the High Wayes: Of Distributors of the Prouision for Noysome Fowle and Vermine: Of the Collectors: Ouerseers: And Gouernors of the Poore: And of the Wardens and Collectors for the Houses of Correction. Collected and Penned by William Lambarde of Lincolnes Inne Gent. 1582* (London: Rafe Newberie and Henrie Middleton, 1583).

M.Y., *The Hartford-Shire Wonder. Or, Strange News from Vvare: Being an Exact and True Relation of One Jane Stretton the Danghter [Sic] of Thomas Stretton, of Ware in the County of Hartford, Who Hath Been Visited in a Strange Kind of Manner by Extraordinary and Unusual Fits, Her Abstaining from Sustenance for the Space of 9 Months, Being Haunted by Imps or Devils in the Form of Several Creatures Here Described the Parties Adjudged of All by Whom She Was Thus Tormented and the Occasion Thereof with Many Other Remarkable Things Taken from Her Own Mouth and Confirmed by Many Credible Witnesses* (London: John Clark, 1669).

Mason, James, MA, *The Anatomie of Sorcerie: Vvherein the Wicked Impietie of Charmers, Inchanters, and Such Like, Is Discouered and Confuted. By Iames Mason, Master of Artes* (London: Vniuersitie of Cambridge, 1612).

Mather, Cotton, *Late Memorable Providences Relating to Witchcrafts and Possessions: Clearly Manifesting, Not Only That There Are Witches, but That Good Men (as Well as Others) May Possibly Have Their Lives Shortned by Such Evil Instruments of Satan* (London: Tho. Parkhurst, 1691).

Mather, Increase, *Cases of Conscience Concerning Evil Spirits Personating Men, Witchcrafts, Infallible Proofs of Guilt in Such as Are Accused with That Crime: All Considered According to the Scriptures, History, Experience, and the Judgment of Many Learned Men* (London: Dunton, 1693).

Michaelis, Sébastien, *The Admirable Historie of the Possession and Conuersion of a Penitent Woman: Seduced by a Magician That Made Her to Become a Witch, and the Princes of Sorcerers in the Country of Prouince, Who Was Brought to S. Baume to Be Exorcised, in the Yeere 1610. In the Moneth of Nouember, by the Authority of the Reuerend Father, and Frier, Sebastian Michaelis, Priour of the Couent Royall of S. Magdalene at Saint Maximin, and Also of the Said Place of Saint Baume. Who Appointed the Reuerend Father, Frier Francis Domptius, Doctor of Diuinity, in the Vniuersity of Louaine ... For the Exorcismes and Recollection of the Acts*, Translated from French (London: William Aspley, 1613).

Misodaimon, B., *The Divels Delvsions, or, a Faithfull Relation of John Palmer and Elizabeth Knott Two Notorious Vvitches Lately Condemned at the Sessions of Oyer and Terminer in St. Albans: Together with the Confession of the Aforesaid John Palmer and Elizabeth Knott, Executed July 16: Also Their Accusations of Severall Vvitches in Hitchen, Norton, and Other Places in the County of Hartford* (London: Richard Williams Stationer, 1649).

Nelson, William, *The Law of Evidence*, 1st edn (London: B. Gosling, 1717; reprint, 1735).

Nettesheim, Agrippa von, *Three Books of Occult Philosophy* (London: Gregory Moule, 1650).

——, *Henry Cornelius Agrippa's Fourth Book of Occult Philosophy, and Geomancy. Magical Elements* (London: s.n., 1655).

Perkins, William, *A Discourse of the Damned Art of Witchcraft: So Farre Forth as It Is Reuealed in the Scriptures, and Manifest by True Experience. Framed and Deliuered by M. William Perkins, in His Ordinarie Course of Preaching, and Now Published by Tho. Pickering Batchelour of Diuinitie, and Minister of Finchingfield in Essex. Whereunto Is Adioyned a Twofold Table; One of the Order and Heades of the Treatise; Another of the Texts of Scripture Explaned, or Vindicated from the Corrupt Interpretation of the Aduersarie* (Cambridge, UK: Vniuersitie of Cambridge, 1608).

Petto, Samuel, *A Faithful Narrative of the Wonderful and Extraordinary Fits Which Mr. Tho. Spatchet (Late of Dunwich and Cookly) Was under by Witchcraft, or, a Mysterious Providence in His Even Unparallel'd Fits: With an Account of His First Falling into, Behaviour under, and (in Part) Deliverance out of Them: Wherein Are Several Remarkable Instances of the Gracious Effects of Fervent Prayer* (London: John Harris, 1693).

Potts, Thomas, *The Vvonderfull Discouerie of Witches in the Countie of Lancaster: Vvith the Arraignement and Triall of Nineteene Notorious Witches, at the Assizes and General Gaole Deliuerie, Holden at the Castle of Lancaster, Vpon Munday, the Seuenteenth of August Last, 1612. Before Sir Iames Altham, and Sir Edward Bromley, Knights; Barons of His Maiesties Court of Exchequer: And Iustices of Assize, Oyer and Terminor, and Generall Gaole Deliuerie in the Circuit of the North Parts. Together with the Arraignement and Triall of Iennet Preston, at the Assizes Holden at the Castle of Yorke, the Seuen and Twentieth Day of Iulie Last Past, with Her Execution for the Murther of Master Lister by Witchcraft. Published and Set Forth by Commandement of His Maiesties Iustices of Assize in the North Parts. By Thomas Potts Esquier* (London: Iohn Barnes, 1613).

R.B., *The Kingdom of Darkness: Or, the History of Daemons, Specters, Witches, Apparitions, Possessions, Disturbances, and Other Wonderful and Supernatural Delusions, Mischievous Feats and Malicious Impostures of the Devil. Containing near Fourscore Memorable Relations, Forreign and Domestick, Both Antient and Modern. Collected from Authentick Records ... And Asserted by Authors of Undoubted Verity. Together with a Preface Obviating the Common Objections ... Of the Sadduces and Atheists of the Age, Who Deny the Being of Spirits, Witches, &C. With Pictures* (London: Nath. Crouch, 1688).

Roberts, Alexander, *A Treatise of Witchcraft: Vvherein Sundry Propositions Are Laid Downe, Plainely Discouering the Wickednesse of That Damnable Art, with Diuerse Other Speciall Points Annexed, Not Impertinent to the Same, Such as Ought Diligently of Euery Christian to Be Considered. With a True Narration of the Witchcrafts Which Mary Smith, Wife of Henry Smith Glouer, Did Practise: Of Her Contract Vocally Made between the Deuill and Her, in Solemne Termes*, 2nd edn (London: Samuel Man, 1616).

Scot, Reginald, *The Discouerie of Witchcraft: Wherein the Lewde Dealing of Witches and Witchmongers Is Notablie Detected, the Knauerie of Coniurors, the Impietie of Inchantors, the Follie of Soothsaiers ...: Hereunto Is Added a Treatise Vpon the Nature and Substance of Spiriits and Diuels, &C* (London: William Brome, 1584).

Sheppard, William, *An Epitome of All the Common & Statute Laws of This Nation Now in Force Wherein More Then Fifteen Hundred of the Hardest Words or Terms of the Law Are Explained, and All the Most Useful and Profitable Heads or Titles of the Law by Way of Common Place, Largely, Plainly and Methodically Handled: With an Alphabetical Table* (London: W. Lee, D. Pakeman, J. Wright, H. Twyford, G. Bedell, Tho. Brewster, Ed. Dod, and J. Place, 1656).

Smith, Sir Thomas, *De Republica Anglorum: The Maner of Gouernement or Policie of the Realme of England, Compiled by the Honorable Man Thomas Smyth, Doctor of the Ciuil Lawes, Knight, and Principall Secretarie Vnto the Two Most Worthie Princes, King Edwarde the Sixt, and Queene Elizabeth. Seene and Allowed*, 1st edn (London: Printed by Henrie Midleton for Gregorie Seton, 1583).

Stearne, John, *A Confirmation and Discovery of Witchcraft: Containing These Severall Particulars: That There Are Witches ... Together with the Confessions of Many of Those Executed since May 1645* (London: William Wilson, 1648).

Stockden, John, *The Seven Women Confessors, or a Discovery of the Seuen White Divels Which Liued at Queen-Street in Coven-Garden: Viz. Katherine Wels, Susan Baker, Anne Parker, Katherine Smith, Elinor Hall, Mary Iones, Dorathy Marsh. Whose Articles Are Herein Declared, and Their Mad Pranks Presented to the View of the World. Discovered by Iohn Stockden a Yeoman. Jan. 22. 1641* (London: Iohn Smith, 1642).

Swan, John, *A Trve and Breife Report of Mary Glovers Vexation, and of Her Deliuerance by the Meanes of Fastinge and Prayer: Performed by Those Whose Names Are Sett Downe in the Next Page* (London: s.n., 1603).

T., R., *The Opinion of Witchcraft Vindicated: In an Answer to a Book Intituled the Question of Witchcraft Debated: Being a Letter to a Friend* (London: Francis Haley, 1670).

Taylor, Zachary, *The Surey Impostor: Being an Answer to a Late Fanatical Pamphlet, Entituled the Surey Demoniack* (London: Printed for John Jones, at the Dolphin and Crown in St Paul's Church-Yard; and Ephraim Hohnson, Bookseller in Manchester, 1697).

W., W., *A True and Iust Recorde, of the Information, Examination and Confession of All the Witches, Taken at S. Ofes in the Countie of Essex: Whereof Some Were Executed, and Other Some Entreated According to the Determination of Lawe. Wherein All Men May See What a Pestilent People Witches Are, and How Vnworthy to Lyue in a Christian Commonwealth. Written Orderly, as the Cases Were Tryed by Euidence* (London: Thomas Dawson, 1582).

Wagstaffe, John, *The Question of Witchcraft Debated, or, a Discourse against Their Opinion That Affirm Witches* (London: Edward Millington, 1669).

Webster, John, *The Displaying of Supposed Witchcraft: Wherein Is Affirmed That There Are Many Sorts of Deceivers and Impostors and Divers Persons under a Passive Delusion of Melancholy and Fancy, but That There Is a Corporeal League Made Betwixt the Devil and the Witch ... Is Utterly Denied and Disproved: Wherein Also Is Handled, the Existence of Angels and Spirits, the Truth of Apparitions, the Nature of Astral and Sydereal Spirits, the Force of Charms, and Philters, with Other Abstruse Matters* (London: J.M., 1677).

Secondary Sources

Almond, Philip, *Demonic Possession and Exorcism in Early Modern England* (Cambridge, UK: Cambridge University Press, 2004).

Anderson, Alan, and Raymond Gordon, 'Witchcraft and the Status of Women – the Case of England', *British Journal of Sociology* 29, no. 2 (1978): 171–84.

Ankarloo, Bengt, and Gustav Henningsen (eds), *Early Modern European Witchcraft: Centres and Peripheries* (Oxford, UK: Clarendon Press, 1990).

Baker, John Hamilton, 'Criminal Courts and Procedure at Common Law 1550–1800', in J.S. Cockburn (ed.), *Crime in England, 1550–1800*, 15–48 (Princeton, NJ: Princeton University Press, 1977).

——, *An Introduction to English Legal History*, 3rd edn (London: Butterworths, 1990).

——, *The Law's Two Bodies: Some Evidential Problems in English Legal History* (Oxford: Oxford University Press, 2001).

Barry, Jonathan, 'Introduction', in Jonathan Barry, Marianne Hester and Gareth Roberts (eds), *Witchcraft in Early Modern Europe: Studies in Culture and Belief*, 1–45 (Cambridge, UK: Cambridge University Press, 1996).

Beattie, J.M., *Crime and the Courts in England, 1660–1800* (Princeton, NJ: Princeton University Press, 1986).

Behringer, Wolfgang, *Witchcraft Persecutions in Bavaria: Popular Magic, Religion, and the State in Early Modern Europe* (Cambridge, UK: Cambridge University Press, 1997).

——, *Witches and Witch-Hunts* (Cambridge: Polity Press, 2004).

Belcort, Willen, 'The Making of the Female Witch: Reflections on Witchcraft and Gender in the Early Modern Period', *Gender & History* 12, no. 2 (2000): 287–309.

Bellamy, John G., *The Criminal Trial in Later Medieval England: Felony before the Courts from Edward I to the Sixteenth Century* (Thrupp, Stroud, Gloucestershire: Sutton, 1998).

Ben-Yehuda, Nachman, 'The European Witch Craze of the 14th to 17th Centuries: A Sociologist's Perspective', *The American Journal of Sociology* 86, no. 1 (1980): 1–31.

Bostridge, Ian, 'Witchcraft Repealed', in Jonathan Barry, Marianne Hester and Gareth Roberts (eds), *Witchcraft in Early Modern Europe: Studies in Culture and Belief*, 309–34 (Cambridge, UK: Cambridge University Press, 1996).

——, *Witchcraft and Its Transformations, c.1650–c.1750*, Oxford Historical Monographs (Oxford; New York: Clarendon Press, 1997).

——, 'Music, Reason, and Politeness', in Peter Burke, Brian Howard Harrison and Paul Slack (eds), *Civil Histories: Essays Presented to Sir Keith Thomas*, 251–63 (Oxford: Oxford University Press, 2000).

Braddick, Michael J., and John Walter (eds), *Negotiating Power in Early Modern Society: Order, Hierarchy and Subordination in Britain and Ireland* (Cambridge, UK: Cambridge University Press, 2001).

Briggs, Robin, 'Women as Victims? Witches, Judges, and the Community', *French History* 5 (1991): 438–50.

——, 'Many Reasons Why: Witchcraft and the Problem of Multiple Explanation', in Jonathan Barry, Marianne Hester and Gareth Roberts (eds), *Witchcraft in Early Modern Europe*, 49–63 (Cambridge, UK: Cambridge University Press, 1996).

——, *Witches and Neighbors: The Social and Cultural Context of European Witchcraft* (New York: Viking, 1996).

——, *The Witches of Lorraine* (Oxford: Oxford University Press, 2007).

Burke, Peter, *Popular Culture in Early Modern Europe* (Aldershot, England: Scholar Press, 1987; reprint, 1994).

——, *A Social History of Knowledge: From Gutenberg to Diderot* (Cambridge, UK: Polity Press, 2000).

Catlow, Charles Richard Arthur, *The Pendle Witches* (Nelson: Hendon Publishing Co., 1976).

Clark, Stuart, 'King James' *Daemonologie*: Witchcraft and Kingship', in Sydney Anglo (ed.), *The Damned Art*, 156–81 (London: Routledge & Kegan Paul, 1977).

——, 'Inversion, Misrule and the Meaning of Witchcraft', *Past and Present* 87 (1980): 98–127.

——, 'The Rational Witchfinder: Conscience, Demonological Naturalism and Popular Superstitions', in Stephen L. Pumfrey, Paolo L. Rossi and Maurice Slawinski (eds), *Science, Culture and Popular Belief in Renaissance Europe*, 222–48 (Manchester: Manchester University Press, 1991).

——, *Thinking with Demons: The Idea of Witchcraft in Early Modern Europe* (Oxford: Oxford University Press, 1997).

——, 'Introduction', in Stuart Clark (ed.), *Languages of Witchcraft: Narrative, Ideology, and Meaning in Early Modern Culture*, 1–18 (New York: St. Martin's Press, 2001).

——, 'Witchcraft and Magic in Europe: The Period of the Witch Trials', in Bengt Ankarloo and Stuart Clark (eds), *Witchcraft and Magic in Europe* (Philadelphia, PA: University of Pennsylvania Press, 2002).

Cockburn, J.S., 'Introduction', in J.S. Cockburn (ed.), *Calendar of Assize Records, Elizabeth I* (London: HMSO, 1975–80).

——, 'The Nature and Incidence of Crime in England 1559–1625: A Preliminary Survey', in J.S. Cockburn (ed.), *Crime in England 1550–1800*, 49–71 (London: Methuen & Co. Ltd, 1977).

—— (ed.), *Crime in England, 1550–1800* (Princeton, NJ: Princeton University Press, 1977).

——, *Calendar of Assize Records: Home Circuit Indictments Elizabeth I and James I. Introduction*, ed. J.S. Cockburn, 11 vols, vol. 1 (London: Her Majesty's Stationery Office, 1985).

Cockburn, J.S., and Thomas Andrew Green (eds), *Twelve Good Men and True: The Criminal Trial Jury in England, 1200–1800* (Princeton, NJ: Princeton University Press, 1988).

Cohen, Esther, 'Law, Folklore and Animal Lore', *Past and Present*, no. 110 (1986): 6–37.

——, 'The Animated Pain of the Body', *The American Historical Review* 105, no. 1 (2000).

Cohn, Norman, *Europe's Inner Demons: The Demonization of Christians in Medieval Christendom*, (1975) (Chicago: University of Chicago Press, 2000).

Craker, Wendel D., 'Spectral Evidence, Non-Spectral Acts of Witchcraft, and Confession at Salem 1692', *The Historical Journal* 40, no. 2 (1997): 331–58.

Davies, Owen, *Witchcraft, Magic and Culture, 1736–1951* (Manchester: Manchester University Press, 1999).

——, *Cunning-Folk: Popular Magic in English History* (London; New York: Hambledon and London, 2003).

Davies, Reginald Trevor, *Four Centuries of Witch-Beliefs, with Special Reference to the Great Rebellion* (New York: B. Blum, 1947; reprint, 1972).

Davis, J.C., *Fear, Myth and History: The Ranters and the Historians*, 1st edn (Cambridge, UK: Cambridge University Press, 1986).

Davis, Natalie Zemon, *Fiction in the Archives: Pardon Tales and Their Tellers in Sixteenth-Century France* (Stanford, CA: Stanford University Press, 1987).

Deacon, Richard, *Matthew Hopkins: Witch Finder General* (London: F. Muller, 1976).

DeWindt, Anne Riever, 'Witchcraft and Conflicting Visions of the Ideal Village Community', *Journal of British Studies* 34 (1995): 427–63.

Douglas, Mary (ed.), *Witchcraft Confessions and Accusations, A.S.A. Monographs 9* (London: Tavistock Publications, 1970).

Dukes, Eugene D., *Magic and Witchcraft in the Dark Ages* (Lanham, MD: University Press of America, 1996).

Durston, Gregory, *Witchcraft and Witch Trials: A History of English Witchcraft and Its Legal Perspectives, 1542 to 1736* (Chichester: Barry Rose Law Publishers, 2000).

Edwards, Kathryn A. (ed.), *Werewolves, Witches, and Wandering Spirits: Traditional Belief and Folklore in Early Modern Europe, Sixteenth Century Essays and Studies; V. 62* (Kirksville, MO: Truman State University Press, 2002).

Ehrenreich, Barbara, and Deirdre English, *Witches, Midwives, and Nurses: A History of Women Healers* (Old Westbury, NY: Feminist Press, 1973).

Eisaman Maus, Katharine, 'Proof and Consequences: Inwardness and Its Exposure in the English Renaissance', *Representations*, no. 34 (1991): 29–52.

Elmer, Peter, 'Saints or Sorcerers', in Jonathan Barry, Marianne Hester and Gareth Roberts (eds), *Witchcraft in Early Modern Europe: Studies in Culture and Belief*, 145–79 (Cambridge, UK: Cambridge University Press, 1996).

——, 'Towards a Politics of Witchcraft in Early Modern England', in Stuart Clark (ed.), *Languages of Witchcraft: Narrative, Ideology and Meaning in Early Modern Culture*, 101–18 (New York: St. Martin's Press, 2001).

——, 'Introduction', in Peter Elmer (ed.), *The Later English Trial Pamphlets*, English Witchcraft 1560–1736 (London: Pickering & Chatto, 2003).

——, 'Introduction', in Peter Elmer (ed.), *The Post-Restoration Synthesis and Its Opponents*, vii–xxii (London: Pickering & Chatto, 2003).

——, 'Science, Medicine and Witchcraft', in Jonathan Barry and Owen Davies (eds), *Witchcraft Historiography*, Palgrave Advances, 33–51 (Houndmills, UK: Palgrave Macmillan, 2007).

Evans-Pritchard, Edward, *Witchcraft, Oracles and Magic among the Azande* (Oxford: Clarendon Press, 1937).

Ewen, Cecil L'Estrange, *Witch Hunting and Witch Trials: The Indictments for Witchcraft from the Records of 1373 Assizes Held for the Home Circuit A.D. 1559–1736* (New York: Lincoln Mac Veagh: The Dial Press, 1929).

——, *Witchcraft and Demonianism: A Concise Account Derived from Sworn Depositions and Confessions Obtained in the Courts of England and Wales* (London: Heath, 1933).

——, 'A Noted Case of Witchcraft at North Moreton, Berks, in the Early 17th Century', *The Berkshire Archaeological Journal* 40, no. 2 (1936).

——, *The Trials of John Lowes, Clerk* (London: C.L. Ewen, 1937).

Fisher, George, 'The Jury's Rise as Lie Detector', *The Yale Law Journal*, no. 107 (1997): 575–713.

Foucault, Michel, *Discipline and Punish: The Birth of the Prison* (New York: Pantheon Books, 1977).

Gage, Matilda Joslyn, *Woman, Church, and State* (New York: Arno Press, 1893).

Gaskill, Malcolm, 'Early Modern Kent', in Jonathan Barry, Marianne Hester and Gareth Roberts (eds), *Witchcraft in Early Modern Europe*, 257–87 (Cambridge, UK: Cambridge University Press, 1996).

——, 'The Devil in the Shape of a Man: Witchcraft, Conflict and Belief in Jacobean England', *Historical Research* 71, no. 175 (1998): 142–71.

——, *Crime and Mentalities in Early Modern England* (Cambridge: Cambridge University Press, 2000).

——, 'Witches and Women in Old and New England', in Stuart Clark (ed.), *Languages of Witchcraft*, 55–80 (London: Macmillan Press Ltd, 2001).

——, *Witchfinders: A Seventeenth-Century English Tragedy* (Cambridge, MA: Harvard University Press, 2005).

——, 'Witchcraft and Evidence in Early Modern England', *Past and Present*, no. 198 (2008): 33–70.

Geertz, Hildred, 'An Anthropology of Religion and Magic, I', *Journal of Interdisciplinary History* 6, no. 1 (1975): 71–89.

Geis, Gilbert, and Ivan Bunn, *A Trial of Witches: A Seventeenth-Century Witchcraft Prosecution* (London: Routledge, 1997).

Gibson, Marion, *Reading Witchcraft: Stories of Early English Witches* (London: Routledge, 1999).

—— (ed.), *Early Modern Witches: Witchcraft Cases in Contemporary Writing* (London: Routledge, 2000).

—— (ed.), *Witchcraft and Society in England and America, 1550–1750* (Ithaca, NY: Cornell University Press, 2003).

Ginzburg, Carlo, *The Night Battles: Witchcraft and Agrarian Cults in the Sixteenth and Seventeenth Centuries* (Baltimore, MD: Johns Hopkins University Press, 1983).

——, *Clues, Myths, and the Historical Method* (Baltimore, MD: Johns Hopkins University Press, 1989).

——, *Ecstasies: Deciphering the Witches' Sabbath* (New York: Pantheon Books, 1991).

Goodare, Julian, 'Women and the Witch-Hunt in Scotland', *Social History* 23, no. 3 (1998): 288–308.

Green, Thomas Andrew, *Verdict According to Conscience: Perspectives on the English Criminal Trial Jury, 1200–1800* (Chicago: University of Chicago Press, 1985).

Gregory, Annabel, 'Witchcraft, Politics and "Good Neighbourhood"', *Past and Present*, no. 133 (1991): 31–66.

Griffiths, Paul, Adam Fox and Steve Hindle (eds), *The Experience of Authority in Early Modern England* (Houndmills: Macmillan Press, 1996).

Groot, D. Roger, 'The Early-Thirteenth-Century Criminal Jury', in J.S. Cockburn and Thomas Andrew Green (eds), *Twelve Good Men and True*, 3–35 (Princeton, NJ: Princeton University Press, 1988).

Guiley, Rosemary, *The Encyclopedia of Witches and Witchcraft* (New York: Facts On File, 1999).

Guskin, Phylis J., 'The Context of Witchcraft: The Case of Jane Wenham (1712)', *Eighteenth-Century Studies* 15 (1981): 48–71.

Haining, Peter (ed.), *The Witchcraft Papers: Contemporary Records of the Witchcraft Hysteria in Essex, 1560–1700* (Secaucus, NJ: University Books, 1974).

Haliczer, Stephen, 'The Jew as Witch: Displaced Aggression and the Myth of the Santo Nino De La Guardia', in Mary Elizabeth Pery and Anne J. Cruz (eds), *Cultural Encounters: The Impact of the Inquisition in Spain and the New World*, 146–56 (Berkeley: University of California Press, 1991).

Hanson, Elizabeth, 'Torture and Truth in Renaissance England', *Representations*, no. 34 (1991): 53–84.

Harley, David, 'Mental Illness, Magical Medicine and the Devil in Northern England, 1650–1700', in Roger French and Andrew Wear (eds), *The Medical Revolution of the Seventeenth Century*, 114–44 (Cambridge: Cambridge University Press, 1989).

Harris, Anthony, *Night's Black Agents: Witchcraft and Magic in Seventeenth-Century English Drama* (Manchester, UK: Manchester University Press, 1980).

Harris, Marvin, *Cows, Pigs, Wars and Witches: The Riddles of Culture* (New York: Vintage Books 1978, 1974).

Heinemann, Evelyn, *Witches: A Psychoanalytic Exploration of the Killing of Women* (London: Free Association Books, 2000).

Helmholz, R.H., *Marriage Litigation in Medieval England* (London: Cambridge University Press, 1974).

Henningsen, Gustav, *The European Witch-Persecution* (Copenhagen: Danish Folklore Archives, 1973).

——, *The Witches' Advocate: Basque Witchcraft and the Spanish Inquisition, 1609–1614* (Reno: University of Nevada Press, 1980).

Herrup, Cynthia B., 'Law and Morality in Seventeenth-Century England', *Past and Present*, no. 106 (1985): 102–23.

——, *The Common Peace: Participation and the Criminal Law in Seventeenth-Century England*, Cambridge Studies in Early Modern British History (Cambridge, UK: Cambridge University Press, 1987).

Hester, Marianne, *Lewd Women and Wicked Witches: A Study of the Dynamics of Male Domination* (London: Routledge, 1992).

——, 'Patriarchal Reconstruction', in Jonathan Barry, Marianne Hester and Gareth Roberts (eds), *Witchcraft in Early Modern Europe*, 288–306 (Cambridge, UK: Cambridge University Press, 1996).

Holdsworth, Sir William Searle, *A History of English Law*, 1st edn, 17 vols, vol. IV (London: Methuen & Co., 1924).

Hole, Christina, *Witchcraft in England* (London: B.T. Batsford, 1945).

——, *A Mirror of Witchcraft* (London: Chatto & Windus, 1957).

——, *Witchcraft in England: Some Episodes in the History of English Witchcraft* (Totowa, NJ: Rowman and Littlefield, 1977).

Holmes, Clive, 'Popular Culture? Witches, Magistrates and Divines in Early Modern England', in S.L. Kaplan (ed.), *Understanding Popular Culture: Europe from the Middle Ages to the Nineteenth Century*, 85–111 (Berlin: Walter de Gruyter & Co., 1984).

——, 'Women: Witnesses and Witches', *Past and Present*, no. 140 (1993): 45–78.

Jackson, Louise, 'Witches, Wives and Mothers: Witchcraft Persecution and Women's Confessions in Seventeenth-Century England', *Women's History Review* 4, no. 1 (1995): 63–83.

Jackson Lualdi, Katharine, and Anne T. Thayer (eds), *Penitence in the Age of Reformations* (Aldershot: Ashgate, 2000).

Keane, Adrian, *The Modern Law of Evidence*, 5th edn (London: Butterworths, 2000).

Kelly, Henry Ansgar, *Inquisitions and Other Trial Procedures in the Medieval West* (Burlington, VT: Ashgate, 2001).

Kelsey, Sean, 'Politics and Procedure in the Trial of Charles I', *Law and History Review* 22, no. 1 (2004): 1–26.

Keynes, Geoffrey, *Harvey* (Oxford: Oxford University Press, 1966).

Kieckhefer, Richard, *European Witch Trials: Their Foundations in Popular and Learned Culture, 1300–1500* (Berkeley: University of California Press, 1976).

Kittredge, George Lyman, *English Witchcraft and James the First* (New York: Macmillan, 1912).

——, *Witchcraft in Old and New England* (Cambridge, MA: Harvard University Press, 1929).

Klaniczay, Gabor, *The Uses of Supernatural Power*, trans. Susan Singerman (Cambridge, UK: Polity Press, 1990).

Knafla, L.A., 'Crime and Criminal Justice: A Critical Bibliography', in J.S. Cockburn (ed.), *Crime in England 1550–1800*, 270–98 (London: Methuen & Co. Ltd, 1977).

Knott, Olive, *Witches of Dorset* (Dorset, UK: Dorset Pub. Co., 1974).

Kors, Alan Charles, *Witchcraft in Europe, 1100–1700: A Documentary History* (Philadelphia, PA: University of Pennsylvania Press, 1972).

Kors, Alan Charles, and Edward Peters (eds), *Witchcraft in Europe, 400–1700: A Documentary History*, 2nd edn (Philadelphia, PA: University of Pennsylvania Press, 2001).

Landau, Norma, *The Justices of the Peace, 1679–1760* (Berkeley: University of California Press, 1984).

Langbein, John H., *Prosecuting Crime in the Renaissance: England, Germany, France*, Studies in Legal History (Cambridge, MA: Harvard University Press, 1974).

——, *Torture and the Law of Proof: Europe and England in the Ancien Regime* (Chicago: University of Chicago Press, 1977).

——, *The Origins of Adversary Criminal Trial*, Oxford Studies in Modern Legal History (Oxford: Oxford University Press, 2003).

——, 'The Legal History of Torture', in Sanford Levinson (ed.), *Torture: A Collection*, 93–103 (Oxford: Oxford University Press, 2004).

Larner, Christina, *Enemies of God: The Witch-Hunt in Scotland* (Baltimore, MD: Johns Hopkins University Press, 1981).

——, *Witchcraft and Religion: The Politics of Popular Belief* (New York, NY: Blackwell, 1984).

Lavi, Shai J., *The Modern Art of Dying* (Princeton, NJ: Princeton University Press, 2005).

Le Roy Ladurie, Emmanuel, *The Peasants of Languedoc*, trans. John Day, ed. Huppert George (Urbana: University of Illinois Press, 1974).

Lehmann, Arthur C., *Magic, Witchcraft, and Religion: An Anthropological Study of the Supernatural* (Mountain View, CA: Mayfield Pub., 1997).

Leonard, David P., *The New Wigmore: A Treatise on Evidence*, ed. Richard D. Friedman (Gaithersburg, NY: Aspen Law & Business, 2001).

Levack, Brian P. (ed.), *Articles on Witchcraft, Magic, and Demonology* (New York: Garland Pub., 1992).

——, *The Witch-Hunt in Early Modern Europe* (1987), 2nd edn (New York: Longman, 1995).

——, 'State-Building and Witch Hunting', in Jonathan Barry, Marianne Hester and Gareth Roberts (eds), *Witchcraft in Early Modern Europe*, 96–115 (Cambridge, UK: Cambridge University Press, 1996).

——, 'The Decline and End of Witchcraft Prosecutions', in Bengt Ankarloo and Stuart Clark (eds), *Witchcraft and Magic in Europe: The Eighteenth and Nineteenth Centuries*, 1–93 (Philadelphia, PA: University of Pennsylvania Press, 1999).

——, 'Crime and the Law', in Jonathan Barry and Owen Davies (eds), *Witchcraft Historiography*, Palgrave Advances, 146–63 (Houndmills, UK: Palgrave Macmillan, 2007).

Loftus, Elizabeth, 'The Devil in Confessions', *Psychological Science in the Public Interest* 5, no. 2 (2005): i–ii.

MacDonald, Michael (ed.), *Witchcraft and Hysteria in Elizabethan England: Edward Jorden and the Mary Glover Case*, Tavistock Classics in the History of Psychiatry (London: Tavistock/Routledge, 1991).

Macfarlane, Alan, *Witchcraft in Tudor and Stuart England: A Regional and Comparative Study* (New York: Harper & Row, 1970).

——, 'Witchcraft in Tudor and Stuart Essex', in J.S. Cockburn (ed.), *Crime in England 1550–1800*, 72–89 (Princeton, NJ: Princeton University Press, 1977).

——, 'Civility and the Decline of Magic', in Peter Burke, Brian Howard Harrison and Paul Slack (eds), *Civil Histories: Essays Presented to Sir Keith Thomas*, 145–59 (Oxford: Oxford University Press, 2000).

Martin, Lauren, 'The Devil and the Domestic: Witchcraft, Quarrels and Women's Work in Scotland', in Julian Goodare (ed.), *The Scottish Witch-Hunt in Context*, 73–89 (Manchester: Manchester University Press, 2002).

Maxwell-Stuart, P.G. (ed.), *The Occult in Early Modern Europe* (New York: St. Martin's Press, 1999).

Maxwell-Stuart, Peter, 'The Contemporary Historical Debate, 1400–1750', in Jonathan Barry and Owen Davies (eds), *Witchcraft Historiography*, Palgrave Advances, 11–32 (Houndmills, UK: Palgrave Macmillan, 2007).

McKenzie, Andrea, '"This Death Some Strong and Stout Hearted Man Doth Choose": The Practice of Peine Forte Et Dure in Seventeenth- and Eighteenth-Century England', *Law and History Review* 23, no. 2 (2005): 279–314.

McLane, Bernard William, 'Juror Attitudes Towards Local Disorder: The Evidence of the 1328 Lincolnshire Trailbaston Proceedings', in J.S. Cockburn and Thomas Andrew Green (eds), *Twelve Good Men and True: The Criminal Trial Jury in England, 1200–1800* (Princeton, NJ: Princeton University Press, 1988).

Megged, Amos, 'The Social Significance of Benevolent and Malevolent Gifts among Single Caste Women in Mid-Seventeenth-Century New Spain', *Journal of Family History* 24, no. 4 (1999): 420–44.

Meyer, Birgit, and Peter Pels (eds), *Magic and Modernity: Interfaces of Revelation and Concealment* (Stanford, CA: Stanford University Press, 2003).

Michelet, Jules, *La Sorciere* (Paris: E. Dentu Libraire-Editeur, 1862).

Mohr, James C., *Abortion in America: The Origins and Evolution of National Policy, 1800–1900* (New York: Oxford University Press, 1978).

Monter, E. William, *European Witchcraft* (New York: Wiley, 1969).

Morgan, Gwenda, and Peter Rushton, 'The Magistrate, the Community and the Maintenance of an Orderly Society in Eighteenth-Century England', *Historical Research* 76, no. 191 (2003): 54–77.

Murray, Margaret Alice, *The God of the Witches* (Manchester: s.n., 1917).

——, *The Witch-Cult in Western Europe: A Study in Anthropology* (Oxford: Clarendon Press, 1921; reprint, 1965).

Newall, Venetia (ed.), *The Witch Figure: Folklore Essays by a Group of Scholars in England Honouring the 75th Birthday of Katharine M. Briggs* (London: Routledge & Kegan Paul, 1973).

Norton, Mary Beth, *In the Devil's Snare: The Salem Witchcraft Crisis of 1692*, 1st edn (New York: Alfred A. Knopf, 2002).

Notestein, Wallace, *A History of Witchcraft in England from 1558 to 1718* (1911), 2nd edn (New York: T.Y. Crowell Co., 1968), available from <http://ets.umdl.umich.edu/cgi/t/text/text-idx?c=acls;cc=acls;idno=heb00177.0001.001;view=toc>.

Oldham, James, *The Jury of Matrons* (2006), available from <www.law.georgetown.edu/alumni/publications/2006/fall/documents/facultyarticle.pdf>.

Oldham, James C., 'On Pleading the Belly: A History of the Jury of Matrons', *Criminal Justice History*, no. 6 (1985): 1–94.

Peel, Edgar, *The Trials of the Lancashire Witches: A Study of Seventeenth-Century Witchcraft* (New York: Taplinger Pub. Co., 1969).

Peters, Edward, *The Literature of Demonology and Witchcraft* (1998), available from <http://historical.library.cornell.edu/cgi-bin/witch/docviewer?did=108>.

Phipson, Sidney L., *Phipson on Evidence*, ed. M.N. and Specialist Editors Howard, 15th edn (London: Sweet & Maxwell, 2000).

Pihlajamäki, Heikki, '"Swimming the Witch, Pricking for the Devil's Mark": Ordeals in the Early Modern Witchcraft Trials', *Journal of Legal History* 21, no. 2 (2000): 35–58.

Pollock, Sir Frederick, and William Maitland, *The History of English Law Before the Time of Edward I*, 2 vols (Cambridge, UK: The University Press, 1895).

Poole, Robert (ed.), *The Lancashire Witches: Histories and Stories* (Manchester: Manchester University Press, 2002).

Porter, Roy, 'The Patient in England, c. 1660–c. 1800', in Andrew Wear (ed.), *Medicine in Society*, 91–118 (Cambridge, UK: Cambridge University Press, 1992).

Purkiss, Diane, 'Women's Stories of Witchcraft in Early Modern England: The House, the Body, the Child', *Gender & History* 7, no. 3 (1995): 408–32.

——, *The Witch in History: Early Modern and Twentieth-Century Representations* (New York, NY: Routledge, 1996).

Quaife, Geoffrey Robert, *Godly Zeal and Furious Rage: The Witch in Early Modern Europe* (New York: St. Martin's Press, 1987).

Rapley, Robert, *A Case of Witchcraft: The Trial of Urbain Grandier* (Montreal: McGill-Queen's University Press, 1998).

Reis, Elizabeth, *Damned Women: Sinners and Witches in Puritan New England* (Ithaca, NY: Cornell University Press, 1997).

Robbins, Rossell Hope, *The Encyclopedia of Witchcraft and Demonology* (New York: Crown Publishers, 1959).

——, 'Introduction', in Cornell Libraries (ed.), *Witchcraft: Catalogue of the Witchcraft Collection in Cornell University Library* (Millwood, NY: KTO Press, 1977).

Roper, Lyndal, *Oedipus and the Devil: Witchcraft, Sexuality, and Religion in Early Modern Europe* (London: Routledge, 1994).

——, 'Early Modern Germany', in Jonathan Barry, Marianne Hester and Gareth Roberts (eds), *Witchcraft in Early Modern Europe*, 207–36 (Cambridge, UK: Cambridge University Press, 1996).

Rosen, Barbara (ed.), *Witchcraft, Stratford-Upon-Avon Library* (New York: Taplinger, 1972).

Rosenthal, Bernard, *Salem Story* (Cambridge, UK: Cambridge University Press, 1993).

Rowlands, Alison, 'Telling Witchcraft Stories: New Perspectives on Witchcraft and Witches in the Early Modern Period', *Gender & History* 10, no. 2 (1998): 294–302.

Rushton, Peter, 'Women, Witchcraft and Slander in Early Modern England: Cases from the Church Courts of Durham, 1560–1675', *Northern History* 18 (1982): 116–32.

——, 'Texts of Authority: Witchcraft Accusations and the Demonstration of Truth in Early Modern England', in Stuart Clark (ed.), *Languages of Witchcraft: Narrative, Ideology, and Meaning in Early Modern Culture*, 21–39 (New York: St. Martin's Press, 2001).

Russell, Jeffrey Burton, *Witchcraft in the Middle Ages* (Ithaca, NY: Cornell University Press, 1972).

Russell, Steven, 'Witchcraft, Genealogy, Foucault', *British Journal of Sociology* 52, no. 1 (2001): 121.

Sawyer, Ronald C., '"Strangely Handled in All Her Lyms": Witchcraft and Healing in Jacobean England', *Journal of Social History* 22 (1989): 461–85.

Scarre, Geoffrey, *Witchcraft and Magic in Sixteenth- and Seventeenth-Century Europe*, Studies in European History (Atlantic Highlands, NJ: Humanities Press International, 1987).

Shapiro, Barbara J., *Probability and Certainty in Seventeenth-Century England: A Study of the Relationships between Natural Science, Religion, History, Law, and Literature* (Princeton, NJ: Princeton University Press, 1983).

——, *'Beyond Reasonable Doubt' and 'Probable Cause': Historical Perspectives on the Anglo-American Law of Evidence* (Berkeley: University of California Press, 1991).

——, *A Culture of Fact: England, 1550–1720* (Ithaca, NY: Cornell University Press, 2000).

——, '"Fact" and the Proof of Fact in Anglo-American Law (c. 1500–1850)', in Austin Sarat, Lawrence Douglas and Martha Merrill Umphrey (eds), *How Law Knows*, 25–71 (Stanford: Stanford University Press, 2007).

Sharpe, J.A., *Crime in Early Modern England*, in J. Stevenson (ed.), *Themes in British Social History* series (London: Longman, 1984).

——, '"Last Dying Speeches": Religion, Ideology and Public Execution in Seventeenth-Century England', *Past and Present* 107, no. 1 (1985).

——, 'Witchcraft and Women in Seventeenth-Century England: Some Northern Evidence', *Continuity and Change* 6, no. 2 (1991): 179–99.

——, *Witchcraft in Seventeenth Century Yorkshire: Accusations and Counter Measures* (Peasholme Green, York: Borthwick Institute of Historical Research, University of York, 1992).

——, *Early Modern England: A Social History 1550–1750*, 2nd edn (London: Arnold, 1997).

——, *The Bewitching of Anne Gunter: A Horrible and True Story of Deception, Witchcraft, Murder, and the King of England* (New York: Routledge, 2000).

——, *Witchcraft in Early Modern England* (Harlow: Longman, 2001).

Sharpe, James A., *Instruments of Darkness: Witchcraft in England 1550–1750* (London: Hamish Hamilton, 1996).

——, 'Introduction: The Lancashire Witches in Historical Context', in Robert Poole (ed.), *The Lancashire Witches: Histories and Stories*, 1–18 (Manchester: Manchester University Press, 2002).

——, 'The Witch's Familiar in Elizabethan England', in G.W. Bernard and S.J. Gunn (eds), *Authority and Consent in Tudor England* (Aldershot: Ashgate, 2002).

——, 'Witch-Hunting and Witch Historiography: Some Anglo-Scottish Comparisons', in Julian Goodare (ed.), *The Scottish Witch-Hunt in Context*, 182–97 (Manchester: Manchester University Press, 2002).

—— (ed.), *English Witchcraft, 1560–1736*, 6 vols (London: Pickering & Chatto, 2003).

——, 'Magic and Witchcraft', in Po-chia R. Hsia (ed.), *A Companion to the Reformation World*, 440–54 (Malden, MA: Blackwell Publishing Ltd, 2004).

Sharpe, Jim, 'Women, Witchcraft and the Legal Process', in Jennifer Kermode and Garthine Walker (eds), *Women, Crime and the Courts in Early Modern England*, 106–45 (Chapel Hill, NC: University of North Carolina Press, 1994).

——, 'The Devil in East Anglia', in Jonathan Barry, Marianne Hester and Gareth Roberts (eds), *Witchcraft in Early Modern Europe*, 237–54 (Cambridge, UK: Cambridge University Press, 1996).

Sidky, H., *Witchcraft, Lycanthropy, Drugs, and Disease: An Anthropological Study of the European Witch-Hunts* (New York: Peter Lang, 1997).

Smith, Bruce P., 'The Presumption of Guilt and the English Law of Theft, 1750–1850', *Law and History Review* 23, no. 1 (2005): 191–200.

Soman, Alfred, 'The Parlement of Paris and the Great Witch Hunt (1565–1640)', *The Sixteenth Century Journal* 9, no. 2 (1978): 31–44.

Steiker, Carol S., and Jordan M. Steiker, 'Sober Second Thoughts: Reflections on Two Decades of Constitutional Regulation of Capital Punishment', *Harvard Law Review* 109, no. 2 (1995): 355–438.

Stein, Alex, *The Foundations of Evidence Law* (Oxford: Oxford University Press, 2005).

Stephen, Sir James Fitzjames, *A History of the Criminal Law of England* (London: Macmillan, 1883).

Stephen, Sir Leslie, and Sir Sidney Lee (eds), *The Dictionary of National Biography*, 22 vols (London: Oxford University Press, 1963–65).

Stephens, Walter, *Demon Lovers: Witchcraft, Sex, and the Crisis of Belief* (Chicago: University of Chicago Press, 2002).

Summers, Montague, *The History of Witchcraft and Demonology* (London: Routledge & Kegan Paul, 1926; reprint, 1965).

——, *The Geography of Witchcraft* (New York: Knopf, 1927).

——, 'Introduction', in *Malleus Maleficarum* (Escondido, CA: Book Tree, 1928; reprint, 2000).

——, 'Introduction', in *The Discoverie of Witchcraft* (1930) (New York: Dover Publications, 1972).

——, *A Popular History of Witchcraft* (London: K. Paul Trench Truber & Co., 1937).

Swain, J.T., 'The Lancashire Witch Trials of 1612 and 1634 and the Economics of Witchcraft', *Northern History* 30 (1994): 64–85.

Thomas, Keith, *Religion and the Decline of Magic* (New York: Charles Scribner's Sons, 1971).

——, 'An Anthropology of Religion and Magic, II', *Journal of Interdisciplinary History* 6, no. 1 (1975): 91–109.

Thompson, Janet A., *Wives, Widows, Witches and Bitches: Women in Seventeenth-Century Devon* (New York: P. Lang, 1993).

Todd, Margo, 'England after 1558', in Andrew Pettegree (ed.), *The Reformation World*, 365–86 (London: Routledge, 2002).

Trevor-Roper, H.R., *The European Witch-Craze of the Sixteenth and Seventeenth Centuries, and Other Essays* (New York: Harper & Row, 1969).

Twining, William, and Alex Stein (eds), *Evidence and Proof*, The International Library of Essays in Law and Legal Theory, ed. Tom D. Campbell (New York: New York University Press, 1992).

Underdown, David, 'The Taming of the Scold: The Enforcement of Patriarchal Authority in Early Modern England', in Anthony Fletcher and John Stevenson (eds), *Order and Disorder in Early Modern England*, 116–36 (Cambridge: Cambridge University Press, 1985).

Unsworth, C.R., 'Witchcraft Beliefs and Criminal Procedure in Early Modern England', in Thomas G. Watkin (ed.), *Legal Record and Historical Reality: Proceedings of the Eighth British Legal History Conference, Cardiff, 1987*, 71–98 (London: The Hambledon Press, 1989).

Valletta, Frederick, *Witchcraft, Magic and Superstition in England, 1640–70* (Aldershot: Ashgate, 2000).

Van Leeuwen, G. Henry, *The Problem of Certainty in English Thought, 1630–1690* (The Hague: Martinus Nijhoff, 1970).

Walker, Garthine, 'Witchcraft and History', *Women's History Review* 7, no. 3 (1998): 425–32.

——, *Crime, Gender and Social Order in Early Modern England* (Cambridge: Cambridge University Press, 2003).

Wear, Andrew, 'Medical Practice in Late Seventeenth- and Early Eighteenth-Century England: Continuity and Union', in Roger French and Andrew Wear (eds), *The Medical Revolution of the Seventeenth Century*, 294–320 (Cambridge, UK: Cambridge University Press, 1989).

——, 'Making Sense of Health and the Environment in Early Modern England', in Andrew Wear (ed.), *Medicine in Society*, 119–47 (Cambridge, UK: Cambridge University Press, 1992).

——, 'The Popularization of Medicine in Early Modern England', in Roy Porter (ed.), *The Popularization of Medicine, 1650–1850* (London: Routledge, 1992).

——, *Knowledge and Practice in English Medicine, 1550–1680* (Cambridge, UK: Cambridge University Press, 2000).

West, Robert Hunter, *Reginald Scot and Renaissance Writings on Witchcraft* (Boston: Twayne, 1984).

Whitney, Elspeth, 'International Trends: The Witch "She"/the Historian "He": Gender and the Historiography of the European Witch Hunts', *Journal of Women's History* 7, no. 3 (1995): 77–101.

Wigmore, John Henry, *Evidence in Trials at Common Law*, 4th edn, 10 vols, vol. 1, *Wigmore on Evidence* (Boston: Little, Brown and Company, 1983).

Willis, Deborah, *Malevolent Nurture: Witch-Hunting and Maternal Power in Early Modern England* (Ithaca, NY: Cornell University Press, 1995).

Index of Names

Subject Index